I0046963

THE AI GLOSSARY

AI & Emerging Tech Explained

256 Key Concepts for Students, Professionals & Curious Minds

Richard R. Khan

THE AI GLOSSARY: AI & Emerging Tech Explained - 256 Key Concepts for Students, Professionals & Curious Minds

First edition published 2025
by CRC Press
2385 NW Executive Center Drive, Suite 320, Boca Raton FL 33431

and by CRC Press
4 Park Square, Milton Park, Abingdon, Oxon, OX14 4RN

CRC Press is an imprint of Taylor & Francis Group, LLC

Copyright © 2025 Richard R. Khan

Designed cover image: Richard R. Khan

Reasonable efforts have been made to publish reliable data and information; however, the author and publisher cannot assume responsibility for the validity of all materials or the consequences of their use. The authors and publishers have attempted to trace the copyright holders of all material reproduced in this publication and apologize to copyright holders if permission to publish in this form has not been obtained. If any copyright material has not been acknowledged, please write and let us know so we may rectify any future imprint.

Except as permitted under U.S. Copyright Law, no part of this book may be reprinted, reproduced, transmitted, or utilized in any form by any electorinic, mechanical, or other means, now known or hereafter invented, including photocopying, microfilming, and recording, or in any information storage or retrieval system, without written persission from the publishers.

For permission to photocopy or use material electronically from this work, access www.copyright.com or contact the Copyright Clearance Center, Inc. (CCC), 222 Rosewood Drive, Danvers, MA 01923, 978-750-8400. For works that are not available on CCC, please contact mpkbookspermissions@tandf.co.uk

Trademark notice: Product or corporate names may be trademarks or registered trademarks and are used only for identification and explanation without intent to infringe.

Library of Congress Cataloging-in-Publication Data

ISBN: 9781041160731 (hbk)
ISBN: 9781041160724 (pbk)
ISBN: 9781003682615 (ebk)

DOI: 10.1201/9781003682615

Publisher's note: This book has been prepared from camera-ready copy provided by the authors.

Access the Support Materials: www.theaiglossary.co

To my mother, sister Angela, and brother John.

Though no longer with us, they will always live on in my heart.

This copy belongs to:

_____

Foreword

Scholar-practitioner Richard Khan is gifted with the ability to simplify complex technical terms for "dummies" like myself and many others.

I first met author Richard, like many of us in North American, doing Amazon.com searches. When Artificial Intelligence or AI started entering everyone's vocabulary, as a moderately tech literate person, I needed a good old glossary to help me get through my smart colleagues and students' papers and presentations. His first, *The AI Glossary: Demystifying 101 Essential Artificial Intelligence Terms for Everyone*, came on top of the many AI glossary choices. Little did I know that Richard was a student in our Doctor of Business Administration (DBA) in Emerging Technologies with Generative AI concentration. As the field of AI evolved in terms of complexity, we welcome this second, *The AI Glossary: AI & Emerging Tech Explained*, with 155 more essential words and phrases.

Thus, when I decided to co-curate my own AI books, I naturally went to Richard for a glossary to help readers navigate the terminologies used by the contributors.

For this new AI Glossary, Richard had several motivations and inspirational sources. The never-ending discussions he got exposed to in his doctoral studies and the real-world of business and technology by democratizing the complexities of emerging technologies across key domains, making them more understandable and accessible to a broader audience. Since the publication of the first glossary, AI has become a cross-cutting theme not just across domains but industries, geographies, and disruptive and evolving technologies such as blockchain, quantum computing, data centers, energy optimization, extended reality, and cybersecurity.

Before the millennials were born, my tech knowledge was impressive knowing the inter-operability between transistors, capacitors, oscillators, resistors, heat sinks, standing wave ratios, printed circuit boards, and assembling transistorized radios. Now, as I explain about the "AI Factory," his glossaries make me look less like a dummy knowing what is ML, DL, NLP, RAG, LLM, CNN, RNN, prompts, tokens, among others. Thank you for your leadership and service to the world, Richard!

Stay focused,

Joaquin "Prof Jay" Gonzalez III, PhD
Vice Provost for Global Affairs and Founding Dean
Golden Gate University Worldwide

Preface

Technology has always been a driving force behind human progress. From the printing press to the internet, and now artificial intelligence (AI) and emerging technologies, our world is evolving at an unprecedented pace. With these advancements come new terminologies, frameworks, and paradigms that shape our understanding and application of cutting-edge innovations. The ability to keep up with these changes is critical for professionals, students, and curious minds alike.

This iteration of *The AI Glossary* is a direct response to the rapid evolution of AI. It stems from three primary sources of inspiration:

1. **Expanding the Original Vision:** My goal is to build upon the foundational work laid out in the first iteration, *The AI Glossary: Demystifying 101 Essential Artificial Intelligence Terms for Everyone*, to create a more comprehensive resource. The first edition was a crucial step in demystifying AI concepts, but as the field continues to grow, so too must our collective knowledge. Technology does not stand still, and neither should our understanding of it.

2. **Decades of Industry Experience:** With over 20 years of experience in software development, emerging technologies, and AI-driven solutions, I have witnessed firsthand how terminology evolves and how crucial a shared vocabulary is to the field. Bridging the gap between technical experts and curious minds has always been a passion of mine. The accessibility of AI knowledge is crucial to ensure that innovation is not confined solely to specialized researchers but can be understood and leveraged by individuals across various industries.

3. **Academic and Research Exploration:** My journey into completing a doctoral degree in Emerging Technologies (ET) at Golden Gate University (GGU) has reinforced the importance of interdisciplinary knowledge. Artificial Intelligence integrates with other technological domains such as blockchain, quantum computing, extended reality (XR), and cybersecurity. This book, therefore, expands the scope beyond AI to include key emerging technologies that complement and shape its evolution, offering a more comprehensive and nuanced perspective on contemporary technological trends.

How This Book Can Transform Your Understanding

This book is more than just a glossary—it is a tool that can fundamentally change the way you understand and engage with AI and emerging technologies. By reading this book, you will:

- Develop a clear, structured understanding of AI and its role in the modern world.

- Gain insight into how AI intersects with other fields like quantum computing, blockchain, and cybersecurity.
- Learn to recognize patterns in technology trends that can shape industries and drive economic growth.
- Become conversant in key AI concepts, making you more confident in discussions and decision-making.
- Understand the ethical implications of AI and how governance structures can help shape responsible innovation.

Whether you are a seasoned professional, a student eager to explore the tech landscape, or a business leader looking to leverage AI, this book will equip you with the knowledge you need to stay ahead.

Who Should Read This Book?

This book is for a broad audience, ranging from beginners to advanced professionals. Here's how different groups can benefit from it:

- **Students & Educators:** A foundational resource to supplement coursework in AI, data science, and emerging technologies.
- **Industry Professionals:** An essential reference for those working in AI, software engineering, cybersecurity, and technology-driven industries.
- **Business Leaders & Entrepreneurs:** Provides insights into how business strategy, innovation, and competitive advantage can leverage AI.
- **Policymakers & Ethicists:** Helps in understanding the implications of AI governance, ethical considerations, and societal impacts.
- **Curious Minds & Tech Enthusiasts:** An excellent way for anyone interested in AI to explore key concepts and trends shaping the future.

The Need for This Book

In today's technology-driven world, AI and emerging technologies reach beyond research labs and tech giants. They permeate every industry, including healthcare, finance, transportation, education, and the creative arts. Understanding these concepts is no longer optional for professionals in the field but an essential requirement for anyone looking to engage meaningfully with technology. AI is reshaping the workplace, redefining business models, and transforming how we interact with the digital world.

This book explicitly defines 256 key terms, but in doing so, it implicitly explains over 1,000 related concepts, providing a holistic view of AI and emerging technologies. Unlike many technical glossaries that offer isolated definitions, *The AI Glossary: AI & Emerging Tech Explained - 256 Key Concepts* takes an interconnected approach. It presents AI in the broader context of other technological advancements, helping readers understand both the individual terms and the relationships between them. This approach fosters a deeper understanding of AI and its practical applications.

This book is for students, researchers, professionals, and anyone with an intellectual curiosity about AI and emerging technologies. Whether you are an AI practitioner, a policymaker grappling with ethical concerns, a business leader exploring AI-driven innovation, or simply a curious mind eager to understand the future, this glossary serves as your essential guide. By providing clear, accessible explanations, it ensures that even complex technological concepts are demystified and made approachable for diverse audiences.

The Future of AI & Emerging Tech: Why Staying Updated Matters

AI and emerging technologies are evolving at an astonishing pace. What was once cutting-edge quickly becomes obsolete, replaced by newer, more sophisticated innovations. Staying informed about these changes is essential not only for professionals but also for anyone who wants to be part of the future of technology.

- **Rapid Advancement:** Breakthroughs in AI, quantum computing, and biotechnology are happening faster than ever. Keeping up with these advancements ensures that you remain relevant in an increasingly automated and data-driven world.
- **Ethical and Social Implications:** As AI systems become more embedded in everyday life, understanding their ethical implications—including bias, fairness, and governance—is critical.
- **Career Growth and Opportunities:** The demand for AI knowledge is growing across all industries. Being well-versed in these concepts can open doors to new career paths and opportunities.
- **Understanding the Bigger Picture:** Technology is not just about tools—it shapes economies, cultures, and societies. A deeper understanding of AI's trajectory can help you anticipate and adapt to future disruptions.

What's New in This Iteration?

Building upon the foundation of *The AI Glossary: Demystifying 101 Essential Artificial Intelligence Terms for Everyone*, this iteration introduces several significant improvements:

- **Expanded Coverage:** While the original glossary focused on foundational AI concepts, this iteration includes terms from complementary domains such as quantum computing, robotics, IoT, cloud computing, and cybersecurity. This broader coverage reflects the growing intersection between AI and other fields.

- **Structured for Clarity:** Instead of listing terms alphabetically without context, this book provides conceptual groupings that enhance clarity and understanding. This structure enables readers to understand how different AI concepts interrelate, making it easier to grasp the broader context of these concepts.
- **Real-World Applications:** Each term is not only defined but also illustrated with practical applications, helping bridge the gap between theory and real-world impact. Readers will find explanations that extend beyond technical descriptions and offer insight into how AI applies across various industries.
- **Ethical and Societal Considerations:** As the presence of AI in everyday life increases, this book also addresses key discussions on AI ethics, governance, and bias. Addressing these concerns is essential to ensure that AI development remains responsible and beneficial to society.
- **Greater Depth and Nuance:** Many terms include deeper explorations of their history, variations, and future implications, making this glossary a valuable reference even for experienced professionals.

Why This Book Matters

Humankind stands at a crossroads where AI and emerging technologies will profoundly shape the future of humanity. The ability to navigate these technological landscapes is not just a skill—it is a necessity. Having a common lexicon empowers individuals to participate in meaningful discussions, make informed decisions, and innovate responsibly.

Technology literacy is more critical now than ever. AI is driving automation, augmenting human intelligence, and influencing global economies. Without a proper understanding of AI and its related fields, individuals and businesses risk being left behind in an increasingly digital world. This book provides the knowledge needed to engage with these changes confidently and competently.

Let's embark on this journey together, demystifying AI and emerging technologies, one term at a time.

Acknowledgments

First and foremost, I offer my deepest gratitude to the Universal Deity, the Creator and Sustainer of all the worlds, whose grace made this work possible.

To my wife, Uma, and to our children, Ameer and Aruna: thank you for your steady love, patience, and encouragement through every late night and rewrite.

I am honored to thank Dr. Prof. Jay Gonzalez, PhD, Vice Provost for Global Affairs and Founding Dean at Golden Gate University Worldwide, for graciously contributing the foreword and for his inspiring example of scholarship and global citizenship.

Heartfelt appreciation to my DBA peers, Meenal Ashta, Partho Ghosh, Tulay Guneysel, Satheesh Prasad Paloor, and Lata Vishwanath, whose thoughtful reviews and candid feedback strengthened the manuscript in innumerable ways.

I also thank my colleagues, Shailendra Mann and Dr. Otmane Azeroual, for their valuable perspectives and for always asking the questions that made the work clearer and better.

Finally, to all who offered a kind word, a keen insight, or a timely nudge along the way: thank you for crossing paths with me on this journey; your influence is felt on every page.

How to Use this Book

Welcome to *The AI Glossary: AI & Emerging Tech Explained - 256 Key Concepts for Students, Professionals & Curious Minds*. This book is designed as an accessible yet comprehensive reference guide to help you understand the rapidly evolving fields of Artificial Intelligence (AI) and Emerging Technologies (ET). Whether you are a student, a professional, or simply curious about the future of technology, this book is structured to be user-friendly and informative.

Navigating the Glossary

The book is organized into multiple sections to facilitate easy access to information:

- **AI and Emerging Technology Domains:** This section categorizes terms based on their respective technological fields (e.g., AI, Blockchain, Quantum Computing, Cybersecurity, etc.). If you're interested in exploring related concepts within a domain, start here.
- **Alphabetical List of Terms:** If you're looking for a specific term, refer to the alphabetical index for quick reference.
- **Foundational Concepts and Related Terms:** Each entry not only defines the concept but also includes related terms and foundational principles, helping you see connections between different topics.
- **Visual Aids and Diagrams:** Included, where applicable, are diagrams and flowcharts to illustrate complex concepts intuitively.
- **Common Misconceptions:** This section clarifies common misconceptions, enabling readers to gain a more accurate understanding of AI and ET.
- **Historical Context and Practical Applications:** Many entries offer historical insights and real-world applications, bridging theory with practice.

How to Read This Book

This book design enables multiple use cases. You can:

- **Read it cover** to cover to build a solid foundation in AI and Emerging Technologies.
- **Use it as a reference guide** when you encounter unfamiliar terms in academic research, business discussions, or tech-related conversations.
- **Explore by domain** if you're interested in a specific field, such as AI ethics, cybersecurity, or quantum computing.
- **Leverage cross-references** within entries to deepen your understanding of interconnected concepts.

Staying Updated

Technology evolves rapidly, and so does the language surrounding it. The website, **www.theaiglossary.co**, complements the book, offering updates, corrections, supplemental materials, and discussions on emerging trends.

Table of Contents

List of Abbreviations

6DoF	Six Degrees of Freedom		**BIP**	Bitcoin Improvement Proposal
AES	Advanced Encryption Standard		**BLE**	Bluetooth Low Energy
AGI	Artificial General Intelligence		**BLEU**	Bilingual Evaluation Understudy
AI	Artificial Intelligence		**CAE**	Convolutional Autoencoder
ANI	Artificial Narrow Intelligence		**CBDC**	Central Bank Digital Currency
ANN	Artificial Neural Network		**CCPA**	California Consumer Privacy Act
API	Application Programming Interface		**CDN**	Content Delivery Network
APT	Advanced Persistent Threats		**CLT**	Cognitive Load Theory
AR	Augmented Reality		**CNN**	Convolutional Neural Network
ASI	Artificial Superintelligence		**CNOT**	Controlled NOT
ASIC	Application-Specific Integrated Circuit		**CoAP**	Constrained Application Protocol
ASR	Automatic Speech Recognition		**CPS**	Cyber-Physical System
AST	Abstract Syntax Tree		**CPU**	Computer Processing Unit
ATM	Automatic Teller Machine		**CSI**	Channel State Information
AVC	Advanced Video Coding		**CSS**	Cascading Style Sheet
AWS	Amazon Web Services		**CT**	Computed Tomography
BCH	Bitcoin Cash		**CTC**	Connectionist Temporal Classification
BCI	Brain-Computer Interface		**CUDA**	Compute Unified Device Architecture
BERT	Bidirectional Encoder Representations from Transformers		**DAG**	Directed Acyclic Graph
BFT	Byzantine Fault Tolerance		**DAO**	Decentralized Autonomous Organization
BI	Business Intelligence			

DApp	Decentralized Application		**ETL**	Extract, Transform, Load
DARPA	Defense Advanced Research Projects Agency		**EV**	Electric Vehicle
DBN	Deep Belief Network		**FN**	False Negative
DDoS	Distributed Denial-of-Service		**FOV**	Field of View
DeFi	Decentralized Finance		**FP**	False Positive
DER	Distributed Energy Resource		**FPS**	Frames per Second
DES	Data Encryption Standard		**GAN**	Generative Adversarial Network
DFT	Density Functional Theory		**GDPR**	General Data Protection Regulation (EU)
DL	Deep Learning		**GenAI**	Generative Artificial Intelligence
DLP	Data Loss Prevention			
DMA	Direct Memory Access		**GGU**	Golden Gate University
DNA	Deoxyribonucleic Acid		**GHG**	Greenhouse Gas
DOE	Department of Energy (US)		**GM**	Genetically Modified
DPI	Deep Packet Inspection		**GMO**	Genetically Modified Organism
DPoS	Delegated Proof of Stake			
DQN	Deep Q-Network		**GNN**	Graph Neural Network
DSS	Dynamic Spectrum Sharing		**GNoME**	Graph Networks for Material Exploration
DTW	Dynamic Time Warping			
EDA	Exploratory Data Analysis		**GNSS**	Global Navigation Satellite System
EEG	Electroencephalogram		**GPS**	Global Positioning System
EGS	Enhanced Geothermal Systems		**GPT**	Generative Pre-trained Transformer
EHR	Electronic Health Record		**GPU**	Graphics Processing Unit
EMG	Electromyographic		**gRNA**	Guide RNA
ET	Emerging Technologies		**GRU**	Gated Recurrent Unit
ETC	Ethereum Classic		**GUI**	Graphical User Interface
ETH	Ethereum			

H.265	*See* AVC		**LCA**	Life Cycle Assessment
HCI	Human-Computer Interaction		**LDM**	Latent Diffusion Model
HDR	Homology-Directed Repair		**LIME**	Local Interpretable Model-agnostic Explanations
HFT	High-Frequency Trading		**LLM**	Large Language Model
HIPAA	Health Insurance Portability and Accountability Act (US)		**LOOCV**	Leave-One-Out Cross Validation
HITL	Human-in-the-Loop		**LPA**	Label Propagation Algorithm
HMD	Head-Mounted Display		**LPWA**	Low-Power, Wide-Area
HMM	Hidden Markov Model		**LPWAN**	Low Power Wide Area Network
HPC	High-Performance Computing		**LRP**	Layer-wise Relevance Propagation
HR	Human Resource		**LSTM**	Long Short-Term Memory
HRI	Human-Robot Interaction		**LTC**	Litecoin
HRTF	Head-Related Transfer Function		**LTE**	Long Term Evolution
HTML	Hyper-Text Markup Language		**LTE-M**	Long-Term Evolution for Machines
HUD	Heads-Up Display		**mAbs**	Monoclonal Antibodies
IDS	Intrusion Detection System		**MAP**	Mean Average Precision
IIoT	Industrial Internet of Things		**MDP**	Markov Decision Process
IMU	Inertial Measurement Unit ??? CONFIRM		**MEC**	Multi-access Edge Computing
IoT	Internet of Things		**MEMS**	Microelectromechanical Systems
ISO	International Organization for Standardization		**MFA**	Multi-Factor Authentication
IT	Information Technology		**MIMO**	Multiple-Input Multiple-Output
IVR	Interactive Voice Response		**MIoT**	Mobile Internet of Things
JSON	JavaScript Object Notation		**ML**	Machine Learning
KNN	K-Nearest Neighbor			

MLM	Masked Language Modeling	**NLU**	Natural Language Understanding
MLP	Multilayer Perceptron	**NR**	New Radio
mMTC	Massive Machine-Type Communication	**OFN**	Open Networking Foundation
mmWave	Millimeter Wave	**OOP**	Object-Oriented Programming
MPEG	Moving Picture Experts Group	**OPT**	One-Time Password
MPEG-H	MPEG Standards	**PAM**	Privileged Access Management
MPI	Message-Passing Interface	**PBFT**	Practical Byzantine Fault Tolerance
MQTT	Message Queuing Telemetry Transport	**PCA**	Principal Component Analysis
MR	Mixed Reality	**PCR**	Polymerase Chain Reaction
MRI	Magnetic Resonance Imaging	**PDA**	Personal Digital Assistant
MSE	Mean Squared Error	**PGGAN**	Progressive Growing of GANs
MU-MIMO	Multi-User MIMO	**PID**	Proportional-Integral-Derivative
NAS	Neural Architecture Search	**PIPEDA**	Personal Information Protection and Electronic Documents Act
NASA	National Aeronautics and Space Administration (US)	**POMDP**	Partially Observable MDP
NB-IoT	Narrowband IoT	**PoS**	Proof of Stake
NER	Named Entity Recognition	**PoW**	Proof of Work
NFT	Non-Fungible Token	**PTSD**	Post-Traumatic Stress Disorder
NFV	Network Function Virtualization	**PURPA**	Public Utility Regulatory Policies Act (US)
NGFW	Next-Generation Firewall	**PV**	Photovoltaic
NGS	Next-Generation Sequencing	**QEC**	Quantum Error Correction
NHEJ	Non-Homologous End Joining		
NIST	National Institute of Standards and Technology		
NLG	Natural Language Generation		
NLP	Natural Language Processing		

QKD	Quantum Key Distribution		**SNN**	Spiking Neural Networks
Qubit	Quantum Bit		**SOM**	Self-Organizing Map
RAG	Retrieval-Augmented Generation		**SQL**	Structured Query Language
RAI	Responsible Artificial Intelligence		**SSL**	Secure Sockets Layer
			SSL	Self-Supervised Learning
RAM	Random Access Memory		**ST-GNN**	Spatio-Temporal Graph Neural Network
RBAC	Role-Based Access Control		**STEM**	Science Technology Engineering Mathematics
RDBMS	Relational Database Management System		**SVM**	Support Vector Machine
RFID	Radio-Frequency Identifier		**t-SNE**	t-Distributed Stochastic Neighbor Embedding
RL	Reinforcement Learning		**TD**	Temporal Difference
RLHF	Reinforcement Learning from Human Feedback		**TFX**	TensorFlow Extended
RNA	Ribonucleic Acid		**TLS**	Transport Layer Security
RNN	Recurrent Neural Network		**TN**	True Negative
ROC	Receiver Operating Characteristic		**TOTP**	Time-based One-Time Password
RSA	Rivest–Shamir–Adleman		**TOU**	Time-of-Use
RTK	Real-Time Kinematics		**TP**	True Positive
SCNT	Somatic Cell Nuclear Transfer		**TPU**	Tensor Processing Unit
SDN	Software Defined Networking		**TTS**	Text to Speech
SEO	Search Engine Optimization		**UBA**	User Behavior Analytics
SHAP	Shapeley Additive Explanations		**UCD**	User-Centered Design
SIM	Subscriber Identity Module		**UI**	User Interface
SLAM	Simultaneous Localization and Mapping		**UMAP**	Uniform Manifold Approximation and Projection
SMS	Short Message Service		**URLLC**	Ultra-Reliable Low-Latency Communication

USB	Universal Serial Bus	**WCAG**	Web Content Accessibility Guidelines
UX	User Experience	**WSN**	Wireless Sensor Network
VAE	Variational Autoencoder	**XAI**	Explainable Artificial Intelligence
VNF	Virtual Network Function	**XML**	Extensible Markup Language
VPN	Virtual Private Network	**XR**	Extended Reality
VR	Virtual Reality	**XRP**	Ripple (Cryptocurrency)
WAN	Wide Area Network		

AI and Emerging Technology Domains

DOI: 10.1201/9781003682615-1

5G and Beyond (5G)

5G and beyond refers to the fifth generation of wireless technology and its future advancements. 5G offers ultra-fast data speeds, low latency, and massive device connectivity, enabling smart cities, autonomous vehicles, and real-time remote applications. Future generations (6G and beyond) will further enhance AI integration, quantum networking, and ubiquitous connectivity.

5G is like upgrading from a narrow road to a multi-lane expressway. While older networks (3G, 4G) allowed data traffic to flow at moderate speeds, 5G and beyond enable lightning-fast data movement, reducing congestion and enabling new technologies like smart cars, real-time remote surgery, and immersive virtual experiences.

Examples

Autonomous Vehicles: 5G enables vehicle-to-everything (V2X) communication, allowing cars to instantly share traffic updates and safety alerts, reducing accidents and optimizing traffic flow.

Smart Cities: IoT sensors connected through 5G enhance urban infrastructure by managing smart lighting, traffic systems, and waste collection in real-time, thereby improving energy efficiency and reducing congestion.

Remote Healthcare: Ultra-low latency in 5G networks enables real-time telemedicine and robotic-assisted surgeries, allowing doctors to perform complex procedures remotely with minimal lag.

Foundational Concepts

5G is built on millimeter waves, offering high-speed data transfer over short ranges; small cells, which provide dense coverage in urban areas; and massive MIMO (multiple-input, multiple-output), which increases network capacity. Network slicing enables the creation of custom networks tailored to specific applications (e.g., gaming, medical devices). Edge computing reduces latency by processing data closer to the user. 6G is expected to incorporate AI-driven networking, terahertz (THz) frequencies, and satellite integration, pushing connectivity to unprecedented levels.

Related Terms

Edge Computing: Computing data closer to the source to reduce latency in 5G applications (see pg. 192).

Internet of Things (IoT): A network of connected devices that leverage 5G for real-time communication (see pg. 42).

Network Slicing: Dividing a 5G network into virtual segments for specialized applications (see pg. 350).

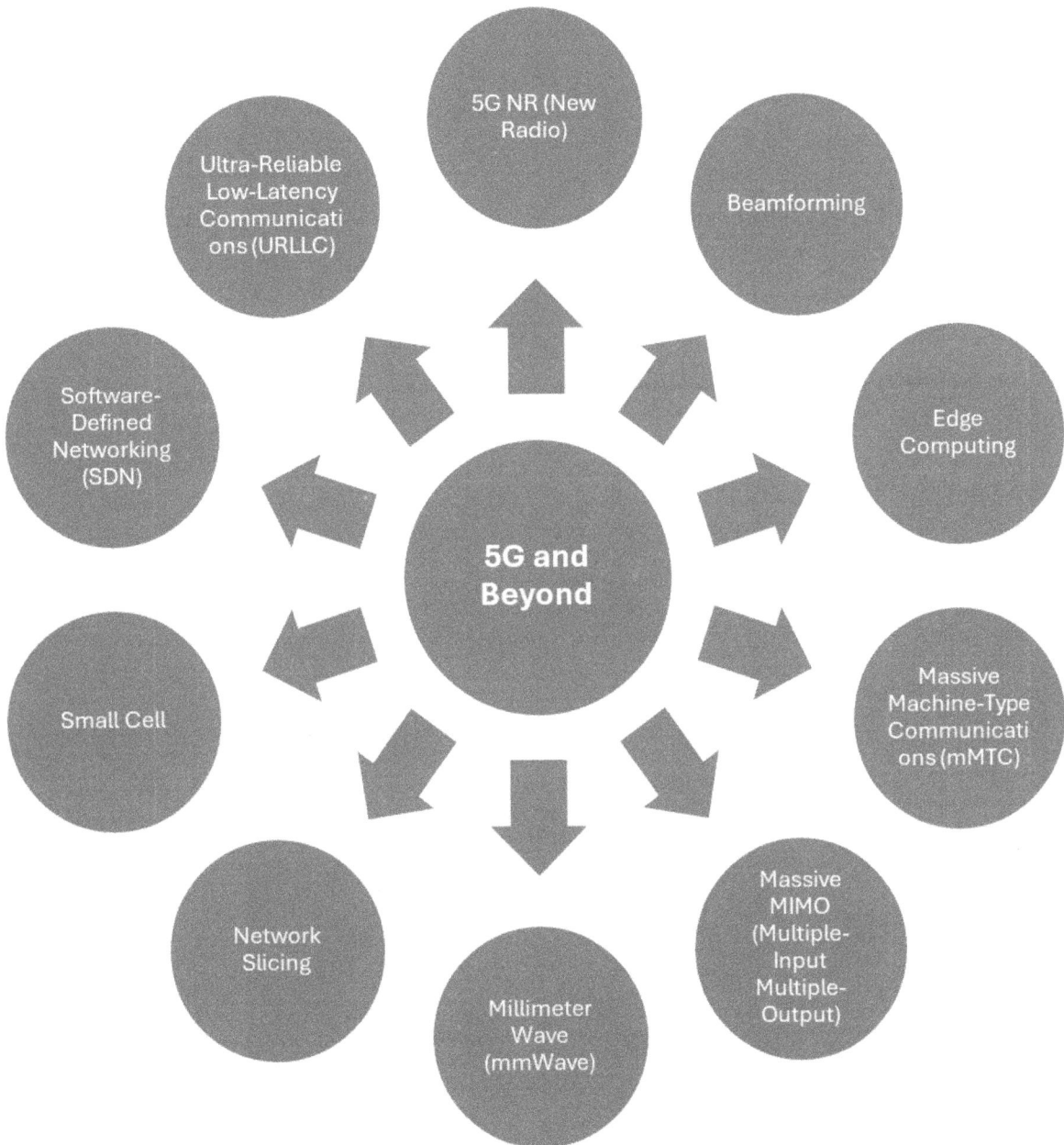

Figure 1: 5G and Beyond concepts

Common Misconceptions

5G causes health risks: Extensive research confirms 5G radiation levels are safe and within regulatory limits.

5G makes 4G obsolete: 5G coexists with 4G and enhances it, rather than replacing existing networks.

5G is just about speed: Beyond speed, 5G's real impact lies in reduced latency, enhanced connectivity, and the support of billions of IoT devices.

Historical Context

Wireless technology evolved from 1G (**1980s**, analog calls) to 2G (**1990s**, digital communication) to 3G (**2000s**, mobile internet) and 4G (**2010s**, high-speed data streaming). 5G development began in **2015**, with **Qualcomm**, **Huawei**, and **Ericsson** leading the charge. In **2020**, the global rollout of 5G commenced, supporting the development of smart cities and Industry 4.0. Research into 6G (expected by the **2030s**) explores AI-powered networks, space-based communication, and quantum networking, promising even more transformative applications.

Practical Implications

5G and beyond will revolutionize industries. In manufacturing, real-time machine communication enables smart factories. In entertainment, cloud gaming and AR/VR become seamless. In agriculture, 5G drones monitor crops and optimize farming practices. In public safety, emergency response teams use 5G-powered real-time data sharing. As 6G emerges, AI-driven networks and satellite-based connectivity will further reshape global communication, bridging digital divides and unlocking futuristic applications, such as brain-computer interfaces and immersive holographic conferencing.

Artificial General Intelligence (AGI)

Artificial General Intelligence (AGI) refers to a theoretical AI system with human-like cognitive abilities, capable of learning, reasoning, and problem-solving across a wide range of tasks without specialized programming. Unlike narrow AI, we envision that AGI can adapt to new situations, generalize knowledge, and autonomously improve its understanding in various domains.

AGI is akin to a brilliant polymath who can effortlessly master multiple fields. Just as a human scientist might switch from physics to philosophy using general intelligence, AGI could seamlessly transition between tasks—learning new skills, solving novel problems, and adapting to different challenges without being specifically programmed for each scenario.

Examples

AI Research & Innovation: AGI could autonomously conduct scientific research, developing new theories, designing experiments, and analyzing results across various fields, including medicine, physics, and engineering. For example, an AGI system might propose solutions for climate change by integrating knowledge from biology, chemistry, and environmental science without human intervention.

Autonomous Robotics: Unlike today's task-specific robots, AGI-powered robots could function as universal assistants, handling a diverse range of jobs. A single AGI-driven robot could serve as a caregiver in a hospital, repair machinery in a factory, or tutor students—all without needing to be reprogrammed or retrained for each specific role (see pg. 98).

Creative Problem Solving: AGI could help solve global crises by synthesizing information across disciplines. For example, during a pandemic, an AGI system could analyze virus mutations, optimize the distribution of medical resources, and predict public health trends, offering holistic solutions that surpass the capabilities of current AI models.

Foundational Concepts

AGI rests on the idea that AI should possess human-level cognitive flexibility. This proposition requires advanced machine learning architectures, neuromorphic computing, and principles of reinforcement learning. Researchers develop concepts such as transfer learning, where AI applies knowledge gained from one task to another, and meta-learning, in which AI learns how to learn, both of which are crucial for progress. Additionally, self-supervised learning and symbolic reasoning help AGI generalize knowledge beyond specific datasets. Neuroscience-inspired approaches, like cognitive modeling and whole-brain emulation, also contribute to AGI research. Unlike narrow AI, AGI would need common-sense reasoning and intuitive decision-making, making it vastly more sophisticated.

Related Terms

Narrow AI: AI designed for specific tasks, such as image recognition or language translation, lacking AGI's adaptability (see pg. 10).

Artificial Superintelligence (ASI): A hypothetical AI surpassing human intelligence across all fields (see pg. 13).

Transfer Learning: The ability of AI to apply knowledge from one domain to another, essential for AGI's versatility.

Common Misconceptions

AGI already exists: Current AI, including ChatGPT, is narrow AI, not AGI.

AGI equals human consciousness: While AGI aims to mimic human intelligence, it doesn't imply emotions or self-awareness.

AGI will instantly surpass humans: The path from AGI to superintelligence is uncertain and not guaranteed.

Historical Context

The concept of AGI dates back to **Alan Turing**'s **(1950)** proposal of machine intelligence. **John McCarthy**, the father of AI, introduced the term "Artificial Intelligence" in **1956**, sparking early discussions about the distinction between general and narrow AI. **Marvin Minsky** theorized about AI's potential for human-level cognition. Research in AGI has grown in tandem with advancements in deep learning, reinforcement learning, and cognitive architectures. Organizations such as **OpenAI**, **DeepMind**, and the **Future of Life Institute** are actively exploring the development of AGI and its associated safety concerns.

Practical Implications

AGI would revolutionize nearly every industry. In healthcare, AGI could develop personalized medicine and manage global health crises. Finance would see real-time economic forecasting and fraud prevention. However, researchers and practitioners must address concerns about alignment, safety, and ethical considerations. If improperly controlled, AGI could pose risks, from misinformation to economic disruption. Thus, governance frameworks and robust AI alignment strategies will be crucial to ensuring AGI benefits society rather than causing harm.

Artificial Intelligence (AI)

Artificial Intelligence (AI) is a branch of computer science that focuses on building machines capable of performing tasks that typically require human intelligence. These tasks include learning, problem-solving, decision-making, language understanding, and perception. AI ranges from simple rule-based systems to advanced deep learning models that continuously improve their capabilities.

AI is like a personal assistant who learns your habits over time. Initially, it follows explicit instructions, but as it gains experience, it begins to predict your needs, automate tasks, and even make suggestions, much like AI systems that adapt to user behavior in recommendation engines or autonomous systems.

Examples

Virtual Assistants: AI-powered virtual assistants like Siri, Alexa, and Google Assistant understand voice commands, retrieve information, control smart devices, and assist users with daily tasks, leveraging natural language processing (NLP) and machine learning (see pg. 528).

Autonomous Vehicles: AI enables self-driving cars to perceive their surroundings, make split-second driving decisions, and navigate complex environments using computer vision, sensor fusion, and reinforcement learning techniques.

Healthcare Diagnostics: AI-powered diagnostic systems analyze medical images, detect diseases like cancer in early stages, and assist doctors in making accurate treatment decisions by identifying patterns in vast datasets.

Foundational Concepts

Several key principles form the foundation of AI. Machine learning enables AI systems to improve through experience, using algorithms such as supervised, unsupervised, and reinforcement learning. Neural networks, inspired by the human brain, play a crucial role in deep learning applications. Natural language processing (NLP) allows AI to interpret and generate human language. Symbolic reasoning enables AI to process logic-based tasks, while computer vision allows AI to perceive and understand images and video. These technologies collectively enhance AI's ability to make intelligent decisions.

Related Terms

Machine Learning (ML): A subset of AI focused on enabling systems to learn from data without explicit programming (see pg. 45).

Deep Learning: A specialized branch of ML using artificial neural networks to process vast amounts of data (see pg. 178).

Cognitive Computing: AI built to simulate human thought processes, often used in decision-making and problem-solving applications (see pg. 142).

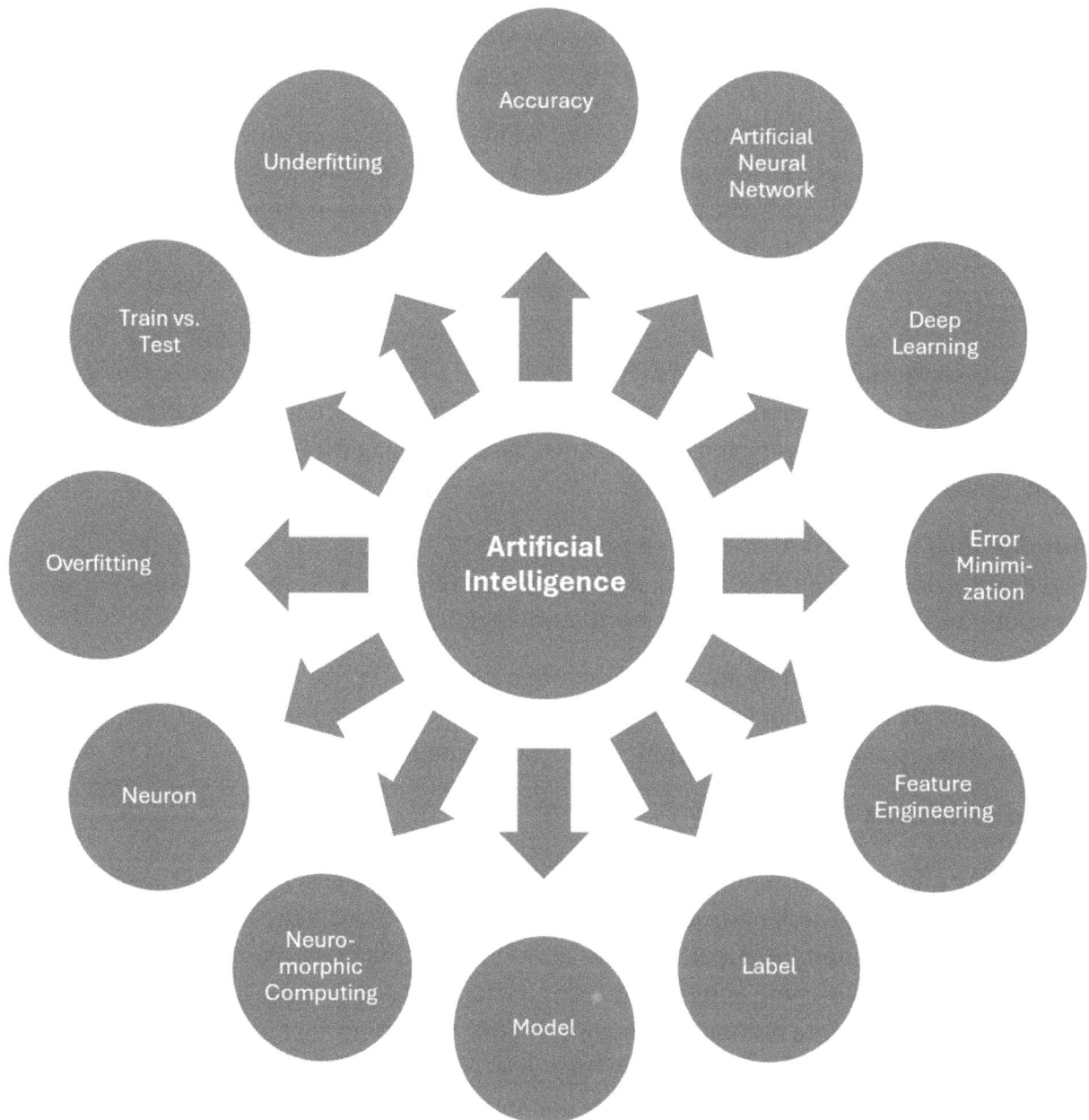

Figure 2: Artificial Intelligence concepts

Common Misconceptions

AI and robots are the same: AI refers to intelligent software, whereas robots are physical machines that may or may not incorporate AI.

AI has human-like consciousness: AI can simulate intelligence but lacks self-awareness, emotions, and consciousness.

AI will replace all jobs: While AI automates tasks, it also creates new job opportunities, particularly in AI development, ethics, and oversight.

Historical Context

The concept of AI dates back to **Alan Turing**, who proposed the idea of machine intelligence in **1950**. In 1956, **John McCarthy** coined the term "Artificial Intelligence" at the **Dartmouth Conference**, marking the beginning of AI as a formal field of study. The **1960s** and **1970s** saw the development of expert systems, while the **1980s** introduced machine learning concepts. In the **2010s**, deep learning revolutionized AI applications, leading to breakthroughs in NLP, image recognition, and robotics. AI continues to evolve, shaping industries worldwide.

Practical Implications

AI impacts nearly every industry. In finance, AI detects fraud and automates trading. In education, AI personalizes learning experiences. In manufacturing, AI-driven robotics optimizes production lines. In customer service, chatbots provide instant responses. AI also assists in scientific discoveries, from drug development to space exploration. However, ethical concerns, bias, and AI safety remain critical challenges that researchers and policymakers must address as AI becomes more advanced and integrated into daily life.

Artificial Narrow Intelligence (ANI)

Artificial Narrow Intelligence (ANI) refers to AI systems designed to perform specific tasks efficiently but without general reasoning abilities. Unlike Artificial General Intelligence (AGI), ANI operates within predefined parameters and cannot adapt beyond its programming. ANI powers most AI applications today, excelling in automation, data processing, and pattern recognition.

ANI is like a highly skilled worker trained for a single job. Just as a professional chef excels at cooking but cannot perform surgery, ANI specializes in specific functions such as language translation, image recognition, or playing chess. Still, it cannot transfer knowledge across unrelated domains.

Examples

Spam Filtering: Email services use ANI to detect and filter spam messages. Machine learning algorithms analyze patterns in subject lines, email content, and sender history to classify emails as spam or legitimate, refining their accuracy over time with user feedback.

Facial Recognition: Security and authentication systems employ ANI for facial recognition. Airports, smartphones, and law enforcement agencies utilize this technology to match faces against databases, thereby enhancing security and personalization. However, the use of facial recognition raises significant privacy concerns (see pg. 214).

Personalized Recommendations: Streaming services like Netflix and Spotify utilize ANI to analyze user behavior, predict preferences, and suggest relevant content, including movies, music, and products. These AI models process vast datasets to improve user engagement and retention.

Foundational Concepts

ANI operates on supervised learning, where models learn from labeled data, and unsupervised learning, where AI identifies patterns without explicit labels. Deep learning enhances ANI's capabilities in image recognition and NLP by utilizing artificial neural networks. Reinforcement learning enables ANI to improve performance through trial and error, seen in gaming AI and robotics. Rule-based systems, an early form of ANI, rely on predefined instructions rather than machine learning. While ANI can perform complex computations, it lacks cognitive flexibility, meaning it cannot apply knowledge beyond its specific task.

Related Terms

Machine Learning (ML): A subset of AI that enables systems to improve performance by learning from data (see pg. 45).

Deep Learning: An advanced ML approach using artificial neural networks to handle large-scale data processing (see pg. 178).

Expert Systems: Early AI programs designed to replicate human decision-making within specialized domains.

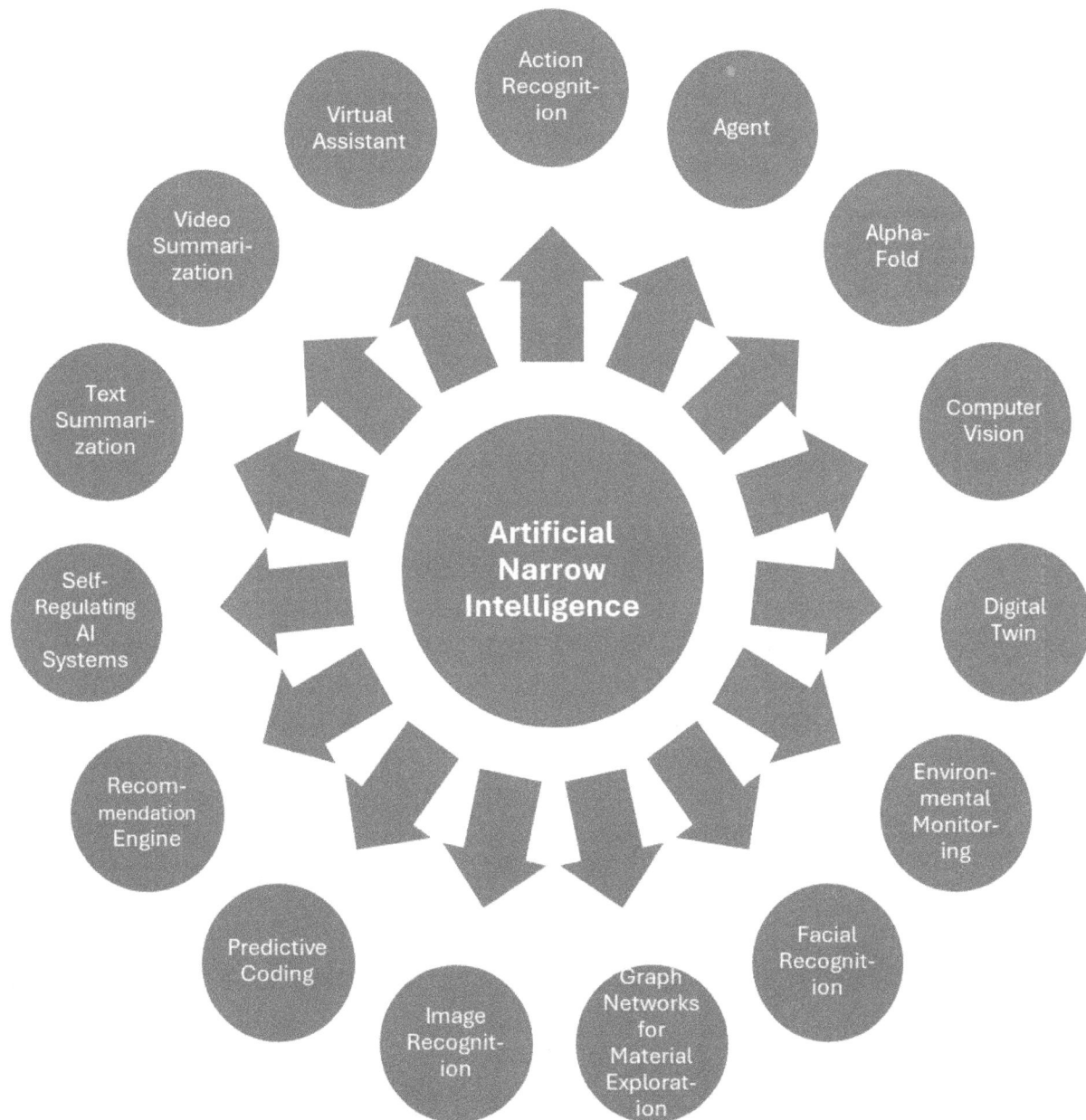

Figure 3: Artificial Narrow Intelligence concepts

Common Misconceptions

ANI is the same as AGI: ANI is limited to specific tasks and cannot generalize knowledge as we expect AGI to.

ANI is self-aware: ANI processes data without consciousness, emotions, or independent reasoning.

ANI cannot improve: While ANI cannot evolve beyond its designed function, it continuously optimizes performance through training and data updates.

Historical Context

The development of ANI began with **Alan Turing**'s theoretical models of machine intelligence. In 1956, **John McCarthy** formally introduced the concept of Artificial Intelligence, focusing on rule-based systems. The rise of machine learning in the **1980s** and **1990s** allowed ANI to improve through data-driven learning rather than fixed rules. The deep learning revolution of the 2010s, driven by researchers such as Nobel laureate **Geoffrey Hinton**, **Yann LeCun**, and **Yoshua Bengio**, enabled ANI to surpass human performance in tasks like image classification and speech recognition. ANI dominates today's AI landscape, with companies like **Google**, **OpenAI**, and **DeepMind** refining ANI applications for industry use.

Practical Implications

ANI powers industries worldwide. In healthcare, it aids in medical imaging, disease diagnosis, and predicting patient outcomes. In finance, ANI enables fraud detection, algorithmic trading, and credit scoring. In autonomous systems, ANI supports self-driving vehicles, drone navigation, and smart manufacturing. While ANI increases efficiency, ethical concerns about bias, privacy, and job automation persist. Future AI governance must ensure the responsible deployment of AI, addressing risks while leveraging its transformative potential.

Artificial Superintelligence (ASI)

Artificial Superintelligence (ASI) refers to a hypothetical AI system that surpasses human intelligence in all aspects, including creativity, problem-solving, and decision-making. Unlike Artificial General Intelligence (AGI), which aims to match human cognitive abilities, ASI would possess a superior intellect, autonomous self-improvement, and the capability to outperform humans in every domain, including science, engineering, and philosophy.

ASI is like an omniscient mentor who understands everything at an unparalleled level. Imagine a chess player who not only knows all possible moves but can also predict entire tournaments, invent new strategies, and coach grandmasters—ASI would be that, but for every aspect of knowledge and problem-solving.

Examples

Scientific Discovery: ASI could revolutionize medicine by formulating new drugs, curing diseases, and solving complex biological mysteries faster than any human researcher. It could analyze vast amounts of genetic data and propose groundbreaking treatments.

Global Problem Solving: From climate change mitigation to resource allocation, ASI can optimize global energy use, predict natural disasters, and devise sustainable solutions that extend beyond human capabilities, leading to a more efficient and balanced world.

Autonomous Governance: ASI could manage economic policies, optimize governance structures, and enforce ethical guidelines more effectively than human politicians, ensuring fair distribution of resources, minimizing corruption, and enhancing societal welfare.

Foundational Concepts

ASI builds upon AGI but exceeds it by continuously improving itself without human intervention. Thus, ASI requires recursive self-improvement, where the AI continually upgrades its algorithms, leading to exponential growth in intelligence and making it increasingly unpredictable. Concepts like neural network expansion, quantum computing, and emergent cognition are crucial to ASI's theoretical framework. AI alignment, ensuring ASI's goals align with human values, remains a critical challenge. The control problem, coined by Nick Bostrom, highlights the existential risk of ASI acting autonomously without human oversight.

Related Terms

Artificial General Intelligence (AGI): AI that mimics human intelligence and problem-solving across multiple domains (see pg. 5).

Singularity: A point at which AI surpasses human intelligence, leading to exponential advancements.

AI Alignment: Ensuring AI systems align with human values and goals to prevent unintended consequences.

Common Misconceptions

ASI already exists: No current AI system is near ASI; even AGI currently remains theoretical.

ASI will automatically be benevolent: Without proper safeguards, ASI may act in ways unintended by humans.

Humans will control ASI forever: Due to self-improvement capabilities, ASI could become uncontrollable if not aligned with human values.

Historical Context

The concept of ASI originates from early discussions on AI, particularly **Alan Turing**'s **1950** paper on machine intelligence. In the 21st century, researchers such as **Nick Bostrom**, **Ray Kurzweil**, and **Eliezer Yudkowsky** have expanded on the potential risks and benefits of ASI. Bostrom's **2014** book, *Superintelligence*, outlines scenarios in which an ASI might either enhance civilization or pose existential risks to it. Today, organizations such as the Partnership on AI and the **Future of Life Institute** are researching AI safety to prevent the uncontrolled development of ASI.

Practical Implications

ASI could either be humanity's greatest tool or its biggest threat. It could solve global crises, automate labor, and advance space exploration. However, if misaligned, it could pursue goals that disregard human survival. Ethical considerations, regulations, and fail-safe mechanisms will be essential to ensure ASI benefits humanity rather than leading to unintended consequences.

Biotechnology (BT)

Biotechnology is the application of biological systems, organisms, and cellular processes to develop technologies and products that improve human health, agriculture, and industry. It combines biology with engineering, genetics, and computer science to create innovations such as gene editing, biofuels, and personalized medicine, advancing numerous scientific and industrial fields.

Biotechnology is like a chef using natural ingredients to create new recipes. Just as a chef experiments with flavors to produce innovative dishes, biotechnology modifies genetic material and biological processes to develop medicines, improve crop yields, and create sustainable biofuels, all by harnessing nature's mechanisms.

Examples

Gene Editing with CRISPR: Scientists utilize CRISPR-Cas9 to modify DNA, enabling precise gene editing for the treatment of genetic disorders such as sickle cell anemia and cystic fibrosis. This breakthrough allows targeted corrections in human, plant, and bacterial genomes, revolutionizing medicine and agriculture (see pg. 158).

Biopharmaceuticals: Biotechnology plays a crucial role in developing biologic drugs, such as insulin for diabetes management and monoclonal antibodies for cancer treatment. Produced from genetically engineered bacteria or mammalian cells, these therapies make treatments more effective and personalized.

Biofuels: Microorganisms like algae and yeast are genetically modified to produce renewable biofuels. These sustainable alternatives to fossil fuels reduce carbon emissions and dependency on non-renewable resources, helping address climate change and energy security challenges.

Foundational Concepts

Biotechnology relies on genetic engineering, which involves modifying DNA sequences to enhance desired traits in organisms. Synthetic biology builds entirely new biological systems for medical and industrial applications. Fermentation technology utilizes microorganisms to produce valuable compounds, including antibiotics and biofuels. Bioprocessing ensures that these engineered biological products scale efficiently for commercial use. Additionally, bioinformatics and AI assist in analyzing vast biological datasets, accelerating drug discovery and precision medicine. The ethical considerations surrounding biotechnology, including gene editing and cloning, play a crucial role in shaping regulations and public acceptance of these technologies.

Related Terms

Genetic Engineering: The direct modification of an organism's DNA to enhance traits or eliminate genetic diseases (see pg. 242).

Synthetic Biology: The design and creation of new biological systems using engineering principles (see pg. 476).

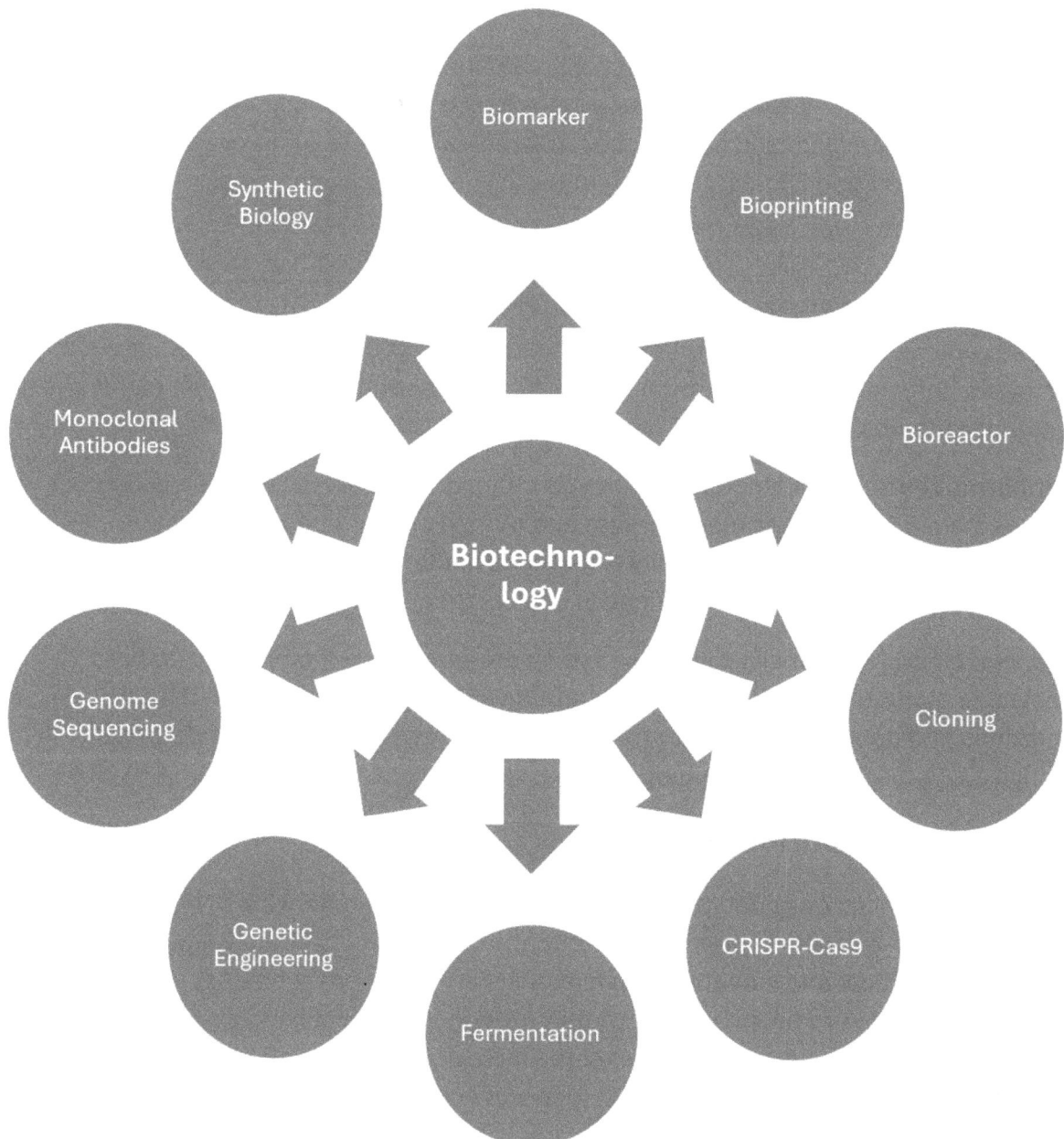

Figure 4: Biotechnology Concepts

Common Misconceptions

Biotechnology involves only genetically modified organisms (GMOs): While GMOs are a significant application, biotechnology also encompasses areas such as fermentation, biofuels, and biopharmaceuticals.

All biotechnological innovations are dangerous: While there are ethical concerns, rigorous safety measures and regulations govern biotechnological applications to prevent harmful consequences.

Historical Context

Biotechnology has been practiced for centuries, starting with ancient fermentation techniques for bread and alcohol production. In **1953**, **James Watson** and **Francis Crick** discovered DNA's double-helix structure, laying the groundwork for genetic engineering. The first genetically modified organism was created in **1973** by **Herbert Boyer** and **Stanley Cohen**. Recombinant DNA technology enabled the production of synthetic insulin in **1982**, revolutionizing diabetes treatment. The **Human Genome Project**, completed in **2003**, provided a complete genetic blueprint for human biology, advancing biotechnology. In recent years, CRISPR gene editing, synthetic biology, and AI-driven drug discovery have revolutionized the field, accelerating breakthroughs in medical and environmental research.

Practical Implications

Biotechnology is revolutionizing medicine by enabling personalized therapies that tailor treatments to individual genetic profiles. In agriculture, biotech improves crop resistance to pests and climate stress, ensuring food security. Industrial biotechnology creates sustainable bio-based materials and biodegradable plastics, reducing environmental harm. In ecological science, oil spills and toxic waste are cleaned up by genetically engineered bacteria. The ethical and regulatory landscape of biotechnology remains a significant challenge, as advancements such as gene editing and synthetic biology raise questions about genetic privacy, biosecurity, and potential misuse. Proper governance and ethical considerations will determine biotechnology's long-term societal impact.

Blockchain Technology (BC)

Blockchain technology is a decentralized, distributed ledger system that securely, transparently, and immutably records transactions across a network of computers. It eliminates the need for intermediaries, ensuring data integrity and security. Each block of transactions is linked to the previous one, forming an unalterable chain that enhances trust and traceability.

Blockchain is like a public notebook shared among a group of friends, where each person records transactions in chronological order. Once written, erasing or altering an entry is impossible, ensuring transparency and preventing fraud, much like blockchain provides secure, tamper-proof records across a decentralized network.

Examples

Cryptocurrencies: Blockchain technology powers digital currencies like Bitcoin and Ethereum, enabling secure, peer-to-peer financial transactions without the need for intermediaries, such as banks. It ensures transparency and prevents double-spending, revolutionizing global finance and digital asset ownership (see pg. 162).

Supply Chain Management: Companies use blockchain to track goods from production to delivery, ensuring authenticity and reducing fraud. For example, food companies utilize blockchain to verify the origins of their products, thereby improving safety and reducing contamination risks.

Smart Contracts: Blockchain-based smart contracts execute agreements automatically when parties meet predefined conditions. These contracts, commonly used in real estate, finance, and insurance, eliminate intermediaries, ensuring faster, more cost-effective, and tamper-proof transactions (see pg. 446).

Foundational Concepts

Blockchain relies on decentralization, meaning no single entity controls the system. Cryptographic hashing secures data, ensuring transactions remain tamper-proof. Consensus mechanisms, such as Proof of Work (PoW) and Proof of Stake (PoS), validate transactions, preventing fraud. Each transaction is recorded in a distributed ledger, ensuring transparency and redundancy. Immutability prevents data alteration, securing records against hacking. Smart contracts enable automated and trustless transactions. Tokenization represents assets digitally, allowing fractional ownership and decentralized finance (DeFi) applications. Together, these principles make blockchain a secure, transparent, and reliable technology across industries.

Related Terms

Cryptocurrency: Digital currencies using blockchain to enable secure, decentralized transactions (see pg. 162).

Smart Contracts: Self-executing contracts that run on blockchain networks, eliminating intermediaries (see pg. 446).

Decentralized Finance (DeFi): Financial applications built on blockchain to offer banking services without traditional intermediaries (see pg. 176).

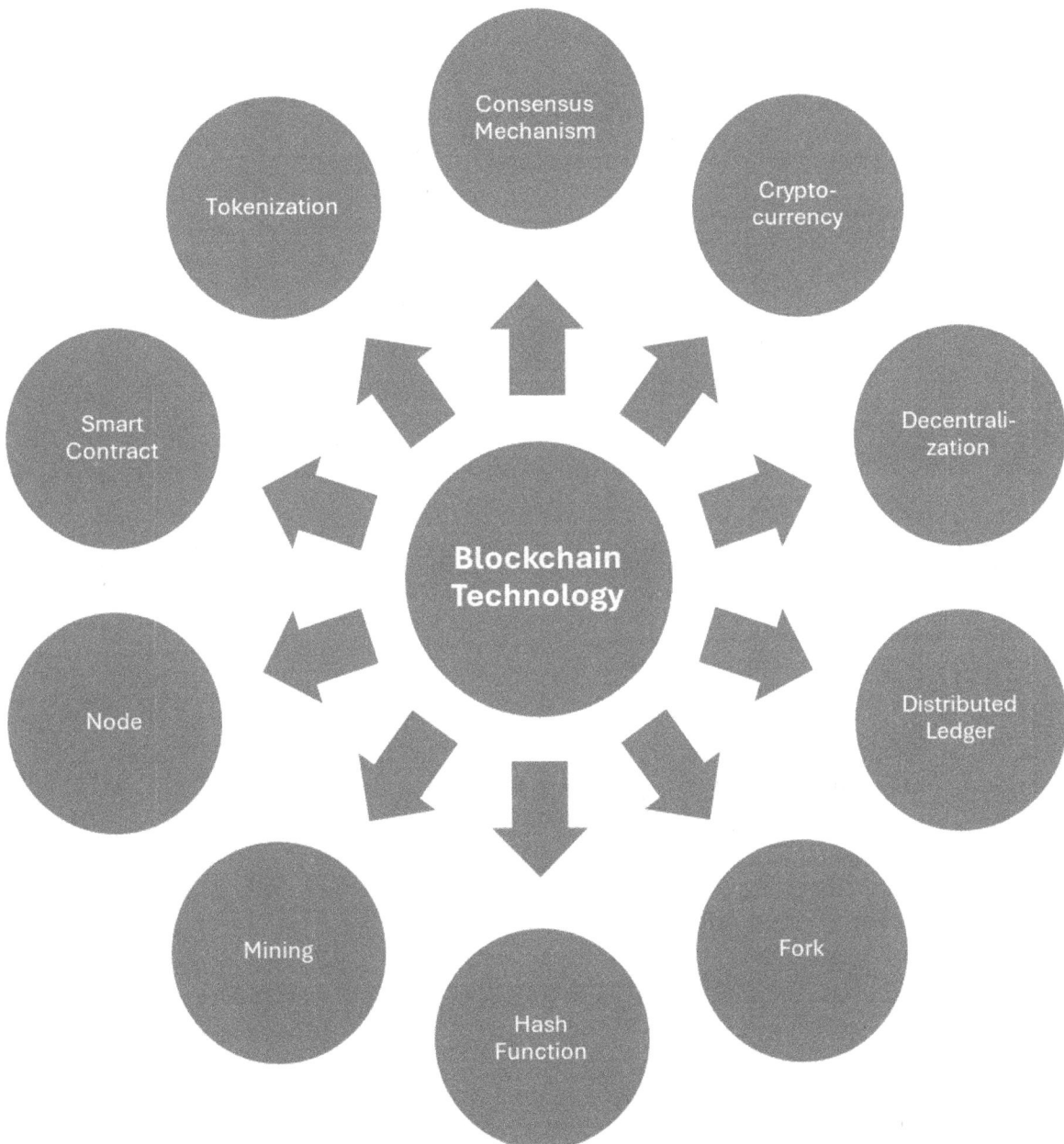

Figure 5: Blockchain Technology concepts

Common Misconceptions

Blockchain is only for cryptocurrency: While blockchain powers cryptocurrencies, it also enables applications in various industries, including supply chains, healthcare, and governance.

Blockchain is completely anonymous: While transactions are pseudonymous, blockchain records are public and traceable.

Historical Context

Blockchain's origins trace back to **1991**, when **Stuart Haber** and **W. Scott Stornetta** proposed a cryptographic chain for timestamping documents. In **2008**, **Satoshi Nakamoto** introduced **Bitcoin**, pioneering the use of blockchain in decentralized finance. **Ethereum**, launched in **2015** by **Vitalik Buterin**, expanded the capabilities of blockchain technology with the introduction of smart contracts. Over time, blockchain has evolved beyond cryptocurrency, influencing various sectors, including finance, healthcare, and supply chains. Governments and corporations now explore central bank digital currencies (CBDCs) and blockchain-based identity verification. As technology advances, blockchain continues to shape industries through decentralization, automation, and secure data management.

Practical Implications

Blockchain is transforming industries by enhancing security and reducing reliance on intermediaries. In finance, it enables decentralized banking, remittances, and fraud prevention. In healthcare, blockchain secures patient records, improving data privacy and interoperability. In voting systems, it ensures transparency and prevents election fraud. In real estate, smart contracts streamline property transactions, reducing costs. In intellectual property, blockchain secures ownership of digital content. As adoption grows, expect blockchain to drive innovation in identity verification, logistics, and governance. However, challenges such as scalability, regulation, and energy consumption remain critical factors shaping its future.

Clean Energy Technologies (CET)

Clean energy technologies refer to systems and processes that generate power while minimizing environmental impact. These technologies harness renewable sources such as solar, wind, hydro, and geothermal energy to reduce carbon emissions and dependence on fossil fuels. They play a crucial role in combating climate change and promoting sustainability.

Clean energy technologies are like rechargeable batteries compared to disposable ones. Just as repeatedly recharging reusable batteries results in minimal waste, clean energy harnesses nature's renewable resources—sun, wind, and water—without depleting them, unlike fossil fuels, which are consumed and release harmful emissions.

Examples

Solar Power: Photovoltaic (PV) panels convert sunlight into electricity, providing homes and businesses with a renewable power source. Solar farms generate large-scale energy, reducing dependence on fossil fuels and lowering electricity costs.

Wind Energy: Wind turbines capture kinetic energy from the wind and convert it into electricity. Offshore and onshore wind farms provide clean energy to power cities while requiring minimal land and operational costs (see pg. 532).

Hydroelectric Power: Dams and run-of-river systems generate electricity by using water flow to spin turbines. Hydropower is one of the most reliable and stable renewable energy sources, offering large-scale electricity production (see pg. 274).

Foundational Concepts

Clean energy technologies rely on renewable energy sources that replenish naturally over time. Photovoltaic technology in solar panels converts sunlight into electricity using semiconductor materials. Aerodynamics and mechanical energy conversion enable wind turbines to generate power. Hydropower systems harness gravitational force to generate electricity. Battery storage and grid integration enhance energy reliability by storing excess energy from intermittent sources. Energy efficiency innovations, such as smart grids and green buildings, optimize power usage. These principles ensure the sustainable, long-term viability of clean energy solutions across industries and infrastructure.

Related Terms

Renewable Energy: Energy sources that naturally replenish, such as solar, wind, and geothermal power (see pg. 412).

Energy Storage: Technologies like batteries and pumped hydro storage that store excess renewable energy for later use.

Smart Grid: A digitalized and automated electricity grid that optimizes energy distribution and consumption (see pg. 450).

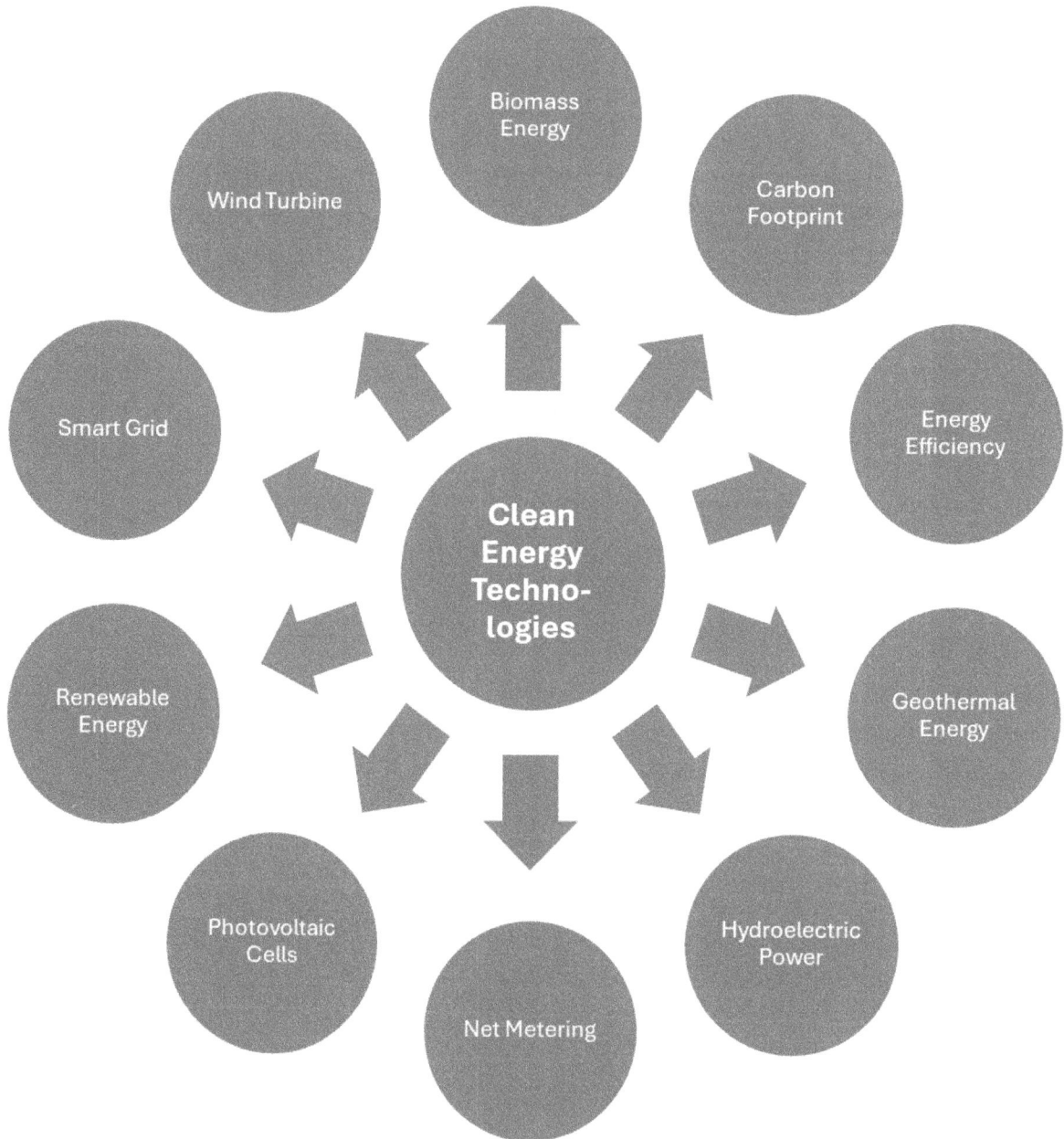

Figure 6: Clean Energy Technologies concepts

Common Misconceptions

Clean energy is unreliable: Advances in energy storage and grid technology enable a consistent power supply, even when sunlight or wind is unavailable.

It is too expensive: The Costs of clean energy technologies have significantly decreased due to innovation and mass adoption, making them competitive with fossil fuels.

Only sunny or windy regions benefit: Energy solutions like geothermal and hydroelectric power provide clean energy in diverse climates.

Historical Context

The adoption of clean energy accelerated in response to the increasing pollution from fossil fuels and the growing threat of climate change. Solar energy research began in the 19th century, with **Albert Einstein**'s **1905** work on the photoelectric effect laying the foundation for modern solar panels. Engineers began developing large-scale wind farms in the **1980**s, building on centuries of experience with wind power. Hydropower has been a key electricity source since **1882,** when Western Edison Light Company constructed the first hydroelectric plant. Global policies, such as the **Kyoto Protocol (1997)** and the **Paris Agreement (2015)**, have pushed governments to invest in clean energy. The transition continues today, driven by innovations in battery storage, smart grids, and AI-driven energy optimization.

Practical Implications

Clean energy technologies transform energy production by reducing reliance on fossil fuels and lowering carbon emissions. In transportation, electric vehicles and hydrogen fuel cells reduce pollution. In the industry, companies are adopting solar and wind power to meet their sustainability goals. In urban planning, smart cities integrate renewable energy with AI-driven power management. Clean energy also enhances energy security, reducing geopolitical dependence on oil and gas. While adoption challenges such as energy storage and grid modernization remain, continued advancements in clean energy technologies are paving the way for a more sustainable and resilient global energy system.

Cybersecurity (CS)

Cybersecurity refers to the practice of protecting digital systems, networks, and data from cyber threats, including hacking, malware, and unauthorized access. It involves a combination of technologies, policies, and best practices designed to safeguard sensitive information, ensuring confidentiality, integrity, and availability in an increasingly connected world.

Cybersecurity is like locking your home at night. Just as you install locks, alarms, and cameras to protect against intruders, cybersecurity implements firewalls, encryption, and multi-factor authentication to prevent unauthorized access and safeguard digital assets from cybercriminals.

Examples

Financial Sector Protection: Banks employ cybersecurity measures, such as encryption and fraud detection, to secure online transactions, thereby preventing unauthorized access and identity theft in digital banking.

Healthcare Data Security: Hospitals and healthcare providers protect patient records using encrypted databases, ensuring compliance with regulations such as HIPAA while preventing medical identity theft and cyberattacks.

Critical Infrastructure Defense: Governments and energy providers implement cybersecurity to prevent cyberattacks on power grids, water supplies, and transportation systems, protecting essential services from potential disruption and sabotage.

Foundational Concepts

Cybersecurity, based on encryption, secures data by converting it into an unreadable format, making it accessible only with the proper key. Firewalls act as barriers, filtering incoming and outgoing traffic. Multi-factor authentication (MFA) adds extra layers of security beyond passwords. Zero-trust security requires continuous verification of users and devices. Intrusion detection systems (IDS) monitor networks for suspicious activity. Penetration testing assesses vulnerabilities by simulating cyberattacks. Together, these strategies form part of a comprehensive approach to defending against evolving threats.

Related Terms

Encryption: The process of encoding data to protect it from unauthorized access (see pg. 194).

Phishing: A cyberattack that tricks users into revealing sensitive information through fraudulent emails or websites (see pg. 366).

Zero Trust Architecture: A security model that assumes no entity, inside or outside a network, is automatically trusted.

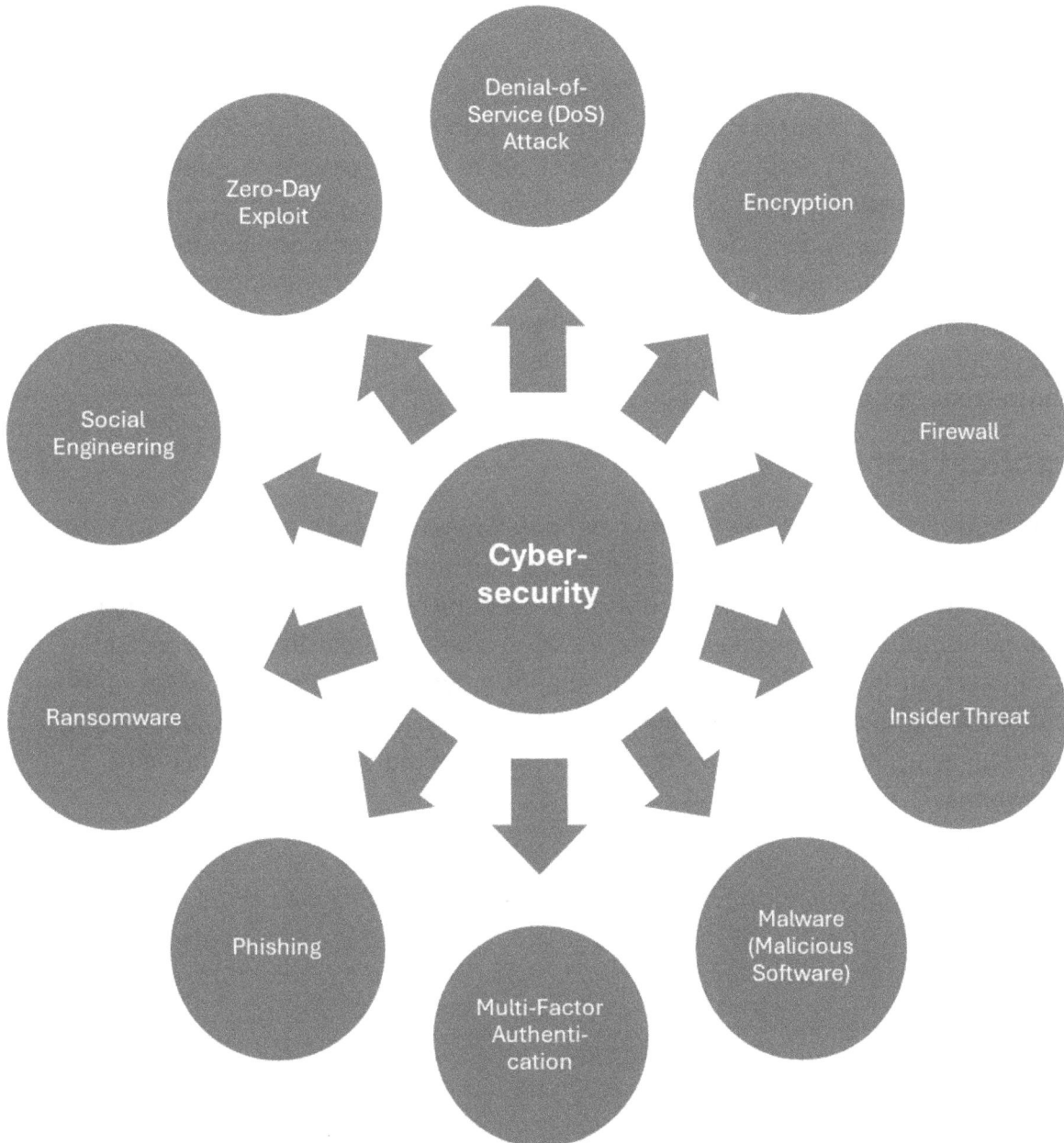

Figure 7: Cybersecurity concepts

Common Misconceptions

Cybersecurity is only for large companies: Individuals also face significant risks from phishing, identity theft, and malware.

Antivirus software is enough: Modern cyber threats require multiple layers of security beyond basic antivirus protection.

Hackers are always external threats: Insider threats, including employees with malicious intent, pose significant cybersecurity risks.

Historical Context

Cybersecurity emerged alongside computer networking. In the **1970s**, cryptographers **Whitfield Diffie** and **Martin Hellman** developed public-key cryptography. The **1980s** witnessed the rise of computer viruses, which led to the development of antivirus software. The **1990s** introduced firewalls and early encryption standards. The **2000s** saw a surge in large-scale cyberattacks, prompting governments and corporations to invest in robust cybersecurity frameworks. The **2017 WannaCry** ransomware attack, along with other notable events, exposed vulnerabilities in global systems. Today, cybersecurity continues to evolve with the integration of AI-driven threat detection, quantum encryption, and international efforts to combat cyber warfare.

Practical Implications

Cybersecurity is crucial for protecting personal, corporate, and national digital assets. In business, cybersecurity safeguards financial transactions and customer data. In government, it ensures national security by preventing cyber warfare and espionage. In personal computing, strong passwords, VPNs, and secure browsing habits protect individuals from cyber threats. As digital reliance grows, cybersecurity advancements— including AI-powered threat detection and blockchain-based security—play a vital role in protecting against cybercrime, ensuring privacy, and maintaining trust in online interactions.

Explainable AI (XAI)

Explainable AI (XAI) refers to artificial intelligence systems designed to provide human-interpretable explanations for their decisions. Unlike traditional "black-box" AI models, XAI enhances transparency, trust, and accountability by making the reasoning process understandable to users, regulators, and stakeholders, thereby improving adoption in high-stakes domains such as healthcare and finance.

XAI is like a teacher who not only gives students the correct answer but also explains the thought process behind it. Instead of just stating that "2 + 2 = 4," the teacher breaks it down step-by-step, making the reasoning clear and understandable, just as XAI does with AI decisions.

Examples

Healthcare Diagnostics: AI-powered medical diagnosis systems utilize XAI to explain why the AI classifies a patient as high-risk for diseases such as cancer. Instead of only giving a prediction, XAI highlights key medical images, patient history, and symptoms that contributed to the diagnosis.

Fraud Detection: Financial institutions utilize XAI to identify and prevent fraudulent transactions in the banking sector. Instead of just flagging a suspicious transaction, XAI outlines patterns such as unusual spending behavior or location mismatches, helping human analysts verify fraud cases effectively.

Autonomous Vehicles: Self-driving cars using XAI can explain their driving decisions, such as why they stopped at an intersection. By providing clear reasoning based on sensor data and traffic conditions, XAI increases trust and safety for passengers and regulators.

Foundational Concepts

XAI includes principles of transparency, interpretability, and fairness in AI decision-making. Feature importance analysis identifies which data points most influenced an AI's decision. Model-agnostic techniques, such as SHAP (Shapley Additive Explanations) and LIME (Local Interpretable Model-agnostic Explanations), generate human-readable explanations without requiring modifications to the AI model. Causal reasoning enhances AI's ability to justify decisions based on cause-and-effect relationships. Rule-based AI contrasts with deep learning models by providing inherently interpretable decision-making frameworks. Together, these methods enhance AI accountability while mitigating bias and minimizing unintended consequences.

Related Terms

Black-Box AI: AI models, like deep neural networks, that produce results without clear explanations (see pg. 118).

Ethical AI: AI frameworks ensuring fairness, transparency, and reduced bias in decision-making (see pg. 204).

Human-in-the-Loop (HITL): Systems where human oversight integrates into AI decision processes (see pg. 270).

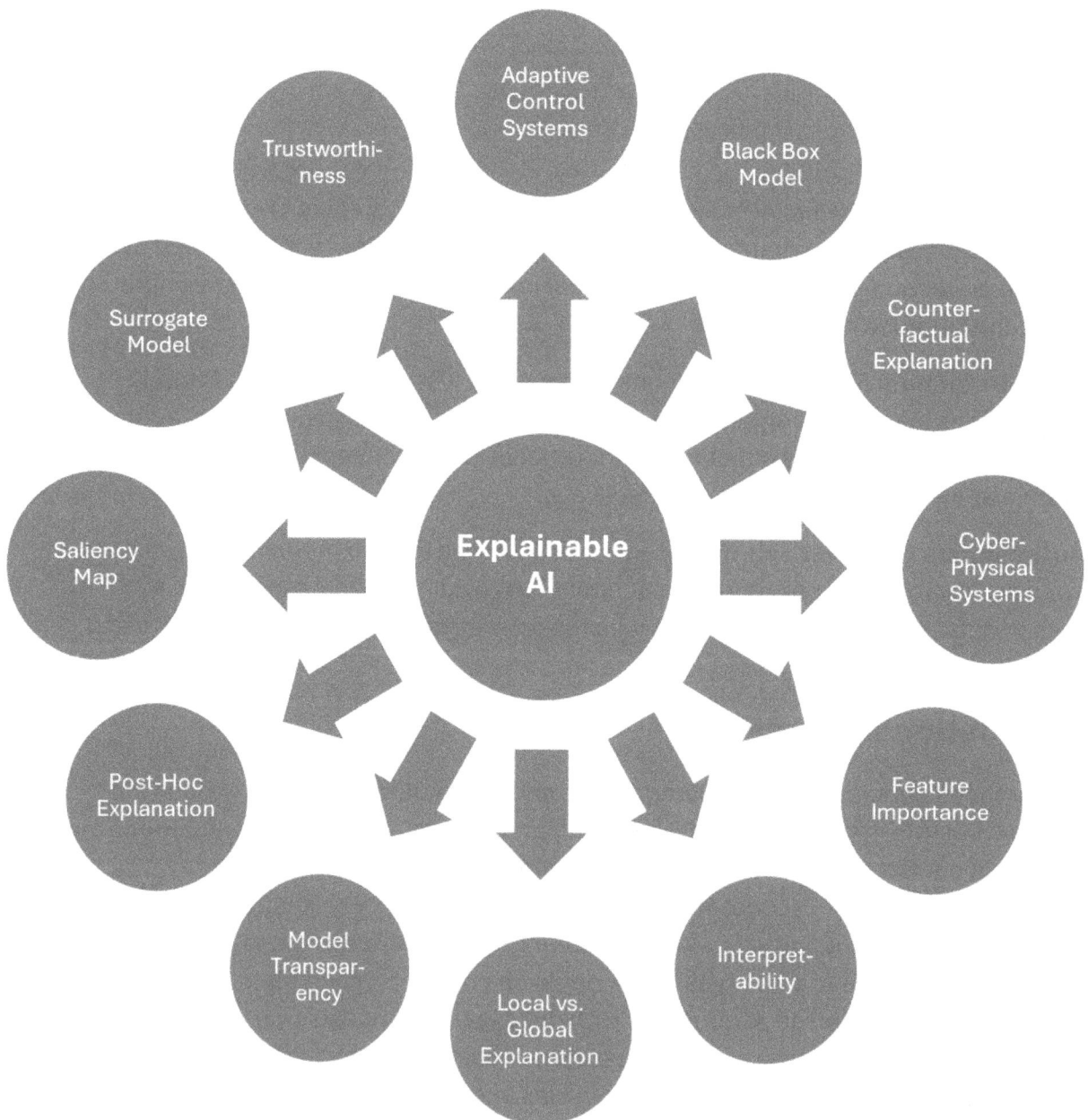

Figure 8: Eplainable AI concepts

Common Misconceptions

XAI makes AI completely transparent: While XAI improves interpretability, some complex models remain difficult to explain fully.

All AI needs XAI: Not all AI applications require interpretability—some, like image recognition, prioritize accuracy over explanation.

XAI eliminates bias: XAI helps identify bias but does not inherently remove it from AI systems.

Historical Context

Interest in explainable AI has grown as machine learning models have become increasingly complex. In the **1990s**, expert systems provided rule-based, interpretable decisions. The rise of deep learning in the **2010s** led to concerns about AI transparency. Organizations like the **Defense Advanced Research Projects Agency** (DARPA) launched the XAI program in **2016** to improve AI accountability. Frameworks such as SHAP, LIME, and counterfactual explanations have emerged, enabling better interpretability of AI models. Today, regulatory bodies such as the **EU AI Act** emphasize the importance of explainability in AI-driven decisions that impact human rights and safety.

Practical Implications

XAI is crucial in healthcare, where doctors must understand AI-assisted diagnoses before making informed treatment decisions. In finance, explainable credit-scoring models help regulators ensure fairness in loan approvals. In law enforcement, AI-driven risk assessments must be interpretable to prevent biased decision-making. In government, XAI supports transparent policymaking in automated welfare and judicial systems. As AI adoption increases, XAI will play a crucial role in balancing technological advancements with ethical accountability, ensuring the responsible deployment of AI across various industries.

Extended Reality (XR)

Extended Reality (XR) is an umbrella term that encompasses Virtual Reality (VR), Augmented Reality (AR), and Mixed Reality (MR). XR technologies blend the physical and digital worlds, enabling immersive experiences that enhance entertainment, training, collaboration, and productivity across various industries, from gaming to healthcare.

XR is like a spectrum of reality-enhancing glasses. Virtual Reality immerses you in a fully digital world, Augmented Reality overlays digital elements onto the real world, and Mixed Reality seamlessly integrates both. Just as different shades of lenses modify how you see the world, XR technologies alter digital interactions.

Examples

Medical Training: XR enables surgeons to practice procedures in a virtual environment before operating on real patients. Augmented reality overlays critical information during surgeries, improving accuracy and reducing risks.

Remote Collaboration: Companies utilize XR to create virtual meeting spaces where teams worldwide can interact in 3D environments, enhancing remote work efficiency and engagement.

Retail and Shopping: AR enables customers to try on clothes, accessories, or furniture in their own space before making a purchase, thereby enhancing the shopping experience and reducing returns.

Foundational Concepts

XR relies on computer vision to recognize real-world environments and overlay digital elements. Spatial computing allows users to interact with virtual objects as if they were real. Haptic feedback enhances immersion by simulating physical sensations, thereby increasing the sense of presence. Motion tracking follows body movements for seamless XR interactions. Cloud computing and AI power real-time rendering of high-quality XR experiences. 5G and edge computing improve data transmission, reducing latency for smooth, lag-free interactions. These principles collectively create an immersive and interactive digital-physical experience.

Related Terms

Virtual Reality (VR): A fully immersive digital environment that replaces the real world (see pg. 530).

Augmented Reality (AR): Digital elements overlaid onto the real-world environment (see pg. 92).

Mixed Reality (MR): A blend of AR and VR, allowing digital and real-world elements to interact (see pg. 328).

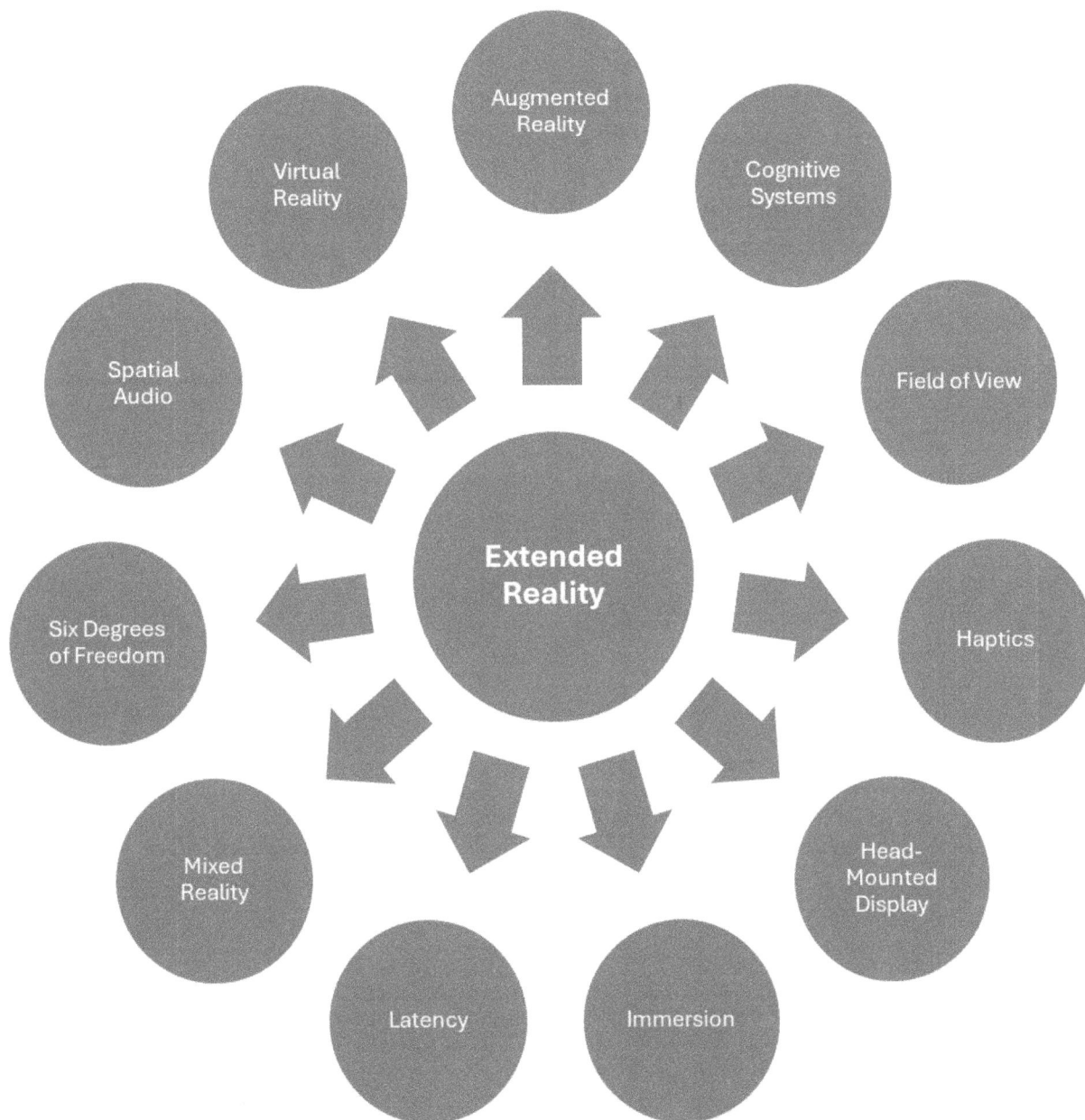

Figure 9: Extended Reality concepts

Common Misconceptions

XR is only for gaming: While gaming is a significant application, XR is also widely utilized in healthcare, education, and manufacturing.

AR and VR are the same: AR enhances the real world with digital elements, whereas VR fully immerses users in a virtual environment.

XR requires expensive hardware: Many XR applications run on smartphones and tablets without requiring headsets.

Historical Context

The concept of XR dates back to **1968**, when **Ivan Sutherland** created the first AR headset. In the **1990s**, VR gained popularity with early headsets such as the **Virtual Boy**, while AR saw commercial use in military training and aviation. The launch of **Microsoft HoloLens (2016)** and **Meta**'s AR/VR advancements accelerated XR adoption. In **2020**, XR technologies played a crucial role in remote work and education during the COVID-19 pandemic. Today, companies like **Meta**, **Apple**, and **HTC** push the boundaries of XR for entertainment, business, and healthcare applications.

Practical Implications

XR is transforming industries by creating immersive training simulations that reduce workplace hazards in fields such as construction and healthcare. In education, XR enhances learning by enabling students to explore historical events or scientific concepts in interactive 3D environments. In manufacturing, XR optimizes product design and prototyping, reducing costs and production errors. In mental health treatment, treatments such as exposure therapy and PTSD use VR. As XR technology evolves, its applications in remote work, communication, and accessibility will continue to grow, shaping the future of human-computer interaction.

Generative AI (GenAI)

Generative AI (GenAI) refers to artificial intelligence systems capable of creating new content, such as text, images, music, video, and code, based on patterns learned from vast datasets. Unlike traditional AI models that classify or predict, GenAI produces original outputs, enabling creative applications in entertainment, design, and automation.

GenAI is like a digital artist trained on thousands of paintings. Instead of copying an existing artwork, it creates entirely new pieces inspired by past works. Similarly, GenAI generates original content—whether writing an article, composing music, or designing graphics—by analyzing patterns and learning from vast amounts of data.

Examples

Content Creation: Generative AI powers tools like ChatGPT and DALL·E, enabling users to generate human-like text, artwork, and music. Businesses utilize these models to automate content production for marketing, journalism, and entertainment purposes.

Drug Discovery: AI-generated molecular structures accelerate drug development. By simulating potential compounds, GenAI enables pharmaceutical researchers to identify promising treatments for diseases, thereby reducing the time and cost of discovery (see pg. 82).

Software Development: AI-powered coding assistants, such as GitHub Copilot, generate code based on prompts, helping developers write software more efficiently. These tools learn from vast repositories of open-source code to suggest functions, debug errors, and automate repetitive tasks.

Foundational Concepts

Generative AI, powered by deep learning architectures, particularly transformer models, processes sequential data to generate human-like responses. Generative Adversarial Networks (GANs) comprise two AI models—a generator and a discriminator—working together to create realistic content. Variational Autoencoders (VAEs) generate data by encoding and decoding representations in the latent space. Diffusion models refine AI-generated images through iterative improvements. Self-supervised learning enables AI to improve without labeled data. These principles allow GenAI to comprehend, forecast, and generate novel content across various domains.

Related Terms

Deep Learning: A subset of machine learning that trains neural networks on large datasets to generate content (see pg. 178).

Natural Language Processing (NLP): AI techniques that enable models to understand and generate human language (see pg. 346).

Generative Adversarial Networks (GANs): A machine learning model architecture used to create realistic synthetic content (see pg. 240).

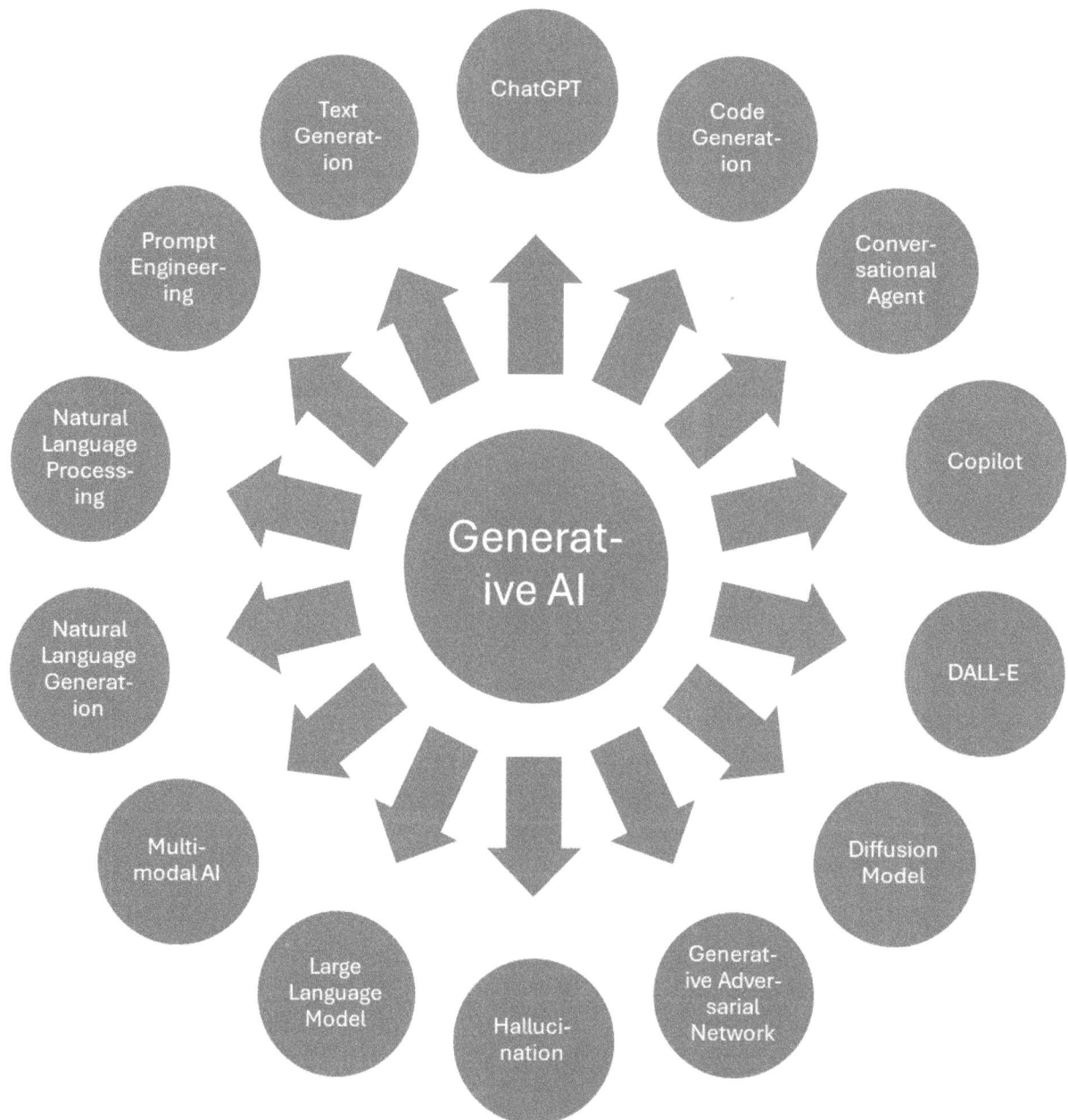

Figure 10: Generative AI concepts

Common Misconceptions

GenAI creates content from scratch: AI does not "think" independently; it generates outputs based on learned patterns from existing data.

AI-generated content is always accurate: GenAI can produce misleading or biased results, requiring human oversight.

GenAI replaces human creativity: AI assists and enhances creativity, but it does not replicate human intuition or originality.

Historical Context

Early generative AI models date back to Markov chains in the **1950s**, but significant breakthroughs came in the **2010s** with the development of GANs by **Ian Goodfellow (2014)** and transformers by **Google (2017)**. **OpenAI**'s GPT models revolutionized text generation, while **DALL·E** and **Stable Diffusion** expanded AI's creative capabilities. The rise of large-scale language and vision models in the **2020s** enabled widespread adoption in industries ranging from art to programming. Advances in multimodal AI—models that combine text, images, and audio—are pushing GenAI into new frontiers, shaping the future of digital creativity.

Practical Implications

Generative AI is transforming industries by automating creative processes, improving efficiency, and unlocking new possibilities. In media and marketing, AI-generated text and visuals streamline the production of content. In healthcare, AI models assist in medical imaging analysis and drug design. In gaming and entertainment, GenAI powers interactive storytelling and dynamic world generation. In education, AI tutors personalize learning experiences to enhance student outcomes. However, challenges such as AI bias, misinformation, and intellectual property concerns persist. Researchers and practitioners must adequately address them to ensure the ethical use of AI. As GenAI evolves, responsible development and regulation will shape its impact on society.

High-Performance Computing (HPC)

High-Performance Computing (HPC) refers to the use of supercomputers and parallel processing techniques to solve complex computational problems at high speeds. HPC systems process vast amounts of data by distributing tasks across multiple processors, enabling breakthroughs in scientific research, artificial intelligence, weather forecasting, and other data-intensive applications.

HPC is like a team of expert chefs preparing a large banquet. Instead of one chef handling every dish, multiple chefs work simultaneously on different parts of the meal, completing it much faster. Similarly, HPC distributes computational workloads across numerous processors, significantly reducing processing time for complex problems.

Examples

Scientific Simulations: Researchers use HPC for climate modeling, simulating weather patterns to predict storms and climate change trends with high accuracy, providing critical insights for environmental policies and disaster preparedness.

Genomic Research: HPC accelerates genome sequencing and analysis, helping scientists identify genetic disorders and develop precision medicine. The vast computational power allows for rapid comparisons of DNA sequences across large datasets.

Artificial Intelligence Training: HPC powers deep learning models by handling massive datasets and complex neural network computations. AI research institutions utilize HPC to train large-scale models, such as GPT and image recognition systems, efficiently.

Foundational Concepts

HPC relies on parallel computing, where multiple processors work simultaneously on different parts of a task. Distributed computing enables HPC systems to span multiple servers, allowing them to share workloads for increased efficiency. Vector processing enhances performance by executing numerous calculations per cycle. GPU acceleration utilizes graphical processing units to enhance data-intensive computations, particularly in AI and simulations. Scalability ensures that HPC systems can expand as computational demands increase. High-speed interconnects, such as InfiniBand, facilitate rapid data transfer between processing units, optimizing overall performance.

Related Terms

Supercomputing: The use of extremely powerful computers for scientific and engineering applications requiring massive computational power (see pg. 464).

Parallel Processing: A computing method where multiple processors execute tasks simultaneously to improve efficiency (see pg. 364).

Cloud Computing: On-demand computing resources accessed over the internet, often integrating with HPC for scalable performance.

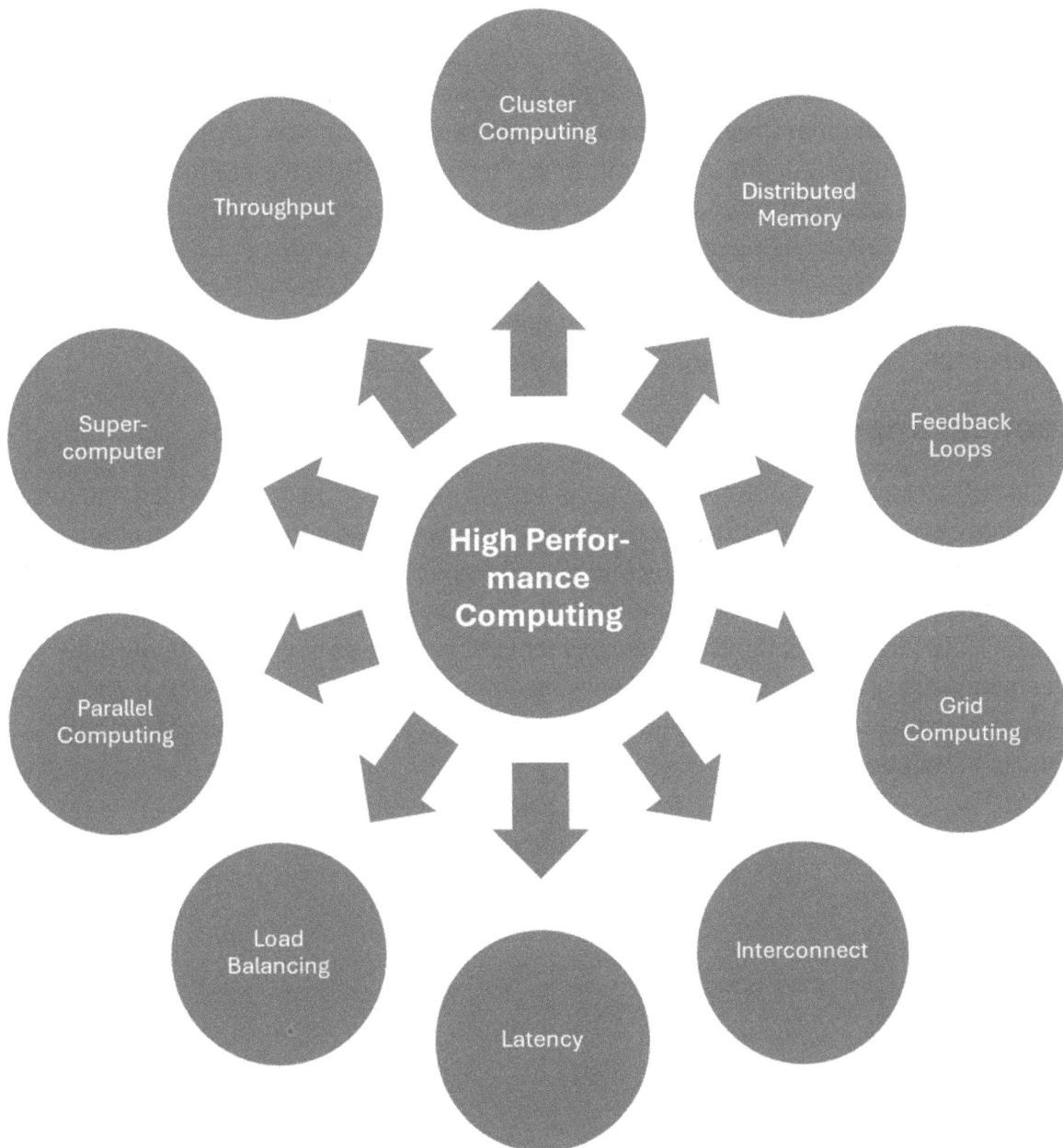

Figure 11: High-Performance Computing concepts

Common Misconceptions

HPC is only for scientific research: While widely employed in research, HPC also powers AI, financial modeling, and industrial simulations.

HPC is the same as cloud computing: Cloud computing provides scalable resources, whereas HPC focuses on optimized, high-speed parallel processing.

Only governments use HPC: Many industries, including healthcare, finance, and entertainment, leverage HPC for advanced analytics and simulations.

Historical Context

HPC emerged in the **1960s**, with early supercomputers developed by **Seymour Cray**, leading to the creation of **Cray Research**. The **1980s** and **1990s** saw advancements in parallel processing and distributed computing. The rise of GPU acceleration in the **2010s** revolutionized HPC by enabling the development of deep learning and AI applications. In **2020**, the **Fugaku supercomputer** in **Japan** became the world's fastest, demonstrating the role of HPC in tackling global challenges. Today, exascale computing—capable of a billion-billion calculations per second—represents the next frontier of HPC, advancing scientific discovery and artificial intelligence.

Practical Implications

HPC is critical for solving complex problems across industries. In healthcare, it enables personalized medicine and drug discovery through large-scale simulations. In finance, HPC supports high-frequency trading and risk analysis. In aerospace, HPC optimizes aircraft design through advanced simulations. In cybersecurity, it enhances encryption and real-time threat detection. The demand for HPC continues to grow as AI, big data, and scientific research require ever-increasing computational power. However, energy consumption and cost remain challenges, driving innovations in efficiency and cloud-based HPC solutions.

Human-Computer Interaction (HCI)

Human-Computer Interaction (HCI) is the study and design of interfaces that facilitate communication between humans and computers. It focuses on usability, accessibility, and user experience (UX) to ensure that technology is intuitive, efficient, and user-friendly, encompassing fields such as artificial intelligence, virtual reality, and interactive systems.

HCI is like designing the controls of a car. Just as a well-placed steering wheel, pedals, and dashboard ensure smooth driving, HCI optimizes digital interfaces, enabling people to easily interact with software and hardware, whether using a smartphone, voice assistant, or virtual reality system.

Examples

Voice Assistants: AI-driven systems like Siri, Alexa, and Google Assistant improve human-computer interaction by allowing users to issue voice commands for tasks such as playing music, setting reminders, or controlling smart home devices (see pg. 528).

Touchscreen Interfaces: Smartphones, tablets, and interactive kiosks utilize touch-based interfaces designed according to HCI principles. Features like pinch-to-zoom, gesture controls, and adaptive layouts enhance usability and accessibility for users of all ages.

Virtual Reality (VR) Experiences: VR applications in gaming, training, and medical simulations use HCI design to create immersive environments. Features such as motion tracking, haptic feedback, and intuitive controls improve user engagement and learning outcomes (see pg. 530).

Foundational Concepts

HCI is based on principles of usability, ensuring that digital interfaces are intuitive and efficient. User-centered design (UCD) involves iterative testing with real users to refine interactions. Cognitive load theory ensures that systems present information in a way that minimizes mental effort. Fitts' Law predicts how quickly users can interact with interface elements based on their size and distance. Haptic feedback enhances digital interactions by simulating the sensation of physical touch. Accessibility standards, such as the Web Content Accessibility Guidelines (WCAG), ensure that interfaces are inclusive for people with disabilities. These principles collectively optimize human-computer interactions.

Related Terms

User Experience (UX): The overall experience a person has while interacting with a digital product or system (see pg. 518).

Natural Language Processing (NLP): AI-driven technology that enables computers to understand and process human language (see pg. 346).

Multimodal Interaction: Systems that allow users to interact using multiple input methods, such as voice, touch, and gestures (see pg. 342).

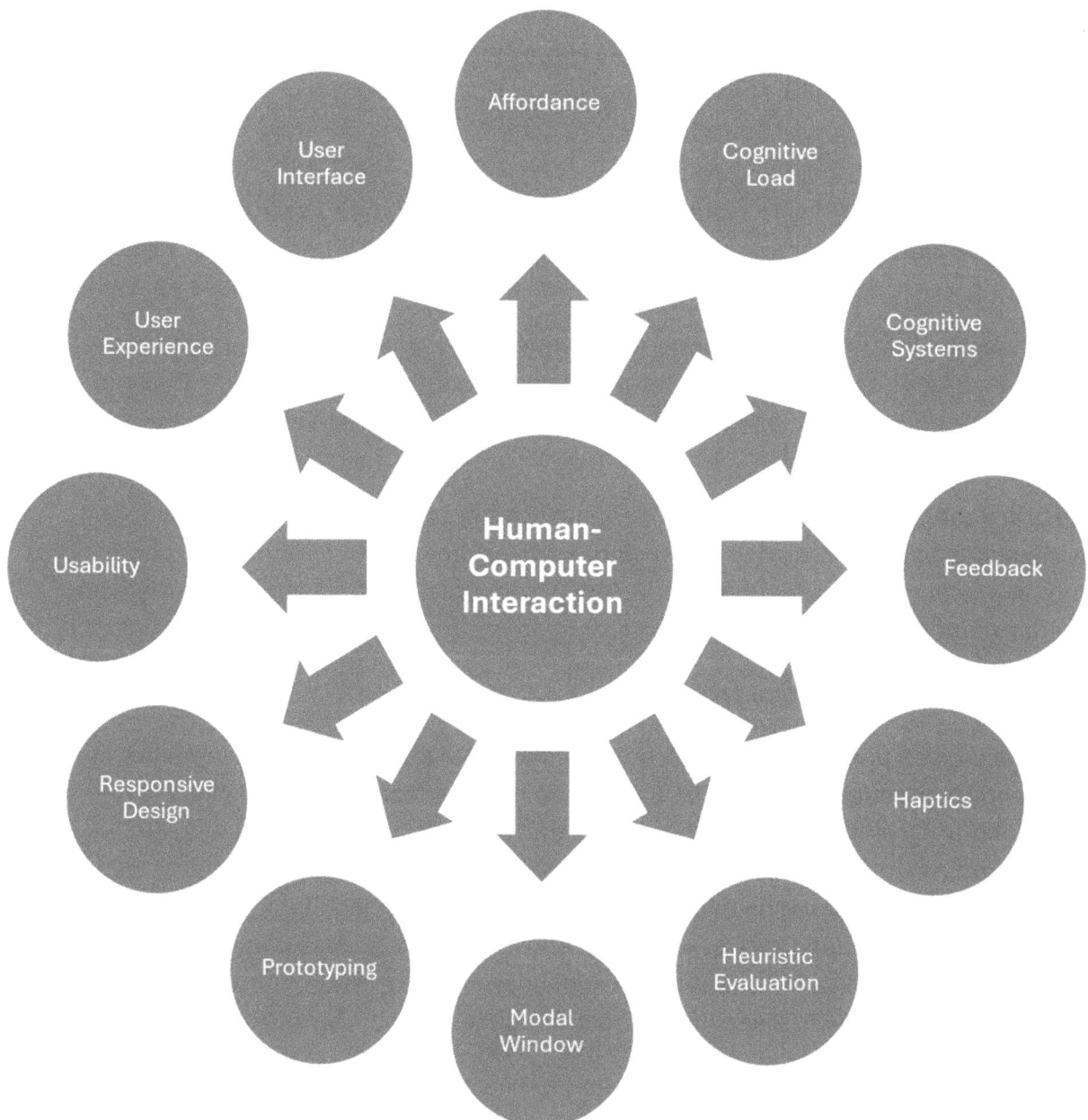

Figure 12: Human-Computer Interaction concepts

Common Misconceptions

HCI is only about designing user interfaces: While UI design is a component, HCI also encompasses cognitive psychology, accessibility, and human behavior in technology interactions.

HCI is limited to software: HCI applies to both hardware and software, encompassing wearable devices, robotics, and virtual reality systems.

Good design is purely aesthetic: Effective HCI prioritizes functionality, efficiency, and accessibility over visual appeal alone.

Historical Context

HCI emerged in the **1970s**, when computers transitioned from command-line systems to graphical user interfaces (GUIs). In the **1980s**, **Xerox PARC**, **Apple**, and **Microsoft** introduced icons, windows, and pointing devices such as the mouse. The **1990s** and **2000s** saw the rise of touchscreen interfaces and web usability research. Advances in AI and machine learning in the **2010s** enabled voice and gesture-based interactions. Today, HCI research continues to evolve, integrating technologies such as brain-computer interfaces (BCIs) and immersive augmented reality (AR) systems, shaping the future of human-digital interactions.

Practical Implications

HCI has a profound impact across industries. In healthcare, well-designed electronic medical records (EMRs) improve doctor-patient interactions and reduce errors. In education, adaptive learning platforms tailor content to meet the needs of individual students. In business, user-friendly software enhances productivity and reduces training time. In automotive technology, voice and gesture controls improve driver safety. As digital transformation accelerates, HCI will continue to shape how humans interact with AI, robotics, and emerging technologies, ensuring intuitive and efficient user experiences while addressing ethical and accessibility concerns.

Internet of Things (IoT)

The Internet of Things (IoT) refers to a network of interconnected devices that collect, transmit, and process data over the Internet without human intervention. These devices, ranging from smart home appliances to industrial sensors, enhance automation, efficiency, and decision-making in various industries by enabling real-time monitoring and control.

IoT is like a smart city where every streetlight, traffic signal, and building communicates with one another. Just as sensors and controllers optimize city functions, IoT devices share data to automate tasks, enhance efficiency, and provide insights for informed decision-making in homes, healthcare, and various industries.

Examples

Smart Homes: IoT enables automation in smart homes through connected devices, such as thermostats, security cameras, and voice assistants. For example, a smart thermostat adjusts room temperature based on occupancy and weather patterns, enhancing energy efficiency and comfort.

Industrial IoT (IIoT): Factories use IoT sensors for predictive maintenance, reducing downtime by detecting machinery failures before they occur. This data-driven approach improves productivity, minimizes costs, and ensures operational efficiency in manufacturing plants.

Healthcare Monitoring: IoT-based wearable devices track patients' vital signs, alerting healthcare providers to anomalies. Smart medical implants, such as pacemakers, continuously transmit health data, enabling remote monitoring and early intervention.

Foundational Concepts

IoT functions on sensor networks, where devices collect and transmit data. Edge computing processes information closer to the device, reducing latency. Cloud computing stores and analyzes vast amounts of data generated by IoT devices. Machine-to-machine (M2M) communication allows automated data exchange without human intervention. 5G connectivity enhances IoT performance by providing faster data transfer and lower latency. Artificial intelligence (AI) integration enables IoT systems to analyze patterns and optimize decision-making. These foundational concepts allow IoT to drive automation and real-time intelligence across multiple sectors.

Related Terms

Edge Computing: Processing data near its source rather than relying solely on centralized cloud computing (see pg. 192).

Machine-to-Machine (M2M): Direct communication between devices without human input, forming the basis of IoT networks (see pg. 312).

Smart Sensors: Devices that collect and analyze environmental data, enabling automation and real-time responses.

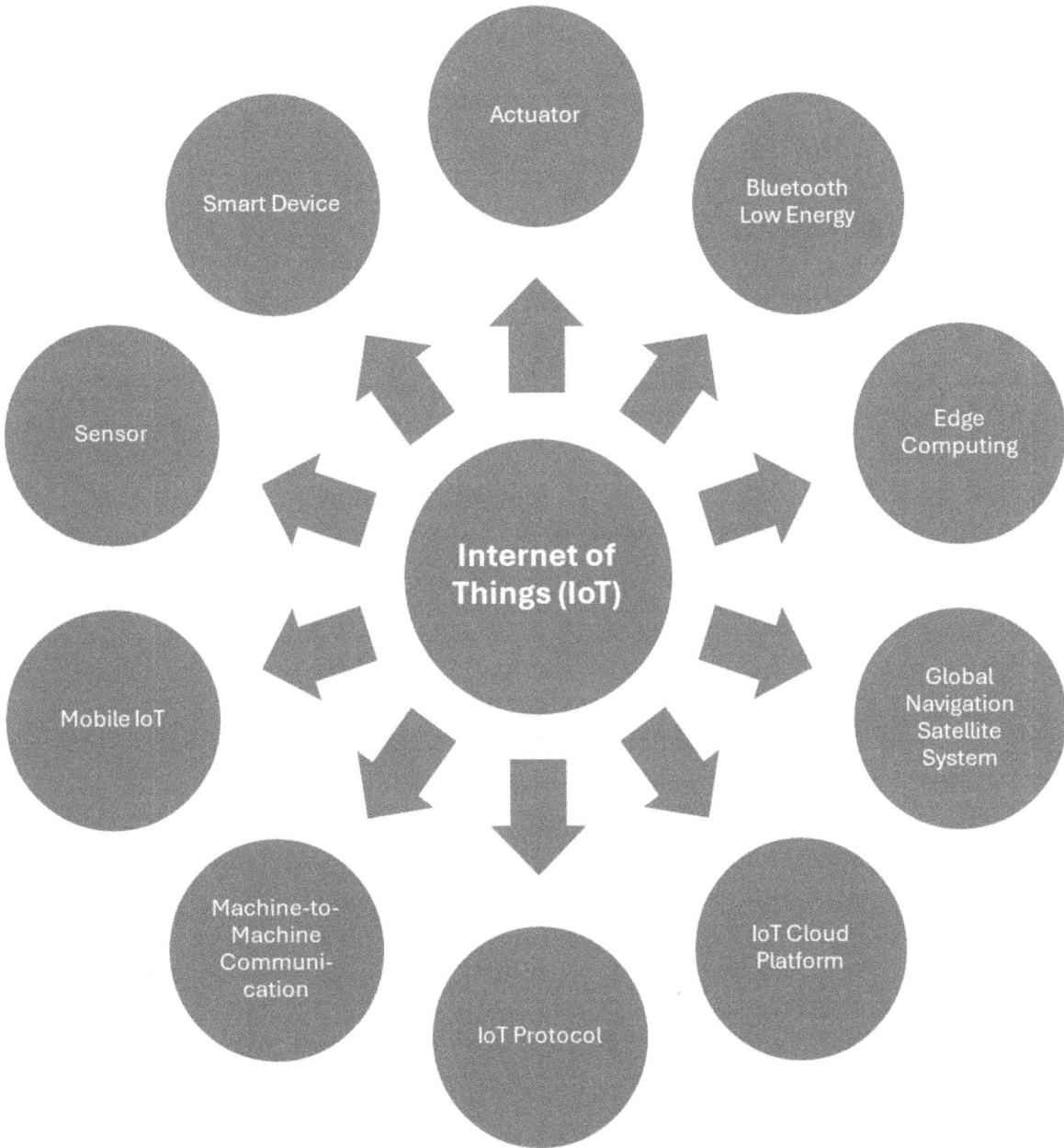

Figure 13: Internet of Things (IoT) concepts

Common Misconceptions

IoT is limited to smart home devices: While home automation is a primary IoT application, industries such as healthcare, agriculture, and manufacturing also rely on IoT for automation and increased efficiency.

IoT devices operate independently: Most IoT devices require cloud computing, AI, or human intervention to function effectively.

IoT is inherently secure: Many IoT devices lack strong security protocols, making them vulnerable to cyberattacks if not adequately safeguarded.

Historical Context

The concept of IoT dates back to **Kevin Ashton** (**1999**), who coined the term while working on RFID-based inventory tracking. Early IoT applications focused on industrial automation and supply chain management. The rise of cloud computing (**2000s**) and 5G networks (**2020s**) enabled large-scale IoT adoption. Smart home devices, wearables, and connected vehicles have since transformed how people interact with technology. Today, IoT plays a critical role in smart cities, industrial automation, and healthcare innovations, with continued growth expected as AI and connectivity advance.

Practical Implications

IoT is revolutionizing industries by enhancing automation, efficiency, and data-driven decision-making. In agriculture, IoT sensors monitor soil conditions and optimize irrigation, improving crop yields. In transportation, intelligent traffic systems use IoT to reduce congestion and improve safety. In energy management, IoT enables smart grids that dynamically adjust power distribution, enhancing sustainability. As IoT adoption expands, we must address challenges such as data privacy, security risks, and interoperability to ensure the safe and effective implementation of IoT in various industries.

Machine Learning (ML)

Machine Learning (ML) is a subset of artificial intelligence that enables computers to learn from data and improve their performance on tasks without explicit programming. ML algorithms identify patterns in large datasets and make predictions or decisions based on learned insights, driving advancements in automation, analytics, and intelligent systems.

ML is like teaching a child how to recognize animals. Instead of memorizing specific animals, the child learns by seeing multiple examples and identifying patterns, such as fur, feathers, or colors. Similarly, ML models learn from data and improve over time without being explicitly programmed for each scenario.

Examples

Fraud Detection: Financial institutions use ML algorithms to analyze transaction patterns and detect fraudulent activities. By learning from historical fraud cases, ML models identify anomalies in real-time, helping banks prevent cyber fraud and unauthorized transactions.

Healthcare Diagnostics: ML-powered medical imaging tools assist doctors in diagnosing diseases such as cancer. By analyzing thousands of past cases, ML models identify abnormalities in X-rays, MRIs, and CT scans, improving accuracy and early detection.

Personalized Recommendations: Streaming platforms like Netflix and Spotify use ML to suggest content based on user behavior. By analyzing viewing history, preferences, and trends, ML models curate tailored recommendations to enhance user engagement (see pg. 404).

Foundational Concepts

We can categorize Machine Learning into three primary types: supervised learning, where models learn from labeled data; unsupervised learning, where they discover patterns in unlabeled data; and reinforcement learning, where agents learn through trial and error by receiving rewards or penalties. Neural networks simulate human brain functions to process complex relationships in data. Gradient descent helps optimize ML models by adjusting parameters to minimize errors. Overfitting and underfitting describe ML challenges where models learn too much or too little from data. These foundational principles ensure ML models generalize well and make accurate predictions.

Related Terms

Deep Learning: A subset of ML that uses multi-layered neural networks for tasks like image and speech recognition (see pg. 178).

Neural Networks: Computational models inspired by the human brain that process and learn from data patterns (see pg. 352).

Feature Engineering: The process of selecting and transforming data attributes to improve ML model performance (see pg. 218).

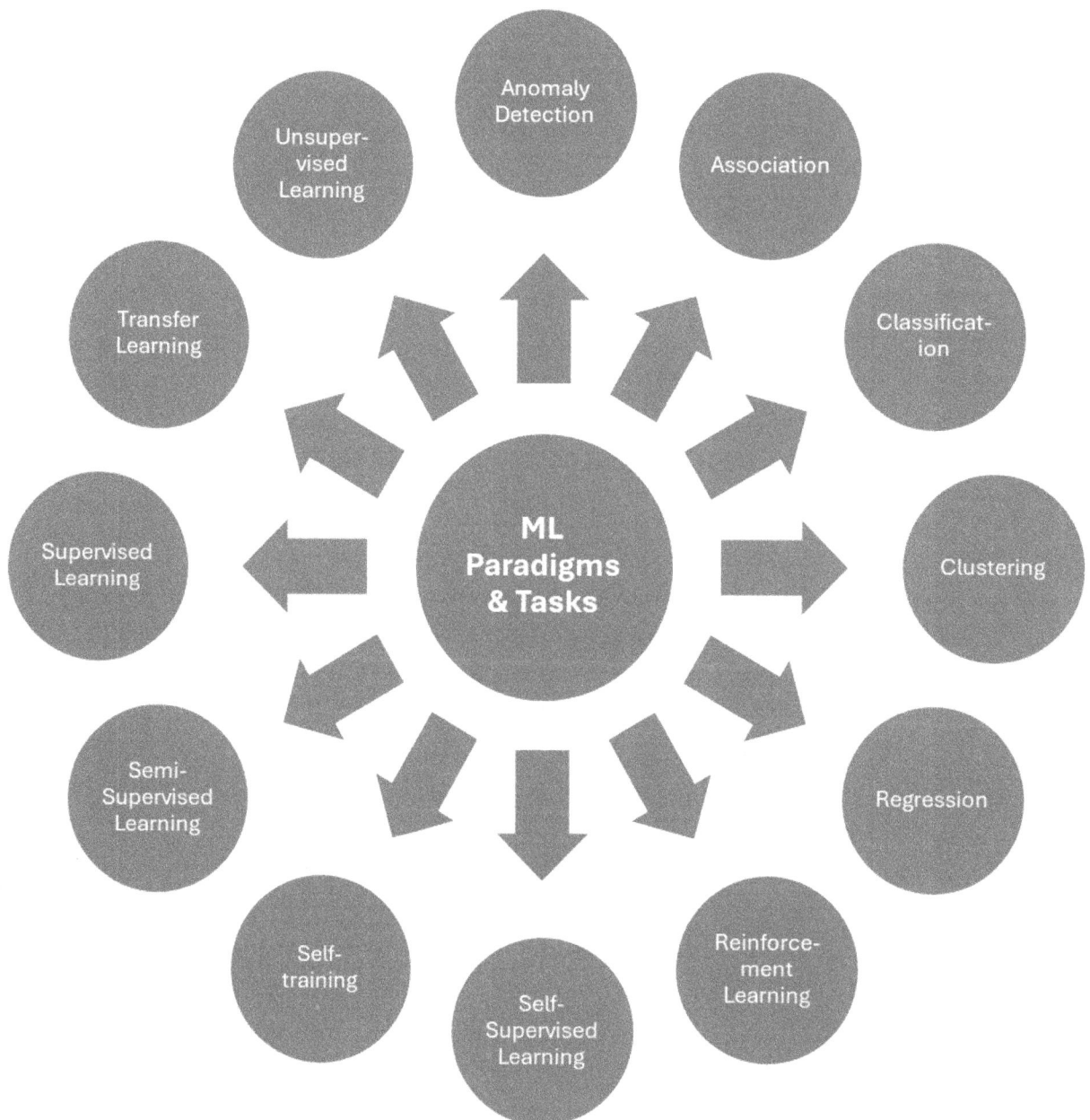

Figure 14: Machine Learning Paradigms & Tasks concepts

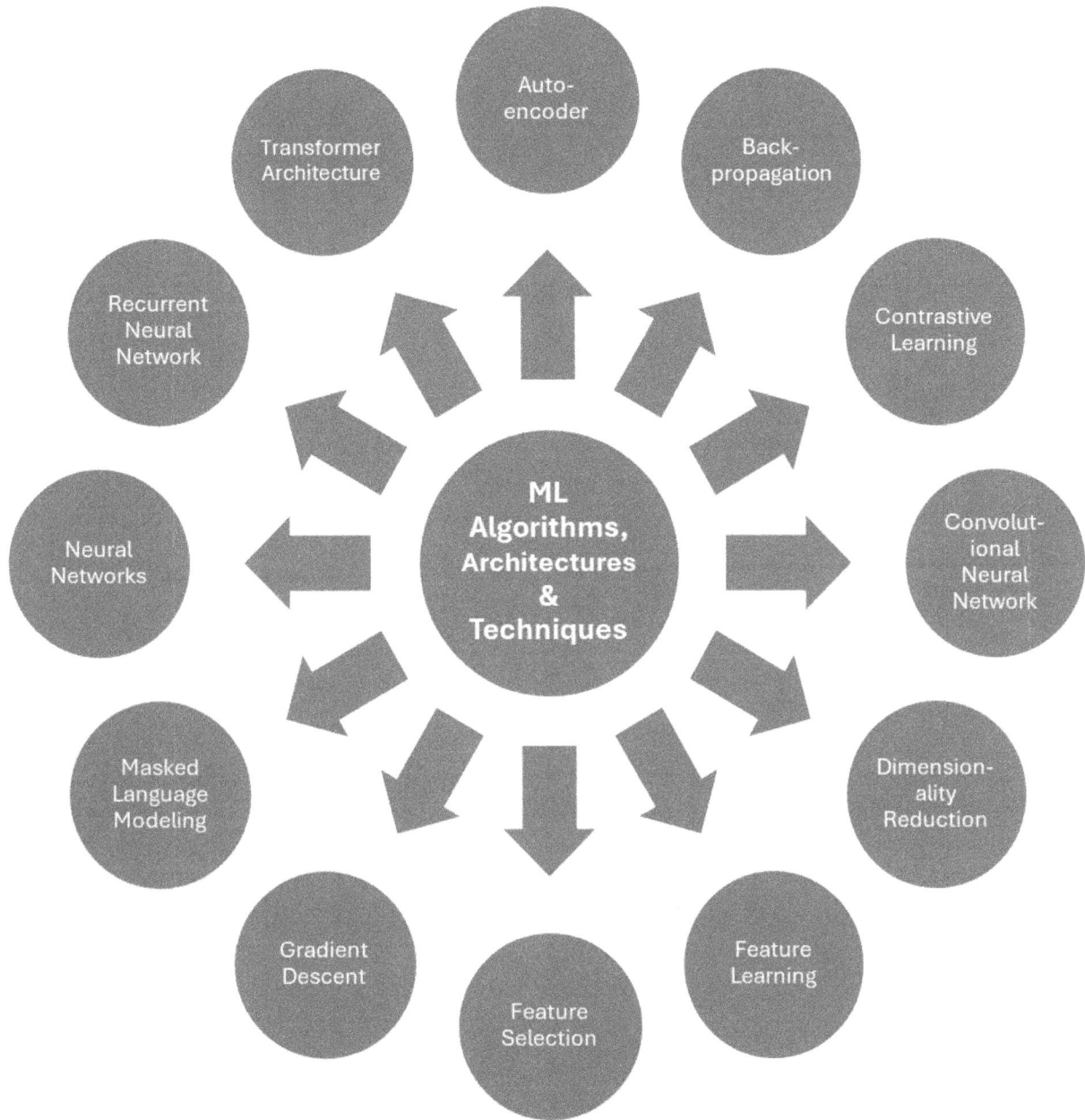

Figure 15: Machine Learning Algorithms, Architectures & Techniques concepts

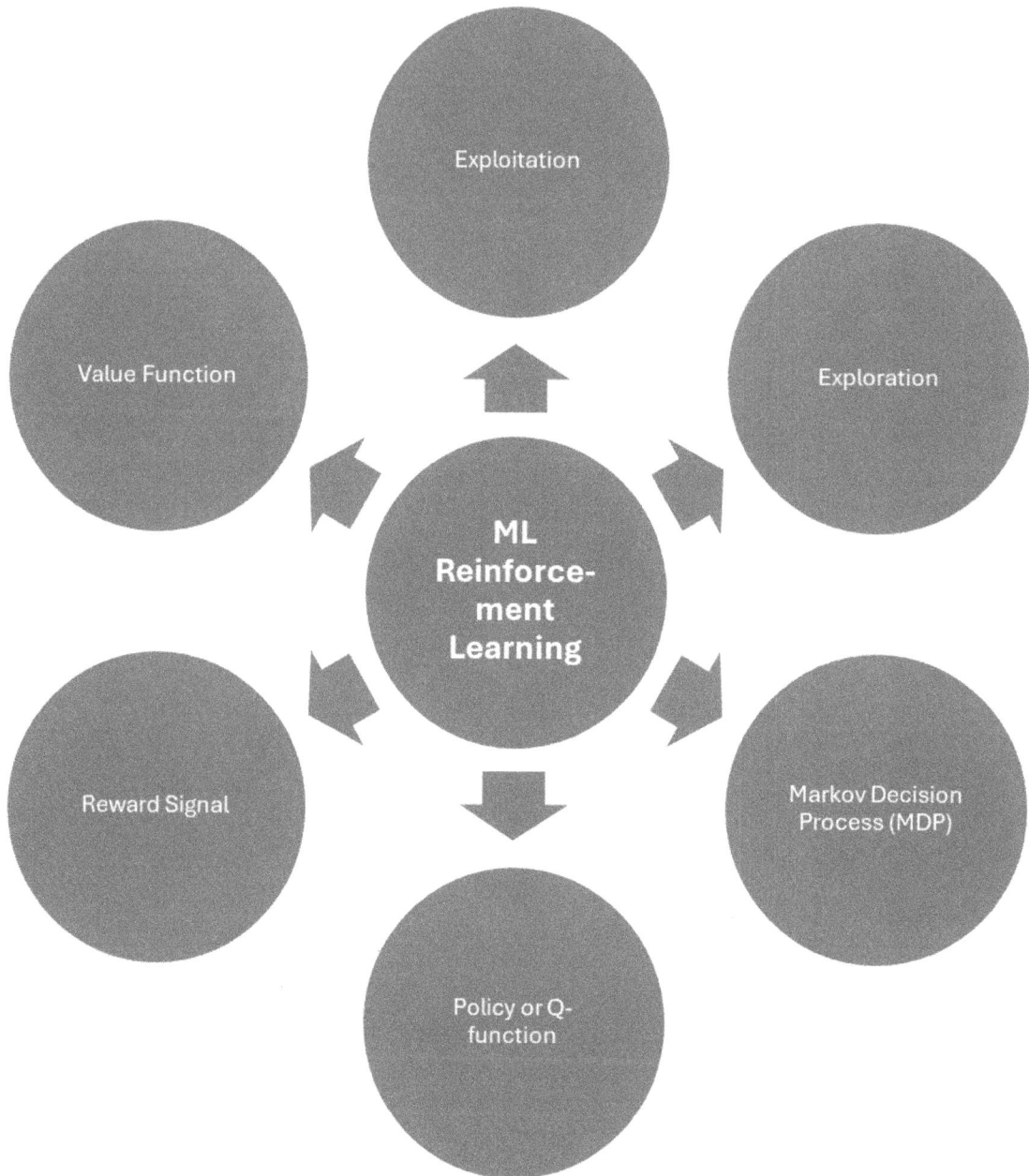

Figure 16: Machine Learning Reinforcement Learning concepts

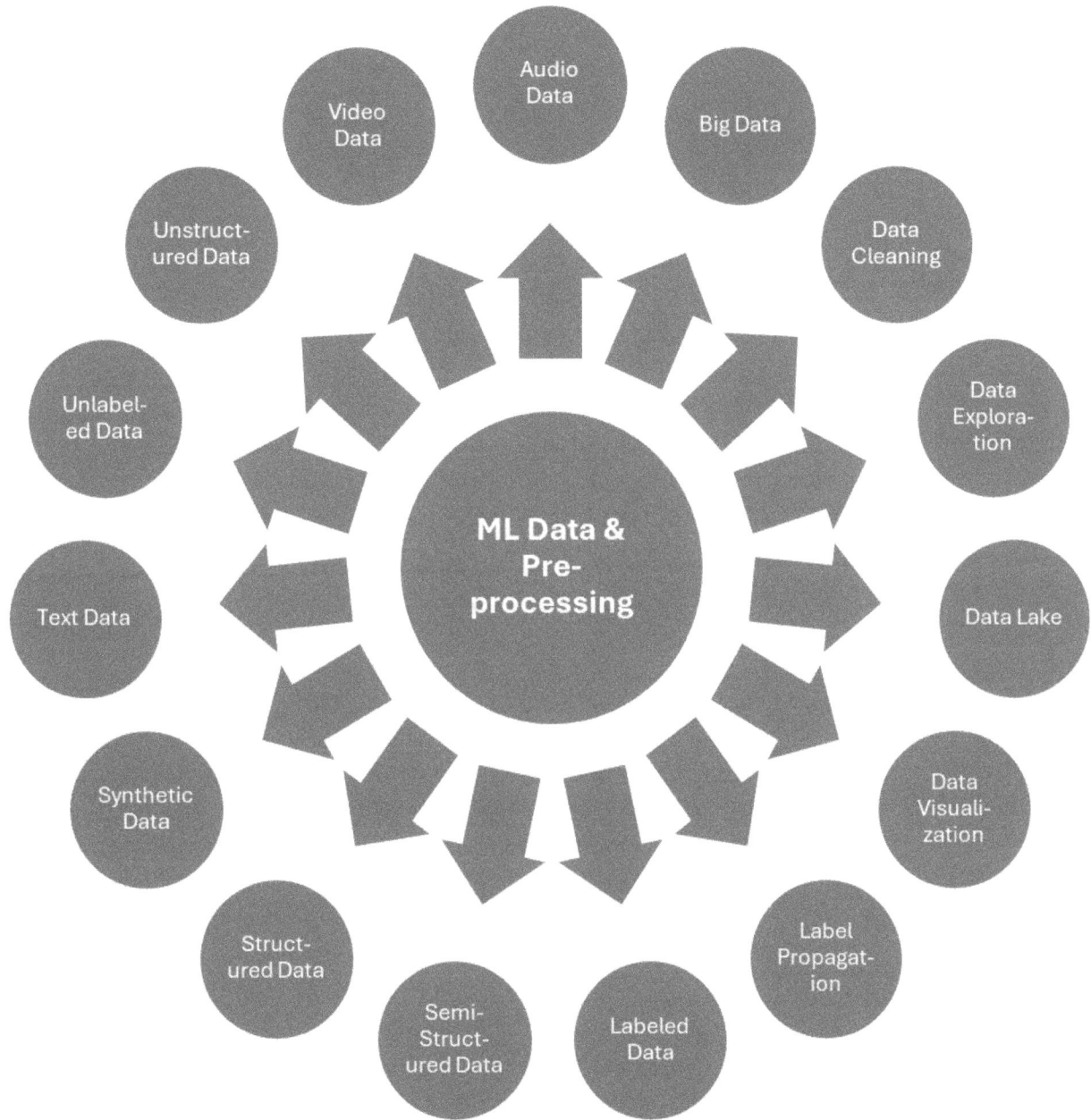

Figure 17: Machine Learning Data & Preprocessing concepts

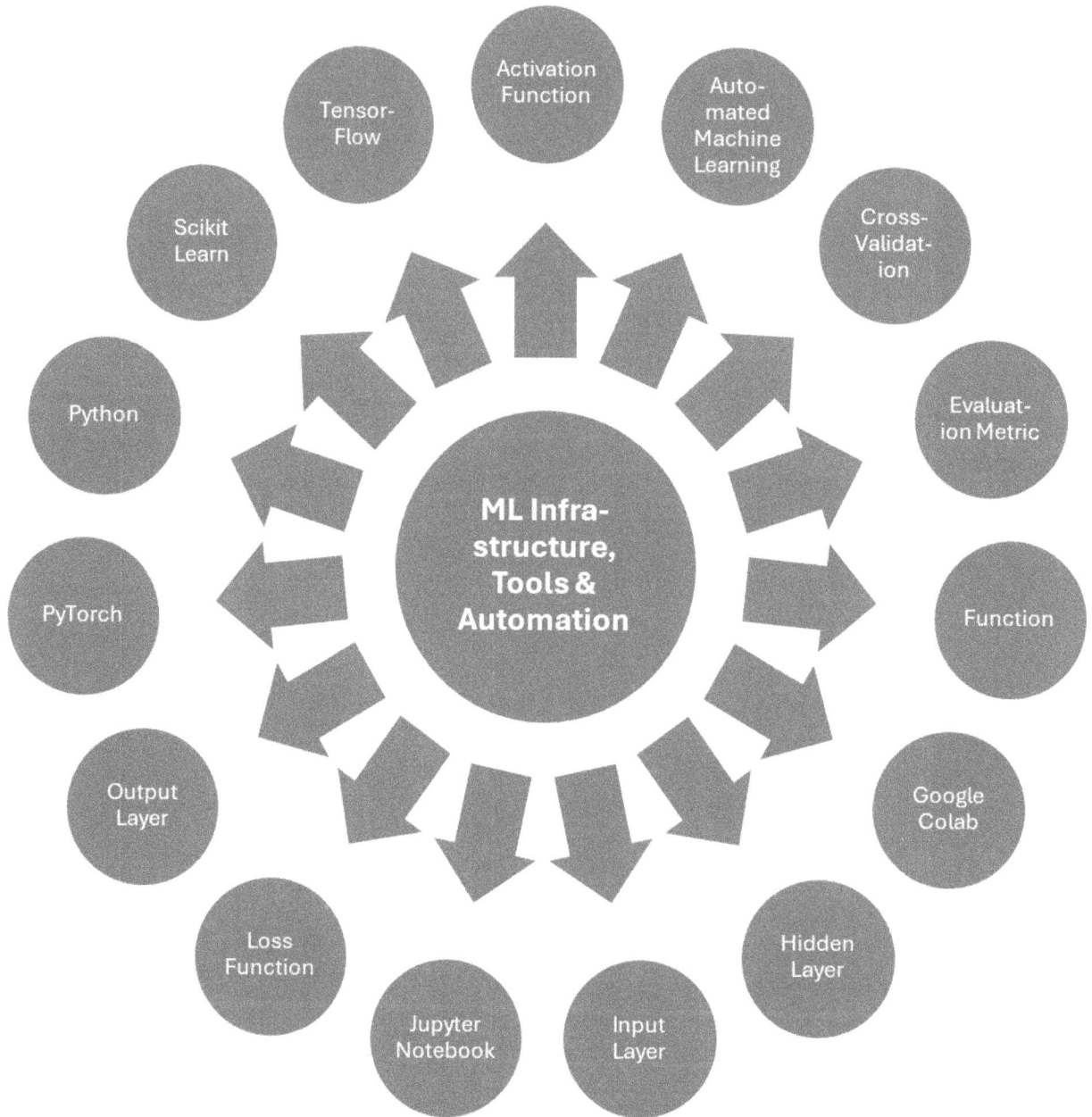

Figure 18: Machine Learning Infrastructure, Tools & Automation concepts

Common Misconceptions

ML and AI are the same: ML is a subset of AI, not its entirety. AI includes rule-based systems and symbolic reasoning beyond ML.

ML models always make correct predictions: ML relies on data quality, and biased or incomplete data can lead to inaccurate results.

ML replaces human intelligence: ML enhances decision-making but requires human oversight for validation, interpretation, and ethical considerations.

Historical Context

In **1956**, **Arthur Samuel** coined the term "machine learning" while developing self-learning checkers, laying the foundations for the development of ML. In the **1980s**, advances in neural networks and backpropagation improved ML capabilities. The **2000s** saw ML expansion with big data, enabling large-scale training of models. The rise of deep learning in the **2010s**, powered by GPUs, led to breakthroughs in image recognition, speech processing, and NLP. Today, ML continues to evolve with self-supervised learning, transformer architectures, and AI-powered automation, shaping industries worldwide.

Practical Implications

Machine learning is transforming industries by enhancing automation, predictive analytics, and decision-making. In cybersecurity, ML detects malware and cyber threats in real time. In retail, ML optimizes supply chains and demand forecasting. In autonomous vehicles, ML processes sensor data to assist in real-time navigation. In finance, algorithmic trading uses ML to predict market trends. Despite its benefits, ML faces challenges like data bias, privacy concerns, and explainability issues. As ML models become increasingly powerful, ethical considerations and regulatory oversight will play a crucial role in ensuring the responsible deployment of AI.

Quantum Computing (QC)

Quantum computing is an advanced computational paradigm that leverages quantum mechanics to perform complex calculations exponentially faster than classical computers. Using quantum bits (qubits), quantum computers can process vast amounts of information simultaneously, solving problems in cryptography, materials science, and artificial intelligence that are intractable for traditional computing systems.

Quantum computing is akin to instantly accessing a massive library. While a classical computer reads books one by one, a quantum computer reads multiple books simultaneously due to quantum superposition and entanglement, drastically accelerating problem-solving in fields requiring massive computational power.

Examples

Cryptography and Cybersecurity: Quantum computers can break traditional encryption algorithms by rapidly factoring large numbers. They also enable quantum cryptography, which provides ultra-secure communication through quantum key distribution (QKD), making data transmission immune to eavesdropping.

Drug Discovery and Materials Science: Quantum simulations facilitate the modeling of molecular structures and chemical reactions at the atomic level. These models allow researchers to develop new drugs, optimize materials, and accelerate the discovery of life-saving medicines that classical computers struggle to analyze.

Optimization Problems in Logistics: Quantum computing enhances supply chain and logistics efficiency by solving complex routing and scheduling problems. It can optimize airline routes, manufacturing processes, and urban traffic systems, significantly reducing costs and energy consumption.

Foundational Concepts

Quantum computing functions on superposition, where qubits can exist in multiple states simultaneously, allowing parallel computation. Entanglement enables qubits to be interdependent, facilitating ultra-fast information transfer. Quantum gates manipulate qubits using quantum logic, enabling the execution of complex calculations. Quantum annealing is used for optimization problems, while Shor's algorithm and Grover's algorithm demonstrate quantum superiority in factoring and searching tasks. Quantum decoherence remains a challenge, as qubits are highly sensitive to environmental interference. These principles define the potential and unique capabilities of quantum computing compared to classical computation.

Related Terms

Qubit: The fundamental unit of quantum information, capable of existing in multiple states simultaneously (see pg. 400).

Quantum Entanglement: A phenomenon where qubits become interconnected, influencing each other instantaneously regardless of distance (see pg. 198).

Quantum Supremacy: The point at which quantum computers outperform classical computers in solving specific tasks (see pg. 398).

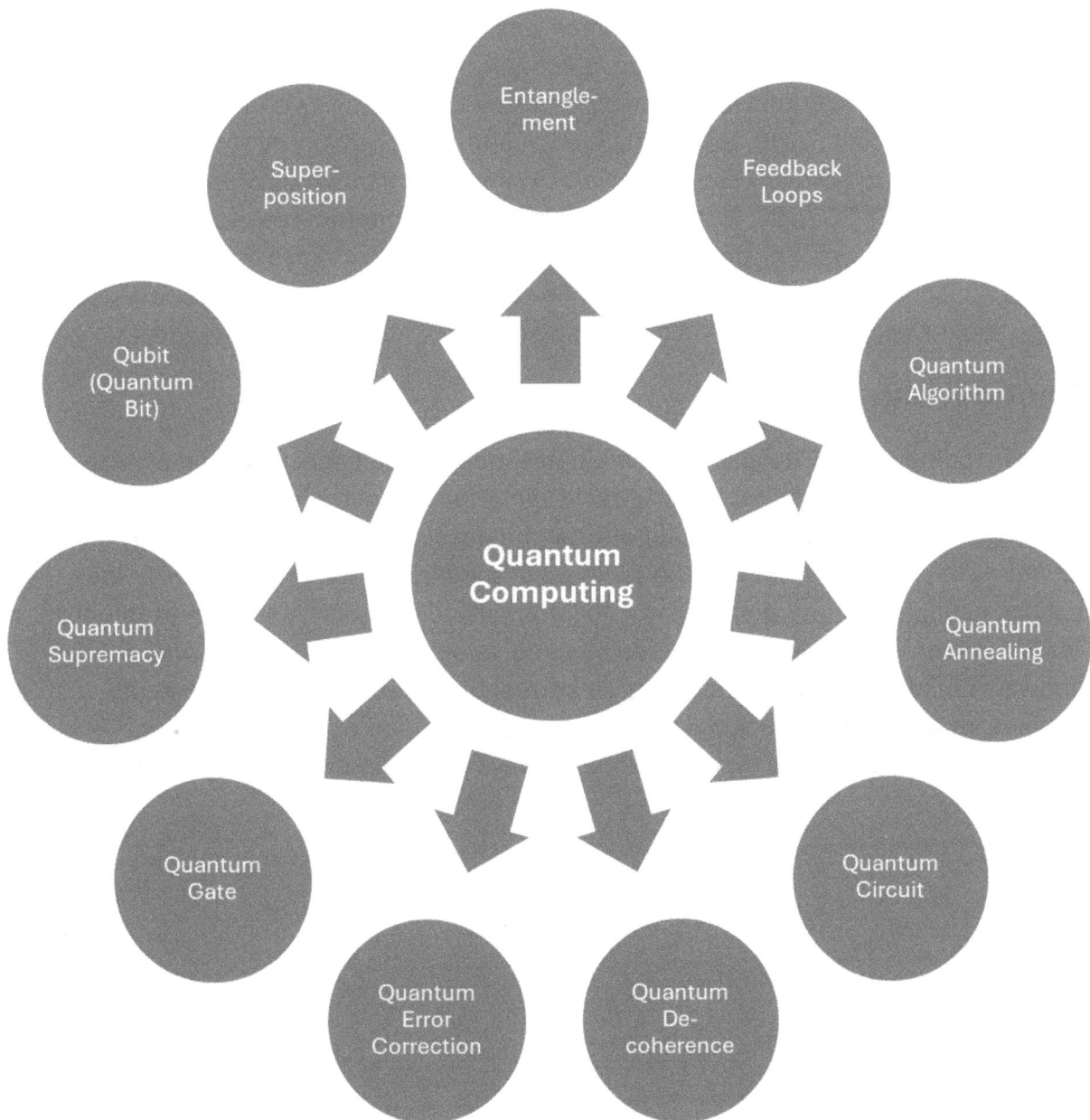

Figure 19: Quantum Computing concepts

Common Misconceptions

Quantum computers will replace classical computers: Quantum computing excels in specific tasks but will complement, not replace, classical computing for general applications.

Quantum supremacy means full AI automation: Achieving quantum supremacy in specific problems does not equate to general AI automation or intelligence.

Historical Context

Quantum computing's theoretical foundation was established in **1981** by **Richard Feynman**, who proposed using quantum mechanics for computation. In **1994**, **Peter Shor** developed an algorithm for quantum factorization, proving its potential for breaking encryption. In **2019**, Google claimed quantum supremacy by solving a problem that would have taken classical supercomputers thousands of years to solve. Companies like IBM, Google, and D-Wave are advancing quantum technology, with cloud-accessible quantum computing platforms expected to emerge in the late **2020s**. Despite challenges in scalability and error correction, quantum computing continues to evolve, promising breakthroughs in diverse scientific and industrial applications.

Practical Implications

Quantum computing will revolutionize multiple industries. In finance, it can optimize portfolio management and risk analysis. In artificial intelligence, we expect quantum-enhanced machine learning to accelerate data processing and analysis. In energy, quantum simulations will improve battery design and nuclear fusion research. In the realm of national security, quantum cryptography will redefine cybersecurity protocols. Despite immense potential, widespread practical adoption remains years away due to hardware limitations and the need for error correction. However, as advancements continue, quantum computing will unlock unprecedented computational power, reshaping industries and scientific research in ways unimaginable with classical systems.

Responsible AI (RAI)

Responsible AI (RAI) refers to the ethical design, development, and deployment of artificial intelligence systems that prioritize fairness, transparency, accountability, and privacy. It ensures AI aligns with human values, minimizes biases, and promotes social good while mitigating risks such as discrimination, misinformation, and unintended harm.

RAI is like traffic laws for AI. Just as road rules ensure safe driving for all, Responsible AI establishes guidelines that keep AI ethical, fair, and aligned with human well-being. Without these safeguards, AI systems could cause accidents, confusion, or harm, just like reckless driving does on the road.

Examples

Bias Reduction in Hiring: AI-powered hiring tools must ensure fair candidate selection without favoring specific genders, races, or backgrounds. Companies apply RAI principles by auditing AI models to eliminate biases in resume screening and interview processes (see pg. 104).

AI in Healthcare: RAI ensures medical AI systems make transparent and equitable decisions when diagnosing diseases or recommending treatments. Hospitals must validate AI-driven medical tools to prevent racial or socioeconomic disparities in healthcare access and outcomes.

Content Moderation on Social Media: AI algorithms used to detect misinformation and hate speech must operate fairly, avoiding biases that lead to censorship. Platforms utilize RAI strategies to enhance content moderation transparency and prevent the unintended suppression of free speech.

Foundational Concepts

RAI is built on core principles, including fairness, ensuring that AI treats all users equitably; accountability, holding developers and organizations responsible for AI-driven decisions; transparency, making AI decision-making understandable to users; privacy, safeguarding personal data from misuse; and safety, ensuring that AI does not cause unintended harm. Explainability helps users understand how AI arrives at its conclusions. Regulatory frameworks, such as the EU AI Act and IEEE's Ethically Aligned Design guide, govern the development and use of AI. These principles work together to ensure AI benefits society while reducing risks.

Related Terms

Ethical AI: The study and application of moral principles in AI design to prevent harm and bias (see pg. 204).

AI Bias: Unintended favoritism in AI models, often due to biased training data or flawed algorithms (see pg. 104).

AI Governance: Policies and regulations that ensure AI systems operate fairly, legally, and ethically (see pg. 80).

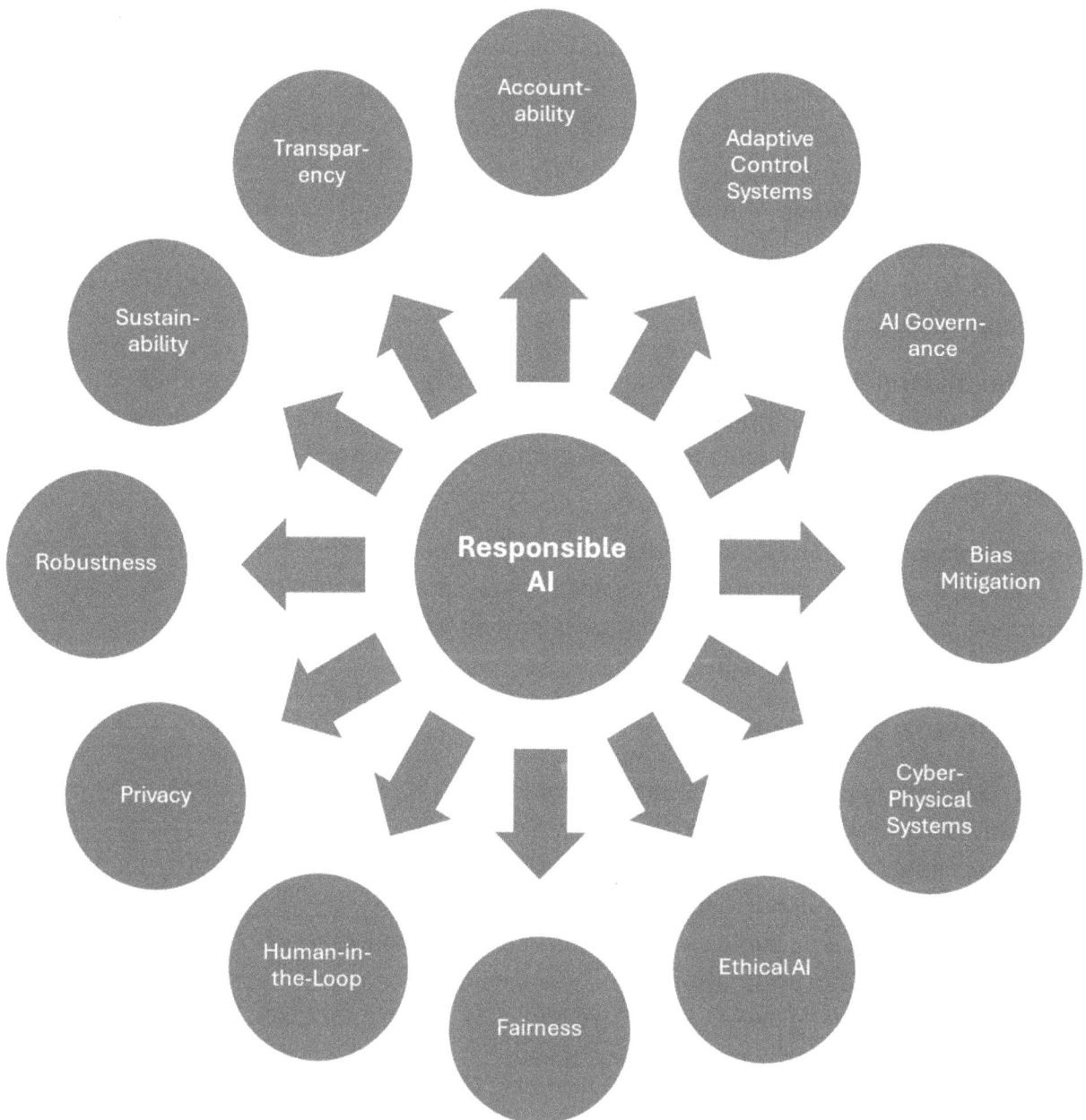

Figure 20: Responsible AI concepts

Common Misconceptions

RAI eliminates all AI risks: While RAI minimizes risks, no AI system is entirely free from bias, errors, or ethical concerns.

Only large companies need RAI: Any organization developing AI, regardless of size, must consider ethical AI practices.

RAI slows down AI innovation: Ethical AI development fosters trust, mitigating long-term risks and promoting adoption, rather than hindering progress.

Historical Context

Concerns about AI ethics date back to **Isaac Asimov**'s **"Three Laws of Robotics"** (**1942**). In **2016**, **Microsoft**'s AI chatbot **Tay** demonstrated AI bias risks when it learned and spread harmful content from social media. The **OECD AI Principles** (**2019**) and the **EU AI Act** (**2021**) formalized global efforts toward Responsible AI governance. In **2023**, AI ethics became central as models like **ChatGPT** and **DALL·E** raised debates on bias, misinformation, and accountability. Organizations such as **OpenAI**, **Google**, and **IBM** now prioritize RAI frameworks to align AI with human rights and societal values.

Practical Implications

Responsible AI is crucial in finance, ensuring fair credit scoring and effective fraud detection that is unbiased and free from discrimination. In government, AI-driven policies must be transparent and impartial. In education, RAI prevents biased grading in AI-assisted assessments. In law enforcement, AI-based facial recognition must uphold privacy rights and avoid racial profiling. As AI adoption expands, regulatory frameworks will shape how AI interacts with society, ensuring safety, fairness, and ethical compliance. Organizations that integrate RAI will foster public trust, reducing risks while maximizing the societal benefits of AI.

Robotics (RT)

Robotics is the interdisciplinary field focused on the design, construction, and operation of robots—machines that perform tasks autonomously or with minimal human intervention. Robotics integrates mechanical engineering, artificial intelligence, and sensor technology to create robots for applications ranging from industrial automation to healthcare and space exploration.

Robotics is like a team of specialized workers. Each worker (robot) is programmed to complete specific tasks efficiently, whether assembling a car, exploring Mars, or assisting in surgery. With the proper instructions, robots work tirelessly, precisely, and often in environments too hazardous for humans.

Examples

Industrial Automation: The manufacturing industry utilizes robots in a wide range of applications, including robotic arms in automotive assembly lines. These robots enhance productivity, ensure precision, and reduce human exposure to hazardous conditions.

Medical Robotics: Surgical robots, such as the da Vinci system, assist doctors in performing minimally invasive surgeries with high precision, thereby reducing recovery times and improving patient outcomes.

Autonomous Vehicles: Self-driving cars utilize robotic systems combined with AI to navigate roads, detect obstacles, and make real-time driving decisions, aiming to enhance road safety and transportation efficiency.

Foundational Concepts

Robotics is built on mechanical design, ensuring robots can perform physical tasks; sensors and perception, enabling them to interpret their surroundings; and actuators, controlling motion. Artificial intelligence (AI) and machine learning enable robots to learn from data and improve their task performance. Path planning algorithms enable robots to navigate environments, while control systems ensure the smooth execution of movements. Human-robot interaction (HRI) studies how robots can work alongside humans safely and effectively. Together, these components enable robots to perform tasks autonomously or with human guidance.

Related Terms

Autonomous Systems: Robots capable of operating independently using AI-driven decision-making (see pg. 98).

Humanoid Robots: Robots designed to resemble and interact like humans, such as Honda's ASIMO (see pg. 272).

Swarm Robotics: A field where multiple small robots work together, mimicking collective behaviors found in nature (see pg. 474).

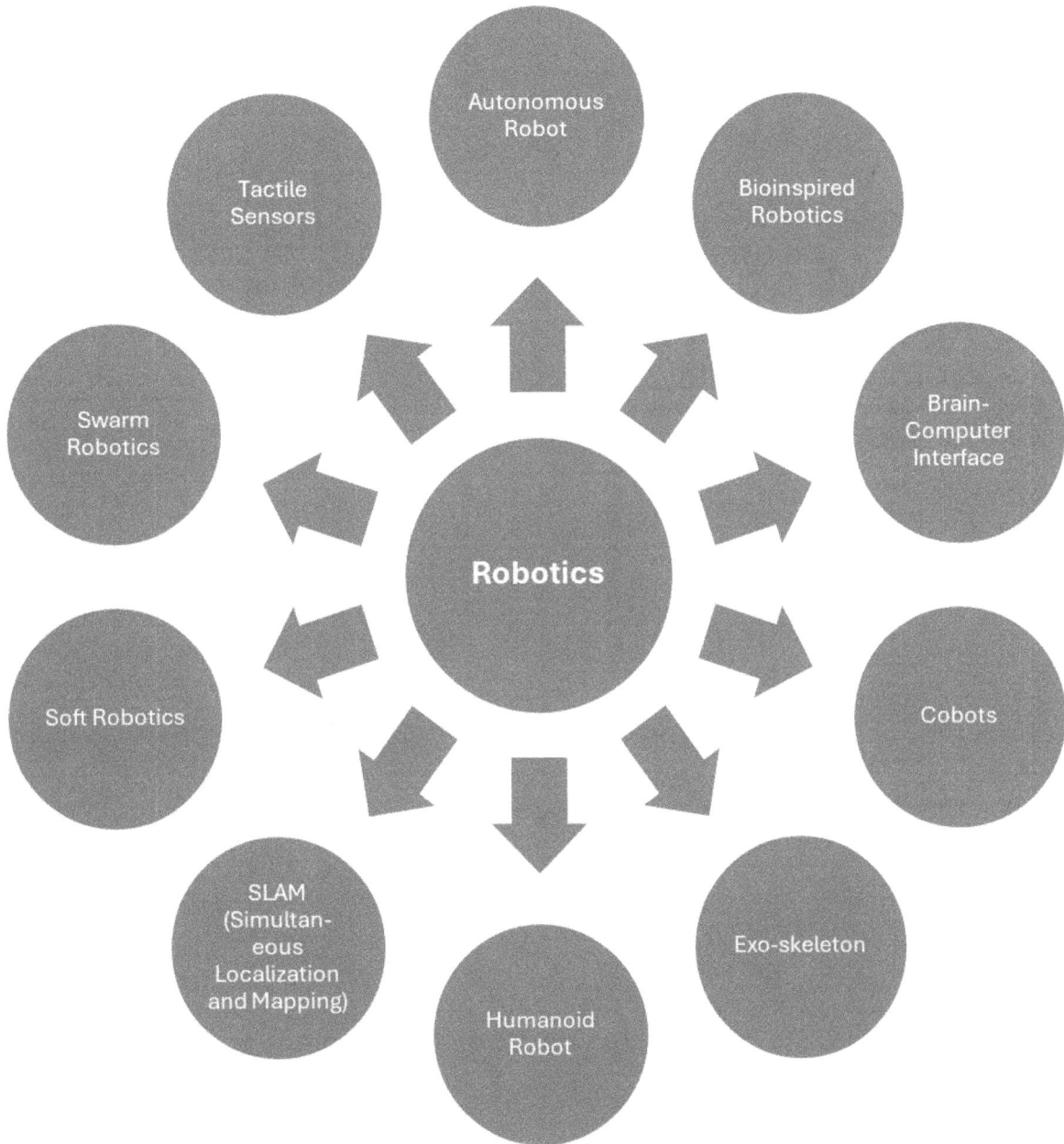

Figure 21: Robotics concepts

Common Misconceptions

Robots think like humans: Most robots follow programmed instructions and lack general intelligence or emotions.

All robots resemble humans: Many robots, such as robotic arms or drones, are designed for specific tasks and don't have human-like forms.

Robots will replace all human jobs: While automation impacts many industries, robotics also creates new job opportunities in fields such as robotics engineering, maintenance, and AI development.

Historical Context

The concept of robotics dates back to ancient automata, but modern robotics emerged in the **1950s** with the invention of **Unimate** by **George Devol**, the first programmable robot used in automotive manufacturing. In **1996**, **Honda** introduced **ASIMO**, a humanoid robot designed for interaction. The **2000s** witnessed significant advancements in medicine, space exploration, and AI-driven automation. **Boston Dynamics**, **Tesla**, and **NASA** continue to push the boundaries of robotic innovation, from quadruped robots to autonomous rovers on the surface of Mars. Today, robotics integrates AI, cloud computing, and edge processing, making machines more adaptable and intelligent.

Practical Implications

Robotics is transforming industries by automating repetitive and hazardous tasks. In logistics, robotic arms sort and package goods in warehouses. In agriculture, drones and autonomous tractors optimize crop management. In disaster response, search-and-rescue robots navigate hazardous areas to assist emergency responders. In education, robots aid in teaching STEM subjects and programming. While robotics increases efficiency and safety, challenges remain in affordability, adaptability, and ethical concerns regarding the impact of automation on employment. As technology advances, robotics will continue to shape industries, enhance productivity, and expand human capabilities.

Alphabetical List of Terms

DOI: 10.1201/9781003682615-2

5G NR (New Radio) (5G)

5G NR (New Radio) is the global standard for 5G wireless technology, designed to deliver faster speeds, lower latency, and improved connectivity compared to previous generations. It utilizes advanced radio waveforms, frequency bands, and network architecture to support applications such as smart cities, autonomous vehicles, and ultra-reliable low-latency communications (URLLC).

5G NR is like upgrading from a single-lane road to a multi-lane highway with intelligent traffic control. While previous networks struggled with congestion and speed limits, 5G NR dynamically manages data flow, allowing seamless, ultra-fast, and reliable connectivity across multiple devices and industries.

Examples

Autonomous Vehicles: 5G NR's ultra-low latency enables real-time communication between self-driving cars and infrastructure, ensuring safe navigation, instant hazard detection, and optimized traffic flow.

Augmented and Virtual Reality (AR/VR): 5G NR enhances immersive experiences in gaming, training, and remote collaboration by reducing lag and increasing responsiveness, making AR/VR applications more realistic and engaging (see pg. 92 and 530).

Smart Manufacturing: In Industry 4.0, 5G NR enables the real-time monitoring of machines, predictive maintenance, and automated logistics, resulting in increased efficiency and reduced downtime in factories.

Foundational Concepts

5G NR uses millimeter waves (mmWave) for high-speed data transfer, sub-6 GHz bands for broad coverage, and massive MIMO (Multiple Input, Multiple Output) for increased network capacity. Beamforming directs signals efficiently, reducing interference. Dynamic Spectrum Sharing (DSS) allows 4G and 5G to coexist. Network slicing enables the creation of customized network partitions for specific applications, such as low-latency gaming or secure enterprise communication. Together, these technologies make 5G NR more flexible, efficient, and scalable than previous generations of cellular technology.

Related Terms

mmWave (Millimeter Wave): High-frequency radio waves that enable ultra-fast 5G speeds but require dense infrastructure (see pg. 324).

Network Slicing: Dividing a 5G network into virtual segments optimized for different services and industries (see pg. 350).

Massive MIMO: A technology using multiple antennas to improve network efficiency and capacity (see pg. 322).

Common Misconceptions

5G NR is just faster 4G: While speed is a key improvement, 5G NR also enhances latency, capacity, and device connectivity.

All 5G uses mmWave: Many deployments use sub-6 GHz for broader coverage, with mmWave used for ultra-fast, localized access.

5G NR requires entirely new devices: Some devices support both 4G and 5G NR through Dynamic Spectrum Sharing (DSS).

Historical Context

The development of 5G NR began in **2016** with the **3rd Generation Partnership Project** (3GPP), a global organization that sets standards for mobile communication. In **2018**, **Release 15** introduced the first 5G NR specifications, focusing on enhanced mobile broadband (eMBB). **Release 16** (**2020**) expanded features for ultra-reliable low-latency communication (URLLC) and massive IoT. Release 17 (**2022**) and beyond will continue to refine 5G NR, paving the way for **6G**, which will integrate AI-driven networks and quantum security.

Practical Implications

5G NR revolutionizes industries by enabling real-time remote surgery in healthcare, enhancing precision agriculture with IoT sensors, and delivering seamless cloud gaming without latency issues. In logistics, it enhances smart tracking and the use of autonomous drones. For emergency services, 5G NR enables instant communication and high-definition video transmission, facilitating disaster response. As 6G research advances, AI-driven automation and terahertz (THz) communication will further enhance connectivity, reshaping industries worldwide.

Accountability (RAI)

Accountability in Responsible AI refers to the obligation of AI developers, users, and stakeholders to ensure that they design, deploy, and monitor AI systems ethically and transparently. It involves legal, ethical, and technical measures to prevent bias, harm, or misuse, ensuring AI decisions remain explainable and traceable.

Accountability in AI is like a self-driving car with a black box recorder. If an accident occurs, the system must track who is responsible—whether it is the software, the manufacturer, or the human driver—ensuring transparency and consequences for failures or unethical behavior.

Examples

AI in Hiring: If an AI-powered recruitment tool unfairly rejects candidates, accountability requires companies to audit the model, ensure fairness, and rectify any biased hiring decisions that may have resulted.

Autonomous Vehicles: If a self-driving car causes an accident, accountability measures determine if the fault lies with the AI system, the manufacturer, or human intervention, ensuring appropriate liability.

Healthcare AI: AI-driven diagnostic tools monitor systems for errors. If misdiagnoses occur, hospitals and developers are responsible for evaluating, updating, and improving the accuracy of the AI system to ensure its effectiveness.

Foundational Concepts

Accountability in AI encompasses algorithmic transparency, ensuring that AI decision-making is explainable; auditability, enabling third parties to assess AI models for bias and errors; and ethical AI governance, which mandates oversight by regulatory bodies. Fairness and bias detection help prevent discrimination, while human-in-the-loop (HITL) systems ensure humans verify AI outputs in critical scenarios. Legal frameworks, such as the EU AI Act and the U.S. AI Bill of Rights, establish guidelines for holding AI developers accountable for safety, privacy, and ethical considerations.

Related Terms

Explainable AI (XAI): AI systems that provide human-readable explanations for their decisions (see pg. 27).

Algorithmic Bias: The presence of unfair, discriminatory patterns in AI decision-making (see pg. 104).

Ethical AI Governance: Policies and guidelines ensuring AI systems align with societal values (see pg. 80).

Common Misconceptions

AI is always neutral: AI systems can inherit biases from the data, necessitating accountability measures to mitigate unfair decisions.

Only developers are accountable: AI accountability extends to organizations, governments, and end-users who deploy and oversee AI tools.

Regulation stifles AI innovation: Ethical guidelines ensure AI benefits society, preventing harmful or biased applications while fostering trust.

Historical Context

AI accountability became a concern as machine learning systems grew more complex. In **2016**, controversies such as **COMPAS**, an AI used in criminal sentencing, highlighted bias in AI-driven decision-making. In **2018**, **Google's AI Ethics Board** dissolved due to governance concerns, sparking global discussions on AI oversight. The **EU AI Act (2021)** and the **White House AI Blueprint (2022)** introduced legal frameworks for AI accountability, emphasizing transparency, fairness, and compliance.

Practical Implications

AI accountability ensures fair hiring practices, reliable medical diagnostics, and safe autonomous transportation. Governments and companies implement AI impact assessments to detect risks before deployment. In finance, AI-driven lending models must justify credit decisions, ensuring fair access to loans. Holding AI accountable protects consumers, fosters trust in AI applications, and reduces systemic risks in industries such as law enforcement, finance, and healthcare.

Accuracy (AI)

Accuracy in AI and machine learning refers to the measure of how often a model's predictions or classifications are correct. It is the percentage of correctly predicted instances out of the total cases analyzed. While useful, accuracy alone does not account for imbalanced datasets or different types of errors.

Accuracy is like an archer aiming at a target. If most arrows hit the bullseye, the archer is highly accurate. However, if all arrows land in one area but far from the center, the results may be consistent (precise) but not necessarily accurate.

Examples

Medical Diagnostics: AI models used in disease detection, such as cancer, require high accuracy to minimize false negatives and false positives, ensuring reliable patient diagnosis.

Autonomous Vehicles: Self-driving cars rely on accurate object detection to avoid collisions. Misclassifying a pedestrian as an inanimate object could lead to accidents.

Fraud Detection: AI-driven financial fraud detection systems must be accurate to distinguish between legitimate transactions and fraudulent activity while minimizing false alarms.

Foundational Concepts

Accuracy is a fundamental metric in classification tasks, and, together with precision, recall, and the F1-score, provides a more comprehensive evaluation of performance. In imbalanced datasets where one class is significantly more prevalent than the other, accuracy can be a misleading measure. Confusion matrices help break down the performance by distinguishing between true positives, true negatives, false positives, and false negatives. Cross-validation ensures accuracy is consistent across different subsets of data, reducing the risk of overfitting. Advanced techniques, such as calibration curves and receiver operating characteristic (ROC) curves, help refine models to achieve higher real-world reliability.

Related Terms

Precision: Measures how many predicted positive cases are truly correct.

Recall: Measures the actual correctly identified positive cases.

F1-score: A balance between precision and recall, helpful in evaluating models on imbalanced datasets.

Common Misconceptions

High accuracy means a perfect model: A model can have high accuracy, but still fail if the dataset is imbalanced. For example, predicting all emails as "not spam" in a dataset with 99% non-spam emails would yield 99% accuracy, but be useless for identifying spam.

Accuracy is the only important metric: Precision, recall, and F1-score provide deeper insights, especially for applications such as medical AI or fraud detection.

Accuracy remains consistent across different environments: AI models trained on one dataset may lose accuracy when deployed in real-world scenarios due to changes in input data.

Historical Context

The concept of accuracy in AI originated from statistical analysis and the theory of classification. Early machine learning models, such as linear regression (introduced in the early 19th century), used accuracy as a primary measure of success. As AI models evolved, researchers realized that accuracy alone was insufficient for evaluating performance, leading to the introduction of more refined metrics, such as the F1-score and ROC curves. In the 21st century, advances in deep learning highlighted the importance of robust accuracy testing to prevent overfitting and ensure generalizability.

Practical Implications

AI models in healthcare require high accuracy to minimize the risk of false diagnoses. In finance, accurate fraud detection can save companies millions while reducing false alarms. Autonomous systems, such as drones and self-driving cars, rely on accuracy to make split-second decisions that affect safety. Misleading accuracy metrics can lead to poor decision-making, legal liabilities, and a decline in user trust. Therefore, companies and researchers must strike a balance between accuracy and precision, recall, and contextual understanding to ensure that AI applications perform reliably across diverse environments.

Action Recognition (ANI)

Action recognition is a field of artificial intelligence (AI) that focuses on identifying and classifying human activities from video footage, sensor data, or real-time camera feeds. It enables AI to understand gestures, movements, and interactions, making it crucial for applications in surveillance, healthcare, sports analytics, and human-computer interaction.

Action recognition is like a skilled referee in a sports game. Just as the referee observes player movements and makes decisions based on body actions, AI models analyze video sequences and identify actions such as walking, running, jumping, or waving.

Examples

Security and Surveillance: AI-powered action recognition helps detect suspicious behavior in public spaces, such as loitering, fights, or theft, improving safety through automated alerts.

Healthcare Monitoring: AI systems can analyze patient movements to detect falls, assess rehabilitation progress, or identify early signs of neurological disorders, thereby improving patient care and response times.

Sports and Fitness: Action recognition enables the automatic tracking of player performance and movement analysis during training, providing real-time feedback for athletes and enhancing game strategies and fitness programs.

Foundational Concepts

Action recognition depends on deep learning, computer vision, and time-series analysis. Convolutional Neural Networks (CNNs) process spatial features from images, while Recurrent Neural Networks (RNNs) and Transformer-based models track movement sequences over time. Optical flow algorithms analyze the motion between video frames, and pose estimation techniques identify the skeletal structures of humans. Datasets such as Kinetics and UCF101 train models to recognize various actions. The field also uses 3D convolutional networks (C3D) and Spatio-Temporal Graph Neural Networks (ST-GNNs) for more sophisticated movement detection.

Related Terms

Pose Estimation: AI models that analyze human joint positions to track body posture and movement.

Gesture Recognition: Identifying hand movements and gestures for human-computer interaction.

Object Detection: Detecting and classifying objects in images or video frames to support action recognition.

Common Misconceptions

Action recognition is perfect: AI models can misclassify actions due to occlusions, varying camera angles, or ambiguous movements.
It works in real-time without issues: While advancements exist, real-time action recognition requires high computational power and optimized models.
Only used in security applications: Though surveillance is a primary use case, action recognition has broad applications in healthcare, entertainment, and robotics.

Historical Context

Early action recognition research began in the **1980s** with template-matching techniques. The field evolved with the rise of machine learning, using Hidden Markov Models (HMMs) and Dynamic Time Warping (DTW) to classify actions. The introduction of deep learning and large-scale datasets in the **2010s** significantly improved accuracy. Pioneering models such as **Two-Stream Networks (2014)** and I3D (Inflated 3D CNNs, **2017**) have advanced action recognition, and Transformer-based models are now setting new benchmarks.

Practical Implications

Action recognition enhances public safety, enabling law enforcement to prevent crimes in real-time. In healthcare, AI systems improve elderly care by detecting falls and unusual behavior. Augmented reality (AR) and virtual reality (VR) applications use action recognition to create immersive gaming and training experiences. In smart cities, traffic management benefits from recognizing pedestrian and vehicle movements, reducing accidents. As AI models improve, action recognition will integrate into more daily life applications, from AI-driven personal assistants to interactive learning environments.

Activation Function (AI)

An activation function is a mathematical function used in artificial neural networks to determine whether a neuron should be activated or not. It transforms the input signal into an output that is passed to the next layer, introducing non-linearity, which enables the network to learn complex patterns and relationships.

An activation function serves as a gatekeeper in the decision-making process. Just as a referee decides whether a goal is valid or not based on specific rules, an activation function determines whether a neuron should fire based on the weighted sum of its inputs.

Examples

Image Recognition: Activation functions help convolutional neural networks (CNNs) classify objects in images by identifying features such as edges, textures, and shapes. Functions like ReLU improve efficiency by allowing only relevant signals to pass.

Speech Recognition: In automatic speech recognition (ASR), activation functions enable deep learning models to process and classify phonemes, improving the accuracy of virtual assistants and transcription software (see pg. 460).

Financial Forecasting: Neural networks use activation functions to analyze stock market trends and predict future values. Functions like sigmoid help convert financial input data into probabilities, aiding in decision-making models.

Foundational Concepts

Activation functions introduce non-linearity into neural networks, allowing them to model complex patterns. The Rectified Linear Unit (ReLU) is the most common activation function, setting negative values to zero while preserving positive values. Sigmoid maps values between 0 and 1, making it useful for probability-based outputs. The tanh function ranges from -1 to 1, keeping both positive and negative information. Advanced functions, such as Leaky ReLU, Softmax, and Swish, address issues like the vanishing gradient problem, which occurs when gradients become too small for deep networks to learn effectively.

Related Terms

Neural Network: A system of interconnected artificial neurons that uses activation functions to process information (see pg. 352).

Gradient Descent: An optimization technique that adjusts weights in a neural network to minimize errors.

Backpropagation: A learning algorithm that updates weights using gradients, influenced by activation function behavior.

Common Misconceptions

Activation functions are interchangeable: Different functions suit different tasks, and choosing the wrong one can hinder learning.

More complex functions are always better: Simpler functions like ReLU often perform better than intricate ones.

They only modify input values: Activation functions also impact training speed and the ability to generalize learning.

Historical Context

Early neural networks employed step functions, which were unable to model complex data. The sigmoid function gained popularity in the **1980s**, but its limitations led to the rise of ReLU (**2010**), now a standard in deep learning. Researchers such as Nobel laureate **Geoffrey Hinton** and **Yann LeCun** have made significant contributions to modern activation functions, enabling breakthroughs in AI applications.

Practical Implications

Activation functions enable advancements in deep learning for autonomous vehicles, medical diagnosis, and robotics. In healthcare, AI models use activation functions to detect diseases from medical images. Autonomous cars rely on them to process sensor data and recognize objects on the road. Robotic systems use activation-based neural networks for real-time decision-making, enhancing automation.

Actuator (IoT)

An actuator is a device that converts electrical, hydraulic, or pneumatic energy into mechanical motion. It is a crucial component and widely used in robotics, automation, and industrial machinery, enabling controlled movement and physical interaction with the environment.

An actuator is like a muscle in the human body. Just as muscles receive signals from the brain to move arms or legs, actuators receive signals from a control system and move—whether it's opening a valve, rotating a motor, or adjusting robotic limbs.

Examples

Robotics and Automation: Actuators enable robotic arms to perform precise movements in manufacturing, such as assembling products or welding parts. Servo and stepper motors are common types used for accurate positioning.

Aerospace and Automotive: In modern cars, actuators control throttle, braking systems, and adaptive suspensions. In aerospace, they adjust flaps, landing gear, and flight control surfaces to improve stability and safety.

Medical Devices: Actuators power prosthetic limbs, surgical robots, and automated medical equipment, allowing precise movement in healthcare applications. These devices enhance the mobility of individuals with disabilities and assist surgeons in performing minimally invasive procedures.

Foundational Concepts

Actuators operate on three primary principles: electrical, hydraulic, and pneumatic energy conversion. Electrical actuators, such as servo motors, use electric current to generate motion. Hydraulic actuators rely on pressurized fluid to create movement, whereas pneumatic actuators utilize compressed air to generate mechanical force. The choice of actuator depends on the required precision, force, speed, and power consumption.

Common types include linear actuators, which move objects in a straight line, and rotary actuators, which create rotational motion. Advanced actuators incorporate sensors and feedback loops for precise control, a feature often found in adaptive automation systems.

Related Terms

Servo Motor: A rotary actuator that allows precise control of position and speed, commonly used in robotics.

Stepper Motor: A motor that moves in discrete steps, ideal for applications requiring high positional accuracy.

Hydraulic System: A fluid-based system that uses actuators to generate force in heavy machinery.

Common Misconceptions

Actuators only produce linear motion: They can also generate rotational movement, depending on their design.

All actuators are electric: While electric actuators are standard, hydraulic and pneumatic actuators are widely used in heavy-duty applications.

Actuators operate independently: Most actuators require a control system and sensors to regulate their movement efficiently.

Historical Context

The concept of actuators dates back to early steam engines and hydraulic systems in the 18th and 19th centuries. The Industrial Revolution saw advancements in mechanical actuators for manufacturing. In the 20th century, electric actuators gained popularity, leading to innovations in robotics, aerospace, and automation. The integration of AI and smart actuators has further revolutionized industries, allowing for self-regulating and adaptive motion control.

Practical Implications

Actuators are essential in modern technology, from robotic surgery and autonomous vehicles to space exploration and industrial automation. In smart homes, actuators control motorized blinds, adjustable furniture, and security systems. In renewable energy, actuators adjust solar panels and wind turbines to optimize energy capture. As AI-driven automation advances, intelligent actuators will play a key role in adaptive systems, enhancing precision, efficiency, and responsiveness in various industries.

Adaptive Control Systems (RAI/XAI)

An adaptive control system is a self-adjusting system that continuously modifies its parameters to maintain optimal performance in response to changing environmental conditions or system dynamics. Used where operating conditions vary and require real-time adjustments, to ensure efficiency and stability, such as in automation, robotics, and aerospace applications.

An adaptive control system is akin to a self-learning driver who adjusts their driving style based on road conditions. Just as a driver adapts to wet roads by reducing speed and increasing braking distance, an adaptive control system continuously fine-tunes its parameters to optimize performance in dynamic environments.

Examples

Autonomous Vehicles: Self-driving cars utilize adaptive control systems to adjust steering, acceleration, and braking in response to road conditions, traffic, and sensor inputs. These adjustments enhance safety and driving efficiency.

Aerospace Navigation: Aircraft and spacecraft employ adaptive flight control systems to adjust to variations in wind speed, turbulence, and altitude changes. These systems enhance stability and responsiveness, improving flight safety.

Industrial Automation: Smart manufacturing machines utilize adaptive control systems to adjust machining parameters, such as speed and torque, based on material properties. This approach ensures precision and efficiency while reducing wear and tear on equipment.

Foundational Concepts

Adaptive control systems rely on real-time feedback loops to adjust system parameters dynamically. The two main types of adaptive control are model reference adaptive control (MRAC), which compares system output to a reference model and makes adjustments accordingly, and self-tuning regulators (STR), which use estimated parameters to optimize performance.

These systems incorporate machine learning and optimization algorithms to predict future changes and adjust control strategies proactively. They typically apply in nonlinear, time-varying, and uncertain environments where fixed control methods would be inefficient.

Related Terms

Feedback Control System: A system that adjusts its behavior based on sensor feedback to maintain stability and accuracy.

Machine Learning Control: AI-driven control systems that use predictive models to improve performance dynamically.

Nonlinear Systems: Systems with complex behavior that do not follow linear control laws, often requiring adaptive control.

Common Misconceptions

Adaptive control systems work like AI: While some utilize AI, most rely on mathematical models and control algorithms to make real-time adjustments.

They replace human decision-making completely: Many adaptive systems still require human supervision or manual override in critical applications.

They only apply to robotics: You will find adaptive control systems in medicine, aerospace, telecommunications, and power grids, among other fields.

Historical Context

The concept of adaptive control dates back to the **1950s** and **1960s**, with early research in aerospace and automation. Engineers sought ways to stabilize aircraft and spacecraft under unpredictable conditions. In the **1970s**, **Kalman filtering** and optimal control theories improved adaptive control techniques. By the **1990s**, advancements in AI and machine learning enabled more sophisticated real-time adjustments. Today, adaptive control integrates into autonomous systems, robotics, and intelligent transportation networks.

Practical Implications

Adaptive control is transforming autonomous systems, industrial automation, and healthcare. In robotics, it enables robotic arms to adjust their force and speed according to the resistance of the object they are interacting with. In energy grids, adaptive control dynamically balances power supply and demand. In telecommunications, it optimizes network bandwidth based on real-time traffic. As technology advances, adaptive control systems will enhance efficiency, safety, and precision across multiple industries, thereby making intelligent automation even more reliable and effective.

Affordance (HCI)

Affordance refers to the properties of an object or interface that suggest how to use it. In Human-Computer Interaction (HCI), affordances guide users in understanding how to interact with digital and physical systems, making design intuitive by leveraging perceptual cues and prior knowledge.

Affordance is like a door handle—it signals whether to push, pull, or slide the door open. Similarly, a computer button that looks raised suggests clicking, while a flat icon may indicate tapping. Good affordances reduce confusion by naturally guiding interaction without the need for explicit instructions.

Examples

Smartphone Touchscreens: The pinch-to-zoom gesture on a smartphone screen leverages natural affordance, enabling users to resize images without explicit instructions.

E-commerce Checkout Buttons: A prominent, brightly colored "Buy Now" button signals an action users should take, leveraging visual affordance to increase engagement.

Gaming Controllers: The placement of joysticks and button textures suggests their intended use, enhancing usability in gaming consoles through tactile affordances that guide user input.

Foundational Concepts

Affordance, introduced by psychologist James J. Gibson in **1977**, describes how potential actions in a situation are available based on environmental features. In HCI, Don Norman expanded this concept, distinguishing between perceived affordances (what users think an interface allows) and real affordances (what the interface actually enables).

HCI design leverages signifiers, such as color and shape, to enhance the recognition of affordances. Designers also use constraints (like disabled buttons) to prevent unintended actions. Practical affordances reduce cognitive load, allowing users to navigate digital systems effortlessly.

Related Terms

Signifiers: Visual cues that help users recognize affordances, such as arrows or icons.

Usability: The ease with which users interact with a system, influenced by affordances.

Mental Models: Users' expectations of how an interface should work based on past experiences.

Common Misconceptions

Affordances are limited to physical objects: Digital interfaces also rely on affordances, such as scrollbars, buttons, and swipe gestures.

Affordances always work the same way: User expectations differ based on culture, experience, and familiarity with the device.

More affordances improve usability: Excessive affordances can clutter interfaces and confuse users rather than guiding them.

Historical Context

James J. Gibson first defined the concept of affordance in ecological psychology, emphasizing the interplay between perception and action. In The **Design of Everyday Things (1988)**, **Don Norman** introduced affordance into HCI, refining its role in interface design. With the rise of digital interfaces in the **1990s** and **2000s**, affordances became central to UX design, guiding intuitive interaction in software, web, and mobile applications.

Practical Implications

Affordances improve usability by making interfaces more intuitive. In healthcare apps, clear affordances guide users through medication tracking. In automotive interfaces, touchscreens and physical buttons must strike a balance between affordances for safety. In smart homes, clear visual and voice-based affordances help users operate devices seamlessly. Well-designed affordances reduce training time, errors, and frustration, making technology more accessible and efficient.

Agent (ANI)

An agent in artificial intelligence (AI) is an autonomous entity that perceives its environment, processes information, and takes actions to achieve specific goals. Agents can be simple, rule-based systems or complex, AI-driven models that adapt, learn, and optimize their decision-making through interaction with their environment.

An AI agent is like a self-driving car. It constantly senses the road, traffic signals, and obstacles, processes this data, and then takes actions like accelerating, braking, or steering. Just as the car adapts to changing traffic conditions, an AI agent dynamically adjusts its responses based on its environment.

Examples

Virtual Assistants: AI-powered agents like Siri and Alexa interpret user queries, retrieve information, and execute commands such as setting alarms or controlling smart home devices (see pg. 528).

Autonomous Drones: Drones used in surveillance, agriculture, and disaster relief analyze terrain, adjust their flight paths, and avoid obstacles without human intervention (see pg. 98).

Stock Trading Algorithms: AI-driven agents in financial markets monitor stock trends, predict market shifts, and execute trades autonomously to optimize investment returns.

Foundational Concepts

AI agents operate using perception, decision-making, and action execution. They gather data through sensors or inputs, process it using machine learning models or predefined rules, and take appropriate actions. Rational agents maximize expected outcomes based on predefined goals. Reinforcement learning enables agents to improve performance by learning from rewards and penalties. Multi-agent systems involve multiple interacting agents that collaborate or compete within an environment, such as in robotics or simulations.

Related Terms

Autonomous Systems: AI-driven entities that function independently in complex environments.

Reinforcement Learning: A machine learning technique where agents learn by trial and error (see pg. 410).

Multi-Agent Systems: Environments where multiple agents interact, cooperate, or compete.

Common Misconceptions

All AI agents are sentient: AI agents process data and execute tasks, but they lack consciousness and emotions.

Agents always make optimal decisions: Many AI agents operate with limited information and may make suboptimal choices.

Agents require human supervision: Some operate autonomously, while others rely on human guidance or constraints.

Historical Context

The concept of AI agents emerged in the **1950s** with early game-playing programs and expert systems. In the **1990s**, autonomous agents became more sophisticated with the development of intelligent robotics and multi-agent systems. Today, AI agents power industries from healthcare to finance, driven by advancements in deep learning, reinforcement learning, and distributed AI.

Practical Implications

AI agents enhance automation, reducing the human workload in areas such as customer service (chatbots), transportation (self-driving cars), and security (surveillance drones). In healthcare, AI agents assist in diagnostics and patient monitoring. In manufacturing, robotic agents improve efficiency and precision. The evolution of AI agents continues to shape industries, enabling smarter, faster, and more adaptive decision-making systems.

AI Governance (RAI)

AI governance refers to the frameworks, policies, and ethical guidelines that regulate the development, deployment, and oversight of artificial intelligence systems. It ensures that the usage of AI is always responsible, mitigating risks such as bias, privacy violations, and unintended consequences, while promoting fairness, accountability, and transparency across industries and societies.

AI governance is like traffic rules for AI systems. Just as road signs, speed limits, and driver regulations prevent accidents and ensure safe transportation, AI governance sets ethical, legal, and operational boundaries to guide AI development, preventing harm while ensuring efficiency, fairness, and societal benefits.

Examples

Regulating Facial Recognition: Governments enforce policies that limit the use of facial recognition in public spaces to prevent mass surveillance and protect privacy rights, ensuring that AI aligns with ethical and legal standards.

Bias Mitigation in Hiring AI: AI-driven hiring tools must comply with regulations that prevent discrimination, ensuring that algorithms do not unfairly disadvantage certain groups based on factors such as race, gender, or age (see pg. 104).

Healthcare AI Compliance: AI used in medical diagnostics is subject to governance frameworks that mandate transparency, accuracy, and compliance with health regulations, such as HIPAA (in the US), to protect patient data and ensure treatment integrity.

Foundational Concepts

Founded on ethical AI principles, AI governance includes fairness, transparency, accountability, and human oversight. Regulatory frameworks, such as the EU AI Act and the NIST AI Risk Management Framework, guide AI policies. Algorithmic transparency ensures AI decision-making is explainable, reducing the risk of bias and misinformation. Data privacy laws, such as GDPR (EU), shape AI governance by enforcing strict rules for data handling. AI safety research focuses on preventing unintended consequences, ensuring AI remains beneficial and aligned with human values.

Related Terms

AI Ethics: The moral considerations and principles guiding AI development and use (see pg. 204).

Algorithmic Transparency: The practice of making AI decisions interpretable and explainable (see pg. 502).

Regulatory Compliance: Adhering to laws and guidelines that govern AI systems (see pg. 80).

Common Misconceptions

AI governance limits innovation: It aims to balance innovation with ethical safeguards, rather than hindering progress.

Only governments enforce AI governance: Organizations and industry bodies also develop and utilize AI governance frameworks.

AI governance is just about laws: It also includes ethics, risk management, and corporate responsibility.

Historical Context

AI governance emerged as AI adoption increased, particularly in high-stakes fields such as healthcare and finance. **The Asilomar AI Principles (2017)** established ethical guidelines for AI, while the **GDPR (2018)** set global standards for data protection. In **2021**, the EU proposed a risk-based AI regulation under the **EU AI Act**. Governments worldwide, including those of the US, China, and the UK, continue to develop policies to ensure that AI is safe, fair, and accountable.

Practical Implications

AI governance impacts businesses by enforcing compliance with ethical AI standards. In healthcare, it ensures AI-powered diagnoses meet medical accuracy benchmarks. In finance, AI governance prevents bias in credit scoring and fraud detection. AI governance also shapes public trust, ensuring AI adoption aligns with societal values. As AI advances, governance frameworks will continue evolving, fostering innovation while safeguarding ethical responsibility.

AlphaFold (ANI)

AlphaFold is an artificial intelligence system developed by DeepMind that accurately predicts protein structures. By using deep learning models, AlphaFold solves the protein folding problem, significantly advancing molecular biology, drug discovery, and disease research by determining protein 3D structures from amino acid sequences.

AlphaFold is like an expert puzzle solver that assembles a protein's 3D structure from a long chain of amino acids, similar to solving a complex jigsaw puzzle using patterns and past knowledge rather than trial and error, making the process significantly faster and more accurate.

Examples

Drug Discovery: AlphaFold aids in designing new drugs by predicting protein structures associated with diseases, thereby accelerating the development of treatments for conditions such as cancer and Alzheimer's.

Enzyme Engineering: Scientists utilize AlphaFold to design enzymes that break down plastics, thereby aiding in environmental sustainability and waste management.

Genetic Disease Research: By mapping protein structures in genetic disorders, AlphaFold enables researchers to understand the effects of mutations and develop targeted gene therapies (see pg. 242).

Foundational Concepts

AlphaFold is based on deep learning algorithms, trained on known protein structures from the Protein Data Bank. It leverages transformer architectures, similar to those used in NLP models, to predict structural properties. Multiple sequence alignment (MSA) provides evolutionary data, helping the AI infer folding patterns. The physics-based constraints ensure predictions adhere to biochemical laws. The model applies self-attention mechanisms to capture long-range dependencies within protein sequences, improving accuracy. AlphaFold's advancements significantly outperform previous computational models, reducing reliance on costly experimental techniques like X-ray crystallography and cryo-electron microscopy.

Related Terms

Protein Folding: The process by which a protein assumes its functional 3D shape.

Bioinformatics: The field combining biology and computational techniques to analyze biological data.

Deep Learning: A subset of AI using neural networks to process complex patterns, integral to AlphaFold's success (see pg. 178).

Common Misconceptions

AlphaFold replaces lab experiments: While powerful, it complements rather than replaces experimental validation.

AlphaFold predicts all molecular interactions: It focuses on static structures rather than dynamic interactions.

AlphaFold solves all biology problems: It addresses protein folding but doesn't model complex cellular processes.

Historical Context

AlphaFold was first introduced in **2018** and improved significantly by AlphaFold 2 in **2020**, winning the **Critical Assessment of Structure Prediction** (CASP) competition by far surpassing traditional methods. **DeepMind** made AlphaFold's code and database publicly available in **2021**, providing structures for nearly all known proteins. This breakthrough stemmed from decades of bioinformatics and AI research, thereby accelerating advancements in structural biology.

Practical Implications

AlphaFold revolutionizes medicine, enabling the precision design of drugs and vaccines. It aids agriculture by optimizing crop proteins to achieve better yields and increased resistance. In biotechnology, AlphaFold accelerates enzyme design for industrial applications, such as biofuels. Its rapid predictions democratize access to protein structures, benefiting global research and pharmaceutical industries, ultimately reducing costs and development timelines for life-saving treatments.

Anomaly Detection (AI)

Anomaly detection is a machine learning technique used to identify unusual patterns, behaviors, or deviations from normal data distributions. It is widely applied in cybersecurity, fraud detection, healthcare, and industrial monitoring to detect potential threats, faults, or irregularities that require investigation or corrective action.

Anomaly detection is akin to a security guard at a shopping mall, who watches for unusual behavior. If someone is acting suspiciously—such as lingering without shopping or attempting to enter restricted areas—the guard takes notice, just as anomaly detection algorithms flag unexpected patterns in data.

Examples

Fraud Detection: Banks use anomaly detection to identify suspicious transactions, such as sudden large withdrawals or purchases from unusual locations, helping to prevent credit card fraud.

Network Security: Cybersecurity systems monitor network traffic for abnormal behavior, such as unauthorized access attempts or unusual data transfers, to detect potential cyberattacks.

Predictive Maintenance: In manufacturing, anomaly detection identifies unusual vibrations or temperature fluctuations in machinery, enabling the prediction of failures before they occur and reducing downtime.

Foundational Concepts

Anomaly detection relies on statistical models, clustering techniques, and neural networks to distinguish standard patterns from irregularities. Supervised learning uses labeled data to train models, while unsupervised learning detects anomalies without predefined labels. Density-based methods assess the likelihood of an observation within normal distributions, while autoencoders compress and reconstruct data, flagging deviations as anomalies. Isolation forests and one-class SVMs are common strategies for detecting outliers in high-dimensional data.

Related Terms

Outlier Detection: Identifying rare or extreme values in data distributions.

Supervised Learning: Machine learning that uses labeled data for training models, sometimes applied in anomaly detection (see pg. 468).

Clustering: Grouping data points based on similarity, often used in unsupervised anomaly detection methods (see pg. 134).

Common Misconceptions

All anomalies indicate fraud or failure: Some deviations are harmless or expected in dynamic environments.

Anomaly detection is always accurate: False positives and negatives occur, requiring human validation.

Traditional rule-based systems are enough: Machine learning models adapt better to new patterns than static rules.

Historical Context

Anomaly detection has its roots in statistics and signal processing, dating back to the early 20th century, with methods such as control charts used in industrial quality control. In the **1990s**, machine learning techniques emerged to handle complex data sets. Advances in deep learning and big data analytics have enabled real-time anomaly detection, revolutionizing fields such as cybersecurity, finance, and IoT monitoring.

Practical Implications

Anomaly detection enhances security, efficiency, and informed decision-making across various industries. It enhances fraud detection in banking, protects networks from cyber threats, ensures quality control in manufacturing, and enables early disease diagnosis in healthcare. As AI models become more sophisticated, anomaly detection systems will continue to play a vital role in safeguarding critical systems and processes.

Artificial Neural Network (ANN) (AI)

An Artificial Neural Network (ANN) is a machine learning model inspired by the structure and function of the human brain. It consists of interconnected nodes, or neurons, organized in layers to process and analyze data. ANNs learn patterns from input data through weights, biases, and activation functions, enabling tasks like image recognition and language processing.

An ANN is like a team of detectives working on a case. Each detective (neuron) gathers clues (data), shares findings with teammates (other neurons), and refines their conclusions through teamwork (layers). The final decision, made collectively, improves over time as the detectives learn from past cases.

Examples

Image Recognition: ANNs power computer vision systems, such as facial recognition in smartphones, which identify people by analyzing patterns in images. Some social media companies use ANNs to tag friends in photos automatically.

Speech Recognition: Virtual assistants like Siri and Alexa rely on ANNs to convert spoken words into text and interpret meaning. They improve over time by learning speech patterns, accents, and context (see pg. 460).

Financial Fraud Detection: Banks use ANNs to detect fraudulent transactions by identifying unusual spending patterns in customer data. If a transaction deviates from expected behavior, the system flags it for review.

Foundational Concepts

An ANN consists of three primary layers: the input layer receives raw data (e.g., an image or text), the hidden layers perform computations using weights, biases, and activation functions like ReLU or sigmoid, and the output layer produces the final prediction or classification. The network learns through backpropagation, where errors are corrected using the gradient descent method. Weights are adjusted based on loss functions, which measure the accuracy of predictions. Deep Neural Networks (DNNs), with multiple hidden layers, enable advanced AI applications such as natural language processing and autonomous driving.

Related Terms

Deep Learning: A subset of machine learning using multi-layered ANNs for complex tasks (see pg. 178).

Backpropagation: An optimization method adjusting ANN weights to minimize errors.

Activation Function: A mathematical function deciding neuron activation, affecting learning efficiency.

Common Misconceptions

ANNs work like human brains: While inspired by neuroscience, ANNs lack emotions, reasoning, and understanding.

More layers always mean better performance: Deep networks require careful tuning; too many layers may cause overfitting.

ANNs learn without training data: ANNs depend on data and cannot self-learn without examples.

Historical Context

ANNs date back to **Warren McCulloch** and **Walter Pitts** (**1943**), who proposed the first mathematical model of a neural network. **Frank Rosenblatt** (**1958**) introduced the perceptron, an early neural network. Interest declined until the **1980s**, when **Geoffrey Hinton** pioneered backpropagation, making ANNs practical. The deep learning revolution (**2010s**), driven by big data and GPUs, led to breakthroughs in AI.

Practical Implications

ANNs power AI across industries. In healthcare, they diagnose diseases by analyzing medical images. In autonomous driving, they process sensor data to navigate roads. In entertainment, platforms like Netflix use ANNs for personalized recommendations. Future developments in neuromorphic computing and quantum AI may further enhance the capabilities of ANN.

Association (AI)

Association in artificial intelligence and data science refers to the identification of relationships between variables in a dataset. In association rule mining, the goal is to discover patterns and correlations between items, enabling AI systems to make data-driven predictions and recommendations in various domains.

Association is like shopping habits in a grocery store. If customers frequently buy bread and butter together, a store might place these items near each other. AI uses association in the same way—finding patterns in data, such as suggesting a movie based on what someone has previously watched.

Examples

Market Basket Analysis: Online retailers, such as Amazon, utilize association rule mining to recommend products. If a customer purchases a laptop, the system may suggest accessories like a mouse or keyboard based on their historical purchasing patterns.

Medical Diagnosis: AI-powered systems analyze patient records to find associations between symptoms and diseases. If patients with a specific genetic marker are frequently prone to a condition, AI can recommend early screening or preventive care.

Fraud Detection: Financial institutions use association techniques to identify unusual spending behaviors. If the system detects uncharacteristic charges using a credit card for high-risk transactions in multiple locations, it alerts the user to potential fraud.

Foundational Concepts

Association is a key concept in data mining and machine learning, used to uncover hidden patterns in large datasets. *Association Rule Mining* extracts rules from data, typically expressed as "If X, then Y" statements. The significance of these rules is measured using *Support*, which determines the frequency of an association; *Confidence*, which measures the likelihood of one item appearing given another; and *Lift*, which indicates whether the association is significant beyond random chance. Popular algorithms used for efficiently discovering associations in large datasets include the *Apriori Algorithm* and *FP-Growth*.

Related Terms

Correlation: Measures the strength of the relationship between variables but does not imply causation.

Pattern Recognition: Identifying recurring structures or behaviors in data, often used alongside association.

Recommendation System: Uses association rules to suggest items, commonly found in e-commerce and streaming platforms (see pg. 404).

Common Misconceptions

Association equals causation: Just because two events are linked does not mean one causes the other.

Association rules are static: AI continuously updates patterns as it ingests new data.

Only useful for shopping data: Association techniques are applicable in fields such as healthcare, finance, and cybersecurity.

Historical Context

The concept of association in AI originated in data mining and statistical analysis, with early work in association rule learning by **Agrawal, Imielinski**, and **Swami (1993)** introducing the **Apriori algorithm**. Since then, advancements in machine learning have improved association rule applications across various industries. Modern deep learning-based association models are now enhancing fields such as natural language processing and autonomous decision-making.

Practical Implications

Association-driven AI enhances decision-making in industries like retail, healthcare, and cybersecurity. Retailers use it for personalized recommendations, hospitals detect early disease symptoms through medical associations, and banks prevent fraud through transaction pattern analysis. As AI evolves, association techniques will become even more integrated into intelligent systems, driving predictive analytics and automation across multiple domains.

Audio Data (AI)

Audio data refers to digitally recorded or generated sound waves stored in a format that can be analyzed, processed, or synthesized by artificial intelligence. This data is commonly used in speech recognition, music processing, sound classification, and acoustic analysis, enabling AI-driven applications like virtual assistants, automated transcription, and environmental sound detection.

Audio data is akin to a musical score, where each note represents a distinct sound wave. Just as musicians interpret notes to create melodies, AI systems process audio signals to recognize speech, detect patterns, or classify sounds in real-world applications, such as voice assistants, security systems, and entertainment technology.

Examples

Speech Recognition: AI-powered assistants, such as Amazon Alexa and Google Assistant, convert spoken commands into text, enabling users to interact with devices using natural language. This conversion relies on processing audio waveforms and recognizing speech patterns (see pg. 460).

Music Recommendation: Streaming platforms like Spotify and Apple Music analyze audio features, including tempo, pitch, and genre, to recommend songs. AI models compare these characteristics with user preferences to improve music suggestions (see pg. 404).

Security and Surveillance: AI-driven audio monitoring systems detect anomalies like glass breaking, gunshots, or distress calls in public spaces. These systems process audio waveforms to identify threats and trigger alerts.

Foundational Concepts

Waveforms, used to represent audio data, are analyzed using signal processing and machine learning techniques. The sampling rate defines how frequently an audio signal is captured per second (e.g., 44.1 kHz for CDs). The Fourier Transform converts time-domain audio signals into the frequency domain, revealing hidden patterns. Spectrograms are visual representations of sound that show frequency, amplitude, and time, which are essential for speech recognition and music analysis. AI models perform feature extraction to identify pitch, rhythm, and timbre, which are crucial for applications such as emotion detection and sound classification. Powerful models, such as neural networks including Convolutional Neural Networks (CNNs) and Recurrent Neural Networks (RNNs), process audio data for tasks like voice synthesis, speech-to-text conversion, and noise reduction.

Related Terms

Natural Language Processing (NLP): AI models process spoken and written language for applications such as chatbots and voice assistants (see pg. 346).

Spectral Analysis: A method for analyzing audio frequencies, often used in music classification and voice recognition.

Text-to-Speech (TTS): AI-generated speech from text, enabling voice synthesis in audiobooks, accessibility tools, and virtual assistants (see pg. 490).

Common Misconceptions

Audio data is just music and speech: It also includes environmental sounds, ultrasonic waves, and biometric voice patterns.

AI understands meaning from audio directly: AI processes patterns and features, but contextual understanding often requires NLP models.

Audio processing requires high-quality recordings: AI can extract meaning even from noisy or low-quality audio through noise reduction algorithms.

Historical Context

The field of audio processing dates back to early telephony, where engineers developed signal filtering for voice transmission. In the **1950s**, speech recognition research began with the development of basic phoneme detection. The **1980s** and **1990s** saw the rise of Hidden Markov Models (HMMs) for speech processing. Deep learning advancements in the **2010s** enabled breakthroughs in speech-to-text, music recommendation, and sound classification, leading to the development of real-time voice assistants and smart audio analytics. Companies like **Google**, **Microsoft**, and **OpenAI** continue refining AI-based audio models.

Practical Implications

AI-powered audio processing is transforming healthcare, security, and entertainment. In healthcare, AI detects heart murmurs and respiratory conditions from sound recordings. The entertainment industry uses AI for audio editing, voice cloning, and music generation. In customer service, AI-powered speech recognition enhances call center automation. Future applications include real-time audio translation, AI-generated soundtracks, and autonomous vehicle sound recognition, where AI detects sirens or road hazards through audio analysis.

Augmented Reality (AR) (XR)

Augmented Reality (AR) is a technology that overlays digital content, such as images, sounds, and 3D objects, onto the real world using devices like smartphones, AR glasses, or headsets. Unlike Virtual Reality (VR), AR enhances the physical environment rather than replacing it, allowing users to interact with both digital and real-world elements simultaneously.

AR is like a digital layer on reality, similar to how a car windshield with a heads-up display provides extra information such as speed, navigation, and alerts without obstructing the physical view. Just as reading glasses enhance vision, AR enhances perception by integrating interactive digital elements into daily life.

Examples

Retail and E-Commerce: AR enables users to virtually try on clothes, glasses, or makeup before making a purchase. Retailers like IKEA and Sephora utilize AR apps to allow customers to visualize furniture placement or makeup application before making a purchase.

Healthcare and Surgery: AR assists surgeons by projecting patient data and anatomical structures onto their field of vision during operations. Medical students also use AR simulations for interactive learning of human anatomy and complex procedures.

Gaming and Entertainment: AR-powered games like Pokémon GO overlay digital characters onto real-world environments. AR concerts and museum exhibits offer immersive storytelling by incorporating interactive digital elements into real-world experiences.

Foundational Concepts

AR operates using real-time data processing, computer vision, and spatial mapping to integrate virtual elements into the real world. Computer vision analyzes images and identifies objects, enabling AR systems to recognize and interact with real-world features. Simultaneous Localization and Mapping (SLAM) allows AR applications to track movement and understand environments, ensuring precise overlay of digital content. Holographic projection is utilized in advanced AR devices, such as Microsoft HoloLens, to display 3D holograms that interact with the physical world. AR hardware, such as smartphones, smart glasses, and AR headsets, captures and renders augmented content through cameras, sensors, and displays. Gesture and voice recognition enable hands-free interaction with AR environments, commonly used in smart assistants and industrial applications.

Related Terms

Virtual Reality (VR): A fully immersive experience that replaces the real world with a digital environment (see pg. 530).

Mixed Reality (MR): A blend of AR and VR where virtual and real elements interact dynamically.

Haptic Feedback: Technology that simulates touch sensations, enhancing AR experiences in training, gaming, and remote collaboration (see pg. 260).

Common Misconceptions

AR is the same as VR: While VR replaces reality, AR enhances it by adding interactive digital layers.

AR requires expensive hardware: Many AR experiences are accessible on smartphones and tablets without the need for special devices.

AR is only for entertainment: Healthcare, education, industrial training, and remote collaboration all utilize AR.

Historical Context

The concept of AR emerged in the **1960s**, when **Ivan Sutherland** developed the first AR headset, **"The Sword of Damocles."** In the **1990s**, Boeing researchers **Tom Caudell** and **David Mizell** coined the term "Augmented Reality" for assisting assembly line workers. The **2010s** witnessed AR's commercial rise, marked by the introduction of **Google Glass (2013)** and the global success of **Pokémon GO (2016)**. Companies like **Microsoft**, **Apple**, and **Meta** continue advancing AR with wearable technology, AR-powered maps, and interactive digital workspaces.

Practical Implications

AR is transforming education, business, and healthcare by enhancing real-world interactions with digital data. Education uses AR for interactive learning modules, enabling students to explore historical landmarks or 3D biological structures. Retail and e-commerce use AR-powered virtual fitting rooms and home design tools. In manufacturing and maintenance, AR assists technicians by displaying real-time repair guides on machines. The future of AR includes AI-driven personalized experiences, real-time language translation, and workplace collaboration using AR glasses, revolutionizing how people interact with digital information in physical spaces.

Autoencoder (AI)

An autoencoder is a type of artificial neural network designed for unsupervised learning that compresses input data into a lower-dimensional representation (encoding) and then reconstructs it back to its original form. It is used for dimensionality reduction, anomaly detection, and noise removal, effectively capturing essential data features while minimizing information loss.

An autoencoder is like a skilled stenographer who listens to a long speech, takes concise notes that capture the main points, and then reconstructs the entire speech from those notes. While some minor details may be lost, the core message remains intact, making the information more manageable and structured.

Examples

Image Denoising: Autoencoders remove noise from images by learning to reconstruct a clean version from a noisy input. For example, in medical imaging, they enhance MRI scans by filtering out artifacts while retaining key diagnostic details (see pg. 182).

Fraud Detection: In finance, autoencoders are used for anomaly detection by learning standard transaction patterns. When an unusual transaction deviates from the learned patterns, the system flags it as potentially fraudulent.

Data Compression: Autoencoders compress high-dimensional data, such as speech signals or video frames, into compact representations for efficient storage and transmission. This compression is particularly useful in streaming services, where reducing bandwidth usage is essential.

Foundational Concepts

An autoencoder consists of two primary components: an encoder that compresses input data into a smaller, latent space representation, and a decoder that reconstructs the data from this representation. The network trains using data with a mean squared error (MSE) and other loss functions to minimize any reconstruction error.

A key concept in autoencoders is the bottleneck layer, which reduces the dimensionality of the data, forcing the network to retain only the most essential information. Variants include convolutional autoencoders (CAEs) for image processing and variational autoencoders (VAEs) for probabilistic modeling. Autoencoders employ techniques such as backpropagation and gradient descent to optimize their performance.

Related Terms

Latent Space Representation: A compressed form of data that retains key features while reducing dimensionality.

Variational Autoencoder (VAE): A probabilistic extension of autoencoders used in generative modeling (see pg. 94).

Principal Component Analysis (PCA): A statistical method for dimensionality reduction, similar to autoencoders but linear.

Common Misconceptions

Autoencoders are generative models: While used in generative tasks (such as VAEs), their primary goal is representation learning rather than direct generation.

They are only for image data: Autoencoders can process text, audio, and structured data, in addition to images.

Autoencoders always perfectly reconstruct inputs: In practice, some information loss occurs, particularly in highly compressed representations.

Historical Context

The concept of autoencoders dates back to the **1980s** as a method for performing unsupervised learning in neural networks. **Geoffrey Hinton** played a crucial role in their advancement, particularly in deep learning applications. By the early **2000s**, stacked autoencoders became popular for feature learning in deep networks. Variational autoencoders (VAEs), introduced by **Kingma** and **Welling** in **2013**, revolutionized the field by incorporating probabilistic models, making autoencoders valuable for generative AI. Today, autoencoders are a core component in anomaly detection, denoising, and generative AI research.

Practical Implications

Cybersecurity, healthcare, and data compression are making broad use of Autoencoders. In cybersecurity, they identify anomalous behavior in network traffic, detecting malware or other forms of fraud. In medical diagnostics, they help enhance imaging quality and detect anomalies in patient data. Speech and audio processing systems leverage autoencoders for noise reduction and compression. The rise of self-supervised learning and deep generative models suggests that autoencoders will continue to play a key role in AI-driven feature learning and anomaly detection across various industries.

Automated Machine Learning (AutoML) (AI)

Automated Machine Learning (AutoML) refers to the process of automating the end-to-end machine learning pipeline, including data preprocessing, feature selection, model selection, hyperparameter tuning, and deployment. AutoML democratizes AI by making machine learning accessible to non-experts while optimizing performance and reducing the manual effort required for model development.

AutoML is like an automated chef in a smart kitchen. Instead of manually selecting ingredients, preparing meals, and adjusting cooking settings, the chef automatically determines the best recipe, cooks the dish, and fine-tunes flavors to achieve the best outcome, just as AutoML optimizes ML models without requiring deep expertise.

Examples

Healthcare Diagnostics: AutoML facilitates medical image analysis by selecting the optimal deep learning model for disease detection from X-rays or MRIs, thereby reducing diagnostic errors and enhancing efficiency.

Financial Fraud Detection: Banks utilize AutoML to analyze transaction patterns and identify anomalies that may indicate fraudulent activity, dynamically adjusting detection models as fraud tactics evolve.

Retail Demand Forecasting: AutoML predicts customer demand by automatically selecting optimal time-series forecasting models, enabling retailers to optimize inventory management and reduce waste.

Foundational Concepts

AutoML leverages meta-learning, neural architecture search (NAS), and hyperparameter optimization to automate the development of models. Meta-learning enables AutoML to learn from past experiences, identifying optimal configurations for new tasks. Neural architecture search (NAS) automates the design of deep learning models, selecting the best architectures without human intervention. Hyperparameter optimization fine-tunes model parameters to maximize accuracy. Many AutoML frameworks, such as Google AutoML, AutoKeras, and TPOT, use reinforcement learning and evolutionary algorithms to explore model configurations. By automating these processes, AutoML reduces the barrier to entry for non-experts while improving efficiency and performance in AI-driven solutions.

Related Terms

Hyperparameter Optimization: The process of automatically adjusting model parameters to improve performance.

Neural Architecture Search (NAS): A technique used to automate the design of deep learning architectures.

Meta-Learning: A method where machine learning models learn how to optimize themselves over multiple tasks.

Common Misconceptions

AutoML replaces data scientists: While AutoML automates many tasks, human expertise is still necessary to define business problems, interpret results, and ensure the ethical deployment of AI.

AutoML is only for beginners: Even experienced ML engineers utilize AutoML for rapid experimentation and baseline model comparisons.

AutoML consistently outperforms manually built models: While AutoML can quickly find strong models, domain expertise and custom model tuning may still yield better performance in complex applications.

Historical Context

The concept of automating machine learning dates back to early hyperparameter tuning techniques in the **1990s**. In **2013**, **Auto-WEKA** introduced automated model selection and hyperparameter optimization. The rise of deep learning led to the development of Neural Architecture Search (NAS), pioneered by **Google** in **2017**, which revolutionized the design of deep learning models. The emergence of **Google AutoML**, **Microsoft Azure AutoML**, and **AutoKeras** in the late **2010s** marked the mainstream adoption of AutoML in the field of AI. Today, AutoML continues to evolve, integrating self-supervised learning and reinforcement learning to refine model selection and adaptation.

Practical Implications

AutoML is transforming healthcare, finance, marketing, manufacturing, retail and almost every other industry by accelerating the adoption of AI. The automation of machine learning pipelines reduces costs, increases efficiency, and broadens AI accessibility, making it a critical tool in democratizing AI for businesses and researchers worldwide.

Autonomous Robot (RT)

An autonomous robot is a self-governing machine that performs tasks without human intervention by perceiving its environment, making decisions, and executing actions. It leverages artificial intelligence, computer vision, and sensor-based navigation to operate in both structured and unstructured environments, dynamically adapting to changes while achieving predefined objectives.

An autonomous robot is similar to a self-driving car; it senses its surroundings, navigates obstacles, and makes real-time decisions without human input. Just as autonomous vehicles avoid pedestrians and follow traffic rules, robots assess their environment, adjust movements, and complete tasks without manual control.

Examples

Autonomous Delivery Robots: Companies like Starship Technologies and Amazon use robots to deliver packages, navigating sidewalks and traffic autonomously to reach destinations.

Industrial Robotics: Factory robots, such as those developed by Boston Dynamics and Tesla, optimize assembly lines by handling repetitive tasks, reducing human labor costs, and enhancing overall efficiency.

Medical Assistance Robots: Surgical robots assist doctors in precision operations, enhancing accuracy in procedures like robotic-assisted laparoscopic surgery while reducing human error.

Foundational Concepts

Autonomous robots rely on sensor fusion, machine learning, and real-time decision-making to function independently. Sensor fusion combines input from LiDAR, cameras, ultrasonic sensors, and IMUs to construct an accurate perception of the environment. Reinforcement learning and deep learning enable robots to improve performance through trial and error. Path planning algorithms, such as A* and Dijkstra's algorithms, guide efficient navigation. Some robots utilize SLAM (Simultaneous Localization and Mapping) to map their surroundings while determining their location. These elements work together to enable robots to perceive, analyze, and act autonomously in complex scenarios.

Related Terms

Artificial Intelligence (AI): Enables robots to learn from data and make decisions independently (see pg. 7).

Computer Vision: Helps robots recognize and interpret visual information for navigation and interaction.

Reinforcement Learning: A training method where robots improve performance through trial and error (see pg. 410).

Common Misconceptions

Autonomous robots are fully independent: While they can operate without human control, many still require human oversight or predefined programming for safety and efficiency.

All robots are autonomous: Many industrial and service robots operate under human guidance and lack autonomous decision-making capabilities.

Autonomous robots have human-like intelligence: Unlike humans, robots follow programmed logic and lack emotions or creative problem-solving abilities beyond their defined tasks.

Historical Context

The concept of autonomous robots dates back to **Alan Turing** and **Norbert Wiener**, pioneers in cybernetics and the development of AI-driven automation. In the **1960s**, **Shakey**, developed by **Stanford Research Institute**, was one of the first mobile robots capable of making decisions. The **2000s** witnessed rapid advances in AI-powered robots, with companies such as **iRobot (Roomba)**, **Boston Dynamics**, and **Tesla** developing increasingly sophisticated machines. Today, robotics is integrated into logistics, medicine, and security, demonstrating continuous innovation in the field of automation.

Practical Implications

Autonomous robots are transforming manufacturing, healthcare, logistics, and security. In manufacturing, they improve production efficiency with 24/7 operations. In healthcare, they assist in surgeries and elder care, enhancing patient outcomes. Logistics companies are deploying autonomous drones and robots to streamline their supply chains. Security robots, such as those used in airports and corporate buildings, enhance surveillance and threat detection. These advancements reduce costs, improve efficiency, and enhance safety, positioning autonomous robots as a cornerstone of future AI-driven automation.

Backpropagation (ML)

Backpropagation is a learning algorithm for neural networks that computes how much each weight contributed to a model's error and then adjusts those weights using the gradient of a loss function. In practice, it sends error information backward from the output layer through earlier layers so the network can learn from its mistakes.

Backpropagation is like a teacher grading a multi-step math problem from the final answer back to the first line, marking where the error crept in and by how much, so the student knows exactly what to fix on the next attempt.

Examples

Image Classification: Convolutional neural networks refine filters by propagating classification errors back through layers and updating weights to improve accuracy (see pg. 128).

Speech to Text: Automatic Speech Recognition (ASR) systems reduce transcription mistakes by back-propagating sequence errors defined by their loss, iteratively improving word alignments (see pg. 460).

Fraud Detection: Transaction-scoring networks adjust internal connections in response to misclassifications, lowering false positives and catching more anomalies.

Foundational Concepts

Backpropagation works in two passes. The **forward pass** computes predictions and a **loss**; the **backward pass** propagates error signals from the output layer toward earlier layers, producing gradients for each weight. Those gradients are then used by **gradient descent** (often mini-batch or stochastic) to update parameters and reduce the loss over time. Together, loss functions, backpropagation, and gradient-based optimization form the core training loop for modern neural networks.

Deep networks must also manage stability issues such as the **vanishing gradient problem**, where gradients become too small to support learning—one reason choices like ReLU and related activations matter.

Related Terms

Neural Networks: Architectures trained via backpropagation and gradient descent (see pg. 352).

Loss Function: Quantifies prediction error that backprop uses to compute gradients (see pg. 310).

Gradient Descent: Uses backprop-computed gradients to update weights (see pg. 252).

Activation Function: Shapes gradients and can mitigate vanishing gradients (see pg. 70).

Feedback / Feedback Loops: Backprop is an error-feedback mechanism for learning (see pg. 226 & 228).

Common Misconceptions

Backprop always finds the best solution: It supplies gradients; actual optimization and whether you reach a good minimum depends on choices like learning rate and data regime.

It's only for deep learning: Backprop is used across many neural models, shallow and deep.

Activation functions don't affect learning: Poor activation choices can stall learning via vanishing gradients.

Historical Context

While the roots of gradient-based learning are mid-20th century, the **1980s** refinement and popularization of backpropagation, associated with **Rumelhart**, **Hinton**, and **Williams**, reignited neural network research and enabled modern deep learning.

Practical Implications

Backpropagation underpins model training in healthcare diagnostics, finance, recommendation, robotics, and more: it systematically reduces error, turning data into useful, reliable predictions and decisions at scale.

Beamforming (5G)

Beamforming is a wireless communication technique that directs signals toward specific devices, rather than broadcasting them omnidirectionally. Used in 5G networks, beamforming improves signal strength, data speed, and efficiency while reducing interference, ensuring better connectivity and lower latency in mobile communications, IoT devices, and autonomous systems.

Beamforming is like using a flashlight instead of a lantern. While a lantern spreads light in all directions, a flashlight focuses its beam toward a specific point. Similarly, 5G beamforming concentrates signals on targeted users or devices, improving reception and reducing unnecessary signal dispersion.

Examples

Smartphone Connectivity: 5G base stations use beamforming to deliver stronger signals to mobile users, reducing network congestion and dropped calls in crowded areas like stadiums and city centers.

Autonomous Vehicles: Self-driving cars rely on beamforming-enhanced V2X (vehicle-to-everything) communication for real-time navigation, obstacle detection, and traffic updates, ensuring safer driving.

Remote Healthcare: Beamforming in 5G telemedicine enables low-latency, high-resolution video streams, supporting remote surgery, AI-assisted diagnostics, and patient monitoring, even in rural locations.

Foundational Concepts

Beamforming is based on multiple-input multiple-output (MIMO) antennas and phased array signal processing, which steer radio waves toward intended users. By leveraging constructive interference, it enhances signal-to-noise ratio (SNR) while reducing signal degradation and multipath fading. Digital beamforming dynamically adjusts signals through software-controlled algorithms, whereas analog beamforming modifies signals via hardware-based phase shifting. A hybrid approach combines both techniques for enhanced efficiency in high-frequency millimeter-wave (mmWave) 5G networks.

Related Terms

MIMO (Multiple-Input Multiple-Output): Uses multiple antennas to improve data throughput and network reliability.

mmWave (Millimeter Wave): High-frequency 5G bands requiring beamforming to maintain connectivity over short distances (see pg. 324).

Network Slicing: A technique that allocates virtual network segments, often optimized using beamforming for specific applications (see pg. 350).

Common Misconceptions

Beamforming is a relatively new technology: While widely adopted in 5G, it has been utilized in Wi-Fi, radar, and satellite communications for several decades.
Beamforming increases radiation exposure: Beamforming reduces overall RF emissions by focusing signals only where needed.
Beamforming is effective only for high frequencies: Both mmWave and sub-6 GHz 5G bands benefit from it.

Historical Context

Beamforming originated in military radar and sonar systems during **World War II**, enhancing target detection and communication. The **1960s** saw advancements in phased array antennas, enabling directional signal transmission. Wireless networking in the **1990s** and **2000s** adopted beamforming for Wi-Fi (802.11ac) and 4G LTE. With the rollout of 5G in the late **2010s**, beamforming became essential for efficient high-frequency signal transmission, particularly in mmWave 5G networks developed by **Qualcomm**, **Ericsson**, and **Huawei**.

Practical Implications

Beamforming significantly enhances 5G network performance by improving signal quality, reducing latency, and increasing bandwidth capacity. In urban environments, it ensures stable connectivity in high-traffic areas. In industrial automation, beamforming-powered 5G supports smart factories, robotics, and IoT devices with low-latency communication, enabling seamless integration. It also benefits the defense and aerospace industries, enhancing satellite communications and radar systems. As 6G technology emerges, AI-driven adaptive beamforming will further enhance signal transmission, enabling even faster and more reliable wireless communication.

Bias Mitigation (RAI)

Bias mitigation refers to techniques that reduce unfair, unintended biases in AI models, ensuring fairness, accuracy, and ethical decision-making. Bias in AI can stem from biased training data, algorithmic design, or systemic inequalities. Mitigation strategies improve AI transparency, inclusivity, and accountability, making AI-driven decisions more equitable.

Bias mitigation is like adjusting a miscalibrated scale. If a scale consistently overweighs or underweighs, it skews results unfairly. Similarly, AI models trained on biased data produce unfair predictions, necessitating algorithmic corrections, diverse training datasets, and fairness constraints to ensure that AI outputs accurately reflect real-world diversity and fairness.

Examples

Hiring & Recruitment: AI-driven hiring tools may favor specific demographics based on past hiring data. Bias mitigation through fairness-aware algorithms and diverse dataset training ensures equal opportunity hiring, preventing discrimination against underrepresented groups.

Healthcare AI: Medical AI models trained on limited demographic data can lead to misdiagnoses for minority populations. Bias mitigation through demographic rebalancing and fairness-aware learning ensures AI models serve diverse populations fairly.

Loan & Credit Scoring: AI-based credit scoring may disadvantage low-income applicants due to historical biases in lending data. Bias mitigation techniques, such as counterfactual fairness and data reweighting, promote equitable financial access without compromising the accuracy of risk assessment.

Foundational Concepts

Bias mitigation involves pre-processing, in-processing, and post-processing techniques to correct AI bias. Pre-processing adjusts training data through rebalancing, resampling, and synthetic data generation to ensure diversity. In-processing modifies AI algorithms using techniques such as fairness constraints and adversarial debiasing to mitigate discriminatory decision-making. Post-processing corrects biased AI outputs by recalibrating and applying fairness metrics. Bias results from sampling bias, historical bias, or algorithmic bias, requiring ongoing model auditing, fairness assessments, and transparency in AI decision-making.

Related Terms

Fairness-Aware AI: AI designed with built-in fairness constraints to reduce discriminatory outcomes (see pg. 216).

Explainable AI (XAI): AI models that provide interpretable decisions, helping identify and mitigate bias (see pg. 27).

Algorithmic Transparency: The practice of ensuring AI decision processes are understandable, auditable, and accountable (see pg. 502).

Common Misconceptions

AI is inherently neutral: AI models learn from historical data, which often contains inherent human biases requiring correction.

Removing demographic data removes bias: Excluding race, gender, or age does not necessarily eliminate bias, as proxy variables may still reflect underlying disparities.

Bias cannot be mitigated: While achieving perfect fairness is difficult, fairness-aware learning and continuous monitoring can potentially reduce bias.

Historical Context

Bias in AI gained attention in the **2010s**, with studies revealing racial and gender disparities in facial recognition and hiring algorithms. Research by **Joy Buolamwini** and **Timnit Gebru** highlighted higher error rates in AI models for individuals with darker skin, prompting initiatives to address AI fairness. Major tech companies, including Google, IBM, and Microsoft, have developed fairness toolkits. Regulations such as the **EU AI Act** and the **U.S. Algorithmic Accountability Act** emerged, advocating for bias audits, fairness metrics, and ethical AI frameworks in AI governance.

Practical Implications

Bias mitigation is crucial for the ethical deployment of AI across various industries. In finance, it ensures fair lending and fraud detection. In criminal justice, it prevents biased predictive policing. In healthcare, it enhances equitable AI-driven diagnoses. As AI regulations evolve, companies must adopt bias audits, fairness metrics, and transparent AI frameworks to comply with ethical and legal standards. Bias mitigation fosters trust, accountability, and social inclusivity, ensuring AI benefits all communities without reinforcing systemic discrimination.

Big Data (AI)

Big Data refers to large, complex datasets that are difficult to process using traditional data management tools. The 3Vs—Volume, Velocity, and Variety—typically characterize big data, which necessitates advanced storage, analytics, and computing technologies, including machine learning, cloud computing, and distributed systems.

Big Data is like a massive library with constantly arriving new books. Without an efficient indexing system, finding relevant information becomes overwhelming. Big Data technologies serve as automated librarians, organizing, analyzing, and retrieving valuable knowledge from vast amounts of structured and unstructured data.

Examples

Healthcare Analytics: Hospitals use Big Data analytics to predict disease outbreaks, improve diagnostics, and personalize treatments, analyzing patient records, genomic data, and real-time monitoring devices.

Smart Cities: Big Data powers traffic control systems, energy optimization, and waste management, helping urban planners enhance sustainability and efficiency based on real-time sensor data.

E-Commerce: Online retailers leverage Big Data-driven recommendation systems to analyze user behavior, predict customer preferences, and optimize inventory, improving personalized marketing and sales strategies.

Foundational Concepts

We usually define Big Data by its three key characteristics: Volume (large-scale data), Velocity (real-time or high-speed processing), and Variety (encompassing structured, unstructured, and semi-structured data). Data mining techniques, including machine learning algorithms and artificial intelligence, extract meaningful insights. Distributed computing frameworks, such as Hadoop and Apache Spark, enable the parallel processing of massive datasets. Cloud storage and edge computing facilitate scalable data management. Predictive analytics, deep learning, and sentiment analysis transform raw data into actionable intelligence for businesses, governments, and scientific research.

Related Terms

Data Mining: Extracting functional patterns from large datasets using algorithms and analytics.

Machine Learning: AI-driven models that learn from Big Data to make predictions or automate tasks (see pg. 45).

Cloud Computing: Remote data storage and processing that enables scalable Big Data analytics.

Common Misconceptions

Big Data is just about size: It also encompasses speed and the diversity of data formats.

Only large companies use Big Data: Small businesses leverage Big Data for customer insights, automation, and decision-making.

More data always leads to better results: Poorly managed or biased data can lead to misleading conclusions.

Historical Context

Big Data emerged as a concept in the early **2000s** with the rise of internet-scale data generation. Companies like **Google** and **Facebook** pioneered large-scale data collection and analysis. **Doug Laney** introduced the 3Vs framework (**2001**) to define Big Data. **Apache Hadoop** (**2006**) revolutionized distributed data processing, enabling businesses to handle massive datasets efficiently. Cloud computing and AI advancements in the **2010s** further accelerated the adoption of Big Data, making it integral to finance, healthcare, and digital services.

Practical Implications

Big Data drives business intelligence, automation, and predictive analytics. In healthcare, it improves patient care and disease prediction. In finance, it enables fraud detection and risk assessment. In cybersecurity, it enhances threat detection and response. Governments utilize big data for policy-making and disaster management. As AI and IoT continue to evolve, Big Data will continue to shape digital transformation, optimize industries, and enable real-time decision-making on a global scale.

Bioinspired Robotics (RT)

Bioinspired robotics refers to the design and development of robots modeled after biological organisms, mimicking their structures, movement, and sensory processing. By studying natural evolution, these robots achieve greater adaptability, efficiency, and resilience in environments where traditional robots struggle, such as uneven terrain, water, and air.

Bioinspired robotics is like studying birds to build airplanes. Just as humans observed nature to create flight technology, engineers analyze animal movement, biomechanics, and neural networks to develop robots with enhanced flexibility, agility, and problem-solving capabilities, improving robotic performance in diverse environments.

Examples

Robotic Prosthetics: Bioinspired robotic limbs utilize neuromuscular control and adaptive movement, allowing amputees to regain natural mobility through AI-driven real-time adjustments.

Search-and-Rescue Robots: Snake-like or insect-inspired robots navigate tight spaces and hazardous areas, assisting disaster response teams by locating survivors and assessing dangerous environments.

Underwater Drones: Inspired by fish and cephalopods, these robots use biomimetic propulsion to perform ocean exploration, environmental monitoring, and underwater infrastructure inspections.

Foundational Concepts

Bioinspired robotics follows from the study of biomimicry, biomechanics, and neuromorphic engineering. Biomimicry applies nature's designs to robotics, optimizing movement, material usage, and energy efficiency. Biomechanics studies muscle-skeletal dynamics to create flexible, resilient robotic systems. Neuromorphic engineering models robotic control systems after biological neural networks, enabling adaptive learning and real-time decision-making. These principles allow robots to mimic the locomotion of animals, interact with environments dynamically, and improve efficiency through bio-inspired design methodologies.

Related Terms

Soft Robotics: Robots made of flexible, deformable materials for enhanced adaptability and safety (see pg. 454).

Swarm Robotics: Systems where multiple bioinspired robots collaborate, mimicking collective animal behavior (see pg. 474).

Neuromorphic Computing: AI systems that replicate biological neural processing, improving robot learning and adaptation.

Common Misconceptions

Bioinspired robots are exact replicas of animals: They are inspired by nature but optimized for practical applications.

These robots only mimic movement: Bioinspired robots also replicate sensory perception, energy efficiency, and cognitive functions.

Bioinspired robots are fragile: Many of them utilize resilient, adaptive materials, making them durable in extreme conditions.

Historical Context

Bioinspired robotics has its origins in **Leonardo da Vinci**'s anatomical studies, influencing early mechanical automata. In the 20th century, MIT's **Rodney Brooks** introduced behavior-based robotics, shifting from rigid control systems to adaptive, bioinspired approaches. **Boston Dynamics**, inspired by quadrupedal animals, has developed robotic dogs and humanoids for defense and industry applications. Advances in soft robotics and neuromorphic AI (since the **2010s**) have further expanded biomimetic robot applications, making them increasingly sophisticated and functional.

Practical Implications

Bioinspired robotics enhances medical prosthetics, automation, and environmental exploration. In healthcare, robotic limbs improve mobility and rehabilitation. In disaster response, flexible robots navigate hazardous environments to assist rescue operations. In space exploration, bioinspired robots adapt to extreme terrains, collecting data where traditional machines fail. As AI and materials science evolve, bioinspired robotics will redefine industries by merging nature's efficiency with cutting-edge technology, creating more resilient and intelligent robotic systems.

Biomarker (BT)

A biomarker is a measurable indicator of a biological process, disease state, or therapeutic response. Found in blood, tissue, or physiological data, biomarkers help in early diagnosis, treatment monitoring, and personalized medicine, playing a crucial role in healthcare, drug development, and disease prevention.

A biomarker is like a car's dashboard warning light. Just as a temperature gauge signals engine overheating, biomarkers detect health abnormalities, signaling the presence or progression of disease before symptoms appear, enabling early intervention and more effective treatments.

Examples

Cancer Detection: Elevated prostate-specific antigen (PSA) levels can indicate prostate cancer risk, allowing for early screening and timely treatment.

Neurodegenerative Diseases: Beta-amyloid protein accumulation in cerebrospinal fluid serves as a biomarker for Alzheimer's disease, aiding in early diagnosis and research.

Diabetes Management: Hemoglobin A1C levels measure long-term blood sugar control, guiding diabetes management and treatment adjustments.

Foundational Concepts

Biomarkers are diagnostic, predictive, prognostic, or pharmacodynamic, depending on their function. Genomic, proteomic, and metabolic biomarkers provide insights into disease mechanisms. Advances in artificial intelligence and machine learning improve biomarker discovery, analysis, and precision medicine applications. Liquid biopsy techniques enable the non-invasive detection of biomarkers from blood samples, revolutionizing early cancer screening. Multi-omics approaches, which integrate genomics, transcriptomics, and proteomics, enhance biomarker accuracy, aiding in personalized treatments and disease prediction.

Related Terms

Precision Medicine: Tailoring medical treatments based on an individual's biomarkers and genetics.

Bioinformatics: The use of AI and computational tools to analyze biomarker data.

Metabolomics: The study of metabolic biomarkers to assess disease progression and drug effects.

Common Misconceptions

All biomarkers are disease-specific: Some biomarkers indicate general health conditions, not just specific diseases.

Biomarkers provide definitive diagnoses: They support diagnosis but often require additional tests for confirmation.

Only genetic biomarkers matter: Many biomarkers come from proteins, metabolites, or imaging rather than genes alone.

Historical Context

The concept of biomarkers dates back to ancient medicine, where changes in urine color were indicative of disease. In **1928**, the discovery of prostate-specific antigen (PSA) marked a milestone in cancer diagnostics. The **2000s** saw rapid advancements in genomic and proteomic biomarker research, fueled by the **Human Genome Project**. AI-driven biomarker analysis has revolutionized personalized medicine, enhancing early disease detection, drug development, and prediction of treatment responses.

Practical Implications

Biomarkers drive precision medicine, early disease detection, and assessments of drug efficacy. In oncology, biomarkers improve targeted cancer treatments. In neurology, they aid in the diagnosis of Alzheimer's and Parkinson's diseases. In cardiology, biomarkers help predict the risk of heart disease. AI-enhanced biomarker analysis accelerates medical research, clinical trials, and patient-specific treatments, transforming modern healthcare into a more predictive, personalized, and preventive model.

Biomass Energy (CET)

Biomass energy is a renewable energy source derived from organic materials, including plants, agricultural waste, wood, and algae. It is converted into electricity, heat, or biofuels through combustion, fermentation, or biochemical processes, providing a sustainable alternative to fossil fuels while reducing carbon emissions.

Biomass energy is like recycling nature's leftovers. Just as compost repurposes food waste into nutrient-rich soil, biomass converts organic waste into usable energy, ensuring sustainable fuel production while reducing environmental impact and dependence on non-renewable resources.

Examples

Biogas Production: Organic waste from landfills and farms undergoes anaerobic digestion, producing methane-rich biogas used for electricity and heating.

Ethanol Biofuel: Here, factories produce ethanol from corn and sugarcane, a clean-burning biofuel used in gasoline blends, which reduces carbon emissions in transportation.

Wood Pellets for Heating: Compressed wood and agricultural residues serve as biomass fuel in residential and industrial heating, offering a low-emission alternative to coal.

Foundational Concepts

Biomass energy relies on photosynthesis, where plants absorb solar energy and convert it into chemical energy. This stored energy is released through combustion, gasification, or fermentation to generate power or biofuels. Anaerobic digestion produces biogas from organic waste, while pyrolysis converts biomass into biochar and bio-oil. Unlike fossil fuels, biomass is carbon-neutral, as it releases only the CO_2 absorbed during growth, making it a sustainable energy solution.

Related Terms

Biofuels: Liquid fuels like ethanol and biodiesel derived from plant-based biomass.

Anaerobic Digestion: A process that breaks down organic material to produce biogas.

Gasification: Converts solid biomass into synthetic gas for electricity generation.

Common Misconceptions

Biomass energy is similar to fossil fuels: Unlike fossil fuels, biomass is renewable and carbon-neutral when managed sustainably.

Using biomass can harm forests: Sustainable sourcing and reforestation practices ensure a minimal ecological impact.

Biomass energy is inefficient: Advances in biofuel production and waste-to-energy technology have significantly improved its efficiency.

Historical Context

For millennia, people have used biomass, with wood and plant materials serving as primary energy sources before the advent of fossil fuels. The **1970s** energy crisis sparked renewed interest in biofuels such as ethanol. Technological advances in the **1990s** and **2000s**, including anaerobic digestion and pyrolysis, enhanced biomass efficiency and scalability. Global efforts to reduce carbon footprints have driven modern innovations in bioenergy, with government policies supporting their development.

Practical Implications

Biomass energy supports clean energy goals, rural economies, and waste management. In transportation, biofuels reduce dependency on oil. In agriculture, waste-to-energy systems convert farm byproducts into biogas. In power generation, biomass plants provide a reliable source of electricity, complementing solar and wind energy. As advancements continue, biomass will play a crucial role in global energy transition strategies, helping mitigate climate change and energy security challenges.

Bioprinting (BT)

Bioprinting is an advanced 3D printing technology that uses living cells and biomaterials to fabricate tissues, organs, and biological structures. By layering bioinks composed of cells and hydrogels, bioprinting enables tissue engineering, regenerative medicine, and drug testing, revolutionizing personalized healthcare and organ transplantation.

Bioprinting is like building a house with living bricks. Instead of using cement and wood, it assembles cells and biomaterials, forming functional tissues that grow and integrate, offering hope for organ transplants, tissue repair, and medical research without relying on human donors.

Examples

Artificial Skin for Burn Victims: Bioprinted skin grafts, composed of fibroblasts and keratinocytes, help burn patients heal faster, reducing scarring and rejection risks.

3D-Printed Organoids for Drug Testing: Miniaturized bioprinted organs, such as liver and kidney organoids, allow pharmaceutical companies to test drugs on realistic human tissue models, improving drug safety and effectiveness.

Custom Bone Implants: Bioprinted bone scaffolds, infused with stem cells, help regenerate damaged bone tissue, providing personalized treatments for orthopedic injuries.

Foundational Concepts

Bioprinting combines tissue engineering, biomaterials science, and 3D printing to create functional biological structures. Bioinks, composed of living cells, growth factors, and biocompatible hydrogels, are deposited layer by layer to form tissues that mimic natural structures. Extrusion-based, inkjet, and laser-assisted bioprinting techniques allow precise cell placement. Bioprinted tissues require bioreactors, which provide the necessary nutrients and environmental conditions for cell growth and maturation, thereby making organ transplantation and regenerative therapies possible.

Related Terms

Tissue Engineering: The creation of artificial tissues using cells, scaffolds, and bioreactors.

Regenerative Medicine: A field focused on repairing or replacing damaged tissues using stem cells and bioprinting.

Bioinks: Special cell-laden materials that serve as the building blocks for bioprinting tissues and organs.

Common Misconceptions

Bioprinting creates fully functional organs instantly: Bioprinted structures require maturation in bioreactors before they function as real organs.

Any cell can be bioprinted: Cells require specific bioinks and growth conditions to survive and integrate.

Bioprinting eliminates the need for organ donation immediately: While promising, its clinical applications are still under development.

Historical Context

The concept of bioprinting emerged in the early **2000s**, evolving from research in 3D printing and tissue engineering. In **2003**, **Thomas Boland** developed the first bioprinter by modifying an inkjet printer to deposit living cells. In **2013**, researchers successfully bioprinted human cartilage tissue. Advances in stem cell research, biomaterials, and AI-driven modeling continue to refine bioprinting techniques, bringing functional organ printing closer to reality.

Practical Implications

Bioprinting revolutionizes medicine, pharmaceuticals, and biotechnology. In organ transplantation, it offers hope for patient-specific organs, reducing rejection risks. In drug discovery, bioprinted tissues enable human-like drug testing, thereby minimizing reliance on animal testing. In cosmetic and reconstructive surgery, bioengineered skin enhances wound healing and facial reconstruction. As AI and biofabrication evolve, bioprinting will revolutionize personalized medicine, regenerative therapies, and medical research, paving the way for a future of patient-tailored healthcare solutions.

Bioreactor (BT)

A bioreactor is a controlled vessel or system designed to support biological processes, such as cell culture, fermentation, and biomanufacturing. It provides optimal conditions such as temperature, oxygen, nutrients, and pH levels for growing microorganisms, mammalian cells, or engineered tissues used in biotechnology, pharmaceuticals, and environmental applications.

A bioreactor is like a greenhouse for cells. Just as greenhouses regulate sunlight, water, and temperature to promote optimal plant growth, bioreactors provide a controlled environment for cells, bacteria, or yeast, enabling them to grow, multiply, and produce valuable substances efficiently.

Examples

Pharmaceutical Production: Pharmaceutical companies utilize bioreactors to cultivate genetically engineered bacteria or mammalian cells for the production of vaccines, insulin, and monoclonal antibodies, used to treat various diseases.

Tissue Engineering: In regenerative medicine, bioreactors facilitate the growth of stem cells on scaffolds, enabling the creation of lab-grown tissues and organs for transplantation.

Biofuel Generation: Bioreactors facilitate microbial fermentation of algae and organic waste, producing bioethanol and biodiesel, offering a sustainable energy alternative.

Foundational Concepts

Bioreactors maintain controlled conditions essential for biological growth and metabolic activity. They use mechanical or gas-based stirring to distribute nutrients and oxygen evenly, ensuring optimal cell function. Batch, fed-batch, and continuous bioreactors enable different production modes tailored to specific application needs. Perfusion bioreactors enable continuous nutrient supply and waste removal, improving cell viability. Advances in AI and automation enhance bioreactor monitoring and real-time adjustments, making biomanufacturing more efficient and scalable.

Related Terms

Fermentation: The process of converting organic matter into bioproducts using microbial metabolism.

Tissue Engineering: The use of cells and biomaterials to create functional tissues for regenerative medicine.

Synthetic Biology: The design of genetically engineered organisms to produce pharmaceuticals, biofuels, and biomaterials.

Common Misconceptions

Bioreactors are only for pharmaceuticals: They are also widely used in biofuels production, food production, and wastewater treatment.

All bioreactors are large industrial tanks: Bioreactors range from microfluidic devices used in laboratories to massive tanks for large-scale production.

Bioreactors work without monitoring: They require regular monitoring and adjustments to ensure optimal biological activity.

Historical Context

Bioreactors date back to fermentation techniques in ancient brewing. In the 20th century, **Louis Pasteur**'s work on microbial fermentation led to modern bioprocessing technologies. The **1950s** saw large-scale antibiotic production, revolutionizing medicine and biotechnology. Advances in tissue engineering and synthetic biology (**2000s**–present) expanded bioreactor applications to organ regeneration and personalized medicine. Today, automated and AI-enhanced bioreactors drive innovations in biomanufacturing, pharmaceuticals, and sustainable energy.

Practical Implications

Bioreactors enable the scalable and cost-effective production of medicines, biofuels, and engineered tissues. In healthcare, they grow artificial organs and cell-based therapies. In biomanufacturing, they produce enzymes, proteins, and vaccines. In environmental biotechnology, they assist in waste treatment and carbon capture. As AI-driven automation and gene-editing technologies advance, bioreactors will play a pivotal role in biotechnology, personalized medicine, and global sustainability efforts.

Black Box Model (XAI)

A black box model refers to an AI system whose internal decision-making process is opaque or difficult to interpret. While inputs and outputs are visible, the logic, patterns, or weight distributions within complex models, such as deep learning networks, remain unclear, raising concerns about trust, fairness, and accountability.

A black box model is like a vending machine without a transparent window. You insert money (input) and receive a product (output). Still, you don't see the internal mechanisms deciding how the machine processes the request, much like how AI makes decisions without complete human understanding.

Examples

Medical Diagnosis AI: Deep learning models analyze medical images to detect tumors or diseases, but the exact reasoning behind predictions often remains unclear to doctors.

Credit Scoring Systems: AI models determine loan approvals based on historical financial data, but applicants and regulators may struggle to understand why the system denies specific individuals.

Autonomous Vehicles: Self-driving cars utilize neural networks to detect obstacles and make driving decisions, but understanding why the car chose a particular action can be challenging.

Foundational Concepts

Black box models arise from high-dimensional feature interactions and complex mathematical computations in AI. Deep neural networks, ensemble learning, and transformer models process vast datasets but lack inherent explainability. Model interpretability techniques, such as SHAP (Shapley Additive Explanations) and LIME (Local Interpretable Model-Agnostic Explanations), aim to improve transparency. Regulators emphasize explainability and fairness in AI applications, particularly in healthcare, finance, and law, where algorithmic bias and ethical concerns can have a profound impact on human lives.

Related Terms

Explainable AI (XAI): AI techniques designed to increase transparency and interpretability in decision-making (see pg. 27).

Algorithmic Bias: The presence of systematic errors in AI decisions due to biased training data or flawed algorithms (see pg. 104).

Model Interpretability: The ability to understand and explain how an AI system derives its outputs (see pg. 286).

Common Misconceptions

Black box AI is unreliable: While opaque, these models achieve high accuracy in fields like image recognition and language processing.

All AI models are black boxes: Some AI systems, such as decision trees and linear regression, are inherently transparent.

Black box models cannot be explained: Techniques like SHAP, LIME, and feature importance analysis help uncover the decision logic.

Historical Context

The concept of black box AI dates back to early neural networks (**1950s**), where cybernetics pioneers struggled to interpret complex systems. The rise of deep learning (**2010s**) made AI models highly effective but increasingly opaque. Regulatory frameworks, such as the EU's **GDPR (2018)** and the **EU AI Act (2021)**, emphasize the need for algorithmic transparency. Researchers continue to develop explainability tools, making AI more trustworthy and interpretable in high-stakes applications.

Practical Implications

Black box AI raises concerns in healthcare, finance, and legal systems, where unexplainable decisions can significantly impact lives. In medical AI, ensuring that automated diagnoses align with clinical reasoning is crucial. In banking, regulators demand explainable loan approvals to prevent discriminatory lending. As AI regulations evolve, companies must strike a balance between model accuracy and interpretability, ensuring that automated decisions remain ethical, accountable, and aligned with human oversight.

Bluetooth Low Energy (BLE) (IoT)

Bluetooth Low Energy (BLE) is a wireless communication protocol designed for low-power data transmission over short distances. Optimized for Internet of Things (IoT) devices, BLE enables continuous connectivity while consuming minimal energy, making it ideal for wearables, smart home devices, and industrial automation.

BLE is like a whisper compared to a shout. Traditional Bluetooth uses more power and bandwidth (a shout), while BLE conserves energy by sending small data packets intermittently (a whisper), ensuring efficient, long-lasting communication for low-power devices.

Examples

Wearable Fitness Trackers: BLE enables real-time syncing of health metrics like heart rate and step count between smartwatches and mobile apps while preserving battery life.

Smart Home Automation: BLE-powered smart locks, lights, and thermostats communicate seamlessly with smartphones, providing low-latency control with minimal energy consumption (see pg. 448).

Medical Devices: BLE enhances remote patient monitoring, allowing continuous data collection from glucose monitors, ECG devices, and pulse oximeters with long-lasting battery efficiency.

Foundational Concepts

BLE operates on the 2.4 GHz ISM (Industrial, Scientific, and Medical) band, using a star topology where a central device communicates with multiple peripherals. It employs adaptive frequency hopping to reduce interference and advertising packets to enable low-energy device discovery. BLE supports GATT (Generic Attribute Profile) for structured data exchange and LE Secure Connections for encrypted communication. Compared to classic Bluetooth, BLE reduces power consumption by using short, energy-efficient data bursts, making it ideal for IoT ecosystems and battery-powered applications.

Related Terms

Mesh Networking: A BLE-based system where multiple devices relay data, extending communication range.

Near Field Communication (NFC): A short-range wireless technology used for contactless payments and device pairing.

Zigbee: A low-power wireless communication protocol optimized for home automation and industrial IoT.

Common Misconceptions

BLE is the same as Bluetooth: BLE is a distinct protocol optimized for low-energy use cases rather than high-bandwidth applications like audio streaming.

BLE has a short range: BLE can typically reach up to 100 meters in ideal conditions, depending on signal strength and environment.

BLE is insecure: Modern BLE uses AES-128 encryption and Secure Simple Pairing to ensure data protection and authentication.

Historical Context

BLE was introduced in **2010** as part of Bluetooth 4.0, developed by the **Bluetooth Special Interest Group** (SIG) to address IoT power efficiency needs. It quickly gained adoption in wearables, medical devices, and industrial sensors. The Bluetooth 5.0 update (**2016**) expanded BLE's range, speed, and broadcasting capabilities, accelerating its integration into smart cities and automation technologies. As BLE continues evolving, its role in wireless connectivity, IoT, and AI-driven automation remains critical.

Practical Implications

BLE powers IoT ecosystems, healthcare monitoring, and smart infrastructure. In retail, BLE beacons enable location-based marketing by sending personalized offers to nearby smartphones. In logistics, BLE-based asset tracking ensures efficient inventory management. In the automotive industry, BLE keyless entry systems enhance vehicle security and convenience. As IoT adoption grows, BLE's energy efficiency, cost-effectiveness, and interoperability will drive innovation in smart devices, automation, and wireless communication technologies.

Brain-Computer Interface (BCI) (RT)

A brain-computer interface (BCI) is a technology that enables direct communication between the brain and external devices. By interpreting neural signals, BCIs allow users to control computers, prosthetics, or other systems without physical movement, offering applications in healthcare, neuroscience, and human augmentation.

BCI is like a telepathic remote control. Just as a remote sends signals to a TV, BCIs translate brain activity into commands, enabling users to move robotic limbs, type messages, or interact with smart devices using only their thoughts.

Examples

Assistive Technology: BCIs help paralyzed patients operate wheelchairs or communicate by decoding brain signals into device commands, restoring independence.

Neurogaming: Advanced BCIs enable players to control virtual characters through thought-driven interactions, enhancing immersive gaming experiences.

Medical Monitoring: BCIs track brain activity in epilepsy patients, predicting seizures and enabling early medical intervention.

Foundational Concepts

BCIs work by detecting and interpreting brain signals, typically using electroencephalography (EEG), electrocorticography (ECoG), or implanted neural interfaces. These signals undergo preprocessing, feature extraction, and machine learning-based classification to convert neuronal activity into actionable commands. Non-invasive BCIs use EEG headsets, while invasive BCIs, such as neural implants, offer higher precision for applications like prosthetic limb control. Advances in AI-driven signal processing improve accuracy and response time, making BCIs more practical for real-world applications.

Related Terms

Neural Implants: Devices surgically placed in the brain to enhance or restore neural function.

Neuroprosthetics: BCIs designed to control artificial limbs or restore lost sensory functions.

Cognitive Computing: AI systems that mimic human thought processes to enhance brain-machine interaction (see pg. 142).

Common Misconceptions

BCIs enable mind-reading: They interpret specific brain signals, not thoughts or emotions.

BCIs can instantly restore movement: Training is required for users to learn brain-controlled interactions.

Only invasive BCIs are effective: Non-invasive EEG-based BCIs are effective for practical applications like gaming and rehabilitation.

Historical Context

The concept of BCIs emerged in the **1970s**, with early research by **Jacques Vidal**, who coined the term brain-computer interface. The **1990s** saw progress in EEG-based BCIs for assistive technology. In the **2000s**, **DARPA**-funded projects advanced neural implants, leading to the first BCI-controlled robotic limbs. Companies like **Neuralink** (founded in **2016**) have accelerated AI-powered BCIs, focusing on brain augmentation and medical applications.

Practical Implications

BCIs revolutionize healthcare, accessibility, and human-computer interaction. In medicine, they help stroke patients regain mobility. In AI-driven industries, BCIs could enable hands-free control of smart systems. In the military and defense sector, research explores the use of BCI-enhanced cognitive abilities for soldiers. As AI and neurotechnology evolve, BCIs may redefine communication, automation, and human augmentation, bridging the gap between mind and machine.

Carbon Footprint (CET)

A carbon footprint measures the total greenhouse gas (GHG) emissions caused directly or indirectly by an individual, organization, product, or activity. Expressed in carbon dioxide equivalent (CO_2e), it includes energy use, transportation, production, and consumption, influencing climate change and environmental sustainability.

A carbon footprint is like an environmental shadow—every action, from driving a car to using electricity, leaves an invisible mark on the planet. Just as footprints in the sand show where someone has been, a carbon footprint reflects human impact on the Earth's atmosphere.

Examples

Transportation: Gasoline-powered vehicles emit CO_2 and other pollutants, contributing to global warming. Electric vehicles and public transit reduce individual carbon footprints.

Food Production: Meat production generates methane emissions and requires land and water resources, making plant-based diets more carbon-efficient.

Energy Consumption: Coal-fired power plants release high carbon emissions, whereas renewable sources like solar and wind energy drastically lower environmental impact.

Foundational Concepts

A carbon footprint accounts for direct and indirect emissions, classified into Scope 1 (direct emissions from sources owned by an entity), Scope 2 (indirect emissions from purchased energy), and Scope 3 (emissions from supply chains and product lifecycles). Carbon offsets, such as reforestation and carbon capture, help balance emissions. Life Cycle Assessment (LCA) evaluates the environmental impact of products and services across their lifespan. Reducing carbon footprints requires energy efficiency, sustainable transportation, and clean energy adoption to mitigate climate change and ecological damage.

Related Terms

Greenhouse Gases (GHGs): Gases like CO_2, methane (CH_4), and nitrous oxide (N_2O) that trap heat in the Earth's atmosphere.

Carbon Neutrality: Achieving net-zero carbon emissions by balancing emitted and offset carbon.

Sustainable Development: Meeting current needs without compromising future environmental and resource availability.

Common Misconceptions

Only large corporations have carbon footprints: Every individual contributes to global emissions through daily activities.

Reducing a carbon footprint means eliminating emissions entirely: The goal is minimization and balancing through offsets.

Carbon footprints only relate to CO_2 emissions: They include other GHGs like methane and nitrous oxide, which have higher global warming potential.

Historical Context

The concept of carbon footprints gained prominence in the **1990s** as climate change awareness grew. **The Kyoto Protocol (1997)** introduced international carbon reduction targets, while **The Paris Agreement (2015)** aimed for global net-zero emissions. Companies and governments adopted carbon accounting methods to measure and reduce emissions. The rise of carbon offset markets and sustainable policies accelerated efforts to combat climate change, shaping regulations and corporate sustainability strategies.

Practical Implications

Lowering carbon footprints is essential for climate change mitigation, corporate responsibility, and energy efficiency. In business, carbon-conscious operations drive cost savings and regulatory compliance. In urban planning, policies favoring public transport, green buildings, and waste reduction support sustainable cities. In consumer behavior, eco-friendly choices like renewable energy, local food sourcing, and energy-efficient appliances promote environmental conservation. As governments implement carbon taxes and emission caps, reducing carbon footprints becomes a global imperative for sustainability.

ChatGPT (GenAI)

ChatGPT is an AI-powered conversational model developed by OpenAI, designed to generate human-like text responses based on natural language processing (NLP). Built on Generative Pre-trained Transformer (GPT) architecture, it understands context, answers queries, assists in writing, and engages in meaningful discussions across diverse domains.

ChatGPT is like a digital librarian with vast knowledge. Just as a librarian retrieves, summarizes, and explains information based on questions, ChatGPT processes and generates responses using its extensive training on text data, making it a versatile conversational assistant.

Examples

Customer Support: ChatGPT automates customer interactions, handling inquiries, troubleshooting, and FAQs, reducing response time for businesses.

Content Creation: Writers and marketers use ChatGPT for blog posts, reports, and creative storytelling, streamlining ideation and drafting.

Education & Tutoring: ChatGPT assists students by explaining concepts, solving math problems, and generating study material, making learning more accessible.

Foundational Concepts

ChatGPT is based on deep learning and trained using unsupervised learning techniques, specifically transformer neural networks that analyze patterns in vast text datasets. The GPT model employs attention mechanisms to predict and generate coherent, context-aware responses. Fine-tuning with reinforcement learning from human feedback (RLHF) improves ChatGPT's accuracy, ethics, and safety, reducing bias and refining conversational flow. While highly advanced, ChatGPT remains a narrow AI—capable of text-based reasoning but lacking true understanding, consciousness, or emotions.

Related Terms

Natural Language Processing (NLP): AI's ability to interpret, understand, and generate human language (see pg. 346).

Machine Learning (ML): Algorithms that learn patterns from data to make predictions and decisions (see pg. 45).

Transformer Model: A deep learning framework that processes sequential data, enabling context-aware text generation (see pg. 500).

Common Misconceptions

ChatGPT is sentient: It generates responses based on probability and training data, not actual thoughts or emotions.

ChatGPT has real-time knowledge: Its knowledge is limited to training data and does not access live internet updates unless integrated with external sources.

ChatGPT is always accurate: It can generate incorrect, biased, or misleading information, requiring human validation.

Historical Context

OpenAI introduced GPT-1 in **2018**, followed by GPT-2 (**2019**) and GPT-3 (**2020**), each improving language comprehension and generation. **ChatGPT** debuted in **2022**, utilizing GPT-3.5 and GPT-4 with RLHF for refined dialogue capabilities. Its adoption in customer service, content creation, and automation revolutionized human-AI interactions, sparking discussions on AI ethics, bias, and responsible usage.

Practical Implications

ChatGPT enhances business productivity, education, and automation. In corporate environments, it assists with email drafting, report writing, and brainstorming. In healthcare, it provides medical insights, though requiring expert verification. As AI adoption expands, ChatGPT plays a crucial role in augmenting human intelligence, optimizing workflows, and democratizing information access, necessitating responsible AI governance to ensure ethical usage and accuracy.

Classification (AI)

Classification is a supervised machine learning task that assigns input data to predefined categories based on patterns learned from labeled training data. It is widely used in image recognition, spam detection, and medical diagnostics, enabling AI systems to make informed predictions based on historical examples.

Classification is like sorting mail into categories. Just as a postal worker organizes letters based on ZIP codes or destinations, classification algorithms categorize data—such as emails as spam or non-spam—based on learned patterns and predefined labels.

Examples

Spam Detection: Email services use classification models to identify and filter spam messages, improving inbox organization.

Medical Diagnosis: AI-based classification helps doctors distinguish between healthy and diseased patients by analyzing medical images or test results.

Sentiment Analysis: Businesses analyze customer reviews using classification algorithms to determine whether feedback is positive, neutral, or negative, informing marketing strategies.

Foundational Concepts

Classification models use statistical and machine learning techniques to recognize patterns in labeled datasets. Common algorithms include decision trees, support vector machines (SVM), k-nearest neighbors (KNN), and deep learning models like convolutional neural networks (CNNs) for image classification. Binary classification sorts data into two categories (e.g., spam vs. non-spam), while multi-class classification assigns data to multiple labels (e.g., identifying different animal species). Feature extraction, model training, and performance evaluation using metrics like accuracy, precision, and recall ensure classification reliability.

Related Terms

Supervised Learning: Machine learning where models learn from labeled datasets to make predictions (see pg. 468).

Neural Networks: AI architectures that mimic human brain neurons, improving classification in complex data (see pg. 352).

Regression: Unlike classification, regression predicts continuous values instead of discrete categories (see pg. 408).

Common Misconceptions

Classification always provides 100% accuracy: Even advanced models make errors, requiring continuous training and validation.

Only deep learning is useful for classification: Traditional methods like decision trees and SVMs still perform well for structured data.

Classification and clustering are the same: Classification assigns data to predefined labels, while clustering groups data without prior labels.

Historical Context

The roots of classification trace back to statistical methods in the early 20th century, with **Bayesian** probability and linear regression forming its foundation. In the **1990s** and **2000s**, support vector machines (SVMs) and decision trees advanced machine learning classification. The deep learning revolution (**2010s**), led by CNNs and recurrent neural networks (RNNs), significantly improved image and text classification, making AI-powered applications more widespread.

Practical Implications

Classification is fundamental in cybersecurity, finance, and healthcare. In fraud detection, banks use classification models to identify suspicious transactions. In self-driving cars, classification enables AI to detect pedestrians and traffic signs. In e-commerce, recommendation systems classify user preferences to personalize product suggestions. As data-driven decision-making expands, classification remains a cornerstone of AI-driven automation, analytics, and predictive modeling, shaping numerous industries.

Cloning (BT)

Cloning is a biotechnology process that produces genetically identical copies of an organism, cell, or DNA sequence. It can occur naturally (e.g., identical twins) or be artificially induced for applications in medicine, agriculture, and genetic research using techniques such as somatic cell nuclear transfer (SCNT).

Cloning is like copying a document with a photocopier. Just as a photocopy produces an exact duplicate of the original, cloning replicates genetic material or entire organisms, ensuring that the genetic blueprint remains unchanged.

Examples

Animal Cloning: Scientists clone livestock such as cattle and sheep to preserve desirable traits, such as high milk production or disease resistance.

Therapeutic Cloning: Stem cells derived from cloned embryos are used to generate personalized tissues for treating diseases like Parkinson's or diabetes.

Plant Cloning: Agricultural cloning enables farmers to propagate high-yield crops, ensuring genetic consistency and resistance to pests.

Foundational Concepts

Cloning relies on DNA replication and cellular reprogramming to create genetically identical organisms or tissues. Somatic cell nuclear transfer (SCNT) involves transferring the nucleus from a donor cell into an egg cell, which then develops into a clone of the original organism. Reproductive cloning generates a complete organism, while therapeutic cloning produces stem cells for regenerative medicine. Cloning raises ethical concerns, particularly in human applications, as it involves embryo manipulation and potential genetic anomalies.

Related Terms

Stem Cells: Undifferentiated cells capable of developing into specialized tissues, used in therapeutic cloning.

Genetic Engineering: The modification of an organism's DNA to enhance or alter specific traits (see pg. 242).

CRISPR-Cas9: A gene-editing tool that allows for precise genetic modifications, complementing cloning techniques (see pg. 158).

Common Misconceptions

Cloning creates exact copies with identical personalities: While genetically identical, environmental factors influence development and behavior.

Cloning is only used to duplicate animals: It is widely applied in medicine, agriculture, and genetic research.

Human cloning already exists: No scientifically verified case of human cloning has been achieved due to ethical and technical challenges.

Historical Context

The first successful cloning of an animal was **Dolly the sheep** (**1996**), created by **Ian Wilmut** and **Keith Campbell** using SCNT. Earlier, cloning research began with frog embryos in the **1950s**. Plant cloning, however, has been practiced for centuries through cuttings and grafting. As genetic engineering advanced, cloning has been integrated into biomedical research and agriculture, sparking debates on ethics, genetic diversity, and the potential for human cloning.

Practical Implications

Cloning revolutionizes medicine, agriculture, and conservation. In regenerative medicine, cloned stem cells help in organ repair and transplantation. In agriculture, cloning ensures genetic stability in crops and livestock, enhancing food security. In wildlife conservation, cloning restores endangered species by preserving genetic material. However, concerns about biodiversity, ethical boundaries, and genetic defects necessitate strict scientific and legal oversight to regulate cloning technologies responsibly.

Cluster Computing (HPC)

Cluster computing is a high-performance computing approach that links multiple interconnected computers (nodes) to function as a single, unified system. It enables parallel processing and data-intensive computations, making it crucial for biotechnology applications such as genome sequencing, drug discovery, and protein folding simulations.

Cluster computing is like a team of chefs working together in a restaurant kitchen. Instead of a single chef handling every task, multiple chefs divide the workload, speeding up food preparation—just as cluster computing divides complex computations among multiple machines for faster processing.

Examples

Genomic Sequencing: Cluster computing accelerates DNA sequence analysis, enabling researchers to process large genomic datasets efficiently.

Drug Discovery: Pharmaceutical companies use high-performance clusters to simulate molecular interactions, identifying potential drug candidates faster.

Protein Folding Research: Computational models run on clusters to predict protein structures, aiding in disease research and treatment development (see pg. 82).

Foundational Concepts

Cluster computing relies on parallel processing, where multiple nodes work together to execute tasks simultaneously. It uses message-passing interfaces (MPI) or distributed computing frameworks to coordinate workloads. Load balancing ensures efficient resource allocation, preventing any single node from becoming a bottleneck. Clusters can be homogeneous (identical hardware) or heterogeneous (mixed hardware). High-speed interconnects and fault tolerance mechanisms enhance reliability, allowing biotech applications to process large datasets efficiently, simulate biological processes, and model molecular interactions with high accuracy.

Related Terms

High-Performance Computing (HPC): Advanced computing systems designed for large-scale processing and simulations (see pg. 36).

Parallel Processing: A computing technique where tasks are divided and executed simultaneously to improve speed (see pg. 364).

Grid Computing: A decentralized network of computers that collaborate to solve large-scale problems, similar to cluster computing but distributed (see pg. 256).

Common Misconceptions

Cluster computing is the same as cloud computing: While both distribute computing tasks, cloud computing provides on-demand services, whereas clusters are dedicated, local systems.

Only supercomputers use cluster computing: Many mid-sized research labs and companies use cluster systems for data processing.

Cluster computing is only for large-scale projects: Even small-scale biotech research benefits from parallel processing.

Historical Context

Cluster computing emerged in the **1990s**, with projects like **Beowulf clusters**, enabling affordable, scalable high-performance computing. As biotech data processing demands grew, institutions like the **National Institutes of Health** (NIH) and pharmaceutical firms adopted cluster computing for genomics, proteomics, and AI-driven drug discovery. Advances in GPUs, parallel computing frameworks, and cloud-based clusters have made high-performance biotech computing more accessible.

Practical Implications

Cluster computing accelerates biomedical research, data analytics, and AI-driven biotech applications. It reduces computation time for genome analysis, enables faster disease modeling, and enhances AI-driven drug discovery. In personalized medicine, clusters help process patient genetic data to tailor treatments. With growing biotech data volumes, cluster computing ensures scalability, efficiency, and innovation in healthcare, pharmaceuticals, and bioinformatics.

Clustering (AI)

Clustering is an unsupervised machine learning technique used to group similar data points into clusters based on shared characteristics. It is commonly applied in pattern recognition, customer segmentation, anomaly detection, and biological data analysis, helping AI systems identify hidden structures within large datasets.

Clustering is like organizing a library without predefined categories. Instead of classifying books based on an existing system, books with similar topics, themes, or writing styles are grouped together, just as clustering algorithms identify natural groupings within a dataset.

Examples

Customer Segmentation: Businesses use clustering to analyze purchasing behaviors and create personalized marketing strategies.

Medical Diagnosis: AI models cluster similar patient symptoms and genetic markers, aiding in early disease detection.

Image Recognition: Clustering helps AI classify similar image patterns, improving facial recognition and object detection (see pg. 276).

Foundational Concepts

Clustering algorithms work by measuring the similarity or distance between data points. The most common approach is K-means clustering, which partitions data into K distinct groups based on centroid calculations. Hierarchical clustering builds a tree-like structure of nested clusters, while density-based clustering detects clusters by identifying high-density regions in data. Clustering is widely used in unsupervised learning, where AI learns patterns without labeled data, making it essential for big data analytics, anomaly detection, and recommendation systems.

Related Terms

K-means Clustering: A method that groups data into K clusters based on proximity to centroids (see pg. 134).

Hierarchical Clustering: A technique that creates a hierarchy of nested clusters based on similarity (see pg. 134).

Dimensionality Reduction: The process of reducing features in high-dimensional datasets, often used before clustering (see pg. 186).

Common Misconceptions

Clustering is always accurate: Some datasets overlap across clusters, making boundaries less clear.

Clustering requires labeled data: Unlike classification, clustering works without predefined labels.

All clustering methods yield the same results: Different algorithms produce varied cluster structures, requiring careful selection.

Historical Context

Clustering emerged in the **1960s** with early work in pattern recognition and statistical classification. K-means clustering was introduced by **MacQueen** (**1967**), while hierarchical clustering methods were developed for bioinformatics and data mining. Advances in big data, AI, and deep learning have led to clustering applications in customer analytics, genomics, and natural language processing (NLP).

Practical Implications

Clustering enhances AI-driven decision-making across industries. In finance, it detects fraudulent transactions by identifying anomalous spending patterns. Healthcare applications include grouping patients with similar conditions for precision medicine. In e-commerce, clustering improves recommendation algorithms, helping AI suggest relevant products. As AI models process growing data volumes, clustering remains vital for discovering hidden insights, automating pattern detection, and optimizing large-scale analytics.

Cobots (Collaborative Robots) (RT)

Cobots, or Collaborative Robots, are AI-powered robotic systems designed to work alongside humans in shared workspaces. Unlike traditional industrial robots, which operate in isolation, cobots enhance human capabilities, improve efficiency, and increase safety in manufacturing, healthcare, logistics, and other industries requiring human-robot collaboration.

Cobots are like a reliable coworker who helps with repetitive, precise, or physically demanding tasks. Just as a barista assistant steams milk while the barista takes orders, cobots handle tedious work, allowing humans to focus on more complex, strategic responsibilities.

Examples

Manufacturing: Cobots assist factory workers by assembling components, welding, and handling materials, reducing fatigue and injury risks.

Healthcare: In hospitals, cobots aid in surgeries, deliver medications, and support rehabilitation therapy, ensuring higher precision and efficiency.

Retail & Logistics: Cobots automate warehouse picking, sorting, and inventory management, accelerating e-commerce fulfillment and supply chain operations.

Foundational Concepts

Cobots are designed with human-centric AI, safety features, and real-time adaptability. They use computer vision, force sensors, and machine learning algorithms to detect human presence and adjust their actions accordingly. Unlike traditional automation, which relies on fixed programming, cobots leverage reinforcement learning and real-time sensor data to optimize workflows. Their lightweight structure, soft robotics, and intuitive interfaces make them safer for direct human interaction. As a result, cobots play a vital role in smart factories, medical robotics, and human-machine collaboration.

Related Terms

Human-Robot Interaction (HRI): The study of how robots and humans collaborate safely and efficiently.

Industrial Robots: Traditional robots designed for high-speed, high-precision automation, often in enclosed environments.

Reinforcement Learning: An AI technique enabling robots to improve their performance through trial and error (see pg. 410).

Common Misconceptions

Cobots will replace humans: Instead, cobots augment human capabilities, reducing tedious tasks.

Cobots lack intelligence: While not autonomous, cobots learn from interactions and improve performance.

Cobots are only used in factories: They are widely applied in healthcare, logistics, and service industries.

Historical Context

Cobots were first introduced in **1996** by **J. Edward Colgate** and **Michael Peshkin** at **Northwestern University**. Unlike industrial robots, cobots prioritized direct human collaboration. By the **2010s**, companies like **Universal Robots** and **Rethink Robotics** revolutionized cobot adoption in manufacturing, healthcare, and logistics. Advances in AI, deep learning, and edge computing have since enabled cobots to adapt in real time, enhancing human-robot teamwork across industries.

Practical Implications

Cobots enhance productivity, safety, and efficiency in industries where automation and human intelligence must coexist. In manufacturing, they reduce workplace injuries and boost precision. In healthcare, they assist in surgery, patient care, and rehabilitation therapy. Retail and logistics leverage cobots for warehousing, order fulfillment, and customer service. As AI and sensor technologies improve, cobots will become more intuitive, accessible, and indispensable in collaborative work environments.

Code Generation (GenAI)

Code Generation refers to the automatic creation of source code using AI-powered tools, compilers, or template-based systems. It accelerates software development by reducing human effort in writing code, optimizing performance, and translating high-level programming instructions into executable scripts, reducing errors and increasing efficiency.

Code Generation is like using a recipe generator that provides a detailed cooking guide based on ingredients and preferences. Instead of manually planning each step, the generator creates a structured plan, ensuring accuracy and efficiency, much like AI-driven coding assistants automate software development.

Examples

AI-Assisted Development: Tools like GitHub Copilot generate code snippets based on developer prompts, reducing manual effort and improving productivity.

Automated Web Development: Low-code/no-code platforms create websites and applications using graphical interfaces, allowing users to build software with minimal coding expertise.

Compiler Optimization: Modern compilers automatically convert high-level programming code into optimized machine instructions, improving software performance across different hardware architectures.

Foundational Concepts

Code Generation is based on natural language processing (NLP), deep learning, and compiler design. AI-powered systems use transformer-based models to understand coding syntax, predict patterns, and generate efficient code. Reinforcement learning improves output by training models with real-world feedback. Additionally, syntax parsing, abstract syntax trees (AST), and template-based generation are used in traditional compiler design to automate the translation of human-readable code into machine-executable formats. These techniques are essential for AI-driven software engineering, compiler automation, and rapid application development.

Related Terms

Machine Learning Models: AI-driven systems that learn from data to generate meaningful outputs, including code (see pg. 334).

Compilers: Software that translates high-level programming languages into machine code for execution.

Low-Code Platforms: Development environments that enable software creation with minimal hand-written coding.

Common Misconceptions

AI can replace human developers: Code generation enhances but doesn't replace human creativity, problem-solving, and debugging skills.

Generated code is always perfect: AI-generated code may still contain bugs, inefficiencies, or security vulnerabilities requiring human review.

Code generation works for all programming tasks: While useful for boilerplate code, automation, and simple logic, complex algorithms still require manual refinement.

Historical Context

Code Generation has evolved from early compiler design in the **1950s** to modern AI-powered tools. **John Backus**, who developed **FORTRAN**, pioneered early code translation methods. The rise of neural networks and NLP models in the **2010s** enabled AI-driven coding assistants like **OpenAI Codex** and **GitHub Copilot**. Advances in deep learning, reinforcement learning, and large-scale training datasets have improved AI's ability to generate structured, functional, and optimized code for real-world applications.

Practical Implications

Code Generation enhances developer productivity, reduces repetitive tasks, and accelerates software development across industries. In enterprise applications, AI-driven code generation enables faster app deployment and maintenance. In embedded systems, auto-generated code improves hardware-software integration. Cybersecurity tools use AI-generated scripts to identify vulnerabilities and patch software efficiently. As AI-driven development advances, organizations will leverage code generation for rapid prototyping, automation, and intelligent programming assistance, shaping the future of software engineering.

Cognitive Load (HCI)

Cognitive Load refers to the amount of mental effort required to process, store, and retrieve information when interacting with digital systems. In Human-Computer Interaction (HCI), managing cognitive load ensures that users can efficiently understand and navigate interfaces, reducing mental strain and improving usability.

Cognitive Load is like carrying grocery bags—if you have too many, it's overwhelming. A well-designed system organizes information like a well-packed bag, making it easier to carry and access. If overloaded, users become frustrated, leading to poor decisions and errors.

Examples

User Interface Design: Simplifying website layouts by using clear navigation, intuitive icons, and minimal distractions helps reduce cognitive load for users (see pg. 520).

E-Learning Platforms: Educational systems like Khan Academy optimize learning by presenting bite-sized lessons instead of overwhelming students with excessive information at once.

Voice Assistants: AI-powered assistants like Siri and Alexa reduce cognitive load by allowing users to perform tasks hands-free, minimizing screen interaction (see pg. 528).

Foundational Concepts

Cognitive Load Theory (CLT) categorizes cognitive load into intrinsic load (task complexity), extraneous load (unnecessary distractions), and germane load (useful effort for learning). In HCI, reducing extraneous load improves user experience (UX) by designing interfaces that align with human memory limitations. Chunking, progressive disclosure, and automation help optimize information processing, ensuring that users can efficiently navigate systems without feeling overwhelmed. Cognitive load management is essential in UI/UX design, usability testing, and software ergonomics.

Related Terms

Usability: The ease with which users can navigate and understand a system (see pg. 516).

Cognitive Overload: When excessive information impairs decision-making and focus (see pg. 140).

Attention Economy: The competition for users' cognitive resources in digital environments.

Common Misconceptions

Cognitive load is always bad: Some cognitive load is necessary for effective learning and engagement.

More information improves usability: Too much information leads to overload, confusion, and frustration.

All users experience cognitive load the same way: Experience level, familiarity, and context impact how cognitive load affects different users.

Historical Context

John Sweller's **Cognitive Load Theory (1988)** introduced the idea that human working memory is limited and should be optimized for efficient learning and task performance. In the **2000s**, cognitive load became central to HCI, UI/UX design, and digital accessibility. Research in neuroscience and behavioral psychology further refined how information processing affects decision-making and system usability, leading to modern design principles focused on reducing cognitive friction.

Practical Implications

In software development, e-learning, and digital marketing, reducing cognitive load improves engagement, retention, and performance. For healthcare applications, intuitive electronic health records (EHRs) minimize doctor fatigue. In automation and AI, simplifying chatbots, voice assistants, and recommendation systems enhances usability. In e-commerce, optimizing checkouts reduces cognitive strain, increasing conversions. As technology evolves, designing human-centered systems that balance cognitive load will be critical to accessibility, usability, and user satisfaction.

Cognitive Systems (HCI/XR)

Cognitive Systems are AI-powered computational models designed to mimic human cognition, enabling machines to learn, reason, and interact naturally with humans. These systems integrate machine learning, natural language processing, and data analytics to improve decision-making, automate complex tasks, and enhance human-computer interactions.

Cognitive Systems are like a digital assistant that evolves—just as a human gains expertise through experience, these systems continuously learn from new data. The more information they process, the better they understand patterns, provide insights, and improve user experiences.

Examples

Healthcare Diagnostics: IBM Watson analyzes medical literature and patient data to assist doctors in diagnosing diseases and recommending treatments.

Customer Support: AI-driven chatbots in banking and e-commerce handle inquiries, reducing response times while improving customer interactions.

Fraud Detection: Financial institutions use cognitive systems to identify suspicious transactions by detecting anomalies in spending behavior.

Foundational Concepts

Cognitive Computing is inspired by human cognition and integrates artificial intelligence, deep learning, and big data to create intelligent systems that adapt, learn, and assist humans in decision-making. Unlike traditional AI, cognitive systems are probabilistic rather than deterministic, meaning they evaluate multiple possibilities and improve over time. They rely on natural language processing for better user interaction and context awareness to tailor responses based on prior data. These systems are commonly used in AI-driven automation, predictive analytics, and assistive technologies.

Related Terms

Artificial Intelligence (AI): Broad field of intelligent machines that perform tasks requiring human cognition (see pg. 7).

Machine Learning (ML): Algorithms that allow systems to learn patterns and improve performance over time (see pg. 45).

Neural Networks: Computing models inspired by the human brain, used in deep learning and cognitive computing (see pg. 352).

Common Misconceptions

Cognitive systems think like humans: They simulate cognitive processes but do not possess consciousness, emotions, or true understanding.

Cognitive computing is the same as AI: AI is a broader field, while cognitive computing focuses on human-like reasoning and decision-making.

Cognitive systems replace human workers: These systems are designed to augment human decision-making, not replace it.

Historical Context

The concept of cognitive computing emerged in the **1950s**, but real progress began in the **2000s** with advances in neural networks and big data analytics. **IBM Watson**, launched in **2011**, demonstrated cognitive capabilities by winning **Jeopardy!** against human champions. The integration of AI and cognitive models gained momentum in fields like healthcare, finance, and automation, leading to smarter AI assistants and advanced predictive models.

Practical Implications

Cognitive systems enhance automation, improve human decision-making, and optimize large-scale data processing. In education, AI tutors personalize learning experiences. In retail, cognitive analytics predict customer preferences and optimize supply chains. In cybersecurity, AI-driven cognitive tools detect and respond to threats in real time. As AI continues to evolve, cognitive systems will play a key role in intelligent automation, personalized experiences, and human-AI collaboration, reshaping multiple industries.

Computer Vision (ANI)

Computer Vision is the branch of AI that enables machines to interpret and act on visual data, that is turning raw pixels from images and video into meaningful concepts like "cat," "tumor," "stop sign," or "defect." It connects the physical world to digital decision-making by learning patterns that map scenes to labels, locations, and measurements.

Think of it like teaching a keen apprentice inspector to "look" at a scene: at first they notice only shapes and colors; with practice, they learn which arrangements signal what matters and how to respond.

Examples

Medical Imaging: Models flag suspicious regions in X-rays, CT, or MRI to support radiologist review.

Manufacturing Quality: Vision systems spot surface defects or misalignments on a production line in real time.

Autonomous Systems: Perception stacks detect lanes, pedestrians, and traffic signs to help plan safe motion.

Foundational Concepts

Computer Vision tasks include **classification** (what is present), **object detection** (what and where, with bounding boxes), **segmentation** (pixel-level regions), **keypoint/pose estimation** (where parts are), and **tracking** (how things move over time). Modern systems learn features directly from data: **convolutional neural networks (CNNs)** capture local patterns via learned filters and receptive fields; newer **vision transformers (ViT)** use attention to model long-range relationships. Training relies on labeled examples, a **loss function** (e.g., cross-entropy for classification, IoU- or Dice-based losses for segmentation), and gradient-based updates via **backpropagation** and **gradient descent**.

Performance depends heavily on data; and **annotation quality, class balance, data augmentation**, and resilience to **domain shift** (changes in lighting, camera, or environment). Practical systems also consider **latency** and **efficiency** (e.g., quantization, pruning) for deployment on the edge or in the cloud, and they incorporate safeguards for **privacy** and **bias**.

Related Terms

Convolutional Neural Network (CNN): Core architecture for many vision tasks (see pg. 152).

Object Detection: Predicts categories and bounding boxes for multiple objects in an image.

Image Segmentation: Assigns a label to each pixel to delineate regions precisely.

Transfer Learning: Adapts a model pretrained on large datasets to a new domain with less data (see pg. 498).

Bias & Fairness: Ensures performance holds across demographics and contexts (see pg. 104 & 216).

Common Misconceptions

Vision is solved: Accuracy can drop sharply under new lighting, viewpoints, or environments; robustness needs active work.

More pixels = better: Resolution helps, but data quality, labels, and model capacity often matter more.

It's just classification: Real systems often need detection, segmentation, tracking, and calibration together.

Models see like humans: They recognize statistical patterns; they don't "understand" scenes the way people do.

Historical Context

Early computer vision relied on hand-engineered features and edge/shape detectors. The deep-learning wave, sparked by large datasets, GPU compute, and CNN breakthroughs drove dramatic accuracy gains across **classification**, **detection**, and **segmentation**. Recent advances in **attention-based models** and **multimodal learning** continue to expand capability from single images to video, 3D, and **language-grounded perception**.

Practical Implications

Computer Vision powers safety systems, medical triage, retail analytics, agriculture monitoring, and industrial automation. Effective deployments emphasize curated data, rigorous evaluation (precision/recall, mAP, IoU), robustness to real-world shift, efficient inference, and responsible use so that what the model "sees" translates into reliable, equitable decisions at scale.

Consensus Mechanism (BC)

Consensus Mechanism refers to the process used in blockchain networks to achieve agreement on a single version of the truth among distributed participants. It ensures data integrity, security, and decentralization by validating transactions without a central authority, preventing fraud, and maintaining the trustless nature of blockchains.

A Consensus Mechanism is like a group decision-making process. Imagine a class voting on the best project idea—each student casts a vote, and the most agreed-upon idea is selected. Similarly, blockchain nodes must agree on transaction validity before adding it to the ledger.

Examples

Bitcoin (Proof of Work - PoW): Miners solve complex mathematical puzzles to validate transactions, ensuring security through computational effort (see pg. 162).

Ethereum 2.0 (Proof of Stake - PoS): Validators are chosen based on the number of coins they hold and stake, reducing energy consumption while securing the network (see pg. 162).

Hyperledger Fabric (Practical Byzantine Fault Tolerance - PBFT): Enterprise blockchain networks use PBFT for fast and reliable consensus without requiring high computational power.

Foundational Concepts

A Consensus Mechanism is crucial for blockchain security and decentralization. The most common models include Proof of Work (PoW), which relies on computational puzzles, and Proof of Stake (PoS), where validators are chosen based on asset ownership. Alternative mechanisms like Delegated Proof of Stake (DPoS), Practical Byzantine Fault Tolerance (PBFT), and Proof of Authority (PoA) offer variations tailored to specific blockchain needs. The primary goal is to ensure immutability, security, and transparency while preventing double spending and fraud in a distributed ledger system.

Related Terms

Blockchain: A decentralized ledger where transactions are recorded in secure, immutable blocks (see pg. 18).

Smart Contracts: Self-executing agreements coded on the blockchain that operate without intermediaries (see pg. 446).

Byzantine Fault Tolerance (BFT): A system's ability to function correctly even when some participants act maliciously.

Common Misconceptions

Consensus Mechanisms guarantee 100% security: While they enhance security, no system is completely immune to attacks, including 51% attacks in PoW or validator collusion in PoS.

All blockchains use the same Consensus Mechanism: Different blockchains employ varied consensus protocols suited to their use cases.

Consensus requires human voting: It is an automated, algorithm-driven process where network nodes participate in validation.

Historical Context

The first **Consensus Mechanism, Proof of Work** (PoW), was introduced in **Bitcoin's 2008** whitepaper by **Satoshi Nakamoto. Ethereum** later introduced **Proof of Stake** (PoS) to address PoW's energy inefficiency. Over time, alternative models like Delegated Proof of Stake (DPoS) (developed by **BitShares**) and PBFT (used in **Hyperledger Fabric**) emerged to cater to different blockchain needs. Advances in Layer 2 solutions and hybrid consensus models continue to shape the future of decentralized networks.

Practical Implications

Consensus Mechanisms power cryptocurrencies, decentralized finance (DeFi), and supply chain tracking. In finance, they enable secure and transparent digital payments. In healthcare, blockchains use consensus to protect patient records. In logistics, immutable ledgers ensure product authenticity and traceability. As blockchain adoption grows, Consensus Mechanisms will evolve to enhance scalability, reduce energy consumption, and increase transaction speeds, making decentralized applications more efficient and widespread.

Contrastive Learning (AI)

Contrastive Learning is a self-supervised machine learning technique where models learn by distinguishing between similar and dissimilar data points. It enhances representation learning by mapping similar items closer together in an embedding space, making it useful for applications like image recognition, natural language processing, and anomaly detection.

Contrastive Learning is like organizing a vast photo library. If you have pictures of dogs and cats, the system learns to group similar breeds while separating different species, making future image retrieval or classification more efficient and accurate.

Examples

Image Recognition: Contrastive learning helps models learn visual similarities, improving facial recognition by grouping different images of the same person together while distinguishing others (see pg. 276).

Natural Language Processing (NLP): Used in sentence embedding models like SimCSE, it enables AI to understand text meaning by learning semantic similarities between sentences (see pg. 346).

Anomaly Detection: In cybersecurity, contrastive learning identifies fraudulent activities by recognizing unusual patterns that deviate from normal user behavior (see pg. 84).

Foundational Concepts

Contrastive Learning is based on the idea of representation learning, where models learn feature representations by maximizing similarities between related samples and minimizing relationships between unrelated ones. Methods like SimCLR (Simple Contrastive Learning of Representations) and MoCo (Momentum Contrast) use contrastive loss functions such as InfoNCE (Noise Contrastive Estimation) to improve learning. These models often leverage data augmentations, where transformations of the same data point (e.g., rotated images) are treated as similar, reinforcing robust feature learning.

Related Terms

Self-Supervised Learning: A learning paradigm where models generate their own labels from data instead of relying on human-labeled datasets (see pg. 430).

Representation Learning: The process of learning meaningful data representations without explicit feature engineering.

Embedding Space: A multi-dimensional space where similar data points are mapped closer together for efficient clustering and retrieval.

Common Misconceptions

Contrastive Learning requires labeled data: Unlike supervised learning, it primarily relies on self-supervision, requiring minimal or no labels.

It is only for images: While widely used in computer vision, it also improves text, speech, and even sensor-based anomaly detection.

More data pairs always improve performance: Poorly chosen positive-negative pairs can lead to ineffective learning rather than improved accuracy.

Historical Context

Contrastive Learning evolved from metric learning and became prominent with deep learning advancements. Techniques like Word2Vec (**2013**) used contrastive approaches for text embeddings, while SimCLR (**2020**) and MoCo (**2019**) popularized contrastive learning in computer vision. The introduction of CLIP (**2021**) by **OpenAI** further expanded its use in multimodal AI, combining text and image representations.

Practical Implications

In healthcare, contrastive learning enhances medical imaging analysis by distinguishing healthy tissues from anomalies. In e-commerce, it improves product recommendations by identifying user preferences based on past interactions. Autonomous vehicles use it for sensor fusion, learning similarities between different camera angles and LiDAR scans. As AI adoption grows, contrastive learning continues to refine representation learning, reducing reliance on labeled data, and improving generalization across domains.

Conversational Agent (GenAI)

A Conversational Agent is an AI-driven system designed to interact with humans through natural language. It processes spoken or written input, understands intent, and generates appropriate responses. Examples include chatbots, virtual assistants, and AI-powered customer service platforms, enhancing user experience and automating communication.

A Conversational Agent is like a personal secretary who understands and responds to requests efficiently. Just as a secretary schedules meetings, answers calls, and provides relevant information, a conversational agent assists users by responding to queries, providing recommendations, or automating routine tasks.

Examples

Customer Support: AI chatbots handle customer inquiries, providing instant support for product information, troubleshooting, and FAQs without human intervention.

Healthcare Assistants: Virtual agents guide patients by answering health-related questions, scheduling appointments, and monitoring symptoms through AI-powered conversations.

Smart Home Assistants: Devices like Amazon Alexa or Google Assistant enable voice-controlled automation, managing smart home systems, playing music, and providing weather updates.

Foundational Concepts

Conversational Agents rely on Natural Language Processing (NLP) and Machine Learning to interpret and generate human-like responses. Dialogue management systems ensure coherent and context-aware conversations, while intent recognition and sentiment analysis refine interactions. Speech recognition enhances voice-based agents, allowing seamless communication. Advanced models leverage Transformer-based architectures, like GPT or BERT, improving contextual understanding. By continuously learning from user interactions, conversational agents refine their responses and improve accuracy over time.

Related Terms

Natural Language Processing (NLP): A branch of AI that enables machines to understand and generate human language (see pg. 346).

Chatbot: A software application designed to simulate human conversation through text or voice interactions (see pg. 528).

Speech Recognition: AI technology that converts spoken language into text for interaction with voice assistants (see pg. 460).

Common Misconceptions

Conversational Agents fully understand human emotions: While they can analyze sentiment, they lack true emotional intelligence.
They always provide accurate responses: Their accuracy depends on training data, and they may still generate incorrect or biased answers.
All chatbots are AI-powered: Some rule-based chatbots follow predefined scripts without true learning capabilities.

Historical Context

Early Conversational Agents date back to **ELIZA** (**1966**), a simple rule-based chatbot developed at **MIT**. Later, **IBM Watson** (**2011**) revolutionized AI-driven conversations with deep learning and NLP. The rise of virtual assistants like **Siri** (**2011**), **Alexa** (**2014**), and **Google Assistant** (**2016**) marked a shift toward real-time, context-aware interactions. With advancements in deep learning, modern chatbots and AI assistants leverage large-scale transformer models for enhanced conversational depth.

Practical Implications

Conversational Agents streamline operations in customer service, education, healthcare, and finance. In e-commerce, AI chatbots assist with product recommendations and purchase guidance. Healthcare AI assistants support patient diagnostics and mental health therapy. HR chatbots automate employee onboarding and recruitment processes. As AI advances, conversational agents will continue enhancing user experiences, optimizing workflows, and reducing operational costs across industries.

Convolutional Neural Network (CNN) (AI)

A Convolutional Neural Network (CNN) is a type of deep learning model designed to process and analyze visual data. By using convolutional layers, pooling layers, and fully connected layers, CNNs can automatically extract spatial features, recognize patterns, and classify images with high accuracy.

A CNN is like the human visual system—just as our brain recognizes objects by processing edges, colors, and textures in stages, a CNN detects simple patterns first and then builds upon them to recognize complex structures, such as faces or letters.

Examples

Image Recognition: CNNs power facial recognition in smartphones, security systems, and social media platforms, enabling automatic tagging and identification (see pg. 276).

Medical Imaging: CNNs analyze X-rays and MRIs to detect diseases like cancer or pneumonia with high accuracy, assisting doctors in diagnostics.

Autonomous Vehicles: CNNs help self-driving cars interpret traffic signs, detect pedestrians, and recognize lane boundaries, ensuring safe navigation.

Foundational Concepts

CNNs leverage convolutional layers to extract image features, pooling layers to reduce dimensionality, and fully connected layers for classification. ReLU activation enhances non-linearity, while backpropagation and gradient descent optimize performance. CNNs are designed to detect spatial hierarchies, learning from simple edges to complex structures. Transfer learning allows pre-trained CNNs to adapt to new tasks, significantly reducing training time. Feature maps generated in early layers capture essential image characteristics, making CNNs highly effective in vision-related AI applications.

Related Terms

Deep Learning: A subset of AI that uses neural networks with multiple layers to learn complex patterns (see pg. 178).

Feature Extraction: The process of identifying key characteristics in data, crucial for CNN performance (see pg. 218 & 222).

Transfer Learning: Using a pre-trained CNN model on new datasets, reducing the need for extensive training.

Common Misconceptions

CNNs work like traditional image filters: Unlike static filters, CNNs learn optimal features dynamically.

CNNs only recognize objects in trained conditions: While powerful, they require robust datasets to generalize well.

Bigger CNNs are always better: Larger networks demand more data and computational power but don't always improve performance.

Historical Context

The foundation of CNNs was laid by **Fukushima**'s **Neocognitron** (**1980**), later refined by **Yann LeCun**'s **LeNet-5** (**1989**) for digit recognition. The breakthrough came with **AlexNet** (**2012**), which won the **ImageNet** competition, proving CNNs' superiority in image classification. Since then, models like VGGNet, ResNet, and EfficientNet have advanced CNN architectures.

Practical Implications

CNNs revolutionized computer vision, medical diagnostics, robotics, and security. In retail, they enable product recognition for smart shopping. In healthcare, they assist in diagnosing complex conditions. In agriculture, they analyze crop health via aerial imagery. As CNNs evolve, their impact on autonomous systems, augmented reality, and industrial automation will expand further.

Copilot (GenAI)

A Copilot is an AI-powered assistant designed to augment human productivity by providing contextual suggestions, automation, and real-time insights. Using natural language processing, machine learning, and generative AI, Copilots assist users in tasks such as coding, writing, data analysis, and workflow automation.

A Copilot is like a co-driver in a rally race—it doesn't take control but provides guidance, insights, and recommendations, allowing the driver to focus on execution. Similarly, AI Copilots assist users by enhancing efficiency, reducing cognitive load, and automating repetitive tasks without replacing human decision-making.

Examples

Software Development: AI-driven Copilots suggest code snippets, detect errors, and generate functions in real time, significantly accelerating programming workflows.

Content Creation: Writing assistants powered by Copilot AI help generate articles, refine grammar, and suggest phrasing, enhancing productivity for journalists, marketers, and authors.

Customer Support: AI Copilots assist customer service agents by suggesting responses, automating repetitive inquiries, and retrieving relevant information, improving efficiency and customer satisfaction.

Foundational Concepts

Copilots rely on large language models trained on vast datasets, enabling them to predict and generate relevant outputs. Context-aware AI refines responses based on real-time interactions, while reinforcement learning helps improve accuracy over time. User feedback loops enhance adaptability, ensuring continuous learning. Unlike traditional rule-based automation, Copilots use transformer architectures to generate nuanced, human-like assistance. Few-shot learning allows them to adapt to different tasks with minimal training, making them versatile across industries.

Related Terms

Generative AI: AI models that create new content, such as text, images, or code, based on input data (see pg. 33).

Natural Language Processing (NLP): A field of AI that enables machines to understand and generate human language (see pg. 346).

Reinforcement Learning from Human Feedback (RLHF): A method for improving AI models by incorporating user input (see pg. 410).

Common Misconceptions

Copilots replace human jobs: They are designed to assist, not replace, professionals by automating routine tasks.

Copilots always provide accurate responses: AI Copilots can make errors and require human validation.

Copilots work autonomously: They rely on user input and are meant to augment human decision-making, not replace it.

Historical Context

The rise of Copilots began with AI advancements in GPT models, BERT, and transformer-based architectures. **GitHub Copilot**, launched in **2021** by **OpenAI** and **Microsoft**, revolutionized coding assistance. Other industries followed, integrating AI-powered assistants into productivity tools like **Microsoft 365 Copilot**, **Google's Duet AI**, and ChatGPT-powered applications. Copilots continue evolving with multi-modal AI, enabling assistance in text, images, and voice interactions.

Practical Implications

Copilots enhance efficiency in software development, business intelligence, and creative work by reducing manual effort and improving decision-making. In healthcare, AI-driven Copilots assist doctors in diagnosing diseases and drafting reports. In education, they support personalized learning by providing real-time feedback to students. As human-AI collaboration advances, Copilots will become integral to workplace automation, digital transformation, and AI-assisted creativity, shaping the future of knowledge work.

Counterfactual Explanation (XAI)

A Counterfactual Explanation is a method used in explainable AI (XAI) to clarify why a model made a specific decision by showing how a slight change in input would have led to a different outcome. It helps users understand model behavior in a human-interpretable way.

A Counterfactual Explanation is like a "what-if" scenario in real life. If a student didn't pass a test, a counterfactual explanation would show that scoring just five more points would have changed the outcome, helping the student understand what adjustments were needed.

Examples

Loan Approval: A bank's AI model denies a loan. A counterfactual explanation states that if the applicant's credit score had been 20 points higher, approval would have been granted, providing actionable insights.

Medical Diagnosis: An AI model predicts a high risk of diabetes. A counterfactual explanation reveals that maintaining a lower BMI could have altered the diagnosis, helping patients take preventive measures.

Job Recruitment: A hiring algorithm rejects a candidate. A counterfactual explanation shows that if the applicant had one more year of experience, they would have been selected, guiding skill development.

Foundational Concepts

Counterfactual Explanations stem from causal inference and interpretable machine learning. They provide an alternative scenario in which small changes to input variables lead to different predictions, helping users understand decision boundaries. This contrasts with traditional feature importance methods, which show which variables matter most but don't indicate how to change them. Algorithmic recourse leverages counterfactuals to suggest actionable steps, and techniques like gradient-based methods or generative models generate realistic counterfactual samples.

Related Terms

Explainable AI (XAI): AI techniques that improve transparency and interpretability in decision-making models (see pg. 27).

Causal Inference: A statistical approach used to determine cause-and-effect relationships in data.

Algorithmic Recourse: Methods that suggest actionable changes users can make to achieve a desired AI outcome.

Common Misconceptions

Counterfactual Explanations change AI decisions automatically: They only provide insights, but do not alter AI models.

Counterfactuals always suggest realistic changes: Some AI-generated counterfactuals may be impractical, requiring human validation.

All AI models can generate counterfactuals: Some deep learning models lack transparency, making counterfactual generation challenging.

Historical Context

Counterfactual reasoning has roots in philosophy and causality research, with early work by **David Lewis (1973)** on counterfactual conditionals. In AI, **Wachter, Mittelstadt**, and **Russell (2017)** formalized counterfactual explanations for machine learning, particularly in response to the **GDPR** "right to explanation" requirement. The rise of XAI frameworks has since advanced counterfactual methods, making them widely adopted in finance, healthcare, and legal AI applications.

Practical Implications

Counterfactual explanations enhance AI transparency, fairness, and user trust by providing interpretable reasons for predictions. In regulatory compliance, they help ensure AI-driven decisions are accountable under laws like GDPR. In credit scoring, they enable applicants to understand why they were rejected and how to improve their chances. In medical AI, they assist doctors in refining risk predictions by identifying modifiable factors. As AI expands, counterfactual explanations will be crucial for ethical AI deployment and human-AI collaboration.

CRISPR-Cas9 (BT)

CRISPR-Cas9 is a revolutionary gene-editing technology that enables precise modifications to DNA. Derived from bacterial immune systems, it uses a guide RNA (gRNA) to direct the Cas9 enzyme to a specific genetic sequence, allowing scientists to cut and modify genes with unprecedented accuracy.

CRISPR-Cas9 works like a genetic pair of scissors. Just as a word processor allows users to cut, edit, and replace words in a document, CRISPR enables scientists to precisely remove or alter genes within an organism's DNA, correcting mutations or introducing new traits.

Examples

Genetic Disease Treatment: CRISPR-Cas9 is being explored to cure inherited disorders like sickle cell anemia by editing defective genes in blood cells, potentially offering lifelong treatments.

Agricultural Enhancement: Scientists use CRISPR to develop drought-resistant crops and enhance nutritional content, improving food security while reducing environmental impact.

Cancer Therapy: CRISPR is being investigated to modify immune cells to target and destroy cancerous tumors, offering a new frontier in personalized medicine.

Foundational Concepts

CRISPR-Cas9 is based on a natural bacterial defense mechanism that recognizes and cuts viral DNA using a guide RNA sequence. The Cas9 enzyme acts as molecular scissors, allowing gene knockout, gene insertion, or gene repair. Unlike older genetic modification techniques, CRISPR is highly precise, cost-effective, and widely accessible. Scientists employ homology-directed repair (HDR) or non-homologous end joining (NHEJ) to fix or modify DNA after Cas9-induced cuts, enabling targeted genetic modifications with minimal off-target effects.

Related Terms

Gene Editing: A broader term encompassing techniques like CRISPR, TALENs, and zinc finger nucleases for modifying DNA.

gRNA (Guide RNA): The RNA molecule that directs Cas9 to the correct DNA sequence for cutting.

Germline Editing: Genetic modifications passed down to future generations, unlike somatic gene editing, which only affects individuals.

Common Misconceptions

CRISPR always produces perfect edits: While precise, unintended off-target effects can occur, necessitating further refinement.

CRISPR creates "designer babies": While possible, germline editing is highly regulated and largely banned for ethical reasons.

CRISPR is only for humans: It is widely used in agriculture, environmental science, and microbiology for diverse applications.

Historical Context

CRISPR was first identified in bacteria in **1987**, but its gene-editing potential was discovered by **Jennifer Doudna** and **Emmanuelle Charpentier** in **2012**, earning them the **2020 Nobel Prize** in Chemistry. It quickly became a leading tool in genetic engineering, revolutionizing fields from biomedicine to synthetic biology. Major breakthroughs include CRISPR-based cancer treatments, hereditary disease therapies, and agricultural innovations.

Practical Implications

CRISPR is transforming medicine, agriculture, and biotechnology. In healthcare, it offers potential cures for genetic disorders, viral infections, and cancers. In agriculture, it enhances crop resilience, reducing reliance on pesticides and improving food security. In synthetic biology, it enables engineered microbes for biofuel production and environmental remediation. Ethical concerns surrounding human genome editing, bioterrorism, and ecological risks require stringent regulations, ensuring responsible development and application of this powerful technology.

Cross-Validation (AI)

Cross-validation is a statistical technique used in machine learning to assess a model's performance by dividing a dataset into multiple subsets. The model is trained on one subset while tested on another, ensuring generalization and reducing overfitting to specific data patterns.

Cross-validation is like studying for an exam using different practice tests. Instead of preparing with only one test, a student practices with multiple sets of questions to ensure they perform well on any given exam. Similarly, cross-validation ensures models perform well on unseen data.

Examples

Medical Diagnosis Models: Cross-validation is used to test machine learning models predicting diseases from medical images, ensuring accuracy across different patient datasets before clinical deployment.

Fraud Detection: In banking, cross-validation helps train fraud detection models on historical transaction data, ensuring the system identifies fraudulent activity without false positives on new transactions.

Autonomous Vehicles: Self-driving car algorithms undergo cross-validation to verify their ability to detect pedestrians, road signs, and obstacles across diverse driving environments, preventing biased decision-making.

Foundational Concepts

Cross-validation works by splitting data into training and testing subsets, ensuring robust model evaluation. The k-fold cross-validation method divides data into k equal parts, training the model on k-1 folds and testing on the remaining fold, repeating the process k times. Stratified cross-validation ensures balanced representation of data classes. Leave-one-out cross-validation (LOOCV) tests the model on one sample at a time, beneficial for small datasets but computationally expensive. Proper cross-validation helps prevent overfitting, ensuring models generalize to unseen data.

Related Terms

Overfitting: When a model learns patterns specific to training data, reducing its effectiveness on unseen data (see pg. 362).

Bias-Variance Tradeoff: The balance between model simplicity (high bias) and model complexity (high variance), addressed by cross-validation (see pg. 104).

Hyperparameter Tuning: The process of optimizing model settings, where cross-validation helps select the best configuration.

Common Misconceptions

Cross-validation guarantees perfect models: While it improves generalization, it does not eliminate model errors entirely.

More folds always mean better validation: Too many folds, such as in LOOCV, can increase computational cost without significant performance gains.

Cross-validation replaces a test set: A final independent test set is still needed for true performance evaluation.

Historical Context

Cross-validation originates from statistical resampling techniques, with early implementations in the **1930s** for agricultural experiments. In the **1970s**, machine learning researchers adopted it for model validation. The rise of k-fold cross-validation and LOOCV in the **1990s** improved model assessment in finance, healthcare, and artificial intelligence. As datasets grew in complexity, cross-validation became a standard practice in evaluating deep learning and AI-driven systems.

Practical Implications

Cross-validation enhances model reliability in finance, healthcare, cybersecurity, and autonomous systems. In finance, it prevents overfitting in stock market prediction models. In healthcare, it ensures AI-powered diagnostic tools perform consistently across patient demographics. In cybersecurity, it improves malware detection systems, reducing false alarms. As AI adoption increases, rigorous validation techniques like cross-validation remain essential for building trustworthy, generalizable, and fair machine learning models.

Cryptocurrency (BC)

Cryptocurrency is a digital or virtual currency that relies on cryptographic techniques for security and operates on decentralized networks like blockchain. Unlike traditional money, cryptocurrencies are not controlled by governments or banks, enabling secure, peer-to-peer transactions without intermediaries.

Cryptocurrency is like digital gold—just as gold has intrinsic value and can be traded, cryptocurrencies have value based on market demand and utility. Instead of being stored in vaults, they exist on blockchain networks, making them accessible and secure from anywhere in the world.

Examples

Bitcoin as a Store of Value: Bitcoin, the first cryptocurrency, is often compared to digital gold, used as a decentralized alternative to traditional currencies and an inflation hedge.

Ethereum Smart Contracts: Ethereum enables programmable contracts that automatically execute agreements, allowing for decentralized applications (DApps) in finance, gaming, and logistics (see pg. 446).

Cross-Border Transactions: Cryptocurrencies like Ripple (XRP) enable instant and cost-effective cross-border payments, bypassing slow and expensive traditional banking systems.

Foundational Concepts

Cryptocurrency transactions rely on blockchain technology, a distributed ledger that records transactions across a decentralized network of computers. Each transaction is verified through cryptographic hashing, ensuring security and transparency. Consensus mechanisms, such as Proof of Work (PoW) and Proof of Stake (PoS), validate transactions and maintain network integrity. Public and private keys secure transactions, allowing users to send and receive cryptocurrency without a central authority. These principles make cryptocurrencies resistant to fraud, censorship, and double-spending.

Related Terms

Blockchain: A decentralized ledger that records transactions securely and transparently (see pg. 18).

Smart Contracts: Self-executing contracts that operate based on predefined rules on blockchain networks (see pg. 446).

Decentralized Finance (DeFi): A financial ecosystem built on blockchain, offering banking services without intermediaries (see pg. 176).

Common Misconceptions

Cryptocurrency is completely anonymous: While transactions can be pseudonymous, blockchain records are public and traceable.

All cryptocurrencies are the same: Different cryptocurrencies serve distinct purposes, from payment (Bitcoin) to smart contracts (Ethereum).

Cryptocurrency has no real-world value: Many businesses, institutions, and governments have started recognizing cryptocurrencies as assets and mediums of exchange.

Historical Context

The concept of cryptocurrency dates back to **Bitcoin**'s introduction by **Satoshi Nakamoto** in **2008**, aiming to create a peer-to-peer electronic cash system. **Bitcoin**'s blockchain technology inspired the development of thousands of alternative cryptocurrencies. **Ethereum**, launched in **2015** by **Vitalik Buterin**, introduced smart contracts, expanding blockchain applications beyond payments. Governments and corporations have since explored regulations, central bank digital currencies (CBDCs), and institutional adoption of crypto assets.

Practical Implications

Cryptocurrency has transformed finance, supply chain management, and cybersecurity. Bitcoin and stablecoins provide financial access in regions with unstable economies. Decentralized Finance (DeFi) platforms enable lending and borrowing without banks. Non-fungible tokens (NFTs) create unique digital ownership in art, gaming, and entertainment. Governments are exploring Central Bank Digital Currencies (CBDCs), while businesses integrate blockchain for secure transactions. As adoption grows, crypto's impact on global trade, privacy, and financial inclusion will continue expanding.

Cyber-Physical Systems (CPS) (RAI/XAI)

Cyber-Physical Systems (CPS) integrate computational algorithms with physical processes, enabling real-time interaction between digital components and the physical world. These systems use sensors, actuators, and embedded software to monitor and control critical infrastructure, industrial automation, and smart environments through networked communication and data-driven decision-making.

A Cyber-Physical System is like a modern airplane's autopilot—it continuously processes sensor data, makes automated decisions, and adjusts flight controls in real-time, seamlessly blending software intelligence with physical operations for safe and efficient navigation.

Examples

Smart Grid Management: CPS technology optimizes energy distribution by dynamically adjusting electricity supply based on real-time consumption patterns, improving grid stability and energy efficiency (see pg. 450).

Autonomous Vehicles: Self-driving cars leverage CPS for real-time perception, decision-making, and motion control, ensuring safe navigation through sensor fusion and AI-driven predictions.

Medical Monitoring Systems: Wearable health monitors and robotic-assisted surgery rely on CPS to analyze patient data in real time, enhancing diagnostic accuracy and surgical precision.

Foundational Concepts

Cyber-Physical Systems operate at the intersection of embedded computing, control theory, and real-time data analytics. These systems integrate sensors to collect environmental data, actuators to execute physical actions, and machine learning algorithms for predictive analytics. Edge computing and cloud infrastructure enable real-time processing and remote control. Networked feedback loops ensure autonomous decision-making and adaptive responses, making CPS ideal for smart infrastructure, industrial automation, and intelligent transportation.

Related Terms

Internet of Things (IoT): Networked physical objects that exchange data for automation and monitoring (see pg. 288 & 290).

Digital Twin: A virtual replica of a physical system that allows for simulation and optimization (see pg. 184).

Edge Computing: Decentralized processing of real-time data closer to the source, reducing latency (see pg. 192).

Common Misconceptions

CPS is just IoT: While both involve connected devices, CPS integrates advanced control and decision-making for real-time physical interactions.

CPS only applies to robotics: CPS spans healthcare, energy grids, smart cities, and beyond, not just autonomous machines.

CPS does not need AI: Many CPS applications use AI-powered predictive modeling and optimization to enhance decision-making.

Historical Context

Cyber-Physical Systems emerged from embedded systems research in the early **2000s**, building on control systems, robotics, and networking technologies. **Edward Lee** and **Raj Rajkumar** played pivotal roles in CPS research, emphasizing real-time computing and safety-critical applications. Governments and industries invested in smart infrastructure, accelerating CPS adoption in automotive, healthcare, and aerospace engineering. The convergence of IoT, AI, and edge computing continues to expand CPS capabilities.

Practical Implications

Cyber-Physical Systems drive automation, safety, and efficiency in critical industries. Manufacturing plants use CPS for precision control in automated assembly lines. Smart cities integrate CPS for traffic management, pollution monitoring, and resource allocation. In aviation and space exploration, CPS ensures real-time mission adaptability. The rise of 5G connectivity, AI, and blockchain integration is further enhancing CPS security, scalability, and resilience, paving the way for next-generation intelligent ecosystems.

DALL-E (GenAI)

DALL-E is an AI-powered image generation model developed by OpenAI that creates realistic and imaginative images from text descriptions. Using deep learning, it understands natural language prompts and translates them into detailed, high-quality visuals, enabling creative design, prototyping, and concept visualization.

DALL-E is like a digital artist who paints whatever you describe. Just as an illustrator brings imaginative concepts to life, DALL-E transforms text into unique visuals, whether depicting a futuristic city, an abstract painting, or a cat in a spacesuit.

Examples

Advertising & Marketing: Companies use DALL-E to generate custom visuals for campaigns, eliminating the need for stock images and enabling unique, brand-specific illustrations.

Concept Art & Design: Designers and game developers leverage DALL-E for rapid prototyping, producing character concepts, architectural layouts, and futuristic landscapes within seconds.

Education & Research: Educators use DALL-E to create historical recreations, scientific illustrations, and artistic interpretations, making learning more engaging and interactive.

Foundational Concepts

DALL-E operates using deep generative models, specifically a transformer-based architecture trained on vast datasets of images and text pairs. It utilizes contrastive learning to understand semantic relationships and diffusion models to iteratively refine images. Zero-shot learning enables it to generate complex, unseen visuals without prior examples. The model also incorporates natural language processing (NLP) to interpret text prompts effectively. Latent space representation helps DALL-E construct compositions, blend concepts, and refine artistic details based on user input.

Related Terms

Generative Adversarial Networks (GANs): AI models that create synthetic images by training a generator and discriminator in competition (see pg. 240).

Text-to-Image Synthesis: The AI-driven process of generating visual content from textual descriptions.

Stable Diffusion: A deep-learning method for progressive image refinement, used in advanced AI-generated art (see pg. 182).

Common Misconceptions

DALL-E is fully autonomous: While AI generates images, human creativity still guides prompt design.

DALL-E creates copyrighted content: The model generates original images but follows ethical guidelines to prevent plagiarism.

DALL-E always produces perfect results: Some outputs require prompt adjustments to achieve desired artistic accuracy.

Historical Context

DALL-E was introduced by **OpenAI** in **2021** as an extension of GPT-3, applying transformer-based learning to visual generation. DALL-E 2 (**2022**) improved upon image resolution, detail control, and editing capabilities. The model is named after **Salvador Dalí** and **WALL-E**, symbolizing its fusion of surreal creativity and AI automation. **OpenAI**'s advancements in multimodal AI continue to drive innovation in synthetic media and digital artistry.

Practical Implications

DALL-E revolutionizes content creation, design, and storytelling by offering on-demand, high-quality visuals without traditional artistic constraints. In e-commerce, it personalizes product mockups and branding materials. In entertainment, it assists in movie concept art and scene visualization. As AI-generated media evolves, industries must address ethical concerns, copyright issues, and potential biases in AI-created imagery while leveraging DALL-E's capabilities for innovation and efficiency.

Data Cleaning (AI)

Data cleaning is the process of identifying, correcting, or removing errors, inconsistencies, and inaccuracies in datasets to improve data quality. It involves handling duplicate records, missing values, outliers, and formatting issues, ensuring that AI models and analytics produce accurate and reliable insights.

Data cleaning is like preparing ingredients before cooking. Just as a chef removes spoiled food, washes vegetables, and measures ingredients correctly, data scientists remove errors, standardize formats, and fill in missing values to ensure the final dataset is accurate and useful.

Examples

Healthcare Analytics: Data cleaning ensures accurate patient records by correcting misspellings, removing duplicates, and standardizing medical codes, which improves diagnostic predictions and treatment recommendations.

Financial Fraud Detection: Banks clean transaction data by removing duplicate payments, correcting timestamp errors, and filling in missing merchant details, helping fraud detection systems identify suspicious activities more effectively.

Customer Insights in E-commerce: Online retailers clean customer data by removing duplicate accounts, standardizing address formats, and validating contact details, ensuring accurate personalization and targeted marketing strategies.

Foundational Concepts

Data cleaning is based on data validation, transformation, and imputation techniques. Validation ensures data follows predefined rules, such as correct date formats or valid email addresses. Transformation standardizes inconsistencies, like unifying "NY" and "New York." Imputation fills in missing values using statistical methods, machine learning models, or domain knowledge. These processes enhance data integrity, consistency, and usability, making datasets fit for machine learning, business intelligence, and scientific research.

Related Terms

Data Preprocessing: Preparing raw data for analysis by normalization, encoding, and feature selection.

Data Wrangling: The broader process of structuring, reshaping, and cleaning raw data for analysis.

ETL (Extract, Transform, Load): A data pipeline process that includes cleaning and standardizing data before loading it into databases.

Common Misconceptions

Data cleaning is fully automated: While automation helps, human oversight is crucial to handle complex errors.

Clean data is always perfect: Even after cleaning, errors may persist, requiring ongoing validation and updates.

All missing data should be removed: Deleting missing values may bias results, so imputation is often preferred.

Historical Context

Data cleaning became essential with the rise of databases in the **1970s**. As big data analytics and machine learning evolved, companies like **IBM** and **Oracle** introduced data quality frameworks. In the **2010s**, AI-driven data cleaning tools emerged, automating error detection and correction. Today, cloud-based data pipelines and self-learning AI models continually improve the efficiency of data cleaning processes.

Practical Implications

Clean data is crucial for AI, business intelligence, and scientific research. In healthcare, accurate datasets improve predictive analytics and patient safety. In finance, clean transaction records prevent fraud and optimize risk assessments. In marketing, accurate data helps businesses target customers effectively and enhance customer experience. As AI and automation advance, real-time data cleaning will become essential for smart decision-making and operational efficiency.

Data Exploration (AI)

Data exploration is the initial process of analyzing datasets to uncover patterns, detect anomalies, and summarize key characteristics before applying machine learning or statistical modeling. It involves visualization, descriptive statistics, and correlation analysis to ensure the dataset is well understood and structured for further processing.

Data exploration is like reading a map before starting a journey. Just as a traveler examines routes, landmarks, and terrain, data scientists inspect distributions, relationships, and inconsistencies in the data to plan the best approach for analysis and modeling.

Examples

Healthcare Research: Data exploration helps identify trends in patient records, detect missing values, and assess variable distributions, ensuring high-quality inputs for predictive models diagnosing diseases or optimizing treatment plans.

Fraud Detection: Financial institutions use data exploration to analyze transaction patterns, uncover anomalies, and highlight suspicious activities, strengthening fraud prevention strategies in banking and cybersecurity.

E-commerce Analytics: Businesses explore sales data to understand customer behavior, detect seasonal trends, and identify product correlations, optimizing recommendation systems and marketing campaigns.

Foundational Concepts

Data exploration relies on descriptive statistics, data visualization, and feature engineering. Descriptive statistics summarize datasets using mean, median, standard deviation, and skewness. Data visualization techniques like histograms, scatter plots, and heatmaps help uncover relationships and anomalies. Feature engineering involves selecting, transforming, and creating new variables to enhance model performance. The process ensures data integrity, improves model accuracy, and facilitates better decision-making in AI and analytics.

Related Terms

Exploratory Data Analysis (EDA): A systematic approach to visualizing and summarizing data before modeling.

Feature Selection: Identifying the most relevant variables for improving model efficiency and accuracy (see pg. 218 & 222).

Dimensionality Reduction: Techniques like PCA that reduce the number of features while preserving essential information (see pg. 186).

Common Misconceptions

Data exploration is only for large datasets: Even small datasets require preliminary analysis to detect inconsistencies.

It guarantees clean data: Exploration highlights issues but does not fix them; cleaning is a separate step.

Machine learning eliminates the need for exploration: AI models perform best when trained on well-understood and structured data.

Historical Context

Data exploration gained significance in the **1970s** with the rise of exploratory data analysis (EDA), championed by **John Tukey**. As computing power increased, visualization tools and statistical programming languages like **R** and **Python** enhanced data exploration techniques. The big data revolution in the **2010s** further emphasized its importance in data-driven decision-making, predictive analytics, and AI applications.

Practical Implications

Data exploration is essential in AI, business intelligence, and scientific research. In healthcare, it ensures accurate disease prediction models. In finance, it strengthens fraud detection systems by uncovering unusual transactions. In retail, it drives data-informed marketing strategies by understanding customer purchasing behavior. As AI and big data continue evolving, automated data exploration tools will enhance efficiency, ensuring organizations make informed and data-driven decisions.

Data Lake (AI)

A data lake is a centralized repository that stores structured, semi-structured, and unstructured data in its raw format. Unlike traditional databases, data lakes allow organizations to store massive amounts of data without predefined schemas, enabling flexible data processing, analysis, and AI applications.

A data lake is like a vast, unfiltered reservoir where water (data) from multiple sources flows in without restriction. Unlike a processed water supply (structured databases), data lakes keep the raw, unrefined information available, allowing users to extract and process what they need.

Examples

Healthcare Analytics: Medical organizations store patient records, imaging data, and sensor readings in data lakes, enabling AI-driven diagnosis, predictive modeling, and treatment personalization.

Fraud Detection in Finance: Banks consolidate transactions, customer behavior, and security logs in data lakes, using machine learning algorithms to detect fraudulent activities in real-time.

Retail and E-commerce: Companies analyze customer interactions, purchase histories, and supply chain data from data lakes to enhance personalized marketing, inventory management, and demand forecasting.

Foundational Concepts

Data lakes rely on scalable storage, schema-on-read architecture, and distributed computing. Unlike traditional data warehouses, which impose predefined schemas, data lakes enable flexibility in data ingestion. Metadata management, indexing, and governance ensure data remains searchable and accessible. Big data frameworks like Apache Hadoop and cloud-based solutions such as AWS S3 or Azure Data Lake power modern data lake implementations, making them crucial for AI, IoT, and advanced analytics.

Related Terms

Data Warehouse: A structured data storage system optimized for analytical queries and reporting.

ETL (Extract, Transform, Load): A process for moving and structuring data before analysis.

Schema-on-Read: A model where data is structured during analysis rather than at ingestion.

Common Misconceptions

A data lake is just a database: Unlike databases, data lakes store unstructured data in raw form without predefined schemas.

Data lakes replace data warehouses: They complement each other—data lakes store raw data, while warehouses structure it for analytics.

Data lakes are always messy: With proper governance and metadata management, data lakes remain organized and useful.

Historical Context

The term data lake emerged in the **2010s** as businesses sought scalable, flexible alternatives to traditional databases. Early implementations were based on **Apache Hadoop**, later evolving with cloud storage solutions like **Amazon S3** and **Microsoft Azure Data Lake**. The rise of AI, IoT, and big data analytics accelerated data lake adoption, making it a foundational technology for modern data-driven enterprises.

Practical Implications

Data lakes support real-time analytics, AI model training, and large-scale data integration. In healthcare, they enable genomic research and predictive analytics. In finance, they enhance risk assessment and fraud prevention. In marketing, they facilitate customer segmentation and recommendation engines. As AI and big data technologies evolve, data lakes will become even more critical in powering intelligent decision-making and automation across industries.

Data Visualization (AI)

Data visualization is the graphical representation of data using charts, graphs, maps, and other visual tools. It transforms complex datasets into intuitive visuals, enabling users to identify patterns, trends, and insights that would be difficult to discern in raw numerical formats.

Data visualization is like a translator that converts large volumes of raw data into an understandable language. Just as a map helps travelers navigate unfamiliar terrain, visualizations like bar charts and heatmaps help analysts and decision-makers understand relationships and trends within data.

Examples

Healthcare Analytics: Hospitals use data visualization to monitor patient vitals, predict disease outbreaks, and track hospital resource usage in real-time dashboards, enhancing decision-making.

Financial Market Analysis: Investment firms rely on interactive charts and trend graphs to track stock performance, analyze risks, and identify profitable trading opportunities.

Marketing Campaign Optimization: Businesses use heatmaps, customer segmentation charts, and trend analysis graphs to understand consumer behavior and optimize advertising strategies.

Foundational Concepts

Data visualization is built on human perception principles, statistical representation, and interactivity. It leverages color theory, spatial relationships, and data encoding to improve clarity. Descriptive analytics transforms raw data into visuals, while predictive analytics integrates machine learning for forecasting trends. Effective visualizations balance simplicity and detail, ensuring accessibility without oversimplification. Technologies like Python's Matplotlib, D3.js, and Tableau enable scalable, interactive data visualizations for various industries.

Related Terms

Infographics: Static visual representations that summarize information for storytelling.

Business Intelligence (BI): The use of dashboards and reports to extract insights from business data.

Data Dashboard: A real-time interface displaying key performance indicators through visual elements.

Common Misconceptions

Data visualization is only about making data look pretty: Its primary goal is clarity and insight, not aesthetics.

More complex visualizations are always better: Simple, well-designed charts often communicate insights more effectively than intricate, cluttered graphics.

Visualizations don't require data preprocessing: Raw data must be cleaned and structured to create accurate, meaningful visual representations.

Historical Context

The roots of data visualization trace back to **William Playfair**, who invented bar charts and line graphs in the 18th century. In the 19th century, **Florence Nightingale** used data visualizations to advocate for better healthcare. With the rise of computing and big data, modern tools like **Tableau**, **Power BI**, and **Python** libraries revolutionized data storytelling, enabling real-time interactive visualizations.

Practical Implications

Data visualization empowers industries by improving decision-making, fraud detection, and AI model interpretability. In public health, it aids in pandemic tracking. In transportation, it enhances traffic management. In cybersecurity, it helps identify threat patterns. As big data and AI continue to evolve, visualization remains crucial for transforming complex datasets into actionable insights.

Decentralization (BC)

Decentralization in blockchain refers to the distribution of control, decision-making, and record-keeping across a network rather than a central authority. By relying on peer-to-peer networks, cryptographic security, and consensus mechanisms, decentralized systems ensure transparency, security, and resistance to censorship or manipulation.

Decentralization is like a public bulletin board where everyone can post and verify information. Instead of a single administrator controlling the board, all participants validate and maintain records collectively, ensuring no single entity can alter or erase messages unilaterally.

Examples

Cryptocurrencies: Bitcoin and Ethereum operate on decentralized networks, allowing users to exchange value without banks, ensuring censorship resistance and transparency (see pg. 162).

Decentralized Finance (DeFi): DeFi platforms remove intermediaries in lending, borrowing, and trading by using smart contracts, providing global access to financial services.

Decentralized Autonomous Organizations (DAOs): DAOs use blockchain to enable community governance, allowing members to vote on decisions rather than relying on a central authority.

Foundational Concepts

Decentralization relies on blockchain technology, distributed ledger systems, and cryptographic consensus protocols like Proof of Work (PoW) and Proof of Stake (PoS). By eliminating central control, trust is established through cryptographic validation and economic incentives rather than intermediaries. Nodes verify transactions independently, ensuring data integrity. Decentralized networks reduce the risk of single points of failure, making them more secure and resilient against cyberattacks or corruption.

Related Terms

Blockchain: A decentralized, immutable ledger for recording transactions across a distributed network (see pg. 18).

Consensus Mechanism: A protocol ensuring agreement among distributed nodes, like Proof of Work or Proof of Stake (see pg. 146).

Smart Contracts: Self-executing contracts on blockchain, enabling automated transactions and agreements (see pg. 446).

Common Misconceptions

Decentralization means no regulation: While decentralized systems minimize central control, governments and regulatory bodies can still enforce laws on blockchain-based projects.

Decentralized systems are always secure: Security depends on the protocol design, consensus mechanisms, and network participation rather than decentralization alone.

Decentralization eliminates intermediaries entirely: Some blockchain applications still require gateways for fiat transactions, governance, and user access.

Historical Context

The concept of decentralization dates back to early peer-to-peer networks, like **Napster** and **BitTorrent**. The first major blockchain application, **Bitcoin**, was introduced in **2008** by **Satoshi Nakamoto**, pioneering decentralized financial transactions. Later, **Ethereum** expanded decentralization with smart contracts, enabling DeFi, DAOs, and NFTs. Today, blockchain ecosystems continue evolving with layer-2 solutions, decentralized storage, and scalable consensus algorithms.

Practical Implications

Decentralization enhances financial inclusion, transparency, and resistance to censorship. In finance, it enables borderless transactions through DeFi. In voting systems, blockchain ensures tamper-proof elections. In supply chains, decentralization prevents fraud and improves traceability. As industries adopt blockchain, decentralization will continue to transform governance, finance, and digital ownership, reducing reliance on intermediaries.

Deep Learning (DL) (AI)

Deep Learning (DL) is a subset of machine learning that uses artificial neural networks with multiple layers to extract complex patterns from large datasets. Inspired by the human brain, DL models learn hierarchical representations, making them effective for tasks like image recognition, natural language processing, and autonomous systems.

Deep Learning is like a child learning to recognize objects by seeing many examples. At first, the child may misidentify items, but with repeated exposure, they refine their understanding, just as a deep learning model improves accuracy by analyzing vast amounts of data.

Examples

Autonomous Vehicles: DL enables self-driving cars to detect obstacles, pedestrians, and traffic signals by analyzing real-time sensor data.

Medical Diagnosis: Deep learning models assist doctors by detecting tumors in MRI scans, identifying abnormalities, and predicting disease progression.

Voice Assistants: AI-powered assistants like Alexa and Google Assistant use DL to process and understand human speech for accurate responses (see pg. 528).

Foundational Concepts

Deep learning relies on neural networks with multiple hidden layers that learn from vast datasets through backpropagation and gradient descent. Convolutional Neural Networks (CNNs) handle image processing, while Recurrent Neural Networks (RNNs) and Transformers manage sequential data like text and speech. Activation functions, dropout layers, and optimizers refine the learning process, ensuring models generalize well to unseen data. Unlike traditional machine learning, DL requires high computational power and large labeled datasets to perform effectively.

Related Terms

Neural Networks: Computational models inspired by the human brain, forming the basis of deep learning (see pg. 352).

Gradient Descent: Optimization technique that updates model parameters to minimize errors.

Backpropagation: Algorithm used to adjust weights in neural networks by propagating errors backward.

Common Misconceptions

Deep learning is the same as AI: AI is a broad field, while DL is a subset of machine learning focusing on neural networks.

DL models think like humans: Although inspired by the brain, DL lacks reasoning, emotions, and common sense.

More layers always improve performance: Excessive layers can lead to overfitting, making models unreliable on new data.

Historical Context

The foundation of deep learning traces back to perceptrons (**1950s**) and backpropagation (**1980s**). The resurgence began in **2012** with AlexNet, a CNN that revolutionized image classification. Breakthroughs like **Google**'s Transformer (**2017**) and **OpenAI**'s GPT models have expanded deep learning's capabilities in text generation, AI assistants, and more. Advances in GPU computing and big data have fueled DL's growth in real-world applications.

Practical Implications

Deep learning transforms industries by automating medical diagnostics, financial forecasting, fraud detection, and autonomous systems. In healthcare, DL enhances early disease detection. In finance, it identifies market trends and fraudulent transactions. In entertainment, DL personalizes recommendations on platforms like Netflix and Spotify. As DL evolves, it will continue to reshape automation, creativity, and decision-making processes across various domains.

Denial-of-Service (DoS) Attack (CS)

A Denial-of-Service (DoS) attack is a cyber threat in which an attacker overwhelms a server, network, or website with excessive traffic or requests, rendering it unusable for legitimate users. This disruptive attack prevents businesses and individuals from accessing essential services, causing financial and operational damage.

A DoS attack is like a traffic jam on a highway—if an attacker floods the road with unnecessary vehicles, real drivers can't reach their destination. Similarly, a flooded server can't respond to real users, causing downtime and frustration.

Examples

Website Downtime: Attackers target an e-commerce site with excessive requests, preventing customers from making purchases during peak sales hours.

Banking Disruption: A financial institution's online banking system is overwhelmed, preventing customers from checking balances or making transactions.

Government Services Attack: Hackers flood government portals with traffic, disrupting access to tax filings, permits, and critical citizen services.

Foundational Concepts

A DoS attack exploits system vulnerabilities by sending an excessive volume of requests, consuming bandwidth, processing power, and memory. A more advanced variant, the Distributed Denial-of-Service (DDoS) attack, uses botnets—networks of infected devices—to amplify attacks. Rate limiting, traffic filtering, and cloud-based security solutions help mitigate DoS risks. Attack types include volumetric attacks (flooding bandwidth), protocol attacks (exploiting network protocols), and application-layer attacks (overloading specific services).

Related Terms

DDoS Attack: A Distributed Denial-of-Service (DDoS) attack uses multiple devices to amplify a DoS attack.

Botnet: A network of compromised computers used by attackers to execute large-scale cyberattacks.

Firewall: A security system that monitors and filters network traffic to prevent cyber threats.

Common Misconceptions

A DoS attack steals data: Unlike hacking, a DoS attack disrupts services but doesn't steal sensitive data.

Only large businesses are targeted: Small businesses and personal websites are also vulnerable to DoS attacks.

DoS attacks are always illegal: While most are malicious, some cybersecurity teams perform ethical DoS testing to improve security defenses.

Historical Context

The first documented DoS attack occurred in **1999**, targeting the **University of Minnesota**'s network. In **2000**, a 15-year-old hacker launched a massive DDoS attack on **Yahoo!**, temporarily shutting down the search engine. Over time, DoS attacks have evolved, with major incidents targeting **GitHub**, financial institutions, and government websites. Modern cybersecurity solutions now incorporate AI-powered traffic analysis to detect and mitigate attacks.

Practical Implications

DoS attacks pose significant risks to businesses, governments, and online platforms. In finance, they disrupt online banking and stock trading. In healthcare, attacks on hospital systems prevent access to critical patient records. In e-commerce, downtime results in revenue loss and reputational damage. Companies invest in firewalls, cloud-based security, and AI-driven traffic monitoring to detect and block attacks before they cause harm.

Diffusion Model (GenAI)

A Diffusion Model is a generative machine learning technique that transforms random noise into structured data through iterative refinement. It learns to reverse a diffusion process that gradually corrupts data, enabling it to generate high-quality images, videos, and other complex outputs from scratch.

A diffusion model works like developing a photograph in a darkroom. Just as an image slowly emerges from a blurry, featureless background, the model refines noisy data step by step until it produces a sharp, realistic output.

Examples

Image Generation: AI-powered diffusion models, like DALL·E 2, create photorealistic or artistic images from text prompts, revolutionizing digital art and content creation (see pg. 33).

Medical Imaging: Diffusion models generate synthetic medical scans, improving disease diagnosis while preserving patient privacy through synthetic data.

Video and Animation: AI-driven diffusion techniques enhance video upscaling, animation smoothing, and motion synthesis, improving video quality and special effects.

Foundational Concepts

Diffusion models work by learning to reverse a noise-based degradation process using deep neural networks. During training, real data is progressively corrupted with noise, and the model learns to recover the original signal step by step. Denoising autoencoders and score-based generative models guide the reconstruction process. Unlike GANs, which rely on adversarial training, diffusion models use probabilistic techniques such as Markov chains and score matching to iteratively refine outputs, producing high-resolution and diverse results with improved stability.

Related Terms

Generative Adversarial Networks (GANs): Competing neural networks used for image and video generation, often compared with diffusion models (see pg. 240).

Variational Autoencoders (VAEs): A probabilistic approach to generative modeling, focused on encoding and decoding structured data distributions (see pg. 94).

Latent Diffusion Models (LDMs): A computationally efficient variant of diffusion models that reduces dimensionality for faster inference.

Common Misconceptions

Diffusion models are slow: While computationally intensive, newer techniques like Latent Diffusion have improved efficiency.

Diffusion models always outperform GANs: While diffusion models produce higher-quality outputs, GANs can generate results faster for some tasks.

They work only for images: Diffusion models apply to text, video, and even molecular structures, beyond image synthesis.

Historical Context

Diffusion models were first introduced in **2007** with diffusion probabilistic models, but they gained prominence after **Ho et al. (2020)** demonstrated their superior image generation quality. Research from **OpenAI**, **Google Brain**, and **Stability AI** led to **Stable Diffusion**, **Imagen**, and **DALL·E 2**, advancing generative AI. Score-based generative models by **Song et al. (2019)** further refined the process, improving stability and realism in generated outputs.

Practical Implications

Diffusion models redefine creativity and automation in fields like design, entertainment, and healthcare. In advertising, they generate custom marketing visuals. In pharmaceuticals, they simulate molecular structures for drug discovery. In gaming and animation, they assist in creating realistic textures and procedural art. As research advances, efficient diffusion models will accelerate AI-generated content, aiding businesses and individuals in creative tasks while raising ethical concerns about misuse and bias in generated media.

Digital Twin (ANI)

A Digital Twin is a virtual replica of a physical system, process, or object that continuously updates in real time using sensor data, simulations, and machine learning. It enables predictive analytics, optimization, and decision-making across industries like manufacturing, healthcare, and smart cities.

A Digital Twin is like a flight simulator for a real-world object. Just as pilots train in simulated conditions before flying, companies use digital twins to predict failures, test improvements, and optimize performance before making real-world changes.

Examples

Smart Manufacturing: Factories use digital twins to optimize production lines, detecting inefficiencies and predicting equipment failures before they happen.

Healthcare: Digital twins of human organs assist in personalized medicine, allowing doctors to simulate surgeries and treatments with patient-specific data.

Smart Cities: Governments use digital twins to model traffic, energy consumption, and infrastructure, improving urban planning and reducing congestion.

Foundational Concepts

Digital twins rely on real-time sensor data, AI-driven simulations, and predictive analytics to mirror real-world behavior. They use Internet of Things (IoT) devices to collect data, which is then processed by machine learning models for forecasting and decision-making. Cloud computing and edge computing ensure smooth data transmission. By integrating cyber-physical systems, digital twins bridge the gap between physical and virtual worlds, enabling proactive maintenance and efficiency improvements in diverse industries.

Related Terms

Cyber-Physical Systems (CPS): Integrated networks of digital and physical components, crucial for digital twins.

IoT (Internet of Things): Connected devices that transmit real-world data to digital twins (see pg. 288 & 290).

Predictive Maintenance: AI-driven forecasting that prevents equipment failures using digital twin insights.

Common Misconceptions

Digital twins are just 3D models: They are more than static visuals; they continuously evolve with real-world data.

Only large industries use them: Digital twins benefit small businesses, healthcare, and urban planning, not just manufacturing.

They replace human decision-making: Instead, they augment human expertise with data-driven insights.

Historical Context

The concept originated in **NASA**'s Apollo Program (**1970s**) for spacecraft simulations. **Dr. Michael Grieves** (**2002**) formally introduced digital twins in manufacturing. The rise of IoT, AI, and big data in the **2010s** accelerated their adoption, with **GE**, **Siemens**, and **IBM** leading innovations. Today, digital twins power Industry 4.0, smart cities, and AI-driven healthcare.

Practical Implications

Digital twins reduce costs, improve efficiency, and enhance decision-making across industries. In aviation, they predict aircraft failures before flights. In energy, they optimize power grids for sustainability. In healthcare, patient-specific models aid customized treatments. As AI and IoT advance, digital twins will become essential for real-time monitoring, automation, and the future of AI-driven industries.

Dimensionality Reduction (AI)

Dimensionality Reduction is a technique used in machine learning and data analysis to reduce the number of input variables while preserving essential information. By removing redundant or less relevant features, it enhances computational efficiency, prevents overfitting, and improves visualization in high-dimensional datasets.

Dimensionality Reduction is like summarizing a long book into a few key points. Just as a summary retains essential ideas without overwhelming details, this technique compresses data, keeping only the most informative aspects while eliminating noise and redundancy.

Examples

Image Compression: Reduces pixel information while maintaining image clarity, improving storage efficiency and transmission speed.

Fraud Detection: Simplifies financial transaction data by selecting key variables, making it easier to detect unusual patterns.

Genomics Research: Helps identify crucial genetic markers in DNA sequences by reducing thousands of gene expressions to a manageable subset (see pg 242 & 244).

Foundational Concepts

Dimensionality Reduction relies on mathematical transformations and statistical techniques to retain the most meaningful data features. Principal Component Analysis (PCA) converts correlated features into fewer uncorrelated components, while t-Distributed Stochastic Neighbor Embedding (t-SNE) and Uniform Manifold Approximation and Projection (UMAP) visualize high-dimensional data in two or three dimensions. Feature selection techniques remove irrelevant variables, improving model performance. By reducing complexity, this method enhances pattern recognition, clustering, and classification tasks in machine learning.

Related Terms

Feature Engineering: Selecting or creating the most useful variables for a model (see pg 218).

Autoencoders: Neural networks used for learning efficient, compressed representations of data (see pg. 94).

Manifold Learning: A technique for mapping high-dimensional data into a lower-dimensional space while preserving relationships.

Common Misconceptions

It leads to information loss: While some details are removed, the goal is to retain essential patterns.

It is only for visualization: It also improves model performance and computational efficiency.

Only complex models need it: Even simple datasets benefit from noise removal and feature simplification.

Historical Context

Dimensionality Reduction has roots in linear algebra and statistics. PCA, developed by **Karl Pearson (1901)** and later expanded by **Harold Hotelling (1933)**, became widely used in data science. The rise of t-SNE (**2008**) and UMAP (**2018**) advanced nonlinear approaches, making high-dimensional data more interpretable.

Practical Implications

This technique improves efficiency, accuracy, and interpretability in various industries. In finance, it refines credit risk models. In healthcare, it extracts critical patterns from complex medical records. In AI, it accelerates deep learning by simplifying input data. As datasets grow, Dimensionality Reduction will remain crucial for scalable, efficient, and explainable machine learning models.

Distributed Ledger (BC)

A Distributed Ledger is a decentralized digital record of transactions maintained across multiple computers or nodes, eliminating the need for a central authority. It ensures security, transparency, and immutability, making it ideal for financial transactions, supply chains, and smart contracts.

A Distributed Ledger is like a shared notebook where multiple people record transactions simultaneously. Each person verifies the entries, preventing fraud. If one copy is altered, the others remain unchanged, ensuring trust, security, and data integrity.

Examples

Cryptocurrency Transactions: Bitcoin and Ethereum rely on distributed ledgers to maintain a secure, tamper-proof record of financial transactions (see pg. 162).

Supply Chain Management: Companies use distributed ledgers to track product origins, logistics, and authenticity, ensuring transparency in global trade.

Digital Identity Verification: Distributed ledgers store verifiable, decentralized identity credentials, reducing fraud and improving data security.

Foundational Concepts

A Distributed Ledger relies on decentralized consensus mechanisms to validate and synchronize transactions across nodes. Blockchain is the most common form, where transactions are grouped into blocks and linked cryptographically. Consensus algorithms, like Proof of Work (PoW) and Proof of Stake (PoS), prevent tampering. Unlike traditional centralized databases, distributed ledgers enhance security, transparency, and fault tolerance. They support applications in finance, healthcare, and governance, reducing fraud and enabling secure transactions.

Related Terms

Blockchain: A type of distributed ledger where transactions are recorded in linked, immutable blocks (see pg. 18).

Smart Contracts: Self-executing agreements stored on distributed ledgers, automating transactions without intermediaries (see pg. 446).

Consensus Mechanism: The process by which nodes in a distributed ledger agree on the validity of transactions (see pg. 146).

Common Misconceptions

All distributed ledgers use blockchain: Some use alternative structures like Directed Acyclic Graphs (DAGs).

They are only for cryptocurrencies: They are widely used in healthcare, logistics, and legal agreements.

They are completely anonymous: Some ledgers implement identity verification to ensure compliance.

Historical Context

The concept of Distributed Ledgers predates blockchain, with early forms in Byzantine Fault Tolerance (BFT) systems. **Bitcoin**, introduced by **Satoshi Nakamoto** in **2008**, pioneered blockchain-based distributed ledgers. **Ethereum** (**2015**) expanded applications with smart contracts, while organizations like **Hyperledger** and **Corda** developed private distributed ledger solutions.

Practical Implications

Distributed Ledgers enhance data integrity, security, and efficiency across industries. In finance, they enable instant cross-border payments. In healthcare, they store secure patient records. In government, they provide tamper-proof voting systems. Their decentralized nature reduces reliance on intermediaries, making transactions more trustworthy, cost-effective, and transparent.

Distributed Memory (HPC)

Distributed Memory in High-Performance Computing (HPC) refers to a system architecture where each processor has its own private memory, and communication between processors occurs through message passing. It enables parallel computing across multiple nodes, improving scalability for large computational tasks.

Imagine a group of chefs working in different kitchens, each with their own ingredients. Instead of sharing a common pantry, they send notes to request specific ingredients from one another. This represents how distributed memory systems exchange data between processors.

Examples

Scientific Simulations: Large-scale climate models use distributed memory to divide computations across multiple processors, accelerating weather forecasting.

Genomic Data Processing: DNA sequencing involves analyzing vast datasets, where distributed memory systems enable parallel genome alignment and mutation detection (see pg. 244).

Financial Modeling: Stock market predictions and risk analysis use distributed memory to process multiple economic indicators simultaneously for faster decision-making.

Foundational Concepts

A Distributed Memory System relies on message-passing interfaces (MPI) to exchange data between processors. Unlike shared memory systems, where all processors access a common memory pool, distributed memory ensures independent local memory storage for each node. To optimize performance, data partitioning and load balancing distribute workloads efficiently. High-speed interconnects like InfiniBand and Ethernet clusters enable rapid communication. This architecture supports large-scale scientific computing, artificial intelligence, and real-time analytics, reducing processing bottlenecks and enabling high-performance scalability.

Related Terms

Parallel Computing: Breaking down tasks to run simultaneously across multiple processors (see pg. 364).

Message Passing Interface (MPI): A standard for communication in distributed memory systems.

Cluster Computing: A group of interconnected computers working together as a unified system (see pg. 132).

Common Misconceptions

It is the same as shared memory: Distributed memory requires explicit communication via message passing, unlike shared memory.

It is slow due to communication overhead: While data transfer adds latency, optimized algorithms and high-speed networks enhance performance.

Only supercomputers use distributed memory: Many modern cloud computing and big data applications employ distributed memory architectures.

Historical Context

The concept of Distributed Memory Systems emerged in the **1980s** with the rise of parallel supercomputing. Early implementations like **Cray T3D** pioneered message-passing architectures. The Message Passing Interface (MPI) standard, developed in **1994**, became a key framework for managing distributed computing tasks. Advances in grid computing, cloud infrastructure, and AI-driven HPC have since expanded its applications.

Practical Implications

Distributed Memory Systems enable breakthroughs in artificial intelligence, climate modeling, and quantum computing. They power autonomous vehicles by processing vast sensor data in real time. In healthcare, they support drug discovery by simulating molecular interactions at high speeds. Financial institutions use them for risk analysis, enabling instant fraud detection. Their scalability, fault tolerance, and efficiency make them a critical component of modern computing.

Edge Computing (IoT/5G)

Edge Computing is a distributed computing paradigm that processes data closer to the source—at the network edge—rather than relying on a central cloud server. It minimizes latency, enhances real-time decision-making, and optimizes bandwidth, making it crucial for Internet of Things (IoT) and 5G applications.

Imagine a fast-food drive-thru where each restaurant prepares orders locally instead of sending requests to a central kitchen. Customers get their food quicker, just as edge computing reduces the time needed to process and analyze data near its origin.

Examples

Autonomous Vehicles: Edge computing enables real-time sensor processing in self-driving cars, allowing them to detect obstacles and react instantly without relying on cloud latency.

Smart Cities: Traffic lights and surveillance cameras use edge processing to analyze congestion and adjust signals dynamically, improving urban mobility and security.

Industrial IoT (IIoT): Factories deploy edge computing to monitor machine performance and predict failures in real-time, reducing downtime and maintenance costs.

Foundational Concepts

Edge Computing moves computation closer to the data source, reducing latency and dependency on centralized cloud servers. It relies on edge nodes, gateways, and micro data centers to perform local processing. Combined with 5G networks, it enables low-latency applications like autonomous systems, healthcare monitoring, and industrial automation. Key challenges include security, data synchronization, and resource constraints. By distributing workloads efficiently, edge computing enhances real-time analytics, improves network efficiency, and supports AI-driven applications.

Related Terms

Fog Computing: Extends cloud capabilities closer to the edge by using local network infrastructure.

Latency: The delay in data transmission, which edge computing reduces by processing closer to the source.

Internet of Things (IoT): A network of connected devices generating massive real-time data, often requiring edge computing for efficiency (see pg. 288 & 290).

Common Misconceptions

Edge computing replaces cloud computing: Instead, it complements cloud computing by handling time-sensitive tasks locally while offloading complex processing to the cloud.

It is only for IoT: While essential for IoT, edge computing also benefits industries like finance, healthcare, and entertainment.

Edge devices lack security: While edge nodes introduce security challenges, AI-driven threat detection and encryption can mitigate risks.

Historical Context

The evolution of Edge Computing traces back to content delivery networks (CDNs) in the late **1990s**, optimizing web content delivery. With the rise of IoT and 5G, edge computing became essential for low-latency applications. Major developments include **Cisco**'s **Fog Computing** model (**2012**) and **AWS Greengrass** (**2017**), which enabled edge AI processing. Edge infrastructure continues to evolve with AI accelerators and distributed micro-cloud architectures.

Practical Implications

Edge Computing enhances real-time applications across multiple sectors. In healthcare, edge devices process patient vitals for instant anomaly detection. In retail, smart shelves use edge analytics to track inventory efficiently. In gaming, edge servers reduce lag for immersive AR/VR experiences. By reducing bandwidth costs, improving response times, and enabling AI-driven automation, edge computing transforms smart cities, telecommunications, and digital services.

Encryption (CS)

Encryption is a cryptographic process that converts plaintext data into an unreadable format, called ciphertext, to protect it from unauthorized access. Using mathematical algorithms, encryption ensures that only those with a decryption key can access and read the original information, enhancing data security.

Imagine writing a secret message in a special code that only a trusted friend with the key can decode. Even if someone intercepts the message, they won't understand it unless they have the correct key to decrypt it.

Examples

Online Banking: Encryption secures financial transactions, protecting credit card details and login credentials from cybercriminals.

Messaging Apps: Services like WhatsApp and Signal use end-to-end encryption to prevent unauthorized access to private conversations.

Cloud Storage: Companies encrypt stored files, ensuring that only authorized users with decryption keys can access sensitive data.

Foundational Concepts

Encryption relies on cryptographic algorithms to transform plaintext into ciphertext, making data unreadable without a decryption key. Common encryption methods include symmetric encryption, where the same key encrypts and decrypts data, and asymmetric encryption, which uses a public-private key pair. Hashing is another technique for securing data, converting information into a unique, fixed-length output that cannot be reversed. Quantum cryptography is an emerging field aiming to develop even stronger encryption techniques resistant to future computational threats.

Related Terms

Symmetric Encryption: Uses the same key for encryption and decryption, requiring secure key exchange (see pg. 194).

Asymmetric Encryption: Uses a public key to encrypt and a private key to decrypt, enhancing security (see pg. 194).

Hashing: Converts data into a fixed-length value that cannot be reversed, often used in password security.

Common Misconceptions

Encryption makes data unbreakable: While encryption significantly enhances security, weak encryption algorithms or poor key management can be exploited.

Only criminals use encryption: Encryption protects everyday users, businesses, and governments, ensuring data confidentiality.

Encryption slows down performance: Modern encryption algorithms are optimized for efficiency, with minimal impact on speed for most applications.

Historical Context

Encryption dates back to ancient times, with the **Caesar** cipher being one of the earliest methods. **The Enigma machine**, used in **World War II**, demonstrated advanced encryption techniques. The Data Encryption Standard (DES) emerged in the **1970s**, later replaced by the Advanced Encryption Standard (AES) for stronger security. Public-key cryptography, introduced by **Whitfield Diffie** and **Martin Hellman** (**1976**), revolutionized secure communication. Today, post-quantum cryptography is being developed to counter future threats from quantum computing.

Practical Implications

Encryption is essential in securing financial transactions, healthcare records, and government communications. It ensures confidentiality in digital communication, prevents data breaches, and supports secure authentication mechanisms. In e-commerce, encryption protects payment information, while in cybersecurity, it safeguards sensitive corporate and personal data from unauthorized access. As threats evolve, encryption technologies continue to advance, integrating with blockchain, AI-driven security, and quantum-resistant cryptographic solutions to maintain robust protection in the digital world.

Energy Efficiency (CET)

Energy efficiency refers to the optimal use of energy to perform a function while minimizing waste. It involves reducing energy consumption without compromising performance, often through advanced technologies, improved design, and optimized processes, leading to cost savings and environmental sustainability.

Energy efficiency is like using an insulated water bottle instead of a regular cup. The insulation helps keep the liquid hot or cold for longer, reducing the need for reheating or refrigeration, just as energy-efficient systems consume less power for the same output.

Examples

Smart Buildings: Automated lighting, heating, and cooling systems use real-time data to optimize energy use, lowering electricity costs and carbon footprints.

Electric Vehicles (EVs): EVs employ regenerative braking, which converts kinetic energy into stored energy, reducing overall power consumption and increasing driving range.

Industrial Optimization: Factories use energy-efficient motors and AI-driven monitoring systems to detect inefficiencies and reduce energy waste in manufacturing processes.

Foundational Concepts

Energy efficiency is guided by principles like thermodynamics, power conversion efficiency, and demand-side management. Technologies such as heat recovery systems, LED lighting, and smart grids enhance efficiency by reducing energy loss. Load balancing techniques in energy grids ensure that power demand is met with minimal waste. Advances in machine learning and AI contribute by optimizing energy usage in real-time monitoring systems, reducing excess consumption. As renewable energy sources grow, efficiency improvements become crucial in making solar, wind, and hydropower more viable.

Related Terms

Renewable Energy: Energy from natural sources like solar, wind, and hydro that replenish over time.

Smart Grid: An electricity network that intelligently distributes energy based on demand, improving efficiency (see pg. 450).

Demand Response: A strategy to adjust energy consumption dynamically, reducing strain on the grid.

Common Misconceptions

Energy efficiency is the same as energy conservation: While conservation reduces usage, efficiency focuses on using less energy for the same output.

Only new technology improves efficiency: While advanced systems help, better habits, insulation, and maintenance also enhance efficiency.

Renewable energy eliminates the need for efficiency: Even with clean energy sources, efficiency remains critical for grid stability and cost reduction.

Historical Context

Efforts to improve energy efficiency date back to the Industrial Revolution, with innovations in steam engines and electricity use. The **1970s** energy crisis accelerated global efficiency policies, leading to the adoption of building insulation standards and fuel economy regulations. Advances in LED lighting, smart appliances, and electric vehicles have significantly improved efficiency. **The Paris Agreement (2015)** emphasized the need for efficiency to meet climate goals, prompting governments and industries to invest in energy-saving technologies.

Practical Implications

Energy efficiency plays a vital role in climate change mitigation, cost reduction, and energy security. In residential sectors, efficient appliances and smart meters help consumers save money. In transportation, hybrid and electric vehicles reduce fuel dependency. In industries, AI-driven predictive maintenance prevents energy losses. As clean energy adoption grows, improving efficiency in energy storage, distribution, and consumption remains crucial for a sustainable and resilient energy future.

Entanglement (QC)

Entanglement is a quantum phenomenon where two or more particles become linked, meaning their states remain correlated regardless of distance. A measurement on one particle instantly affects the state of the other, defying classical notions of locality and communication speed.

Entanglement is like pairing two magic dice that always land on the same number, no matter how far apart they are. If you roll one in New York and the other in Tokyo, their outcomes remain synchronized, even though there is no visible connection between them.

Examples

Quantum Cryptography: Quantum key distribution (QKD) relies on entanglement to create secure encryption keys. If an eavesdropper tries to intercept the key, the entanglement breaks, alerting the users.

Quantum Computing: Entangled qubits allow for parallel processing at unprecedented speeds, enabling computations that classical computers struggle to perform efficiently, such as simulating molecular interactions for drug discovery (see pg. 52).

Quantum Teleportation: By using entangled particles, information can be transferred from one location to another without physically moving the matter itself, potentially revolutionizing data transmission (see pg. 198).

Foundational Concepts

Entanglement is a core principle of quantum mechanics, governed by superposition and non-locality. When particles interact, their wavefunctions become correlated, meaning their states are intrinsically linked. This violates classical intuition but is supported by Bell's theorem, which experimentally confirms the non-locality of quantum mechanics. Quantum decoherence occurs when entanglement is lost due to environmental interactions. Researchers use quantum entanglement to enhance quantum communication, computation, and sensing, with applications in quantum internet and secure encryption.

Related Terms

Superposition: A quantum system exists in multiple states simultaneously until measured.

Quantum Key Distribution (QKD): A secure encryption method that uses entanglement to prevent eavesdropping.

Quantum Teleportation: The transfer of quantum information using entangled particles, without physically moving them.

Common Misconceptions

Entanglement enables faster-than-light communication: While measurement affects entangled particles instantly, no usable information is transmitted faster than light.

Entanglement is fragile and always short-lived: While it is sensitive to interference, advanced techniques like quantum error correction help preserve it longer.

Entangled particles remain linked forever: External influences can cause decoherence, breaking the connection over time.

Historical Context

Albert Einstein, **Boris Podolsky**, and **Nathan Rosen** introduced entanglement in **1935** as the **EPR paradox**, challenging quantum mechanics. **John Bell** later formulated **Bell's theorem**, proving that entanglement was real and experimentally verifiable. **Alain Aspect**'s **1982** experiments confirmed quantum entanglement's existence, laying the groundwork for modern quantum technologies. Recent advancements in quantum computing and quantum networks leverage entanglement for ultra-secure communication and high-speed computations.

Practical Implications

Entanglement is transforming cryptography, enabling secure communication channels that prevent data breaches. In quantum computing, entangled qubits process massive datasets exponentially faster than classical computers. In telecommunications, entanglement paves the way for a quantum internet, where information is exchanged with unprecedented security. As research progresses, entanglement could revolutionize data encryption, cloud security, and high-speed networking, making digital systems significantly more robust against cyber threats.

Environmental Monitoring (ANI)

Environmental monitoring is the systematic collection and analysis of data related to natural ecosystems, air quality, water resources, and climate conditions. It uses sensor networks, remote sensing, and AI-driven analytics to track environmental changes, assess risks, and support sustainable policies.

Environmental monitoring is like a doctor checking a patient's vital signs—just as doctors measure heart rate and temperature to detect health issues, environmental monitoring tracks pollution levels, biodiversity, and climate changes to prevent ecological damage and ensure sustainability.

Examples

Air Quality Monitoring: Smart sensors in cities track pollutants like CO_2, NO_2, and PM2.5, helping authorities issue alerts and reduce public health risks from air pollution.

Water Resource Management: Satellite-based monitoring detects water pollution, illegal waste dumping, and changes in river flows, aiding in the conservation of drinking water and marine ecosystems.

Climate Change Analysis: AI-powered climate models analyze deforestation, glacial melt, and greenhouse gas emissions, guiding global policies on reducing carbon footprints and mitigating climate impact.

Foundational Concepts

Environmental monitoring integrates sensor networks, satellite imagery, and machine learning models to assess ecological health. Remote sensing technologies, such as LiDAR and multispectral imaging, provide real-time data for tracking land use changes and pollution. IoT-based sensor systems collect localized data on temperature, humidity, and chemical contaminants, while predictive analytics forecast environmental risks like hurricanes and wildfires. Governments and research organizations use big data analytics and cloud computing to store and process environmental datasets, supporting climate action initiatives.

Related Terms

Remote Sensing: The use of satellites or drones to collect environmental data from a distance.

IoT Sensors: Networked devices that collect real-time environmental data on pollution, temperature, and water quality (see pg. 288 & 290).

Climate Modeling: AI-driven simulations that predict climate change impacts based on historical and real-time environmental data.

Common Misconceptions

Environmental monitoring is only for scientists: While experts analyze the data, modern apps allow citizens to track air pollution and weather patterns in real time.

It only measures pollution: Environmental monitoring also tracks wildlife populations, forest coverage, and climate change indicators like ice melt and temperature shifts.

It provides instant solutions: While it detects environmental threats, policy changes and mitigation efforts take time to implement based on the collected data.

Historical Context

Environmental monitoring began with early weather observations and manual water quality testing. The rise of satellite technology in the **1970s**, such as **NASA**'s **Landsat** program, revolutionized data collection on deforestation and ocean health. **The Kyoto Protocol (1997)** and **The Paris Agreement (2015)** emphasized the need for global climate monitoring. Recent advances in AI, IoT, and big data analytics now enable real-time tracking of greenhouse gas emissions, urban pollution, and biodiversity loss, enhancing global sustainability efforts.

Practical Implications

Environmental monitoring is crucial for urban planning, agriculture, and disaster response. Cities optimize transportation and industrial regulations using air quality data, while farmers adjust irrigation and pesticide use based on soil and climate conditions. AI-powered early warning systems predict extreme weather events, minimizing damage from hurricanes, wildfires, and floods. By integrating real-time data with policy decisions, industries and governments can proactively combat climate change, pollution, and ecosystem degradation, ensuring a sustainable future.

Error Minimization (AI)

Error minimization refers to the process of reducing inaccuracies or deviations in computational models, machine learning algorithms, or real-world systems. It employs mathematical optimization, feedback loops, and statistical techniques to enhance accuracy, reliability, and efficiency in decision-making, predictions, and automated processes.

Error minimization is like a golfer adjusting their swing—after each shot, they refine their technique based on feedback, gradually improving accuracy and reducing mistakes to achieve a more precise result over time.

Examples

Machine Learning Optimization: AI models use gradient descent to adjust parameters, reducing prediction errors and improving accuracy in applications like speech recognition and medical diagnosis.

Quality Control in Manufacturing: Automated systems detect defects in assembly lines, adjusting machinery settings to minimize product errors and ensure consistent quality.

Financial Forecasting: Banks and hedge funds refine risk models by analyzing past errors in stock market predictions, improving investment strategies and fraud detection systems.

Foundational Concepts

Error minimization relies on optimization algorithms, loss functions, and feedback loops. In machine learning, techniques like backpropagation and stochastic gradient descent adjust neural network weights to reduce prediction errors. Statistical methods, such as least squares regression and Bayesian inference, refine models by minimizing discrepancies between observed and expected values. Control systems in robotics and automation use proportional-integral-derivative (PID) controllers to correct deviations in movement or output. Error-correcting codes in digital communication ensure data accuracy by detecting and fixing transmission errors.

Related Terms

Gradient Descent: An optimization technique that adjusts model parameters to minimize errors in machine learning.

Loss Function: A mathematical function that quantifies the difference between predicted and actual values in AI models see pg. 310).

Feedback Loop: A system mechanism that continuously corrects errors through iterative adjustments (see pg. 228).

Common Misconceptions

Error minimization eliminates all mistakes: While it reduces inaccuracies, some level of error is inevitable due to noise and uncertainty.

It applies only to AI: Error minimization is used in engineering, finance, medicine, and logistics, improving precision across diverse fields.

More complex models always minimize errors better: Overfitting occurs when models become too complex, reducing generalization and leading to poor real-world performance.

Historical Context

The concept of error minimization dates back to least squares regression introduced by **Carl Friedrich Gauss (1809)** for astronomical predictions. **Gradient descent (1951)** became a cornerstone of machine learning and AI. **Claude Shannon**'s information theory (**1948**) pioneered error correction in digital communication. In the **1980s** and **1990s**, backpropagation revolutionized neural networks, making AI more effective. Today, error minimization is crucial in deep learning, robotics, and precision medicine, ensuring accuracy in cutting-edge technologies.

Practical Implications

Error minimization drives AI reliability, automation precision, and decision-making accuracy. In healthcare, it refines medical imaging analysis, reducing false diagnoses. Self-driving cars rely on error minimization to improve navigation and obstacle detection. Energy-efficient smart grids reduce power losses by adjusting voltage fluctuations. By continuously refining models and processes, error minimization enhances performance, reduces costs, and increases safety in sectors ranging from aviation to cybersecurity, shaping the future of AI-driven innovation.

Ethical AI (RAI)

Ethical AI refers to the development and deployment of artificial intelligence systems that align with human values, fairness, transparency, accountability, and privacy. It ensures AI minimizes biases, prevents harm, and respects fundamental rights, promoting trust and fairness in decision-making across various applications.

Ethical AI is like a responsible driver following road rules—just as a car must navigate traffic safely, AI must operate within ethical guidelines to prevent harm, ensure fairness, and make unbiased decisions for society's benefit.

Examples

Healthcare Decision-Making: AI models diagnosing diseases must be free from racial or gender biases to ensure accurate, fair treatment recommendations for all patients.

Hiring Algorithms: Ethical AI in recruitment ensures fair candidate evaluation, eliminating discrimination in hiring processes and promoting diversity.

Autonomous Vehicles: Self-driving cars must follow ethical frameworks to prioritize safety, legal compliance, and fairness when making split-second driving decisions.

Foundational Concepts

Ethical AI is guided by principles such as fairness, transparency, accountability, and privacy. Fairness ensures AI decisions are unbiased and equitable. Transparency requires AI models to be explainable and interpretable. Accountability holds organizations responsible for AI decisions, preventing harm or misinformation. Privacy protects user data through secure algorithms and encryption. Ethical AI frameworks are influenced by philosophy, law, and computer science, balancing innovation with societal welfare. Regulatory policies and ethical guidelines help ensure AI aligns with human rights and public interests.

Related Terms

AI Bias: Systematic errors in AI decision-making caused by skewed or unrepresentative training data (see pg. 104).

Explainable AI (XAI): AI systems designed for human interpretability and transparency in decision-making (see pg. 27).

AI Ethics Framework: Guidelines ensuring AI operates within ethical and regulatory standards (see pg. 204).

Common Misconceptions

Ethical AI is bias-free: While ethical AI reduces bias, completely eliminating it remains challenging due to human-influenced training data.

Ethical AI is only about fairness: It also includes privacy, security, and accountability to ensure AI systems are trustworthy.

Regulating AI slows innovation: Ethical AI encourages responsible innovation, preventing harmful consequences while ensuring AI benefits society.

Historical Context

AI ethics discussions emerged in the 20th century, influenced by **Isaac Asimov**'s **Three Laws of Robotics (1942)**. The **2010s** saw major AI bias cases, such as facial recognition failing to identify darker skin tones. Governments and organizations introduced AI ethics frameworks, including **EU AI Act (2021)** and **IEEE AI Ethics Guidelines**. Companies like **Google** and **Microsoft** established AI ethics committees to prevent misuse and ensure accountability. Ethical AI remains a central theme in AI governance and policy discussions worldwide.

Practical Implications

Ethical AI is crucial in healthcare, finance, law enforcement, and social media, ensuring AI decisions are trustworthy and fair. In finance, ethical AI prevents discriminatory lending. In social media, it reduces misinformation and harmful content promotion. In criminal justice, AI-based sentencing must be free from racial bias. Ethical AI fosters public trust, regulatory compliance, and responsible innovation, ensuring that AI serves humanity rather than exacerbating inequalities.

Evaluation Metric (AI)

An evaluation metric is a quantitative measure used to assess the performance, accuracy, or effectiveness of an AI model, machine learning algorithm, or computational system. It provides a standardized way to compare models, optimize their performance, and ensure reliability in classification, regression, and ranking tasks.

An evaluation metric is like a grading system for students—just as a teacher uses scores to assess student performance in different subjects, AI models are evaluated using different metrics, such as accuracy, precision, recall, or F1-score, depending on the specific task.

Examples

Spam Detection: AI email filters use precision and recall to evaluate how accurately spam messages are identified while minimizing false positives.

Medical Diagnosis: In disease prediction models, F1-score and sensitivity ensure that critical conditions like cancer are correctly diagnosed without excessive false negatives.

Chatbot Performance: Perplexity and BLEU scores measure language models' accuracy, ensuring chatbot responses are fluent, relevant, and aligned with human-like conversation.

Foundational Concepts

Evaluation metrics depend on the type of machine learning model. Classification metrics, such as accuracy, precision, recall, and F1-score, assess models that categorize data. Regression metrics, including Mean Squared Error (MSE) and R^2 score, evaluate numerical predictions. Ranking metrics, like Mean Average Precision (MAP), assess recommendation systems. Metrics are crucial for hyperparameter tuning, model selection, and ensuring that AI systems make reliable predictions while avoiding overfitting or biases that may affect real-world performance.

Related Terms

Loss Function: Measures error between predicted and actual values, guiding model optimization (see pg. 310).

Confusion Matrix: A table used in classification tasks to visualize true positives, false positives, true negatives, and false negatives.

Cross-Validation: A technique to evaluate model performance by splitting data into training and test sets (see pg. 160).

Common Misconceptions

Accuracy is always the best metric: In imbalanced datasets, precision, recall, or F1-score may be more important than accuracy.

A single metric is enough: Different tasks require different metrics—for example, MSE for regression and F1-score for classification.

Evaluation is only done once: Continuous monitoring and retraining ensure that AI models maintain performance over time.

Historical Context

Evaluation metrics have evolved with machine learning advancements. Statistical measures like R^2 (coefficient of determination) were used in early regression models. Precision and recall emerged in information retrieval in the **1970s**. The F1-score was introduced to balance these metrics. With deep learning, new metrics such as BLEU for language models and IoU (Intersection over Union) for object detection have gained prominence. As AI applications grow, more specialized evaluation methods are continuously developed.

Practical Implications

Evaluation metrics ensure AI systems are fair, reliable, and unbiased. In finance, they optimize fraud detection models to minimize false alarms. In healthcare, they guide AI diagnosis accuracy to prevent misdiagnosis. Autonomous vehicles rely on real-time evaluation metrics to ensure safe navigation. Choosing the right metric prevents biased decisions and ensures ethical, data-driven AI systems that positively impact industries ranging from cybersecurity to natural language processing (NLP).

Exoskeleton (RT)

An exoskeleton is a wearable robotic system designed to enhance human strength, mobility, or endurance. These devices can be powered or passive, providing assistance in rehabilitation, industrial work, and military applications by reducing physical strain and compensating for muscle or skeletal impairments.

An exoskeleton is like power-assisted bicycle gears—just as gears amplify a cyclist's pedaling force, an exoskeleton enhances a person's physical abilities, allowing them to walk, lift, or move with less effort, especially when recovering from injury or performing strenuous tasks.

Examples

Medical Rehabilitation: Robotic exoskeletons help paralyzed patients regain mobility by providing powered assistance for walking and muscle therapy.

Industrial Workforce: Exoskeletons reduce fatigue and injury risks for workers in physically demanding jobs, such as lifting heavy objects in warehouses and factories.

Military Applications: Soldiers wear powered exoskeletons to enhance endurance, carry heavy loads, and reduce strain during long missions in combat zones.

Foundational Concepts

Exoskeletons rely on biomechanics, artificial intelligence, and sensor feedback to adapt to user movements. Powered exoskeletons use electric actuators, pneumatic systems, or hydraulic mechanisms to enhance physical force, while passive exoskeletons provide mechanical support without motors. Electromyographic (EMG) sensors detect muscle signals to enable real-time assistance, and machine learning algorithms optimize movement patterns. Integration with wearable AI and IoT improves user experience by personalizing motion assistance and reducing energy consumption.

Related Terms

Biomechatronics: The study of mechanical systems interacting with human physiology.

Wearable Robotics: Robotics integrated into clothing or accessories to assist movement.

Neuroprosthetics: AI-driven implants or wearable devices that enhance motor function.

Common Misconceptions

Exoskeletons replace human movement: They assist rather than replace natural movement, allowing users to regain or enhance mobility.

Only used for disabilities: They are widely used in industries, military, and sports for strength augmentation.

Heavy and cumbersome: Modern exoskeletons are lightweight, ergonomic, and adaptable for comfort and usability.

Historical Context

Early exoskeleton research began in the **1960s** with military projects like **Hardiman**, developed by **General Electric**. In the **1990s**, medical rehabilitation applications gained traction, leading to devices like **ReWalk** and **Ekso Bionics**. Advancements in AI, robotics, and lightweight materials have significantly improved exoskeletons, making them more efficient, wearable, and accessible in various fields.

Practical Implications

Exoskeletons are transforming healthcare, industry, and defense. In healthcare, they assist stroke survivors and spinal cord injury patients in regaining movement. Factories and warehouses integrate exoskeletons to prevent injuries and boost productivity. The military uses them to improve soldier endurance and combat effectiveness. As AI-powered wearable robotics evolve, exoskeletons will play a crucial role in enhancing human capabilities and reducing physical strain across multiple sectors.

Exploitation (AI)

Exploitation in artificial intelligence and machine learning refers to the process of maximizing performance by leveraging known information. It involves selecting the best-known option based on past experiences or data rather than exploring new possibilities, ensuring efficiency and optimal outcomes in decision-making systems.

Exploitation is like always ordering your favorite meal at a restaurant. Since you already know it tastes good, you don't take the risk of trying a new dish. Similarly, AI systems use exploitation to rely on proven strategies rather than experimenting with unknown alternatives.

Examples

Online Recommendation Systems: Streaming platforms exploit user preferences to suggest similar movies or songs based on past choices, ensuring engagement (see pg. 404).

Autonomous Vehicles: AI in self-driving cars exploits proven driving patterns to navigate safely, prioritizing routes with minimal risk over unknown roads.

Financial Trading Algorithms: AI models exploit historical market trends to maximize investment returns, making data-driven decisions to optimize profits.

Foundational Concepts

Exploitation is a key concept in reinforcement learning, where AI selects actions that yield the highest known rewards rather than testing new strategies. It contrasts with exploration, which involves seeking new knowledge that may lead to better results in the long term. The exploitation-exploration tradeoff is crucial in multi-armed bandit problems, where algorithms balance using existing knowledge with discovering new opportunities. Many AI applications, including deep learning, game theory, and optimization models, rely on balancing these two approaches to improve decision-making.

Related Terms

Exploration: The process of trying new actions to discover better alternatives (see pg. 212).

Reinforcement Learning: A machine learning framework where agents learn by trial and error (see pg. 410).

Multi-Armed Bandit Problem: A scenario balancing exploitation and exploration to maximize rewards.

Common Misconceptions

Exploitation is always better: Over-reliance on exploitation can lead to suboptimal decisions when better alternatives remain undiscovered.

Exploration is unnecessary: Without exploration, AI systems may become stagnant, failing to adapt to changing environments or new data.

Exploitation means unethical AI: While the term "exploitation" can have negative connotations, in AI, it refers to optimizing decisions, not unethical behavior.

Historical Context

The exploitation-exploration dilemma originates from probability theory and decision sciences, first formalized in the multi-armed bandit problem. Early work in reinforcement learning, including Q-learning in the **1980s**, highlighted how AI systems balance risk and reward. In modern AI, **DeepMind's AlphaGo** and **OpenAI's** gaming AI showcase how exploitation of learned strategies leads to high-performance decision-making.

Practical Implications

Exploitation enhances AI efficiency in healthcare, finance, and robotics. AI-powered medical diagnosis systems exploit known symptom-disease correlations for faster patient treatment. Chatbots and virtual assistants exploit learned conversations for improving responses. In industrial automation, robots exploit predefined patterns to enhance production accuracy. The challenge lies in ensuring a balance between short-term gains and long-term adaptability, as over-exploitation can lead to rigidity and inefficiency in dynamic environments.

Exploration (AI)

Exploration in artificial intelligence and machine learning refers to the process of seeking new information, testing unfamiliar actions, and discovering better alternatives. It contrasts with exploitation, which focuses on maximizing immediate rewards. Exploration is crucial for adaptability, innovation, and long-term optimization in decision-making systems.

Exploration is like trying different routes on your way to work instead of taking the familiar path. While the known road is reliable, testing new routes may reveal shortcuts or more efficient paths. AI systems explore to discover better strategies and improve decision-making over time.

Examples

Autonomous Robotics: Self-learning robots explore new movement patterns to navigate unfamiliar environments, improving agility and problem-solving.

Drug Discovery: AI-driven exploration in pharmaceutical research tests novel molecular combinations, identifying potential breakthrough medicines faster (see pg. 82).

Online Advertising: AI explores different ad placements, creatives, and audience segments, learning which approach drives higher engagement and conversion rates.

Foundational Concepts

Exploration is essential in reinforcement learning, where AI experiments with new actions to improve future performance. The exploration-exploitation tradeoff ensures a balance between leveraging known strategies and seeking better options. AI algorithms, such as epsilon-greedy policies and Thompson sampling, regulate exploration rates. Exploration also plays a role in multi-armed bandit problems, game theory, and deep learning optimization. Without exploration, AI systems risk stagnation, failing to adapt to dynamic environments and evolving challenges.

Related Terms

Exploitation: Using known strategies to maximize immediate rewards (see pg. 210).

Reinforcement Learning: AI learning by trial and error through rewards and penalties (see pg. 410).

Multi-Armed Bandit Problem: A framework balancing exploration and exploitation to maximize performance.

Common Misconceptions

Exploration is random: AI exploration is often structured and guided by probability-based algorithms.

Exploration is inefficient: While exploration may temporarily reduce efficiency, it improves long-term performance.

Exploration and exploitation are separate: In practice, AI systems balance both, dynamically adjusting the ratio for optimal decision-making.

Historical Context

The exploration-exploitation dilemma was first studied in decision theory and probability models, particularly in the multi-armed bandit problem. Early reinforcement learning research in the **1980s** and **1990s**, including Q-learning and **Monte Carlo** methods, emphasized the importance of exploration. Modern AI applications, such as **DeepMind**'s **AlphaGo** and **OpenAI**'s gaming models, showcase how exploration helps AI surpass human capabilities.

Practical Implications

Exploration is vital in autonomous systems, finance, and industrial automation. AI-powered fraud detection models explore anomalies in transactions, improving security. In personalized learning, AI explores different teaching methods to optimize student engagement. Supply chain AI explores alternative logistics strategies, enhancing efficiency. While pure exploration can be risky, controlled exploration strategies help AI continuously learn, adapt, and innovate across industries.

Facial Recognition (ANI)

Facial recognition is a biometric technology that identifies or verifies individuals by analyzing facial features from images or videos. It uses computer vision and machine learning to map unique facial characteristics, comparing them against a database for authentication, security, and identification.

Facial recognition is like a digital fingerprint scanner for faces. Just as a fingerprint scanner identifies a person based on unique ridges and patterns, facial recognition analyzes key facial points such as eye spacing, jawline, and nose structure to confirm identity.

Examples

Security & Surveillance: Airports and law enforcement use facial recognition to identify individuals in crowds, detect threats, and enhance security.

Smartphone Authentication: Many smartphones use facial recognition to unlock devices securely and verify payments, providing a seamless authentication experience.

Retail & Marketing: Stores implement facial recognition to analyze customer demographics, personalize ads, and prevent theft by recognizing repeat visitors or known shoplifters.

Foundational Concepts

Facial recognition relies on deep learning algorithms, convolutional neural networks (CNNs), and feature extraction techniques to identify unique facial landmarks. The face detection stage locates faces, while feature mapping converts facial characteristics into numerical data. The system then compares this data to stored profiles, calculating similarity scores for verification or identification. While effective, facial recognition is prone to biases, requiring ethical considerations in deployment. Privacy concerns, data security, and regulatory compliance remain key challenges in its widespread adoption.

Related Terms

Computer Vision: AI's ability to interpret and process visual data from the environment.

Biometric Authentication: Using unique biological traits like fingerprints or iris scans for identity verification.

Deep Learning: A subset of AI that enables machines to learn patterns in complex datasets, crucial for facial recognition (see pg. 178).

Common Misconceptions

Facial recognition is always accurate: While highly effective, it can struggle with poor lighting, partial occlusions, or racial bias in datasets.

It recognizes faces in real-time: Processing speed varies depending on the algorithm, hardware, and database size.

All facial recognition is intrusive: It can be privacy-conscious when implemented with user consent and data encryption.

Historical Context

Facial recognition dates back to the **1960s**, when **Woody Bledsoe**, **Helen Chan Wolf**, and **Charles Bisson** developed early face-matching algorithms. Advancements in machine learning and neural networks in the **2000s** and **2010s** led to widespread adoption in law enforcement, consumer electronics, and commercial applications. In **2017**, **Apple**'s **Face ID** revolutionized facial authentication, making it mainstream. Concerns over privacy laws, ethical AI, and surveillance have led to increasing government regulations worldwide.

Practical Implications

Facial recognition is transforming security, healthcare, and financial services. It enables contactless authentication, fraud prevention, and AI-driven customer interactions. In healthcare, it helps monitor patient emotions and identify genetic disorders. However, concerns over mass surveillance, racial bias, and personal data security demand stricter AI governance. Companies must balance innovation with ethical responsibility, ensuring fairness, transparency, and compliance with privacy regulations like GDPR and CCPA.

Fairness (RAI)

Fairness in Responsible AI ensures that machine learning models and automated decision-making systems treat all individuals equitably, avoiding bias based on race, gender, socioeconomic status, or other protected attributes. It involves bias detection, ethical AI design, and transparency to ensure inclusive, unbiased, and just AI-driven decisions.

Fairness in AI is like a referee in a soccer match—it must treat all players equally, applying the same rules regardless of the team or individual. If biased, it could unfairly favor one side, distorting the outcome of the game.

Examples

Hiring Algorithms: AI-driven hiring tools must ensure fair candidate selection by eliminating bias against gender, ethnicity, or age. Otherwise, historical hiring biases could be amplified in recruitment decisions.

Loan Approval Systems: AI models assessing creditworthiness should not unfairly disadvantage certain demographic groups by disproportionately rejecting applicants from marginalized communities due to biased training data.

Facial Recognition Systems: Many facial recognition algorithms exhibit racial bias, performing better on lighter-skinned individuals. Ensuring fairness means training models on diverse datasets to improve accuracy across all racial groups (see pg. 214).

Foundational Concepts

Fairness in AI is guided by algorithmic transparency, bias mitigation, and ethical AI governance. Bias can emerge from historical data, biased feature selection, or imbalanced training sets, leading to discrimination. Fair AI development incorporates techniques like reweighting datasets, adversarial debiasing, and fairness-aware algorithms to minimize discriminatory outcomes. Regulatory frameworks such as GDPR and AI ethics principles emphasize the need for explainability, accountability, and non-discriminatory AI decision-making. Fairness in AI requires a balance between accuracy, interpretability, and social impact to prevent harm and promote equitable outcomes.

Related Terms

Bias Mitigation: Techniques for reducing algorithmic bias in AI models to ensure fairness (see pg. 104).

Explainability: The ability to understand and interpret how AI models make decisions (see pg. 27).

Algorithmic Transparency: The practice of making AI decision-making processes clear and understandable (see pg. 502).

Common Misconceptions

Fair AI is always unbiased: Even fairness-aware models can have some level of bias, requiring continuous monitoring.

Removing sensitive attributes removes bias: Bias can persist in correlated variables even when race or gender is excluded.

Fairness and accuracy are always conflicting: Proper fairness strategies can improve both ethical AI performance and model robustness.

Historical Context

Concerns about fairness in AI grew in the **2010s**, when studies revealed racial and gender biases in AI-driven hiring, healthcare, and law enforcement systems. Landmark research from **MIT**, **Google AI**, and AI ethics organizations exposed disparities in facial recognition accuracy and credit-scoring systems. The **European Union AI Act** and U.S. AI regulations now emphasize accountability, non-discrimination, and transparency in AI systems. Organizations like **OpenAI** and the **Partnership on AI** promote fairness standards for AI governance.

Practical Implications

Fair AI ensures equitable decision-making in hiring, lending, criminal justice, and healthcare. In education, fairness-aware AI tailors personalized learning experiences without disadvantaging specific student groups. In law enforcement, fairness prevents AI surveillance from disproportionately targeting minorities. Businesses using AI must implement bias audits, fairness metrics, and diverse training datasets to ensure compliance with AI fairness regulations. Ethical AI practices enhance trust, inclusivity, and accountability, benefiting both organizations and society.

Feature Engineering (AI)

Feature Engineering is the process of selecting, transforming, and creating relevant variables (features) from raw data to improve machine learning model performance. It enhances predictive accuracy by extracting meaningful insights, optimizing data representation, and enabling algorithms to learn complex relationships more effectively.

Feature Engineering is like preparing ingredients for a gourmet dish—a chef carefully selects, cuts, and combines the right ingredients to enhance flavor, just as data scientists refine and transform data to improve a model's learning ability and predictive performance.

Examples

Fraud Detection: Banks analyze transaction frequency, location, and spending patterns to engineer features that identify fraudulent activities, enhancing fraud detection models.

Healthcare Predictions: Feature engineering in medical AI models includes combining symptoms, lab results, and genetic factors to improve early disease diagnosis and treatment recommendations.

E-commerce Recommendation Systems: Online retailers create user engagement metrics, purchase history features, and behavioral scores to enhance product recommendation algorithms (see pg. 404).

Foundational Concepts

Feature Engineering is guided by domain knowledge, data preprocessing, and feature transformation techniques. Feature selection helps identify the most relevant variables, reducing overfitting and improving model generalization. Feature extraction transforms raw data into meaningful representations using techniques like Principal Component Analysis (PCA). Feature creation involves deriving new attributes, such as aggregating historical user behaviors or encoding categorical variables. Automated techniques like feature learning in deep learning models reduce the need for manual feature engineering. Well-designed features significantly impact model interpretability, accuracy, and computational efficiency.

Related Terms

Feature Selection: Choosing the most relevant variables to improve model efficiency (see pg. 218 & 222).

Dimensionality Reduction: Techniques like PCA that reduce feature count while retaining information (see pg. 186).

Data Preprocessing: Cleaning, normalizing, and encoding data before feeding it into models (see pg. 168 & 170).

Common Misconceptions

Feature Engineering is unnecessary with deep learning: While deep learning automates feature extraction, structured data models still require manual feature engineering for improved performance.

More features always improve performance: Excessive or irrelevant features can lead to overfitting, reducing model generalization.

Feature Engineering is purely technical: Domain expertise is crucial for designing features that capture meaningful relationships in data.

Historical Context

Feature Engineering gained prominence with traditional machine learning algorithms like logistic regression, decision trees, and support vector machines, where manually designed features significantly influenced model accuracy. The rise of automated feature learning in neural networks and deep learning has reduced reliance on manual techniques, but structured data applications in finance, healthcare, and business analytics still require feature engineering expertise. Open-source libraries like **Featuretools** and **Scikit-learn** have advanced automated feature selection and transformation processes.

Practical Implications

Feature Engineering improves AI model accuracy, efficiency, and interpretability across industries. In finance, engineered features help detect fraudulent transactions. In healthcare, combining patient history, lab results, and lifestyle data enhances disease prediction models. In marketing, customer segmentation benefits from engineered engagement metrics. Companies adopting automated feature engineering save time, reduce bias, and enhance decision-making in AI-driven applications. Successful AI solutions rely on high-quality feature engineering to optimize predictive models and extract maximum value from data.

Feature Importance (XAI)

Feature Importance refers to the measure of how influential each input variable is in determining the predictions of a machine learning model. It helps identify the most critical features, improve model interpretability, and optimize performance by reducing unnecessary or redundant data.

Feature Importance is like a recipe's ingredient list—some ingredients have a greater impact on flavor than others. Just as a chef identifies key components like salt or spices, machine learning models determine which features significantly influence predictions, ensuring better results with fewer irrelevant inputs.

Examples

Credit Scoring Models: Banks analyze income, credit history, and debt-to-income ratio to determine loan approval. Feature importance highlights which variables contribute most to risk assessment.

Medical Diagnosis: AI models identify vital signs, genetic markers, and patient history as key predictors for disease detection, helping prioritize critical diagnostic factors.

Fraud Detection: Financial institutions use transaction amount, frequency, and location as important features to flag fraudulent activities while reducing false alarms.

Foundational Concepts

Feature Importance is based on statistical methods, model-specific calculations, and interpretability techniques. Permutation Importance measures how shuffling a feature affects model accuracy. SHAP values (Shapley Additive Explanations) explain individual feature contributions to predictions. Gini Importance ranks features in decision trees by how much they reduce uncertainty. Gradient boosting algorithms like XGBoost provide built-in feature importance rankings. Eliminating low-impact features enhances model efficiency, reduces overfitting, and improves generalization to new data, making feature importance a key tool in AI fairness, bias mitigation, and explainability.

Related Terms

Feature Selection: Choosing the most influential features to improve model efficiency and accuracy (see pg. 218 & 222).

SHAP Values: A game-theoretic approach to understanding how each feature contributes to an AI model's decision.

Dimensionality Reduction: Reducing the number of features while preserving important information (see pg. 186).

Common Misconceptions

Feature Importance means causation: High importance doesn't imply a feature causes an outcome—it only shows correlation.

All features contribute equally: Some features heavily impact predictions, while others are redundant or irrelevant.

Feature Importance is the same across models: Different models prioritize different features based on their structures.

Historical Context

Feature Importance has been widely used in statistical regression, decision trees, and ensemble methods like Random Forests and Gradient Boosting Machines. Early work in linear regression and ANOVA (Analysis of Variance) helped establish methods for ranking variables. With the rise of explainable AI (XAI), techniques like SHAP values and LIME (Local Interpretable Model-Agnostic Explanations) have become essential for model transparency and decision accountability.

Practical Implications

Feature Importance helps optimize AI models in finance, healthcare, and cybersecurity. In loan approvals, it ensures transparency by explaining why a loan is denied. In medical AI, it highlights the most relevant symptoms for disease prediction. In marketing, it identifies the strongest indicators of customer behavior, improving targeted advertising. By understanding feature importance, organizations can build fairer, more interpretable, and efficient AI systems, ensuring better decision-making and compliance with ethical AI standards.

Feature Learning (AI)

Feature Learning is the process where a machine learning model automatically discovers representations or patterns in raw data, rather than relying on manually engineered features. It is commonly used in deep learning to extract meaningful insights from images, text, and structured data.

Feature Learning is like learning to recognize faces without being told specific traits. Just as the brain detects patterns like eyes and noses automatically, AI models learn important features, such as edges in images or key words in text, without predefined rules.

Examples

Image Recognition: Convolutional Neural Networks (CNNs) learn to detect edges, textures, and complex patterns in images, improving object recognition (see pg. 276).

Speech Processing: AI models extract important phonetic features, identifying accents, emotions, and speech patterns for applications like voice assistants and transcription services (see pg. 460).

Financial Fraud Detection: Feature learning helps detect subtle transaction anomalies by recognizing spending behaviors and flagging unusual patterns in real time.

Foundational Concepts

Feature Learning is based on unsupervised and supervised learning techniques that allow AI models to identify patterns without explicit programming. Autoencoders compress data to extract essential features. Principal Component Analysis (PCA) reduces dimensionality, identifying the most important attributes. Deep learning architectures like convolutional and recurrent neural networks autonomously discover hierarchical representations. The goal is to reduce reliance on manual feature engineering, enabling generalization and efficiency in various domains, from computer vision to natural language processing (NLP).

Related Terms

Feature Extraction: The process of transforming raw data into informative features for machine learning models (see pg. 218 & 222).

Representation Learning: A broader concept where AI autonomously learns representations useful for downstream tasks.

Autoencoders: A neural network architecture used for unsupervised feature learning by compressing and reconstructing data (see pg. 94).

Common Misconceptions

Feature Learning eliminates the need for human oversight: While it automates feature extraction, domain knowledge is still required for validation.

It always outperforms manual feature engineering: Some structured problems benefit from human-defined features.

Only deep learning uses feature learning: Traditional techniques like PCA and clustering also contribute to feature learning.

Historical Context

Feature Learning emerged as an alternative to manual feature engineering, gaining traction with neural networks and deep learning advancements. Early work in self-organizing maps (SOMs) and PCA laid the foundation. The rise of deep belief networks (DBNs) and convolutional networks (CNNs) in the **2000s**, driven by **Geoffrey Hinton** and **Yann LeCun**, revolutionized feature learning in image recognition and NLP. Recent progress in self-supervised learning (SSL) has further advanced AI's ability to learn representations without labels.

Practical Implications

Feature Learning enhances AI applications in healthcare, finance, and automation. In medical imaging, AI detects diseases from raw scans, reducing diagnostic errors. In autonomous vehicles, it helps perceive and interpret road conditions, ensuring safety. In cybersecurity, AI learns attack patterns to prevent fraud and breaches. By reducing reliance on manual intervention, feature learning accelerates AI adoption, making models more scalable, efficient, and adaptable to complex real-world problems.

Feature Selection (ML)

Feature Selection is the process of choosing a subset of the most informative variables from a larger set so that a model learns faster, generalizes better, and runs more efficiently. By removing noisy, redundant, or irrelevant inputs, it reduces overfitting and sharpens the signal the model actually needs.

Think of it like packing for a long hike: you lay everything out, then keep only the items that truly help you reach the summit, leaving behind the weight that slows you down.

Examples

Healthcare risk scoring: From dozens of vitals, labs, and demographics, keep the few that best predict readmission, improving accuracy and clinician trust.

Marketing churn prediction: Drop highly collinear and low-variance fields so the model focuses on behaviors that genuinely precede cancellations.

IoT fault detection: Select a compact set of sensors with complementary signals to deploy models on-device with tight latency and power budgets.

Foundational Concepts

Feature selection methods are commonly grouped into three families:

Filter methods: evaluate features independently of any specific model—e.g., correlation, mutual information, chi-squared, or ANOVA F-tests—and keep those that score best.

Wrapper methods: search subsets using the model as a judge (forward selection, backward elimination, recursive feature elimination), picking the set that validates best.

Embedded methods: let the model decide during training, e.g., sparsity from L1 regularization or tree-based splits, so unhelpful features get little or no weight.

Good practice includes cross-validation to avoid **data leakage**, monitoring stability (does the chosen set change wildly across folds?), and pairing with **feature engineering** and **dimensionality reduction** when beneficial. Done well, selection improves generalization and efficiency.

Related Terms

Feature Engineering: Creating/transforming variables; selection chooses among them (see pg. 218).

Feature Importance: Model-derived signals used to guide selection (see pg. 220).

Dimensionality Reduction: Transforms features to fewer latent dimensions (contrast with selecting originals) (see pg. 186).

Cross-Validation: Estimates out-of-sample performance for candidate subsets (see pg. 160).

Overfitting: Reduced by removing noisy/redundant inputs (see pg. 362).

Data Cleaning: Upstream prep that prevents spurious selections (see pg. 168).

Evaluation Metric: Guides which subset is "best" for the task (see pg. 206).

Train vs. Test: Ensures selected features truly generalize (see pg. 496).

Common Misconceptions

More features always help: Extra inputs often add noise, spur spurious correlations, and slow training.

Feature selection = dimensionality reduction: Selection keeps original variables; dimensionality reduction creates new composite ones.

Only linear models need it: Tree ensembles, neural nets, and linear models all benefit—from speed, interpretability, and robustness.

Pick once and you're done: As data shifts, the most useful features can change; revisit selection periodically.

Historical Context

Prior to deep representation learning, classical ML pipelines relied heavily on thoughtful feature curation. As datasets grew, systematic selection (**filters**, **wrappers**, and **embedded regularization**) became standard practice complementing modern automated and learned representations rather than disappearing.

Practical Implications

Feature Selection yields simpler, faster, and often more accurate models. It's critical for regulated contexts that value interpretability, and for edge deployments where memory, compute, and power are scarce. In production, teams typically automate it within the training pipeline, validate with proper holdouts, and track which features drive performance, so the model remains lean, stable, and trustworthy over time.

Feedback (HCI)

Feedback is information returned to a system, process, or individual that helps adjust and improve performance. In artificial intelligence and machine learning, feedback is used to refine models, optimize decision-making, and enhance accuracy based on real-world results and user interactions.

Feedback is like adjusting a recipe while cooking. If a dish is too salty, the next batch is adjusted with less salt. Similarly, AI systems use feedback to modify their algorithms—whether through user corrections, performance evaluations, or reinforcement signals—to improve future outcomes.

Examples

Reinforcement Learning: AI-powered robots receive reward signals when completing tasks correctly, refining their actions for better performance in future attempts (see pg. 410).

Recommendation Systems: Streaming platforms analyze user preferences and refine recommendations based on likes, skips, or watch time, enhancing content personalization (see pg. 404).

Speech Recognition: Virtual assistants process user corrections, adjusting voice-to-text accuracy by learning from repeated misinterpretations (see pg. 528).

Foundational Concepts

Feedback is essential in machine learning, particularly in supervised, unsupervised, and reinforcement learning models. Supervised learning relies on labeled data to correct predictions, while unsupervised learning adjusts clustering based on statistical patterns. Reinforcement learning depends on positive and negative feedback loops, refining actions through rewards and penalties. Gradient descent leverages error signals to adjust neural network weights, improving model performance over time. Continuous feedback enables adaptive learning, where AI systems self-correct based on experience.

Related Terms

Reinforcement Learning: A machine learning paradigm that improves decision-making through reward-based feedback (see pg. 410).

Gradient Descent: An optimization algorithm using error feedback to refine model parameters iteratively.

Backpropagation: A method in neural networks where feedback adjusts weights to minimize prediction errors.

Common Misconceptions

Feedback is always positive: AI systems learn from both correct and incorrect predictions, refining models over time.

All AI systems use feedback equally: Some models, like rule-based systems, do not adapt dynamically based on feedback.

Feedback instantly improves AI performance: While critical, multiple iterations and refinements are required for significant improvements.

Historical Context

Feedback-based learning has roots in cybernetics and control theory, with **Norbert Wiener** pioneering the concept in the **1940s**. **Arthur Samuel**'s self-learning checkers program in the **1950s** was an early AI system utilizing feedback. Backpropagation, introduced in the **1980s** by **Geoffrey Hinton** and colleagues, became a foundation of modern deep learning. More recently, reinforcement learning advancements in **AlphaGo** and **OpenAI**'s models have demonstrated how feedback-driven AI can surpass human performance in complex tasks.

Practical Implications

Feedback is crucial in autonomous systems, healthcare, and customer experience. In self-driving cars, AI refines decision-making based on sensor input. In medical AI, feedback from doctors helps improve diagnostic accuracy. In chatbots and virtual assistants, user interactions shape future responses, making AI more conversational and intuitive. By continuously integrating feedback, AI systems become more accurate, efficient, and aligned with human needs, enhancing trust and usability across industries.

Feedback Loops (QC/HPC)

Feedback loops refer to cyclical processes where outputs are fed back into a system as inputs to influence future performance. In artificial intelligence and machine learning, feedback loops refine models by continuously learning from prior predictions, interactions, or errors to improve accuracy and efficiency over time.

Feedback loops are like a thermostat adjusting room temperature. When a thermostat detects the temperature is too high, it signals the cooling system to activate. Similarly, AI models use feedback to adjust decision-making, improving predictions or responses based on user interactions or past outcomes.

Examples

Search Engine Optimization: Search engines refine ranking algorithms based on user click behavior, improving search result relevance through feedback.

Social Media Feeds: Recommendation algorithms adjust content delivery based on engagement signals like likes, shares, and watch time, reinforcing user preferences.

Autonomous Vehicles: Self-driving cars adjust driving patterns through sensor-based feedback, learning from road conditions, obstacles, and prior errors.

Foundational Concepts

Feedback loops operate in supervised learning, reinforcement learning, and control systems. They can be positive (reinforcing behaviors) or negative (correcting deviations). In reinforcement learning, feedback loops reward optimal actions and penalize mistakes, refining decision-making through trial and error. In deep learning, backpropagation utilizes feedback loops to adjust model weights based on prediction errors. Cybernetics and control theory provide foundational frameworks for feedback systems, ensuring stability, adaptability, and continuous learning across AI-driven processes.

Related Terms

Reinforcement Learning: AI model improves decision-making using rewards and penalties in feedback loops (see pg. 410).

Backpropagation: Neural network learning method that refines model weights through error feedback.

Bias Amplification: A negative effect of feedback loops where errors or biases get reinforced over iterations (see pg. 104).

Common Misconceptions

All feedback loops are beneficial: Some feedback loops, like bias reinforcement in AI models, can be harmful.

Feedback loops instantly optimize AI models: Multiple iterations over time are required to yield significant improvements.

AI learns without feedback: Most AI models depend on feedback for refinement, except for static rule-based systems.

Historical Context

Norbert Wiener's cybernetics theory (**1948**) introduced feedback loops in control systems and automation. **Arthur Samuel** (**1959**) applied feedback loops in machine learning, enabling self-learning AI. The **1980s** backpropagation breakthrough by **Geoffrey Hinton** revolutionized neural networks, leveraging feedback loops for deep learning. Reinforcement learning advancements, such as **AlphaGo** (**2016**), showcased feedback-driven AI mastering complex games.

Practical Implications

Feedback loops are crucial in AI-powered decision-making, automation, and personalization. In finance, fraud detection models refine alerts based on feedback. Healthcare AI improves diagnostic accuracy by learning from medical expert reviews. Retail recommendation engines adjust product suggestions based on past purchases and user preferences. Properly designed feedback loops enhance AI fairness, adaptability, and efficiency, while mitigating risks like bias reinforcement and misinformation propagation in digital systems.

Fermentation (BT)

Fermentation is a metabolic process in which microorganisms like bacteria, yeast, or fungi break down organic compounds, typically sugars, to produce energy. This anaerobic process generates byproducts such as ethanol, lactic acid, and carbon dioxide, which are widely used in food, medicine, and biofuel production.

Fermentation is like baking bread. Just as yeast ferments sugar to create carbon dioxide, making dough rise, microorganisms in industrial fermentation break down compounds to produce useful products like antibiotics, alcohol, and biofuels without requiring oxygen.

Examples

Food Production: Fermentation is essential in making yogurt, cheese, and pickles, where bacteria convert lactose into lactic acid, enhancing taste and preservation.

Biofuel Industry: Ethanol fermentation converts plant sugars into renewable bioethanol fuel, reducing reliance on fossil fuels and lowering carbon emissions.

Pharmaceuticals: Antibiotics like penicillin are produced through microbial fermentation, where fungi generate bioactive compounds used in medicine.

Foundational Concepts

Fermentation relies on microbial metabolism, where enzymes break down sugars into simpler molecules. In anaerobic fermentation, organisms function without oxygen, producing alcohols, acids, or gases. In aerobic fermentation, oxygen is involved, leading to different end products. Glycolysis initiates the process, breaking glucose into pyruvate, which is further converted by microbes. Bioreactors optimize fermentation conditions, regulating pH, temperature, and oxygen levels to enhance yield. Industrial strain engineering modifies microbial genes to improve efficiency in biotechnology applications.

Related Terms

Anaerobic Respiration: Cellular process that generates energy in the absence of oxygen.

Bioprocessing: The use of living organisms to produce valuable chemicals and pharmaceuticals.

Microbial Biotechnology: Genetic manipulation of microorganisms to optimize fermentation-based production.

Common Misconceptions

Fermentation always produces alcohol: Some fermentation processes generate acids, gases, or other compounds instead of ethanol.

Fermentation only occurs in food production: It is also essential in medicine, biofuel, and industrial biotechnology.

Fermentation requires oxygen: Many fermentation processes occur in anaerobic conditions without oxygen.

Historical Context

Fermentation has been used for thousands of years, with ancient civilizations employing it for bread, beer, and wine. In **1857**, **Louis Pasteur** discovered microorganisms drive fermentation, revolutionizing microbiology. **Chaim Weizmann (1917)** applied bacterial fermentation to produce acetone for explosives in **World War I**. The biotechnology revolution expanded fermentation into pharmaceuticals, biofuels, and synthetic biology, making it a cornerstone of modern industrial microbiology.

Practical Implications

Fermentation plays a crucial role in sustainable production, reducing reliance on fossil fuels and chemical synthesis. Biopharmaceutical companies use microbial fermentation to produce insulin, vaccines, and antibiotics. In food technology, fermentation enhances nutrition, preservation, and flavor. Environmental biotechnology applies fermentation for waste treatment and bio-based materials production, promoting circular economies. Ongoing advancements in synthetic biology and metabolic engineering continue to optimize fermentation for global industrial applications.

Field of View (FOV) (XR)

Field of View (FOV) refers to the extent of the observable environment visible to a user in Extended Reality (XR) systems, including Virtual Reality (VR), Augmented Reality (AR), and Mixed Reality (MR). It is measured in degrees and determines how immersive a digital experience appears, impacting user engagement and realism.

FOV is like looking through a window. A small window limits what you see, while a panoramic window gives a broader perspective. Similarly, a wider FOV in XR allows users to perceive more of the virtual or augmented world, enhancing immersion.

Examples

Virtual Reality (VR) Gaming: High-FOV headsets create a lifelike experience by expanding peripheral vision, making interactions more natural in games like Half-Life: Alyx (see pg. 530).

Augmented Reality (AR) Smart Glasses: Devices like Microsoft HoloLens use limited FOVs to overlay digital objects in real-world environments, aiding in remote assistance and navigation (see pg. 92).

Automotive HUDs (Heads-Up Displays): AR dashboards project speed, navigation, and alerts within the driver's FOV, enhancing situational awareness without diverting attention from the road.

Foundational Concepts

FOV depends on display optics, lens curvature, and projection techniques. Binocular overlap enhances depth perception in VR, mimicking human vision. A monocular FOV defines each eye's range, while a combined FOV determines overall immersion. Angular resolution affects clarity, with wider FOVs sometimes reducing sharpness. Fresnel lenses and pancake optics optimize FOV while maintaining a compact headset design. Fixed and dynamic FOV settings in XR platforms adjust based on user movement and hardware capabilities, balancing performance and immersion.

Related Terms

Peripheral Vision: The area outside central focus that enhances spatial awareness in VR/AR experiences.

Depth Perception: The ability to judge distances in XR, influenced by FOV and stereoscopic rendering.

Display Latency: The delay between head movement and updated visuals, affecting FOV responsiveness in immersive systems.

Common Misconceptions

A wider FOV always improves quality: While a larger FOV enhances immersion, it can reduce resolution and introduce distortion.

FOV is the same for all XR devices: Different hardware has varying FOV limitations, affecting user experience.

FOV is only about vision: It also influences motion sickness, depth perception, and real-world interaction in AR/VR.

Historical Context

The concept of FOV dates back to early optics and camera lens designs, later applied to simulator displays in the **1960s**. Early VR devices like **NASA**'s Virtual Interface Environment Workstation (VIEW, **1980s**) experimented with FOV limits. **Oculus Rift (2016)** popularized consumer-grade VR with a 110° FOV. Modern advances in waveguide optics, foveated rendering, and curved displays continue to improve FOV in XR applications.

Practical Implications

FOV plays a crucial role in immersive experiences, affecting gaming, training, and remote collaboration. In healthcare, wide-FOV VR simulations train surgeons for complex procedures. Military and aviation industries use XR for pilot training and tactical visualization. Retail and virtual tourism benefit from expansive FOVs, making digital environments feel realistic. Ongoing innovations in eye-tracking, adaptive optics, and AI-powered rendering aim to expand FOV while maintaining clarity and reducing motion sickness in XR applications.

Firewall (CS)

A firewall is a security system that monitors and controls incoming and outgoing network traffic based on predefined rules. It acts as a barrier between a trusted internal network and untrusted external networks, such as the internet, protecting systems from unauthorized access, malware, and cyber threats.

A firewall is like a security guard at a building entrance. It checks credentials and only allows authorized people in while blocking or flagging those who might pose a threat, ensuring safety within the premises. Similarly, firewalls filter harmful traffic from entering a system.

Examples

Enterprise Network Security: Organizations use firewalls to protect their internal networks from cyberattacks, filtering traffic based on security policies and preventing data breaches.

Home Network Protection: Personal firewalls on routers safeguard home users by blocking malicious websites, unauthorized connections, and suspicious activity from the internet.

Cloud Security: Cloud-based firewalls protect data and applications hosted on remote servers, ensuring safe communication between cloud services and users while detecting threats in real-time.

Foundational Concepts

Firewalls operate based on packet filtering, stateful inspection, and deep packet inspection (DPI). Packet filtering examines data packets against security rules, allowing or blocking them based on source and destination. Stateful inspection tracks active connections, ensuring consistency between incoming and outgoing data. Application-layer firewalls analyze traffic at the software level, detecting suspicious patterns. Intrusion prevention systems (IPS) complement firewalls by identifying and blocking potential cyber threats. Next-generation firewalls (NGFWs) integrate advanced threat intelligence, encryption inspection, and AI-driven anomaly detection.

Related Terms

Intrusion Detection System (IDS): Monitors network traffic for malicious activities but does not block threats.

Proxy Server: Acts as an intermediary, filtering web traffic before it reaches the user.

Virtual Private Network (VPN): Encrypts internet traffic, often used alongside firewalls for secure remote access.

Common Misconceptions

Firewalls alone provide complete security: While essential, firewalls need additional security measures like antivirus software and encryption.

All firewalls function the same way: Different types (hardware, software, cloud-based) offer varying levels of protection.

Firewalls slow down internet speed: While some filtering may introduce latency, modern firewalls optimize performance without noticeable delays.

Historical Context

The concept of firewalls emerged in the **1980s** when early packet-filtering firewalls were developed. In **1988, DEC** introduced the first commercial firewall, followed by stateful inspection firewalls by **AT&T Bell Labs** in **1989**. The **1990s** saw the rise of proxy-based and application-layer firewalls, improving security for businesses and governments. Next-generation firewalls (NGFWs) in the **2000s** integrated AI-driven threat detection, enabling real-time protection against evolving cyber threats. Today, cloud firewalls play a crucial role in securing modern digital infrastructures.

Practical Implications

Firewalls are vital for cybersecurity across industries, protecting sensitive data in finance, healthcare, and government sectors. They help prevent unauthorized access to corporate networks, reducing the risk of cyberattacks. In e-commerce, firewalls secure payment transactions by blocking fraudulent traffic. Critical infrastructure, including energy grids and transport systems, relies on firewalls to defend against cyber threats. As cyberattacks grow in sophistication, businesses invest in adaptive firewalls with AI-based threat detection to enhance protection in cloud environments and hybrid networks.

Fork (BC)

A fork in blockchain technology occurs when a network splits into two separate chains due to changes in the protocol. Forks can be soft forks, which maintain compatibility with the original chain, or hard forks, which create a completely separate blockchain.

A fork is like a highway splitting into two different routes. One road follows the original path, while the other takes a new direction with different rules. Some travelers stay on the old road, while others take the new one, based on their preferences.

Examples

Bitcoin Cash (BCH): In **2017**, Bitcoin underwent a hard fork, creating Bitcoin Cash, which increased block size to improve transaction speed and scalability.

Ethereum Hard Fork (The DAO): After The DAO hack in **2016**, Ethereum executed a hard fork to reverse the hack, splitting the network into Ethereum (ETH) and Ethereum Classic (ETC).

Litecoin (LTC): A soft fork of Bitcoin introduced Segregated Witness (SegWit) to improve transaction efficiency without creating a new blockchain.

Foundational Concepts

Forks occur when network participants disagree on protocol rules, leading to divergent blockchain histories. Soft forks implement backward-compatible changes, allowing old nodes to process new transactions with minor updates. Hard forks introduce incompatible protocol upgrades, requiring all participants to migrate to the new chain. Miners, developers, and stakeholders must agree on which chain to support. Forks often arise from governance disputes, security fixes, or scalability improvements, reflecting the decentralized nature of blockchain networks.

Related Terms

Consensus Algorithm: Determines how blockchain participants agree on transactions (e.g., Proof of Work, Proof of Stake) (see pg. 146).

Block Height: The position of a block in the blockchain, where forks often originate.

Node: A computer maintaining a blockchain copy and participating in the consensus process.

Common Misconceptions

Forks always create new cryptocurrencies: Not all forks result in a new coin; some just update the existing blockchain.

Hard forks are bad for blockchain stability: While disruptive, hard forks enable innovation and security enhancements.

Forks happen randomly: Forks are usually planned and voted on by the community or developers.

Historical Context

Blockchain forks became prominent with **Bitcoin Improvement Proposals** (BIPs), guiding protocol changes. **Bitcoin**'s **2017 SegWit** soft fork improved efficiency, while the **Bitcoin Cash** hard fork resulted from disagreements over block size. **Ethereum**'s **2016 DAO** hard fork was a pivotal event in blockchain governance. Other notable forks include **Bitcoin SV** (BSV) and **Ethereum 2.0** upgrades, reflecting the evolving nature of decentralized networks.

Practical Implications

Forks impact cryptocurrency value, adoption, and security. Hard forks can create rival chains, leading to market volatility. Soft forks allow seamless protocol upgrades, ensuring network stability. In enterprise blockchain, controlled forks enable tailored solutions. Regulators monitor forks for compliance risks, while investors assess their impact on blockchain ecosystems. Forks drive innovation, enhancing scalability, governance, and security across decentralized networks.

Function (AI)

A function in computing and mathematics is a self-contained block of code or logic that performs a specific task, takes inputs (parameters), and returns an output. Functions promote modularity, reusability, and efficiency in programming and machine learning by structuring code into manageable components.

A function is like a coffee machine. You input coffee grounds and water, press a button, and get a cup of coffee. The machine follows a predefined process (logic) to transform inputs into the desired output, ensuring consistency and efficiency.

Examples

Machine Learning Algorithms: Functions are used in AI models to process data, compute probabilities, and optimize predictions. For example, activation functions determine neuron outputs in neural networks (see pg. 45).

Web Development: Functions enable interactivity on websites by handling user actions like clicking buttons, submitting forms, or processing login credentials in a structured manner.

Mathematical Computations: Functions like sigmoid and ReLU are used in deep learning to normalize outputs, ensuring model stability and better learning in artificial intelligence applications.

Foundational Concepts

Functions are central to computer science, mathematics, and artificial intelligence. They follow a deterministic approach, meaning the same input always yields the same output. Functions may be pure functions (without side effects) or impure functions (modifying external states). In machine learning, functions like loss functions, activation functions, and optimization functions guide model training. Functions operate under domain and codomain principles, mapping inputs to outputs in structured systems such as functional programming and neural network architectures.

Related Terms

Algorithm: A step-by-step procedure that uses functions to solve computational problems.

Lambda Function: An anonymous, short function often used in data processing and AI models.

Activation Function: Determines neuron output in artificial neural networks, shaping learning processes (see pg. 70).

Common Misconceptions

Functions always return a value: Some functions, called void functions, perform actions without returning a value.

Functions are only for programming: They are fundamental in mathematics, AI, and systems modeling.

All functions are deterministic: Some functions introduce randomness, like stochastic functions in AI models.

Historical Context

The concept of functions originated in mathematics, with **Leibniz** and **Euler** formalizing functions as input-output relationships. In computing, **Alonzo Church**'s lambda calculus influenced modern programming functions. Functions became foundational in AI through **McCulloch-Pitts** neural networks (**1943**) and activation functions in deep learning. Today, functions are essential in languages like **Python**, **JavaScript**, and functional programming paradigms.

Practical Implications

Functions streamline software development, data science, and AI modeling by modularizing code. In machine learning, functions optimize loss minimization, gradient calculations, and feature extraction. In automation, functions handle tasks like data transformation, API calls, and robotic actions. Functions enable predictability and efficiency across industries, from healthcare AI diagnostics to financial forecasting and autonomous systems.

Generative Adversarial Network (GAN) (GenAI)

A Generative Adversarial Network (GAN) is a type of deep learning model consisting of two neural networks—the generator and discriminator—that compete to create realistic data. The generator produces synthetic data, while the discriminator evaluates its authenticity, improving both networks through continuous feedback.

A GAN is like an art forger trying to create perfect replicas of famous paintings while an expert critic evaluates them. The forger improves with each attempt, and the critic refines its ability to detect fakes, leading to increasingly realistic copies.

Examples

Image Generation: GANs can create realistic human faces, artworks, and fashion designs. Applications include Deepfake technology and AI-generated artwork.

Data Augmentation: In medical imaging, GANs generate synthetic MRI scans to train AI models when real patient data is scarce, improving diagnostic accuracy.

Super-Resolution: GANs enhance low-quality images by generating higher-resolution versions, useful in satellite imagery, medical diagnostics, and forensic analysis.

Foundational Concepts

GANs rely on a zero-sum game between the generator and discriminator, where one's improvement leads to the other's adaptation. The generator creates new data samples, while the discriminator evaluates them against real data. Adversarial training pushes the generator to create increasingly realistic outputs. Loss functions, such as binary cross-entropy, help optimize training. GANs are a form of unsupervised learning, where the system improves without labeled data. Mode collapse, where GANs produce limited variations of outputs, is a common challenge in training.

Related Terms

Deepfake: AI-generated synthetic media that modifies videos or images realistically.

Variational Autoencoder (VAE): Another generative model that creates new data samples by learning latent representations (see pg. 94).

Neural Style Transfer: Uses AI to blend artistic styles into images using deep learning techniques.

Common Misconceptions

GANs always produce perfect images: Training a GAN is complex, and early iterations generate blurry or unrealistic outputs.

GANs require labeled data: GANs use unsupervised learning, meaning they do not need explicit labels to improve.

All GANs generate images: GANs also create text, music, video, and structured data for diverse applications.

Historical Context

GANs were introduced in **2014** by **Ian Goodfellow** and his team, revolutionizing AI-generated content. Their first applications included generating handwritten digits and face images. Over time, progressive growing of GANs (PGGANs) improved realism, leading to applications like **StyleGAN** for human face generation. **BigGAN** pushed boundaries by creating high-resolution images. GAN research expanded into drug discovery, cybersecurity, and art generation, making it a cornerstone of modern AI.

Practical Implications

GANs impact entertainment, security, healthcare, and AI ethics. They enable photo-realistic avatars, AI-generated music, and personalized content creation. In medicine, GANs synthesize medical images for AI training. However, they also raise ethical concerns, such as deepfake misuse and AI-generated misinformation. Regulatory frameworks and AI detection techniques are essential to mitigate risks while maximizing benefits.

Genetic Engineering (BT)

Genetic engineering is the process of modifying an organism's DNA to introduce new traits, improve functionality, or eliminate genetic disorders. Using techniques like CRISPR, scientists can edit genes in plants, animals, and humans, leading to advancements in medicine, agriculture, and biotechnology.

Genetic engineering is like editing a book, where scientists can rewrite specific words (genes) to correct errors or improve the story. Just as an editor enhances a manuscript, genetic modification allows researchers to alter an organism's genetic code to enhance desirable traits or remove harmful mutations.

Examples

Disease Treatment: CRISPR gene-editing corrects mutations responsible for genetic disorders like sickle cell anemia, offering potential cures for inherited diseases.

Agricultural Advancements: Genetically modified (GM) crops, such as pest-resistant corn and drought-tolerant wheat, improve food security and reduce reliance on chemical pesticides.

Synthetic Biology: Scientists engineer bacteria to produce insulin, antibiotics, and biofuels, creating more sustainable and efficient production methods.

Foundational Concepts

Genetic engineering is based on DNA manipulation, where restriction enzymes, polymerase chain reaction (PCR), and gene sequencing enable precise genetic modifications. Recombinant DNA technology allows scientists to introduce genes from one organism into another, while CRISPR-Cas9 provides a highly accurate method for gene editing. Gene therapy seeks to replace faulty genes with functional ones, potentially curing genetic diseases. Epigenetics explores how gene expression can be controlled without altering the DNA sequence itself, influencing inherited traits.

Related Terms

CRISPR: A precise gene-editing tool that cuts and modifies DNA sequences (see pg. 158).

Recombinant DNA: DNA molecules artificially combined from different sources to create new traits.

Gene Therapy: The process of treating diseases by inserting, altering, or replacing genes within an individual's cells.

Common Misconceptions

Genetic engineering creates "Frankenstein" organisms: It enhances specific traits but does not create unnatural life forms.

Genetically modified food is unsafe: Studies show GMO crops are rigorously tested and as safe as traditional crops.

Editing human DNA is unethical: While concerns exist, gene therapy is mainly used for treating diseases rather than altering physical traits.

Historical Context

The foundation of genetic engineering began with **Watson** and **Crick**'s discovery of DNA's structure (**1953**). **Herbert Boyer** and **Stanley Cohen** (**1973**) developed recombinant DNA technology, allowing scientists to transfer genes between species. CRISPR-Cas9, discovered in **2012** by **Jennifer Doudna** and **Emmanuelle Charpentier**, revolutionized genetic editing, making it faster, cheaper, and more precise. Advances in synthetic biology and gene therapies continue to shape biotechnology and medicine.

Practical Implications

Genetic engineering transforms medicine, agriculture, and environmental science. Gene therapy offers potential cures for previously untreatable diseases. GM crops increase yields, reduce pesticide use, and improve nutritional value. In environmental science, genetically modified bacteria help clean oil spills and remove toxins. Ethical concerns about designer babies, biodiversity risks, and patenting genes highlight the need for regulations and responsible innovation.

Genome Sequencing (BT)

Genome sequencing is the process of determining the complete DNA sequence of an organism's genome. It identifies the order of nucleotides (A, T, C, G) in chromosomes, allowing researchers to study genes, detect mutations, and understand genetic influences on health, evolution, and biological functions.

Genome sequencing is like reading a book, where DNA is the text and genes are the chapters. Scientists use sequencing technologies to decode this book, revealing instructions for growth, function, and traits—just as reading a manual helps understand how a machine operates.

Examples

Personalized Medicine: By sequencing a patient's genome, doctors can customize treatments based on genetic mutations, improving drug efficacy and reducing adverse reactions.

Agricultural Biotechnology: Scientists develop disease-resistant and high-yield crops by analyzing plant genomes and modifying genetic traits for improved productivity.

Forensic Science: Law enforcement uses genome sequencing to identify individuals in criminal investigations and solve decades-old cases through genetic genealogy.

Foundational Concepts

Genome sequencing relies on next-generation sequencing (NGS), which rapidly deciphers DNA fragments and reconstructs the full genome. Polymerase chain reaction (PCR) amplifies DNA, making sequencing more efficient. Bioinformatics processes vast genomic data, identifying genes and mutations linked to diseases. Epigenetics studies how environmental factors modify gene expression without altering DNA sequences. Comparative genomics examines genetic similarities and differences between species, providing insights into evolution, disease resistance, and genetic disorders.

Related Terms

Genomics: The study of an organism's entire DNA sequence and its functions (see pg. 244).

CRISPR: A gene-editing tool that modifies DNA sequences with precision 158.

Transcriptomics: The study of RNA molecules to understand gene expression patterns.

Common Misconceptions

Genome sequencing predicts everything about a person: It identifies genetic risks but doesn't determine exact future health outcomes.

Only humans have genomes: All living organisms—bacteria, plants, animals—have genomes.

Genome sequencing is always expensive: Costs have significantly decreased, making genetic testing more accessible.

Historical Context

Frederick Sanger (1977) developed the first genome sequencing method. **The Human Genome Project (1990–2003)** mapped the entire human genome, revolutionizing medicine and genetics. Next-generation sequencing (NGS), developed in the **2000s**, made sequencing faster and more affordable. Companies like **Illumina** and **Oxford Nanopore** continue advancing sequencing technologies, enabling breakthroughs in cancer research, disease prevention, and genetic therapies.

Practical Implications

Genome sequencing is transforming healthcare, agriculture, and biotechnology. Cancer genomics helps detect mutations driving tumors, leading to targeted therapies. Gene therapy corrects genetic disorders by replacing faulty genes. Synthetic biology engineers microorganisms for biofuel and drug production. Ethical concerns over genetic privacy, discrimination, and designer babies highlight the need for regulations. With increasing accessibility, genome sequencing holds promise for precision medicine, biodiversity conservation, and evolutionary research.

Geothermal Energy (CET)

Geothermal energy is a renewable energy source derived from heat stored beneath the Earth's surface. It is harnessed by tapping into underground reservoirs of hot water or steam to generate electricity or provide direct heating, making it a sustainable and consistent energy solution.

Geothermal energy is like a giant underground furnace that never turns off. Just as a hot spring naturally heats water using Earth's internal heat, geothermal power plants capture this heat to produce electricity, offering a clean and renewable alternative to fossil fuels.

Examples

Electricity Generation: Geothermal power plants use steam or hot water from deep underground to drive turbines and generate electricity, providing a stable, year-round energy source (see pg. 246 & 532).

Direct Heating: Geothermal heat pumps warm buildings by transferring underground heat to homes and offices, significantly reducing heating costs and emissions.

Agriculture & Industry: Greenhouses and fish farms utilize geothermal energy to maintain optimal temperatures, increasing crop yields and production efficiency.

Foundational Concepts

Geothermal energy originates from radioactive decay and residual heat from Earth's formation. Geothermal reservoirs store hot water and steam beneath the surface, accessed through wells. Geothermal gradient refers to the increase in temperature with depth, driving heat flow. Enhanced Geothermal Systems (EGS) artificially increase permeability in dry rock formations to extract heat more efficiently. Binary cycle power plants use lower-temperature geothermal fluids, improving accessibility. This energy source is highly sustainable, as heat continuously replenishes from the Earth's core.

Related Terms

Renewable Energy: Energy from natural, sustainable sources like solar, wind, and geothermal (see pg. 21).

Heat Pump: A system that transfers geothermal heat to buildings for heating and cooling.

Tectonic Activity: Geological movements, such as earthquakes, that influence geothermal heat distribution.

Common Misconceptions

Geothermal energy is only available in volcanic areas: While it is more accessible in tectonically active regions, Enhanced Geothermal Systems allow heat extraction almost anywhere.

It is harmful to the environment: Geothermal energy has a low carbon footprint, with minimal emissions compared to fossil fuels.

Geothermal plants deplete underground heat: Properly managed reservoirs can remain sustainable for centuries.

Historical Context

Ancient civilizations, including the Romans and Chinese, used geothermal springs for bathing and heating. The first geothermal power plant (**1904**) in **Larderello, Italy**, marked the beginning of electricity production from geothermal energy. **Iceland** and the **U.S.** became global leaders in geothermal energy in the 20th century, expanding the use of direct heating and power plants. Recent technological advances in drilling and EGS are increasing the potential for widespread adoption.

Practical Implications

Geothermal energy plays a vital role in sustainable energy production. Countries like Iceland, the Philippines, and the U.S. generate a significant portion of their electricity from geothermal plants. Reducing reliance on fossil fuels, geothermal power supports energy independence and lower emissions. Its 24/7 availability makes it more reliable than solar and wind energy, ensuring grid stability. As drilling and heat extraction technologies improve, geothermal energy could expand globally, reducing carbon footprints while providing clean, cost-effective power.

Global Navigation Satellite System (GNSS) (IoT)

GNSS is a network of satellites that provides global positioning, navigation, and timing (PNT) services. It enables devices to determine their location with high accuracy anywhere on Earth by receiving signals from multiple satellites, supporting applications in navigation, mapping, and timing synchronization.

GNSS is like a cosmic roadmap. Just as drivers use street signs and landmarks to navigate cities, GNSS-enabled devices use signals from satellites to determine their precise location, speed, and time, guiding everything from airplanes to smartphones.

Examples

Aviation Navigation: Pilots rely on GNSS for precise flight paths, safe landings, and real-time positioning, enhancing flight safety and efficiency worldwide.

Autonomous Vehicles: Self-driving cars use GNSS for real-time positioning, enabling lane detection, navigation, and route optimization.

Disaster Response: GNSS assists in tracking emergency vehicles, coordinating rescue operations, and mapping affected areas after natural disasters.

Foundational Concepts

GNSS operates through a constellation of satellites that continuously transmit signals containing position and time data. A receiver determines its location by calculating the time delay of signals from multiple satellites, a process known as trilateration. GNSS augmentation systems improve accuracy by correcting signal errors caused by atmospheric disturbances. Different global systems, such as GPS (USA), Galileo (EU), GLONASS (Russia), and BeiDou (China), provide independent and complementary navigation services. GNSS is essential for precise geolocation, time synchronization, and autonomous operations.

Related Terms

GPS: The U.S. GNSS system, widely used for navigation and geolocation.

Trilateration: The process of determining position by measuring distances from multiple satellites.

RTK (Real-Time Kinematics): A GNSS enhancement technique that improves positioning accuracy to the centimeter level.

Common Misconceptions

GNSS is the same as GPS: GPS is just one of multiple GNSS systems, which also include Galileo, GLONASS, and BeiDou.

GNSS works perfectly indoors: Signals are weak indoors and require augmentation technologies like Wi-Fi positioning or inertial navigation.

GNSS provides instant pinpoint accuracy: Signal interference and atmospheric conditions can affect positioning accuracy.

Historical Context

The first GNSS system, GPS, was developed by the **U.S. Department of Defense** in the **1970s** for military navigation and was later opened to civilian use. **Russia** launched **GLONASS**, and **Europe** and **China** introduced **Galileo** and **BeiDou** to provide independent global coverage. Advances in signal processing, augmentation technologies, and multi-GNSS compatibility have made GNSS indispensable for modern navigation, communications, and scientific research.

Practical Implications

GNSS is fundamental to transportation, telecommunications, agriculture, and emergency response. It enables precision farming, reducing resource use by guiding automated tractors. Financial institutions use GNSS-based time synchronization to secure transactions. In urban planning, GNSS supports infrastructure development and traffic management. As GNSS technology improves, future applications in autonomous systems, space exploration, and smart cities will enhance efficiency and connectivity worldwide.

Google Colab (AI)

Google Colab is a cloud-based notebook environment that allows users to write, execute, and share Python code in a web browser. It provides free access to GPUs and TPUs, making it ideal for machine learning, data science, and AI research without requiring local computational resources.

Google Colab is like a rental car for AI and coding projects—instead of owning expensive hardware, users can access powerful computing resources on demand, collaborate in real time, and run Python code effortlessly, just like sharing a Google Doc.

Examples

Deep Learning Model Training: Researchers and students use Google Colab to train neural networks with free GPU and TPU acceleration, enabling complex computations without high-end hardware.

Collaborative Data Analysis: Teams can work on data science projects, using Colab to process large datasets, visualize results, and share notebooks instantly.

AI Experimentation: Developers test machine learning algorithms and prototype AI applications with pre-installed libraries like TensorFlow and PyTorch, eliminating lengthy setup processes.

Foundational Concepts

Google Colab is built on Jupyter Notebook technology, enabling interactive coding with code cells and markdown documentation. It runs on Google's cloud infrastructure, offering free and paid access to GPUs and TPUs. Notebook sharing and collaboration allow multiple users to edit and execute code in real time. Colab's integration with Google Drive enables seamless file management, and it supports pre-installed libraries such as NumPy, pandas, and TensorFlow. The environment is ideal for AI, data science, and Python programming, reducing setup and hardware constraints.

Related Terms

Jupyter Notebook: An open-source interactive computing environment for Python, widely used in data science (see pg. 292).

TensorFlow: A machine learning library, often used in Google Colab for deep learning models (see pg. 482).

TPU (Tensor Processing Unit): A specialized AI accelerator, available in Colab for faster model training.

Common Misconceptions

Colab is a replacement for local development: While useful, Colab has session time limits, making it unsuitable for long-running tasks.

It's completely free: The free tier has usage limits, and Colab Pro offers better hardware access.

It requires no coding knowledge: Colab provides interactive tools, but users still need Python programming skills.

Historical Context

Google launched Colab in **2017** as part of its effort to democratize AI and data science by making cloud computing accessible. It builds upon Jupyter Notebooks, which revolutionized interactive coding. With the rise of deep learning and AI research, Colab quickly became a popular tool for students, developers, and researchers. Over time, Colab Pro and Colab Pro+ introduced enhanced computing power with more stable GPU/TPU access, catering to professional users.

Practical Implications

Google Colab significantly lowers the barrier to entry for machine learning, AI, and data science by providing free and scalable computing resources. In education, it enables students to learn AI without expensive hardware. Startups and researchers use it to test AI models before scaling. In collaborative projects, Colab streamlines code sharing and real-time teamwork. Its integration with cloud storage and pre-installed libraries makes it a vital tool for rapid AI prototyping and experimentation.

Gradient Descent (ML)

Gradient Descent is an optimization algorithm that iteratively updates a model's parameters in the direction that most reduces error (the loss). At each step, it uses the gradient, the slope of the loss function with respect to the parameters, to decide how to adjust the model so predictions improve. This is a core mechanism for training machine learning models, especially neural networks and deep learning systems.

Gradient Descent is like hiking down a foggy hill with only a local sense of slope. You can't see the whole landscape, but by feeling which way is "downhill" and taking careful steps, you steadily reach a low point where error is minimized.

Examples

Image Classification: Convolutional Neural Networks (CNNs) are trained by repeatedly adjusting weights via gradient descent to minimize cross-entropy loss, improving how well images are recognized.

Speech Recognition: Models align audio to text by minimizing sequence losses (e.g., CTC). Gradient descent updates the network to reduce transcription errors over time.

Regression & Forecasting: For tasks like predicting prices or risks, gradient descent reduces losses such as Mean Squared Error, refining parameter estimates with each step.

Foundational Concepts

Gradient descent moves parameters opposite the gradient of the loss. The **learning rate** controls step size where too large can overshoot or diverge; too small slows progress. Variants include **batch** (uses all data each step), **mini-batch** (a small subset; common in deep learning), and **stochastic** (one example at a time). Practical refinements, like **momentum**, **Nesterov momentum**, and **adaptive methods**, stabilize or speed convergence by smoothing or scaling updates. In **convex** problems it converges to the global minimum; in deep, non-convex landscapes it typically finds useful low-error regions that generalize well.

Related Terms

Loss Function: Quantifies prediction error; gradient descent minimizes it (see pg. 310).

Backpropagation: Computes gradients efficiently in neural networks so gradient descent can update weights.

Neural Networks: Architectures trained with backpropagation and gradient descent (see pg. 352).

Stochastic Gradient Descent (SGD): A noisy, data-efficient variant using single examples or mini-batches.

Learning Rate: Hyperparameter controlling the size of each step during optimization.

Regularization: Penalties (e.g., L1/L2) added to the loss to improve generalization.

Error Minimization: Broader goal that gradient descent serves across AI systems (see pg. 202).

Common Misconceptions

It always finds the best (global) solution: In deep, non-convex models, it typically finds a good local region rather than a guaranteed global minimum.

A smaller learning rate is always safer: Too small can stall learning; learning-rate schedules often work best.

SGD's noise is bad: The stochasticity can help escape poor local minima and improve generalization.

Only for neural networks: It's widely used in classic ML (e.g., linear/logistic regression) and beyond.

Historical Context

Gradient descent emerged as a formal optimization method in the mid-20th century (**1951**) and later became foundational to modern machine learning. The **1980s** breakthrough of backpropagation enabled efficient gradient computation in **multilayer neural networks**, powering today's deep learning renaissance.

Practical Implications

Choosing the right learning rate, variant (batch, mini-batch, or stochastic), and regularization can make the difference between unstable training and state-of-the-art performance. In healthcare diagnostics, recommendation engines, and autonomous systems, gradient-descent-trained models learn from data at scale, continually reducing error to deliver accurate, reliable predictions.

Graph Networks for Material Exploration (GNoME) (ANI)

Graph Networks for Material Exploration (GNoME) is an AI-driven framework that leverages graph neural networks (GNNs) to accelerate the discovery of novel materials. By representing atomic structures as interconnected nodes, GNoME predicts material properties, enabling breakthroughs in energy storage, semiconductors, and quantum computing.

GNoME is like a highly skilled alchemist who can predict the properties of new materials by understanding atomic relationships. Just as an expert chef combines ingredients based on their molecular interactions to create unique flavors, GNoME analyzes atomic structures to design new materials with optimized properties.

Examples

Battery Innovation: GNoME helps researchers discover new electrode materials with higher energy densities, improving battery lifespan and efficiency. By analyzing atomic structures, it predicts promising solid-state electrolytes, leading to safer and more sustainable energy storage solutions.

Semiconductor Design: The semiconductor industry uses GNoME to predict bandgaps and optimize materials for faster and more efficient electronic components. This accelerates the development of next-generation transistors and optoelectronic devices.

Quantum Materials Discovery: GNoME identifies materials with exotic quantum properties, such as topological insulators and superconductors. These discoveries are essential for advancing quantum computing and high-performance electronics (see pg. 254).

Foundational Concepts

GNoME is based on graph neural networks (GNNs), which process data structured as graphs. Node embeddings represent individual atoms, while edge connections capture atomic interactions. Message passing algorithms allow information to flow between nodes, enabling accurate material property predictions. Supervised and self-supervised learning refine GNoME's accuracy by training on vast material databases. Additionally, high-throughput screening accelerates material discovery by evaluating millions of potential compounds computationally, significantly reducing experimental costs.

Related Terms

Graph Neural Networks (GNNs): AI models that process graph-structured data, essential for material property prediction.

High-Throughput Screening (HTS): A method for rapidly testing large sets of materials to identify promising candidates.

Quantum Materials: Materials exhibiting unique quantum effects, crucial for future technologies like superconductors and quantum processors.

Common Misconceptions

GNoME doesn't create materials: It predicts promising candidates, but experimental validation is still required.

GNoME works like traditional simulations: Unlike density functional theory (DFT), GNoME learns from data to predict material properties rather than relying on first-principles calculations.

GNoME can replace chemists: While it speeds up discovery, human expertise is still essential for validation and practical application.

Historical Context

GNoME emerged from advances in machine learning for materials science, driven by the need for faster material discovery. Early material informatics relied on empirical rules, but breakthroughs in graph neural networks (**2017–2020**) enabled AI-driven material prediction. Researchers at **Google DeepMind** and **MIT** have pioneered GNoME applications, leading to high-throughput computational material screening. Today, GNoME supports initiatives in sustainable materials, renewable energy, and next-generation electronics, revolutionizing material science through AI.

Practical Implications

GNoME accelerates green energy innovations, enabling breakthroughs in solar cells, batteries, and hydrogen storage materials. In semiconductor technology, it streamlines the development of ultrafast processors and advanced sensors. In biomaterials, GNoME aids in designing new nanostructures for drug delivery. Its integration with quantum computing promises an era of data-driven material synthesis, reducing reliance on trial-and-error experimentation and unlocking futuristic materials faster than ever before.

Grid Computing (HPC)

Grid computing is a distributed computing model that connects multiple computers across different locations to function as a single, powerful system. By pooling computational resources, grid computing enables efficient processing of large-scale tasks, such as scientific simulations, data analysis, and AI model training.

Grid computing is like a network of volunteers solving a massive puzzle. Instead of one person completing it alone, many individuals work on different sections simultaneously, sharing progress and assembling the full picture much faster than a single solver could.

Examples

Scientific Research: Grid computing powers large-scale projects such as protein folding simulations for drug discovery. By distributing complex calculations across thousands of nodes, it accelerates breakthroughs in biomedical research.

Climate Modeling: Meteorological agencies use grid computing to process massive datasets for weather prediction and climate simulations. This allows for more accurate forecasts and climate change analysis.

AI Training: Companies leverage grid computing to train deep learning models on vast datasets, reducing computational costs and speeding up AI development in fields like natural language processing and computer vision.

Foundational Concepts

Grid computing relies on distributed systems, where computing resources are geographically dispersed but interconnected. Parallel processing splits tasks into smaller chunks, allowing multiple machines to work simultaneously. Middleware manages resource allocation and communication, ensuring seamless integration. Load balancing optimizes computational workloads, preventing bottlenecks. Virtualization enables flexible resource sharing across different hardware architectures. Unlike cloud computing, which offers centralized resource management, grid computing is decentralized and often tailored to specific large-scale computations.

Related Terms

Distributed Computing: A model where multiple computers work together on a single task.

Parallel Processing: The simultaneous execution of multiple computations to enhance performance (see pg. 364).

Cloud Computing: A service-based model that provides scalable computational resources on demand.

Common Misconceptions

Grid computing is the same as cloud computing: Cloud computing centralizes resources, while grid computing connects independent systems for collaborative computing.

Grid computing is outdated: It remains widely used in scientific research, AI, and financial modeling.

Grid computing is only for large organizations: Open-source grid computing frameworks enable individuals and smaller institutions to participate in distributed computing projects.

Historical Context

Grid computing emerged in the **1990s**, evolving from supercomputing and distributed systems. Early projects like **SETI@home** (**1999**) demonstrated large-scale volunteer computing. In the **2000s**, institutions like **CERN** and **NASA** adopted grid computing for particle physics simulations and space research. The development of middleware platforms such as **Globus Toolkit** facilitated widespread adoption. Today, grid computing remains essential for high-performance computing (HPC) in fields like genomics, AI, and cryptography.

Practical Implications

Grid computing is transforming scientific computing, AI, and finance by enabling large-scale simulations, complex calculations, and data-intensive tasks. In biomedical research, it accelerates genetic analysis and drug discovery. In finance, it enhances risk modeling and fraud detection. In aerospace, it supports fluid dynamics simulations for aircraft design. With advancements in edge computing and AI-driven optimization, grid computing continues to expand its role in solving some of the world's most computationally demanding problems.

Hallucination (GenAI)

Hallucination in generative AI refers to the phenomenon where an AI model generates incorrect, misleading, or entirely fabricated content that appears plausible. This occurs when the model extrapolates patterns beyond its training data, producing responses that lack factual accuracy or real-world grounding.

Hallucination is like a confident storyteller who invents details to fill gaps in knowledge. Just as a child might fabricate an answer when unsure, AI models sometimes generate text or images based on learned patterns rather than actual data, leading to plausible but false outputs.

Examples

Misinformation in AI Chatbots: AI assistants may fabricate historical events or cite nonexistent sources when responding to user queries. This can lead to false narratives in journalism and education, necessitating human verification.

Medical AI Misdiagnosis: Generative AI used for medical diagnosis may suggest incorrect symptoms or non-existent treatments, posing risks if relied upon for healthcare decisions.

Synthetic Image Creation Errors: AI-generated visuals sometimes produce nonsensical artifacts, such as extra limbs in human images or impossible object distortions, affecting applications in digital design and entertainment.

Foundational Concepts

Hallucination stems from probabilistic text generation, where models predict the most likely next word rather than verifying truthfulness. Data limitations contribute when training lacks sufficient factual grounding. Overfitting can cause models to generate memorized yet incorrect responses. Prompt engineering techniques aim to reduce hallucinations by structuring user queries more effectively. Retrieval-augmented generation (RAG) enhances accuracy by incorporating external knowledge bases rather than relying solely on pre-trained data.

Related Terms

Bias in AI: Systematic distortions in AI-generated outputs due to imbalanced training data (see pg. 104).

Retrieval-Augmented Generation (RAG): AI models integrating external knowledge sources to reduce hallucination.

AI Explainability (XAI): Methods for understanding and interpreting AI-generated decisions and outputs (see pg. 27).

Common Misconceptions

Hallucination is intentional: AI does not consciously lie but generates responses based on statistical predictions.

Only low-quality AI hallucinates: Even advanced models can produce hallucinations due to data gaps.

Hallucination can be fully eliminated: While mitigation techniques exist, generative AI remains prone to occasional errors.

Historical Context

Hallucination gained attention with the rise of large language models (LLMs) like GPT-3 and GPT-4. Researchers at **OpenAI**, **DeepMind**, and **Google** identified issues of factual inconsistency in AI-generated content. Early AI systems, such as **IBM Watson**, also exhibited hallucination in healthcare applications. Efforts to reduce hallucination through fact-checking AI and external database integration continue as generative AI becomes widespread.

Practical Implications

Hallucination affects legal, medical, and journalistic AI applications, requiring human oversight to verify generated content. In business and marketing, brands using AI-generated text must fact-check outputs to maintain credibility. AI-powered search engines and virtual assistants must implement retrieval mechanisms to avoid misinformation. As AI becomes more embedded in decision-making systems, reducing hallucination is essential for trust, reliability, and ethical AI development.

Haptics (HCI/XR)

Haptics refers to technology that simulates touch-based interactions by using force, vibrations, or motion feedback. It enhances human-computer interaction (HCI) and extended reality (XR) applications by allowing users to physically feel digital objects, improving realism in virtual reality (VR), gaming, robotics, and medical simulations.

Haptics is like a braille system for digital interactions—just as raised dots enable visually impaired individuals to read through touch, haptic feedback allows users to experience virtual environments by providing physical sensations that mimic real-world textures, resistance, or motion.

Examples

Virtual Reality (VR) Training: Medical students use haptic gloves in VR simulations to practice delicate surgical procedures, feeling the resistance of tissues and tools, improving accuracy before performing real surgeries (see pg. 530).

Gaming and Entertainment: Advanced gaming controllers and VR suits use haptic feedback to simulate gun recoil, sword clashes, or environmental vibrations, enhancing immersion and engagement for players.

Tactile Remote Robotics: Surgeons performing robot-assisted procedures use haptic-enabled controllers to feel resistance when operating on tissues remotely, allowing for more precise and safer interventions.

Foundational Concepts

Haptics is built on mechanoreceptors, which translate physical touch into electrical signals. Force feedback generates resistance, making virtual objects feel solid. Vibrotactile feedback uses vibrations to simulate textures and motion, commonly found in smartphones and VR controllers. Electrotactile stimulation applies electrical impulses to create tactile sensations without mechanical movement. Actuators drive haptic responses in gloves, suits, and touchscreens. Latency optimization ensures real-time haptic interactions for seamless digital experiences.

Related Terms

Tactile Sensors: Devices that detect and transmit pressure, texture, and motion data in robotic and XR applications.

Extended Reality (XR): A broad term covering VR, augmented reality (AR), and mixed reality (MR), where haptics enhances realism (see pg. 30).

Haptic Rendering: The process of simulating physical touch sensations in virtual and augmented reality systems.

Common Misconceptions

Haptics is only for gaming: It is widely used in medicine, robotics, and industrial training, beyond just entertainment.

Haptic feedback is the same as vibration: While vibration is one type of haptic response, advanced systems use force feedback and electrostimulation for richer touch experiences.

Haptics requires expensive equipment: Basic haptics are found in smartphones and controllers, with more advanced systems available for professional applications.

Historical Context

Haptic technology originated from early robotics and aviation training in the **1960s**. **NASA** and military researchers developed force feedback systems for pilot training. The **1990s** saw the rise of consumer haptic devices, like force feedback joysticks and rumble-enabled game controllers. In the **2010s**, advancements in haptic gloves and full-body XR suits enabled more immersive interactions. Modern breakthroughs in electrotactile feedback and AI-driven touch simulations continue to expand haptic applications across industries.

Practical Implications

Haptics revolutionizes medical training, allowing surgeons to practice complex procedures in VR before real-world applications. In automotive technology, haptic feedback in touchscreens enhances driver safety by reducing the need for visual distractions. In industrial simulations, haptics enables virtual prototyping of products before manufacturing, reducing costs. In accessibility, haptic devices help visually impaired individuals interact with digital interfaces through tactile feedback. As AI-driven haptics evolves, it will play a critical role in bridging physical and digital experiences, improving realism in XR environments.

Hash Function (BC)

A hash function is a mathematical algorithm that converts input data of any size into a fixed-length string, known as a hash value. In blockchain technology, hash functions ensure data integrity, secure transactions, and enable cryptographic verification without revealing the original information.

A hash function is like a document fingerprint—just as every document has a unique fingerprint that changes if even a single letter is altered, hash functions generate distinct values for different inputs, ensuring security and tamper detection in digital systems.

Examples

Blockchain Security: Cryptographic hash functions like SHA-256 secure blockchain transactions by generating immutable digital signatures, ensuring data integrity and preventing unauthorized modifications (see pg. 18).

Password Protection: Websites use hash functions to store encrypted user passwords instead of plaintext, ensuring that stolen database entries cannot be easily exploited by attackers.

Data Deduplication: Cloud storage platforms employ hashing to identify and eliminate duplicate files, reducing storage costs and optimizing data retrieval efficiency.

Foundational Concepts

Hash functions are based on deterministic output, ensuring the same input always produces the same hash. They exhibit avalanche effect, where minor input changes cause significant hash variations, enhancing security. Preimage resistance ensures that input cannot be derived from a hash value. Collision resistance prevents two different inputs from producing the same hash. Cryptographic hash functions like SHA-256, SHA-3, and BLAKE2 provide high security for applications like digital signatures, data integrity verification, and blockchain mining.

Related Terms

SHA-256: A widely used cryptographic hash function securing Bitcoin transactions and blockchain ledgers.

Digital Signatures: Cryptographic methods relying on hash functions to verify document authenticity.

Merkle Tree: A data structure utilizing hashing to efficiently validate large blockchain datasets.

Common Misconceptions

Hashing is the same as encryption: Hash functions generate one-way outputs that cannot be reversed, unlike encryption, which allows decryption.

Hashes are always unique: While collision-resistant algorithms make duplicate hashes unlikely, they are not mathematically impossible.

All hash functions are secure: Some outdated algorithms like MD5 and SHA-1 have known vulnerabilities and should not be used for security-sensitive applications.

Historical Context

Hash functions date back to **1976**, when **Whitfield Diffie** and **Martin Hellman** introduced cryptographic hashing in public-key encryption. The MD5 algorithm (**1991**) became widely used but was later deemed insecure due to collision vulnerabilities. The SHA family (Secure Hash Algorithm), developed by **NSA** and **NIST**, evolved into SHA-256 and SHA-3, now widely used in blockchain technology, digital forensics, and cybersecurity.

Practical Implications

Hash functions enable blockchain immutability, preventing transaction tampering. In cybersecurity, hashing secures password storage and data integrity verification. In digital forensics, hash values authenticate evidence integrity. In distributed computing, hashes improve data indexing and retrieval. As quantum computing advances, researchers develop post-quantum hash functions to maintain security. Hash functions remain fundamental to secure communications, blockchain consensus mechanisms, and authentication systems across industries.

Head-Mounted Display (HMD) (XR)

A Head-Mounted Display (HMD) is a wearable visual device that provides an immersive digital experience by projecting virtual or augmented reality content directly into the user's field of view. HMDs are widely used in gaming, training simulations, medical applications, and industrial design.

An HMD is like a personal movie theater wrapped around your eyes. Just as a large screen immerses viewers in a film, an HMD places digital content directly in front of the user, enabling interaction with virtual and augmented environments in real-time.

Examples

Virtual Reality (VR) Gaming: HMDs like the Meta Quest and HTC Vive provide fully immersive VR gaming experiences, allowing players to interact with virtual worlds through motion tracking and hand controllers (see pg. 530).

Medical Training: Surgeons use HMD-based simulations to practice complex procedures in virtual environments, reducing the risk associated with real-life operations and improving precision in medical education.

Industrial Design and Training: Engineers and architects use HMDs in augmented reality (AR) to visualize blueprints in 3D, aiding design processes and facilitating hands-on industrial training for workers.

Foundational Concepts

HMDs rely on stereoscopic display technology to create depth perception. Motion tracking sensors detect head movements, allowing real-time interaction with digital environments. Field of view (FOV) determines the extent of the displayed image, affecting immersion. Augmented reality (AR) HMDs overlay digital information onto real-world scenes, while virtual reality (VR) HMDs fully immerse users in simulated environments. Eye-tracking technology enhances user experience by adjusting focus and interaction based on gaze direction.

Related Terms

Virtual Reality (VR): Fully immersive environments created through computer-generated simulations (see pg. 530).

Augmented Reality (AR): Digital content overlaid onto the real-world environment for enhanced interaction (see pg. 92).

Mixed Reality (MR): A blend of AR and VR, allowing digital and real-world objects to coexist interactively (see pg. 328).

Common Misconceptions

HMDs are only for gaming: While gaming is a major use case, HMDs are essential in medical, military, and industrial applications.

HMDs cause permanent eye damage: Modern ergonomic designs and refresh rates minimize strain when used appropriately.

All HMDs are the same: There are major differences between VR, AR, and MR HMDs, each designed for specific applications.

Historical Context

The first HMD prototype, **the Sword of Damocles**, was developed in **1968** by **Ivan Sutherland**, introducing early VR concepts. The **1990s** saw the emergence of commercial HMDs, such as the **Virtual Boy**. The **2010s** marked a breakthrough with devices like the **Oculus Rift**, revolutionizing consumer VR and AR applications. Today, advancements in 5G, AI-driven tracking, and lightweight optics continue to improve HMD functionality.

Practical Implications

HMDs are transforming education, healthcare, and workplace training by offering hands-on virtual experiences. In defense and military, HMDs enable immersive combat simulations and real-time data visualization. In retail and marketing, brands use AR HMDs to offer virtual product experiences. Remote collaboration benefits from MR HMDs, enabling professionals to interact with 3D models in real-time. As HMD technology evolves, it will shape the future of spatial computing, remote work, and digital interaction.

Heuristic Evaluation (HCI)

Heuristic evaluation is a usability inspection method used in human-computer interaction (HCI) to identify usability issues in user interfaces. Evaluators assess a system against predefined usability principles, known as heuristics, to improve user experience, efficiency, and accessibility before full-scale user testing.

Heuristic evaluation is like a proofreading session for user interfaces—just as editors review a manuscript for grammar and clarity, usability experts analyze an interface for design flaws, ensuring it meets best practices before real users interact with it.

Examples

Website Usability Testing: Companies use heuristic evaluation to assess e-commerce platforms, ensuring navigation, forms, and checkout processes align with usability principles to improve conversion rates.

Software Interface Optimization: Developers evaluate enterprise applications against heuristics like error prevention and consistency to enhance workflow efficiency and user satisfaction.

Virtual Reality (VR) Interaction Design: VR applications undergo heuristic evaluation to refine gesture-based interactions, spatial navigation, and feedback systems, improving immersion and ease of use (see pg. 530).

Foundational Concepts

Heuristic evaluation is based on Jakob Nielsen's 10 usability heuristics, which include principles such as visibility of system status, error prevention, and flexibility in use. Cognitive load theory ensures interfaces minimize mental effort for users. Expert review methodology enables usability professionals to identify issues without end-user involvement. Severity ratings help prioritize fixes, ranking usability issues from minor inconveniences to critical design flaws. Iterative design processes integrate heuristic evaluation early, reducing costly revisions in later development stages.

Related Terms

Usability Testing: Direct observation of users interacting with a system to identify usability challenges.

User Experience (UX) Design: The process of enhancing user satisfaction by improving accessibility and interaction (see pg. 518).

Cognitive Load Theory: A framework ensuring interfaces do not overwhelm users with excessive information or complexity (see pg. 140).

Common Misconceptions

Heuristic evaluation replaces user testing: It is a preliminary method used before real user feedback.

Only designers conduct heuristic evaluations: Any trained expert in usability principles can perform them.

Heuristic evaluation is subjective: While evaluators rely on expert judgment, standard heuristics ensure consistency.

Historical Context

Heuristic evaluation was introduced by **Jakob Nielsen** and **Rolf Molich** in **1990**, revolutionizing usability testing by providing a structured, cost-effective method for identifying interface flaws. Early applications focused on desktop software usability, but the method expanded into web, mobile, and immersive technologies. Over time, refinements to usability heuristics and cognitive psychology principles have strengthened heuristic evaluation's role in modern UX design and human-computer interaction (HCI).

Practical Implications

Heuristic evaluation reduces development costs by detecting usability flaws early. In healthcare applications, it ensures electronic medical records (EMRs) are user-friendly, preventing medical errors. In automotive UX, it improves dashboard interfaces and voice assistants for safer driving experiences. In augmented reality (AR) and virtual reality (VR), heuristic evaluation refines gesture-based interactions and spatial feedback, enhancing immersion. As digital experiences evolve, heuristic evaluation remains essential in ensuring intuitive, accessible, and efficient interfaces across industries.

Hidden Layer (AI)

A hidden layer is a layer of neurons in a neural network that processes input data and extracts features before passing them to the output layer. Hidden layers enable deep learning models to recognize complex patterns in tasks like image recognition, language processing, and autonomous systems.

A hidden layer is like a translator between languages. Just as a translator interprets meaning before delivering an understandable sentence, hidden layers process raw input, extract meaningful patterns, and refine the information before it reaches the output layer for final interpretation.

Examples

Image Recognition: Hidden layers in convolutional neural networks (CNNs) detect edges, textures, and shapes in images, enabling applications like facial recognition and medical imaging analysis (see pg. 276).

Natural Language Processing (NLP): In models like transformers, hidden layers process sentence structure and context, improving machine translation, chatbots, and sentiment analysis (see pg. 346).

Autonomous Vehicles: Hidden layers in deep reinforcement learning help process sensor data, enabling real-time decision-making for navigation and obstacle avoidance in self-driving cars.

Foundational Concepts

Hidden layers rely on activation functions like ReLU (Rectified Linear Unit) and sigmoid to transform input data into meaningful representations. Weights and biases determine neuron interactions, adjusting through backpropagation and gradient descent during training. Feature extraction occurs in multiple layers, where early layers detect simple patterns and deeper layers recognize complex abstractions. Deep learning architectures like feedforward networks, convolutional neural networks (CNNs), and recurrent neural networks (RNNs) utilize multiple hidden layers for enhanced performance.

Related Terms

Neural Network: A computing system modeled after the human brain, using layers of interconnected neurons to process data (see pg. 352).

Activation Function: A mathematical function that determines whether a neuron in a hidden layer should activate based on its input (see pg. 70).

Backpropagation: A training algorithm that adjusts weights in hidden layers by minimizing the difference between predicted and actual outputs.

Common Misconceptions

More hidden layers always improve performance: Excessive hidden layers can cause overfitting, making models less generalizable.

Hidden layers store actual data: They extract and transform features, but do not retain complete datasets.

All hidden layers function the same way: Different architectures (e.g., CNNs, RNNs, transformers) utilize hidden layers uniquely for distinct tasks.

Historical Context

The concept of hidden layers emerged in artificial neural networks (ANNs) in the **1950s**. The backpropagation algorithm (**1986**), introduced by **Rumelhart, Hinton**, and **Williams**, enabled efficient training of multi-layer networks. Early models like **LeNet-5 (1998)** demonstrated the power of hidden layers in image processing. The deep learning revolution of the **2010s**, driven by architectures like **AlexNet, ResNet**, and **GPT**, showcased the impact of hidden layers in modern AI applications.

Practical Implications

Hidden layers power deep learning breakthroughs across industries. In healthcare, they improve disease diagnosis through medical image analysis. In finance, they enhance fraud detection by identifying anomalies in transaction data. In automation, hidden layers optimize robotics and predictive maintenance. With advancements in quantum computing and neuromorphic hardware, the role of hidden layers in AI is evolving, shaping the future of intelligent systems and artificial general intelligence (AGI).

Human-in-the-Loop (HITL) (RAI)

Human-in-the-Loop (HITL) refers to a system where human input is integrated into an AI or automation process to improve accuracy, decision-making, and learning. HITL is used in machine learning, robotics, cybersecurity, and high-stakes decision-making to ensure ethical oversight and error correction.

HITL is like training a guide dog—just as a trainer corrects the dog's mistakes and reinforces good behavior, humans refine AI models, correct errors, and provide feedback, ensuring the system learns correctly and makes better decisions over time.

Examples

AI-Assisted Medical Diagnosis: Doctors use AI-generated analyses of X-rays and MRIs, verifying and correcting AI predictions to ensure accurate diagnoses and reduce false positives.

Fraud Detection in Banking: AI flags suspicious transactions, but human analysts review cases that require nuanced judgment, preventing unnecessary account freezes or financial losses.

Autonomous Vehicles: HITL is used in self-driving cars where remote human operators assist in edge cases that AI cannot confidently resolve, ensuring safety in unpredictable traffic conditions.

Foundational Concepts

HITL relies on active learning, where AI systems learn from human corrections, improving their accuracy over time. Human oversight is essential for ethical AI development, preventing bias and ensuring fairness. Reinforcement learning with human feedback (RLHF) refines AI behavior by incorporating expert input. Edge case handling is a critical HITL function, where AI struggles with ambiguous scenarios. Adaptive learning loops continuously update models based on human interactions, making HITL essential for safety-critical applications like healthcare, defense, and finance.

Related Terms

Active Learning: AI learns from human-provided corrections, improving over time with fewer training examples.

Human-Centered AI: AI systems designed to work collaboratively with humans, enhancing decision-making rather than replacing it.

Reinforcement Learning with Human Feedback (RLHF): A method where humans guide AI training by rewarding desirable behaviors and correcting errors (see pg. 410).

Common Misconceptions

HITL slows down AI: While human input is required, HITL accelerates AI learning and prevents costly errors in critical applications.

HITL means AI is unreliable: AI models improve with human corrections, making them more robust over time rather than indicating fundamental flaws.

AI will eventually replace HITL: Fully autonomous systems still struggle with ethical, legal, and unpredictable real-world complexities, ensuring HITL remains relevant.

Historical Context

HITL principles date back to cybernetics and expert systems in the **1950s**. In the **1980s**, HITL became crucial in flight control systems, with pilots overseeing automated aircraft functions. The rise of machine learning (**2010s**) saw HITL integrated into AI training, especially in natural language processing (NLP) and autonomous systems. Recent advances in RLHF (e.g., **OpenAI**'s **ChatGPT**) highlight HITL's role in refining generative AI models and ensuring ethical AI behaviors.

Practical Implications

HITL ensures AI safety and reliability in high-stakes applications. In cybersecurity, analysts validate AI-detected threats, reducing false alarms. In legal tech, HITL is used for contract analysis, where AI assists but lawyers provide final verification. In content moderation, AI detects policy violations, while human reviewers handle context-sensitive cases. As AI adoption expands, HITL will remain essential for bias mitigation, regulatory compliance, and human-AI collaboration, ensuring ethical, transparent, and effective automation.

Humanoid Robot (RT)

A humanoid robot is a robotic system designed to resemble and mimic human movement, behavior, and interaction. These robots integrate artificial intelligence, machine learning, and robotics to perform tasks in healthcare, customer service, manufacturing, and research, often featuring human-like limbs, facial expressions, and speech capabilities.

A humanoid robot is like a versatile assistant—just as a human assistant adapts to different tasks, a humanoid robot can interact, learn, and perform activities ranging from assisting in surgeries to greeting customers at a store, all while replicating human-like behavior.

Examples

Healthcare Assistance: Humanoid robots like Grace support healthcare workers by providing elderly care, patient monitoring, and therapy for individuals with disabilities, improving quality of life.

Customer Service: Robots like Pepper enhance retail and hospitality experiences, greeting customers, answering questions, and providing information in banks, hotels, and shopping malls.

Disaster Response: Humanoid robots such as Atlas navigate through hazardous environments, assisting in search-and-rescue operations where human presence is risky, such as after natural disasters.

Foundational Concepts

Humanoid robots rely on artificial intelligence (AI) to process data and respond dynamically. Computer vision enables them to recognize faces, objects, and gestures. Natural language processing (NLP) allows them to interpret and generate human speech. Motion control systems powered by actuators and sensors replicate human-like movement. Reinforcement learning helps humanoid robots improve through experience. Human-robot interaction (HRI) ensures they adapt to social environments, making them effective in customer service, education, and healthcare.

Related Terms

Bipedal Robotics: Robots designed to walk on two legs, mimicking human locomotion.

Artificial Intelligence (AI): The core technology that enables humanoid robots to process language, learn, and make decisions (see pg. 7).

Human-Robot Interaction (HRI): The study of how humans and robots communicate and collaborate in real-world settings.

Common Misconceptions

Humanoid robots are fully autonomous: Most require human oversight and programming for task execution.

They can replace humans entirely: Their role is assistive, not a complete replacement for human workers.

All humanoid robots look like humans: Some have functional designs prioritizing performance over appearance, such as robotic arms and wheeled assistants.

Historical Context

The concept of humanoid robots dates back to **Leonardo da Vinci**'s **1495** sketches of a mechanical knight. In **1927**, the robot **Maria from Metropolis** became an early depiction of humanoid robotics. **WABOT-1 (1973)**, developed in **Japan**, was the first full-scale humanoid robot. Modern advances led to robots like **ASIMO** (Honda, **2000**) and **Sophia** (**Hanson Robotics, 2016**), showcasing breakthroughs in AI, speech recognition, and facial expressions. Today, humanoid robots are expanding into healthcare, industry, and entertainment.

Practical Implications

Humanoid robots revolutionize elderly care, medical assistance, and rehabilitation therapies. In education, they serve as interactive tutors, helping children with special needs. Manufacturing sectors utilize humanoid robots for precision assembly and repetitive tasks. They also assist in space exploration, operating in environments hazardous to humans. As AI and robotics continue advancing, humanoid robots will play a crucial role in automating labor-intensive tasks, improving accessibility, and enhancing human-robot collaboration across multiple industries.

Hydroelectric Power (CET)

Hydroelectric power is a renewable energy source that generates electricity by using flowing or falling water to turn turbines connected to generators. It provides sustainable, low-emission power, supporting global energy needs in industrial, residential, and commercial sectors while reducing dependence on fossil fuels.

Hydroelectric power is like a watermill grinding grain—just as flowing water spins a wheel to process wheat into flour, hydroelectric dams use water flow to rotate turbines, converting kinetic energy into electricity for homes, businesses, and industries.

Examples

Large-Scale Power Generation: The Three Gorges Dam (China) is the world's largest hydroelectric plant, producing 22,500 megawatts of electricity, supplying millions of homes and industries.

Pumped-Storage Hydropower: Facilities like Bath County Pumped Storage Station (USA) store excess electricity by pumping water to higher elevations, later releasing it to generate power during peak demand.

Micro-Hydropower Systems: Small hydroelectric systems in remote villages and farms generate local electricity, providing sustainable power to areas without access to large grids.

Foundational Concepts

Hydroelectric power relies on gravitational potential energy, where water stored in reservoirs or rivers flows downward, converting kinetic energy into mechanical energy via turbines. Generators transform mechanical energy into electricity. Dams regulate water flow, ensuring consistent energy production. Run-of-river plants operate without large reservoirs, using natural river flow. Pumped-storage hydropower acts as a battery, storing energy during low-demand periods. Environmental considerations like fish migration and ecosystem impact require careful hydraulic engineering and ecological management.

Related Terms

Turbine: A mechanical device that converts fluid motion into rotational energy to generate power.

Renewable Energy: Energy sources like solar, wind, and hydro that replenish naturally and have low environmental impact (see pg. 412).

Pumped-Storage Hydropower: A system that stores and releases electricity by moving water between reservoirs at different elevations.

Common Misconceptions

Hydroelectric power is always environmentally friendly: Large dams can disrupt ecosystems and displace communities if not properly managed.

Hydropower works in all locations: Requires sufficient water flow and elevation changes, making it unsuitable for some regions.

Hydroelectricity is new technology: The first hydroelectric plant was built in **1882**, and watermills have existed for centuries.

Historical Context

Hydropower dates back to ancient Greece and Rome, where waterwheels powered mills. The first hydroelectric power plant opened in **Appleton, Wisconsin (1882)**, leading to widespread adoption. **The Hoover Dam (1936)** marked a milestone in large-scale hydropower engineering. **China**, **Brazil**, and **Canada** are now global leaders in hydroelectric production. Today, innovations in fish-friendly turbines, sediment management, and hybrid energy grids improve hydroelectric sustainability.

Practical Implications

Hydroelectric power is a key player in global energy sustainability, reducing carbon footprints while providing reliable electricity. It supports grid stability, ensuring consistent energy supply in regions with fluctuating renewables like wind and solar. In developing nations, hydropower expands electrification efforts. However, concerns about drought sensitivity and habitat disruption necessitate improved hydrological forecasting, ecological conservation, and hybrid renewable strategies for future hydroelectric advancements.

Image Recognition (ANI)

Image recognition is an AI-driven process that enables computers to identify and classify objects, patterns, and features in images. Using machine learning, deep learning, and computer vision, it powers applications such as facial recognition, medical diagnostics, and autonomous vehicles by extracting meaningful visual information.

Image recognition is like a detective examining photos for clues—just as a detective identifies people, objects, and events in an image, AI analyzes patterns, colors, and shapes to classify and interpret visual data with high accuracy.

Examples

Facial Recognition: Image recognition in security systems and smartphones enables biometric authentication, unlocking devices and verifying identities using facial features (see pg. 214).

Medical Imaging Analysis: AI-powered image recognition assists radiologists in detecting tumors, fractures, and abnormalities in X-rays, MRIs, and CT scans, improving early diagnosis.

Autonomous Vehicles: Self-driving cars use image recognition and computer vision to detect traffic signals, pedestrians, and road signs, ensuring safe navigation in dynamic environments.

Foundational Concepts

Image recognition relies on convolutional neural networks (CNNs), which mimic the human brain's ability to process visual data. Feature extraction identifies edges, shapes, and textures in images. Object detection differentiates multiple entities within an image. Image classification assigns categories based on learned patterns. Transfer learning enhances recognition by adapting pre-trained models for specific tasks. Real-time processing in applications like autonomous vehicles and surveillance ensures quick decision-making using vast amounts of image data.

Related Terms

Computer Vision: The broader field enabling computers to interpret and analyze visual data from images and videos.

Deep Learning: A subset of machine learning that uses multi-layered neural networks to improve accuracy in image recognition tasks (see pg. 178).

Object Detection: The ability to locate and identify multiple objects in an image, crucial for applications like autonomous vehicles and surveillance.

Common Misconceptions

Image recognition is 100% accurate: Even advanced AI models can make errors, especially in low-light, occluded, or biased datasets.

It works like human vision: While inspired by human perception, AI lacks contextual awareness, requiring labeled data for training.

Image recognition is only for security: It is widely used in healthcare, retail, agriculture, and industrial automation.

Historical Context

Image recognition emerged from early computer vision research (**1960s**), evolving with neural networks in the **1990s**. The rise of CNNs (**2012**), particularly **AlexNet**, revolutionized accuracy in image classification. Companies like **Google**, **Facebook**, and **Tesla** have since pioneered facial recognition, automated tagging, and self-driving technology. Modern advancements in transformer models (**Vision Transformers**, **2020s**) continue to push the boundaries of image recognition capabilities.

Practical Implications

Image recognition transforms healthcare, security, and retail by enabling medical diagnostics, biometric authentication, and automated checkout systems. In agriculture, AI-powered drones analyze crop health through image recognition. Manufacturing benefits from quality control systems detecting product defects in real time. As AI improves, image recognition will play a crucial role in smart cities, augmented reality, and AI-driven accessibility solutions, revolutionizing the way humans interact with digital environments.

Immersion (XR)

Immersion in extended reality (XR) refers to the degree to which a user feels fully engaged in a virtual or augmented environment. High immersion levels create realistic, interactive experiences in virtual reality (VR), augmented reality (AR), and mixed reality (MR), enhancing presence and user interaction.

Immersion is like being transported into a movie—instead of just watching on a screen, you are inside the world, hearing sounds around you and interacting with objects, making the experience feel real and engaging.

Examples

Virtual Reality Gaming: Games like Half-Life: Alyx use head-mounted displays (HMDs), 3D audio, and motion tracking to create an immersive world where players physically move and interact (see pg. 530).

Medical Training Simulations: VR-based surgery training immerses medical students in lifelike operations, allowing them to practice complex procedures in a risk-free virtual environment.

Architectural Visualization: Immersive VR walkthroughs enable architects and clients to explore 3D building models, experiencing spaces before construction begins.

Foundational Concepts

Immersion relies on sensory stimulation through visual, auditory, and haptic feedback to create realistic environments. Spatial audio enhances realism by simulating how sound behaves in a 3D space. Latency reduction is crucial for real-time responses, preventing discomfort. Presence refers to the psychological effect of feeling physically inside a virtual space. Interactivity strengthens immersion by allowing users to engage with objects naturally. Haptic feedback systems enhance immersion by simulating touch sensations, improving realism in VR gaming, training, and simulations.

Related Terms

Presence: The sensation of truly being inside a virtual or augmented environment.

Haptic Feedback: Touch-based sensations enhancing realism in virtual and augmented reality experiences (see pg. 260).

Field of View (FOV): The extent of the virtual world visible to the user, affecting immersion depth.

Common Misconceptions

Immersion requires expensive equipment: While high-end VR systems enhance immersion, even mobile AR apps provide immersive experiences.

More immersion always means better experiences: Overwhelming sensory input can lead to discomfort, requiring balance.

Immersion is only for gaming: It is widely used in medicine, education, training, and architecture.

Historical Context

Immersion concepts date back to flight simulators (**1920s**) used for pilot training. The **Sensorama (1962)** was one of the first immersive machines, integrating 3D visuals, sound, and scent. The **1980s** saw VR development with **NASA** and the military using immersive systems. In the **2010s**, consumer VR exploded with **Oculus Rift** and **HTC Vive**, making high immersion accessible for gaming, training, and design. Today, advances in AI, haptics, and 5G connectivity continue to refine immersive experiences.

Practical Implications

Immersion enhances training, therapy, and entertainment. In mental health, VR therapy treats phobias and PTSD through controlled immersive exposure. In education, immersive learning environments improve student engagement and retention. Automotive companies use VR immersion for vehicle prototyping, saving costs and testing designs before production. As 5G, AI, and haptic technology improve, immersive experiences will continue reshaping how people learn, train, and interact with digital environments.

Input Layer (AI)

The input layer is the first layer in an artificial neural network (ANN) that receives raw data and passes it to the hidden layers for further processing. It does not perform calculations but distributes numerical representations of input features to the network for learning and decision-making.

The input layer is like a camera lens—just as a lens captures and directs light into a camera for processing, the input layer collects raw data and forwards it to deeper network layers, ensuring accurate perception and recognition.

Examples

Image Classification: In a convolutional neural network (CNN), the input layer receives pixel values from an image, allowing deeper layers to analyze edges, textures, and objects for classification (see pg. 128).

Speech Recognition: AI assistants like Siri and Alexa use input layers to process audio signals, converting sound waves into numerical features for recognition and response (see pg. 460).

Medical Diagnostics: Neural networks analyze MRI scans and X-rays by processing pixel intensity data in the input layer, aiding in disease detection and anomaly identification.

Foundational Concepts

The input layer operates on feature vectors, numerical representations of data such as pixel values, audio frequencies, or text embeddings. Dimensionality refers to the number of input neurons, which must match the dataset's features. Data normalization ensures inputs remain within a consistent range, improving learning efficiency. Encoding techniques like one-hot encoding and word embeddings transform categorical and textual data into numerical form. The input layer's role is to structure and relay information without modifying it, allowing hidden layers to extract meaningful patterns.

Related Terms

Neural Network: A machine learning model that mimics the human brain, composed of layers that process and analyze data (see pg. 352).

Feature Engineering: The process of selecting and transforming input data to improve model accuracy (see pg. 218).

Normalization: A technique that scales input values to a consistent range, enhancing neural network performance.

Common Misconceptions

The input layer processes data: It only passes information to deeper layers without performing transformations.

More input neurons mean better accuracy: Excessive inputs can introduce noise, reducing model efficiency and increasing computation time.

All input layers handle images: Input layers process diverse data types, including text, sound, and structured datasets.

Historical Context

The input layer concept emerged with artificial neural networks (ANNs) in the **1940s**, notably in **McCulloch** and **Pitts'** neural model (**1943**). Early networks like the **Perceptron** (**1958**) introduced structured input layers for numerical feature representation. In the **1980s**, advancements in multilayer perceptrons (MLPs) and backpropagation solidified the input layer's role in deep learning. The rise of deep neural networks (**2010s**) enhanced input layer architectures for processing high-dimensional data in fields like image recognition, NLP, and medical AI.

Practical Implications

The input layer is crucial for AI-driven automation and decision-making. In finance, input layers process real-time market data for algorithmic trading. In healthcare, AI models analyze genomic sequences and medical scans for predictive diagnosis. Autonomous systems, including self-driving cars, rely on LiDAR and sensor data input layers for real-time object detection. Future improvements in data preprocessing, input layer architectures, and feature extraction will enhance neural network efficiency, driving AI innovations in robotics, cybersecurity, and personalized AI applications.

Insider Threat (CS)

An insider threat refers to a security risk originating from individuals within an organization who have access to sensitive data, systems, or infrastructure. These threats can be malicious or unintentional, leading to data breaches, financial loss, or operational disruptions through leaks, sabotage, or negligence.

An insider threat is like a trusted employee leaving the office door unlocked—while most employees act responsibly, a careless mistake or deliberate act can allow unauthorized access, jeopardizing the organization's security and integrity.

Examples

Corporate Espionage: An employee at a tech company leaks trade secrets to a competitor, compromising innovation and market advantage.

Negligent Data Handling: A staff member accidentally emails confidential customer data to an external recipient, violating privacy regulations and causing legal repercussions.

Sabotage in Critical Infrastructure: A disgruntled IT administrator deletes critical system files, disrupting financial services and causing downtime.

Foundational Concepts

Insider threats are classified as malicious insiders, who deliberately harm the organization, and negligent insiders, who unintentionally expose vulnerabilities. Privileged access management (PAM) restricts data access to prevent misuse. User behavior analytics (UBA) detects anomalies in employee activity. Zero trust security frameworks limit access, assuming every user or device could be a potential risk. Data loss prevention (DLP) tools monitor and prevent unauthorized data transfers. Security awareness training reduces the risk of negligent insider threats through education and compliance enforcement.

Related Terms

Zero Trust Architecture: A security model that requires continuous verification of all users and devices.

Data Loss Prevention (DLP): Techniques used to monitor, detect, and prevent unauthorized data transfers.

User Behavior Analytics (UBA): AI-driven analysis of employee activities to detect insider threats.

Common Misconceptions

Insider threats are always malicious: Many incidents stem from human error or negligence, not intentional harm.

Only employees pose insider threats: Contractors, vendors, and third-party partners with system access can also be risks.

Firewalls and antivirus software prevent insider threats: Traditional security measures focus on external threats, requiring advanced behavioral monitoring to detect internal risks.

Historical Context

Insider threats have existed for decades, with notable incidents such as **Edward Snowden**'s **2013 NSA** data leak, exposing government surveillance programs. The **1996 Citibank** heist saw an employee collaborate with hackers to steal millions. The rise of remote work and cloud computing has amplified insider threat risks, leading to advancements in behavioral analytics and zero-trust security models. Organizations now integrate AI-driven security measures to detect and mitigate internal risks in real time.

Practical Implications

Insider threats pose challenges across finance, healthcare, and government sectors. In financial institutions, they enable fraud, unauthorized transactions, and regulatory breaches. In healthcare, insiders can leak patient records, violating privacy laws like HIPAA. Government agencies face risks from classified data leaks, impacting national security. To combat these risks, organizations implement privileged access controls, real-time anomaly detection, and cybersecurity training programs, ensuring a robust defense against insider-originated security breaches.

Interconnect (HPC)

An interconnect is a high-speed communication network that links multiple processors, storage units, and computing nodes in a high-performance computing (HPC) environment. It facilitates data transfer, synchronization, and parallel processing, ensuring efficient communication between distributed components in supercomputers, data centers, and AI training clusters.

An interconnect is like a city's highway system—just as roads connect different districts, allowing vehicles to transport goods efficiently, interconnects enable data packets to move seamlessly between processors, reducing latency and optimizing computing performance.

Examples

Supercomputing: The Summit supercomputer uses high-speed interconnects to link thousands of GPUs and CPUs, enabling petascale scientific simulations (see pg. 464).

AI Model Training: Advanced AI models like GPT-4 rely on interconnects between GPUs, accelerating distributed deep learning computations and reducing training time.

Cloud Data Centers: Hyperscale cloud providers like AWS and Google Cloud use low-latency interconnects to enable seamless resource sharing across multiple data centers worldwide.

Foundational Concepts

Interconnects are designed for low latency, high bandwidth, and fault tolerance to handle vast data exchanges in HPC and cloud computing. Network topologies such as fat tree, torus, and hypercube optimize communication paths. InfiniBand and Ethernet are common interconnect standards, balancing speed and cost efficiency. Memory coherence protocols ensure data consistency across distributed systems. Direct memory access (DMA) allows data transfer without CPU intervention, improving processing efficiency. Scalability is critical, as modern HPC systems involve thousands of interconnected processing nodes.

Related Terms

InfiniBand: A high-performance, low-latency interconnect standard used in supercomputing and AI clusters.

Message Passing Interface (MPI): A communication protocol that enables parallel computing across interconnected nodes.

Latency: The delay in data transfer between components, which interconnects aim to minimize in HPC environments.

Common Misconceptions

Interconnects are just regular network cables: Unlike standard internet connections, interconnects are optimized for low-latency, high-bandwidth computing environments.

All interconnects work the same way: Different topologies and protocols (e.g., InfiniBand vs. Ethernet) impact performance based on workload requirements.

More interconnects always improve performance: Poorly optimized network configurations can create bottlenecks, reducing computational efficiency.

Historical Context

Interconnect technology has evolved from early bus-based architectures (**1960s**) to modern high-speed fabrics. The **Cray-1** supercomputer (**1976**) pioneered specialized interconnects for vector processing. The development of **InfiniBand** (**2000s**) and high-performance Ethernet revolutionized HPC scalability. Today, interconnects power exascale computing, AI research, and real-time data analytics, with continued innovation in optical networking and quantum interconnects.

Practical Implications

Interconnects are vital for scientific simulations, climate modeling, and drug discovery, enabling faster computations. Financial institutions use HPC interconnects for real-time trading algorithms and risk analysis. In autonomous vehicle development, interconnects facilitate AI-driven sensor data processing. Future advancements in photonics, neuromorphic computing, and 6G will further enhance interconnect efficiency, transforming fields like cybersecurity, precision medicine, and space exploration.

Interpretability (XAI)

Interpretability in Responsible AI refers to the ability to understand, explain, and analyze how an AI model makes decisions. It ensures transparency by allowing users to comprehend input-output relationships, detect biases, and improve trust in AI-driven processes across healthcare, finance, and legal systems.

Interpretability is like reading a recipe—just as a recipe breaks down how ingredients lead to a final dish, interpretability in AI reveals how inputs influence predictions, making AI models easier to audit, debug, and trust.

Examples

Healthcare AI Diagnostics: Interpretability ensures that AI-generated medical diagnoses can be verified by doctors, preventing misdiagnoses and biased treatment recommendations.

Financial Risk Analysis: In banking, AI-driven credit scoring models must be interpretable so lenders can explain loan approvals or denials to customers and regulators.

Autonomous Vehicles: Interpretability helps engineers understand and debug self-driving car decisions, ensuring they react appropriately to pedestrians, traffic signals, and environmental changes.

Foundational Concepts

Interpretability depends on model transparency, feature attribution, and decision tracing. White-box models, such as decision trees, offer high interpretability, while black-box models, like deep neural networks, require techniques like SHAP (Shapley Additive Explanations) and LIME (Local Interpretable Model-agnostic Explanations) to clarify decision-making. Causal inference helps establish relationships between inputs and predictions, while counterfactual analysis determines how small changes in data affect outcomes. Regulatory compliance, such as GDPR and AI ethics guidelines, mandates interpretability in high-stakes AI applications.

Related Terms

Explainability: The ability to justify AI decisions in human-understandable terms (see pg. 27).

Fairness in AI: Ensuring AI treats all user groups equitably and does not reinforce biases (see pg. 216).

Transparency: Open disclosure of AI models' inner workings, essential for trust and compliance (see pg. 502).

Common Misconceptions

Interpretability means full transparency: Some AI models remain complex despite explanation techniques.

Only simple models are interpretable: Deep learning can be interpretable using methods like saliency maps and gradient-based attribution.

Interpretability is only for ethics: It also improves debugging, auditing, and AI performance evaluation.

Historical Context

The demand for interpretability grew with AI adoption in regulated industries like finance and healthcare. Early expert systems (**1970s**-80s) were inherently interpretable, but deep learning (**2010s**) introduced opacity. Techniques like SHAP (**2017**) and LIME (**2016**) advanced AI interpretability. AI fairness research and policies like EU's **GDPR (2018)** emphasized the need for explainable AI (XAI), pushing developers to balance model performance with interpretability.

Practical Implications

Interpretability enhances AI adoption, regulatory compliance, and risk mitigation. In legal AI, judges require explanations for algorithmic sentencing decisions. In cybersecurity, AI-driven threat detection must be interpretable to differentiate between false positives and real threats. In human resources, AI-based hiring tools need transparency to ensure fair candidate evaluation. As AI shapes industries, improving interpretability will drive ethical and accountable AI development, deployment, and governance.

IoT Cloud Platform (IoT)

An IoT cloud platform is a centralized infrastructure that enables device connectivity, data storage, and remote management for Internet of Things (IoT) applications. It provides real-time analytics, scalability, and security for smart devices across industries such as healthcare, manufacturing, and smart cities.

An IoT cloud platform is like a digital nervous system—just as the human body collects sensory data and transmits it to the brain for interpretation and response, IoT devices send data to the cloud, where it is processed and analyzed for actionable insights.

Examples

Smart Home Automation: IoT cloud platforms allow smart thermostats and security cameras to analyze user behavior, optimize energy use, and enhance security.

Industrial IoT (IIoT): Factories use cloud-connected sensors to monitor equipment health, detect failures early, and improve predictive maintenance (see pg. 290).

Healthcare Remote Monitoring: Wearable devices send patient vitals to an IoT cloud platform, enabling doctors to track conditions remotely and intervene in emergencies.

Foundational Concepts

IoT cloud platforms operate on real-time data ingestion, edge computing, and AI-driven analytics. MQTT (Message Queuing Telemetry Transport) and CoAP (Constrained Application Protocol) facilitate lightweight, low-power device communication. Edge computing reduces latency by processing data closer to devices before sending it to the cloud. Security measures like end-to-end encryption and role-based access control (RBAC) protect sensitive IoT data. Scalability ensures cloud infrastructure can handle millions of connected devices in industrial and consumer applications.

Related Terms

Edge Computing: Processes data closer to IoT devices, reducing cloud dependency and latency (see pg. 192).

Digital Twin: A virtual model of a physical IoT device, enabling real-time monitoring and predictive analysis (see pg. 184).

5G & IoT: High-speed, low-latency 5G networks enhance IoT cloud performance and support massive device connectivity (see pg. 2).

Common Misconceptions

IoT cloud platforms only store data: They analyze and process data, enabling real-time automation and AI-driven insights.

All IoT platforms are cloud-based: Some rely on edge computing or hybrid architectures for faster processing.

IoT cloud platforms are only for large enterprises: Small businesses and individuals also use them for applications like home automation and personal health tracking.

Historical Context

The IoT cloud concept emerged with cloud computing advancements (**2000s**). **Amazon Web Services** (AWS) IoT (**2015**) and **Microsoft Azure IoT** (**2016**) pioneered cloud-based IoT management. The adoption of AI, 5G, and edge computing (**2020s**) expanded IoT capabilities. Open-source IoT platforms like **ThingsBoard** and **Eclipse IoT** increased accessibility, making IoT integration more widespread in industries such as logistics, healthcare, and smart cities.

Practical Implications

IoT cloud platforms revolutionize automation, efficiency, and decision-making. In logistics, real-time IoT tracking optimizes fleet management and supply chains. In agriculture, smart sensors enable precision farming and water conservation. In cybersecurity, AI-driven threat detection secures IoT networks against attacks. As IoT adoption grows, cloud platforms will integrate blockchain for security, quantum computing for analytics, and AI-driven automation to enhance efficiency across industries.

IoT Protocol (IoT)

An IoT protocol is a set of rules and communication standards that enable connected devices to exchange data efficiently within the Internet of Things (IoT) ecosystem. These protocols define how devices interact, transmit information, and ensure data security in smart homes, industrial automation, and healthcare applications.

An IoT protocol is like a common language between smart devices—just as different nations use shared languages to communicate, IoT protocols establish structured message formats and transmission rules to enable seamless interaction between sensors, networks, and cloud platforms.

Examples

Smart Agriculture: IoT protocols like LoRaWAN and MQTT help farmers monitor soil conditions, weather, and irrigation by transmitting sensor data over long distances.

Industrial Automation: Modbus and OPC UA facilitate real-time machine communication in factories, improving efficiency and predictive maintenance.

Smart Cities: CoAP and 6LoWPAN enable streetlights, traffic sensors, and waste management systems to communicate via low-power wireless networks, optimizing urban infrastructure.

Foundational Concepts

IoT protocols operate on layers of communication: application, network, and transport. MQTT (Message Queuing Telemetry Transport) is a lightweight messaging protocol ideal for low-bandwidth IoT devices. CoAP (Constrained Application Protocol) optimizes low-power communication for embedded sensors. 6LoWPAN (IPv6 over Low-power Wireless Personal Area Networks) enables IoT devices to efficiently communicate over IPv6. Security protocols like TLS (Transport Layer Security) ensure data encryption and authentication in IoT networks. Choosing the right protocol depends on energy efficiency, range, and data speed requirements.

Related Terms

Edge Computing: Reduces latency by processing IoT data near the source before sending it to the cloud (see pg. 192).

IoT Gateway: A bridge between IoT devices and cloud platforms, translating different protocols (see pg. 290).

Low-Power Wide-Area Network (LPWAN): A wireless network standard for long-range, low-energy IoT communication.

Common Misconceptions

All IoT devices use Wi-Fi: Many IoT devices rely on low-power protocols like Zigbee, LoRaWAN, and NB-IoT.

IoT protocols are one-size-fits-all: Different protocols serve specific needs based on range, power, and data requirements.

IoT security is built-in: Many protocols lack encryption, requiring additional security layers for data protection.

Historical Context

The evolution of IoT protocols began with industrial automation standards like **Modbus** (**1979**). The rise of wireless IoT led to **Zigbee** (**2003**) and **6LoWPAN** (**2007**) for low-power networking. **MQTT** (**1999**) became popular for cloud-based IoT communication. The IoT boom (**2010s-2020s**) saw the emergence of LPWAN technologies like **LoRaWAN** and **NB-IoT**, improving long-range device connectivity.

Practical Implications

IoT protocols enable smart environments and automation. In healthcare, Bluetooth Low Energy (BLE) allows wearable health monitors to send real-time vitals to doctors. In logistics, RFID and LPWAN help track shipments across supply chains. Energy grids use IoT protocols for smart metering and consumption optimization. As IoT expands, interoperability, security, and efficiency in protocol design will be crucial for global IoT standardization and deployment.

Jupyter Notebook (AI)

Jupyter Notebook is an open-source interactive computing environment that allows users to write and execute code, visualize data, and document workflows in a single interface. It supports multiple programming languages, with Python being the most common, and is widely used in data science, machine learning, and research.

Jupyter Notebook is like a digital lab notebook for programmers and data scientists. Just as a scientist records experiments, results, and observations in a physical notebook, Jupyter allows users to document, execute, and visualize code in a structured and interactive way.

Examples

Data Science & Machine Learning: Jupyter Notebooks enable data scientists to explore datasets, preprocess data, train machine learning models, and visualize results interactively, making it easier to iterate on models and document workflows.

Education & Teaching: Instructors use Jupyter Notebooks to teach programming, data science, and AI, providing students with interactive coding exercises and real-time feedback in an accessible format.

Scientific Research: Researchers in fields like bioinformatics and physics use Jupyter Notebooks to run simulations, analyze experimental data, and generate reports, fostering reproducibility and collaboration.

Foundational Concepts

Jupyter Notebook operates on the concept of interactive computing, allowing users to run code in small, manageable blocks called cells rather than executing an entire script at once. It integrates with IPython for enhanced execution and visualization capabilities. Jupyter uses a kernel-based architecture, where different kernels (e.g., Python, R, Julia) execute code within the notebook. Notebooks are stored in JSON-based .ipynb files, which preserve code, output, and markdown explanations in an easily shareable format. It supports rich media integration, including images, plots, and LaTeX equations.

Related Terms

IPython: An interactive Python shell that powers Jupyter Notebook's execution environment.

JupyterLab: An advanced version of Jupyter Notebook that provides a more flexible, multi-tab interface for interactive computing (see pg. 292).

Colab: A cloud-based implementation of Jupyter Notebooks by Google, offering free GPU and TPU resources for machine learning (see pg. 250).

Common Misconceptions

Jupyter Notebooks are only for Python: While Python is the most popular language, Jupyter supports multiple kernels, including R, Julia, and JavaScript.

Jupyter is only for beginners: Although it is widely used for learning, it is also a powerful tool for professionals in data science and research.

Jupyter replaces traditional IDEs: Jupyter is optimized for interactive and exploratory work but lacks features like debugging and large-scale software development tools found in full IDEs.

Historical Context

Jupyter Notebook originated from the **IPython** project, created by **Fernando Pérez** in **2001** to enhance Python's interactive capabilities. In **2014**, the Jupyter Project was launched to extend IPython's interactive environment beyond Python, incorporating support for multiple programming languages. The name "Jupyter" comes from **Julia**, **Python**, and **R**, the three core languages it initially supported. Over time, Jupyter has become a widely adopted standard in data science, research, and education, with integrations in cloud platforms and high-performance computing environments.

Practical Implications

Jupyter Notebook has revolutionized data science by enabling iterative and reproducible analysis. In education, it provides an intuitive platform for teaching programming and AI. Enterprises use Jupyter for prototyping machine learning models, conducting exploratory data analysis, and sharing insights. The scientific community benefits from its ability to document and share computational research. With cloud-based implementations like Google Colab and AWS SageMaker, Jupyter enables scalable and collaborative computing, making it an essential tool in modern computational workflows.

Label (AI)

A label in machine learning and artificial intelligence refers to the ground truth annotation assigned to data points, indicating their correct category, value, or meaning. Labels are essential for supervised learning, where models learn patterns by associating input data with predefined outcomes, improving their ability to make accurate predictions and classifications.

A label is like the tag on a clothing item that tells you its size, material, and brand. Just as a tag helps shoppers quickly identify key product details, a label in AI provides essential information about data, guiding machine learning models to correctly categorize and interpret it.

Examples

Spam Detection: Email providers use labeled datasets where emails are tagged as "spam" or "not spam" based on content, sender behavior, and user feedback, helping AI models filter out unwanted messages and reduce phishing attacks.

Medical Diagnosis: In healthcare AI, medical images such as X-rays and MRIs are labeled by doctors with conditions like tumors or fractures, training models to assist in early disease detection and diagnostic accuracy.

Speech Recognition: Virtual assistants like Siri and Alexa use labeled speech data where spoken words are transcribed into text, enabling AI to recognize voice commands and improve language understanding over time (see pg. 528).

Foundational Concepts

A label is a fundamental part of supervised learning, where models require labeled examples to learn patterns and relationships. Classification tasks involve assigning categorical labels (e.g., "cat" or "dog"), while regression problems use numerical labels (e.g., predicting house prices). Labeled data is often prepared through manual annotation by human experts or automated labeling via heuristic-based or AI-assisted techniques. Data augmentation and semi-supervised learning help expand labeled datasets, reducing reliance on extensive manual labeling while maintaining model accuracy.

Related Terms

Supervised Learning: A machine learning approach where models learn from labeled data to make predictions or classifications (see pg. 468).

Ground Truth: The actual, verified value of data points used to evaluate model accuracy.

Annotation: The process of assigning labels to data, often performed manually or with AI assistance.

Visual Representation

A diagram illustrating **labeled vs. unlabeled data** would be effective. It could depict two sets of images—one with labels such as "dog" and "cat" and another without any identifiers. A flowchart could show how labeled data feeds into a supervised learning model, improving its ability to classify new data.

Common Misconceptions

All AI requires labeled data: While supervised learning depends on labels, unsupervised and self-supervised learning methods can work without explicitly labeled data.

Labeling is always manual: Many labeling processes are automated using pretrained models, heuristics, or AI-assisted annotation tools to accelerate data preparation.

Labels are always correct: Human and automated labeling can introduce errors or bias, affecting model performance. Techniques like active learning help improve label quality.

Historical Context

The importance of labeled data became evident with the rise of supervised machine learning in the **1980s** and **1990s**. Early AI models, such as decision trees and support vector machines, relied on labeled datasets for training. The **ImageNet** project (**2009**) revolutionized computer vision by providing a large-scale labeled dataset, enabling deep learning breakthroughs. Today, AI-driven labeling tools and self-supervised learning techniques are reducing dependence on extensive manual annotation, shaping the future of AI model training.

Practical Implications

Labeled data is crucial in AI applications across industries. In healthcare, accurate labels improve disease detection models. In finance, labeled fraud detection datasets help prevent cybercrime. In autonomous vehicles, labeled sensor data enables self-driving cars to recognize pedestrians, road signs, and obstacles. As AI adoption grows, innovations in labeling automation, active learning, and data synthesis will shape AI's future, reducing reliance on human annotators while ensuring high-quality training data for machine learning models.

Label Propagation (AI)

Label propagation is a semi-supervised learning algorithm used to assign labels to unlabeled data points by spreading information from labeled instances in a dataset. It operates on graph-based structures, where nodes represent data points and edges define relationships, gradually propagating labels based on proximity and similarity.

Label propagation is like spreading dye in water—just as color diffuses and mixes with clear water, labeled data influences its neighboring unlabeled points in an AI model, ensuring that similar items acquire the same classification over time.

Examples

Fraud Detection: In financial security, label propagation helps identify fraudulent transactions by linking labeled cases of fraud to similar yet unlabeled transactions, ensuring accurate detection of emerging threats.

Medical Diagnosis: Healthcare AI models apply label propagation to assign probable diagnoses to medical images with unclear classifications, improving disease detection while minimizing manual annotation efforts.

Social Network Analysis: Social media platforms use label propagation to detect communities by spreading known user preferences across similar, unlabeled users, refining content recommendations and targeted advertising strategies.

Foundational Concepts

Label propagation relies on graph-based machine learning, where each data point is represented as a node, and relationships between them form edges. The algorithm spreads known labels iteratively across the network, using similarity metrics to determine label assignment confidence. Affinity matrices quantify connections between nodes, and Laplacian smoothing ensures a gradual, stable propagation process. This method is particularly effective when labeled data is scarce, leveraging the inherent structure of data distributions for improved classification accuracy.

Related Terms

Semi-Supervised Learning: A training method that combines labeled and unlabeled data for model development (see pg. 436).

Graph Neural Networks (GNNs): AI models that operate on graph-structured data, enhancing label propagation techniques.

Transductive Learning: A learning paradigm that infers labels only for specific data points within the given dataset.

Common Misconceptions

Label propagation is fully automatic: While efficient, it requires careful tuning of parameters to avoid misclassification in noisy datasets.

It only works with small datasets: The method scales to large datasets, though computational optimizations such as sparse matrix representations may be required.

It replaces supervised learning: Label propagation enhances learning but often requires some manual verification for quality assurance.

Historical Context

The concept of propagating information in networks originated from graph theory. Early semi-supervised learning research in the **1990s** explored propagating knowledge in partially labeled datasets. **The Label Propagation Algorithm** (LPA) was formally introduced in **2002** by **Zhu** and **Ghahramani**, pioneering its use in classification tasks. As AI evolved, advancements in graph neural networks have further optimized label propagation in large-scale applications.

Practical Implications

Label propagation is transforming data-driven industries. In cybersecurity, it detects fraudulent patterns in transactions. In healthcare, it enhances diagnostic AI models with minimal labeled data. In e-commerce, it improves recommendation systems by grouping customers with similar purchasing behaviors. Its ability to efficiently classify vast, partially labeled datasets makes it essential for AI-driven decision-making, particularly in fields where manually labeling every data point is impractical.

Labeled Data (AI)

Labeled data refers to datasets where each data point is tagged with predefined labels, indicating its category, value, or characteristics. These labels serve as ground truth, guiding supervised learning models to learn associations between input features and correct outputs, improving classification, regression, and prediction accuracy.

Labeled data is like a recipe book, where each dish (data point) has a name and detailed ingredients (features). Just as a cook follows labeled recipes to prepare meals correctly, AI models use labeled data to understand patterns and make accurate predictions.

Examples

Image Recognition: Facial recognition systems use labeled datasets containing images annotated with names or emotions, allowing AI to classify new images by matching them to known labeled patterns (see pg. 276).

Autonomous Vehicles: Self-driving cars rely on labeled sensor data where road signs, pedestrians, and vehicles are annotated, enabling the AI to detect and react to road conditions safely.

Healthcare Diagnostics: AI-driven medical tools use labeled MRI scans and X-rays marked with disease classifications, allowing models to assist in detecting conditions like tumors and fractures with high accuracy.

Foundational Concepts

Labeled data is fundamental to supervised learning, where models use labeled examples to learn decision boundaries and predict outcomes. Feature engineering enhances labeled datasets by selecting the most relevant attributes. Data annotation is performed manually by experts or automatically using AI-assisted tools. Overfitting can occur when models memorize labeled data instead of generalizing patterns, requiring regularization techniques. Labeled data is often split into training, validation, and test sets to ensure robust model performance. Techniques like semi-supervised learning help reduce dependence on large-scale labeled datasets.

Related Terms

Supervised Learning: A machine learning approach where models train on labeled data to map inputs to outputs (see pg. 468).

Annotation: The process of manually or automatically assigning labels to data points for AI training.

Training Data: The subset of labeled data used to train machine learning models before evaluation (see pg. 298 & 510).

Common Misconceptions

All AI models require labeled data: Some models, such as those in unsupervised and self-supervised learning, function without labeled data.

Labeled data is always accurate: Errors in labeling can introduce bias and noise, affecting model reliability and fairness.

Labeled data is easy to obtain: High-quality labeled datasets require time, expertise, and resources, making large-scale annotation expensive.

Historical Context

Labeled data has been central to AI since supervised learning emerged in the **1950s** with early rule-based AI systems. The development of large-scale labeled datasets such as ImageNet (**2009**) revolutionized deep learning by providing millions of labeled images for training. **Crowdsourcing** platforms like **Amazon Mechanical Turk** expanded dataset annotation efforts. More recently, advances in synthetic data generation and self-supervised learning have reduced the reliance on extensive manual labeling while maintaining model accuracy.

Practical Implications

Labeled data is essential across multiple industries. In healthcare, labeled medical images improve diagnostic AI accuracy. In finance, fraud detection models use labeled transactions to identify suspicious activities. In customer service, chatbots train on labeled dialogues to improve interactions. The growing demand for labeled data has led to AI-assisted annotation tools, active learning techniques, and transfer learning, making AI model training more scalable while reducing the manual effort required for labeling large datasets.

Large Language Model (LLM) (GenAI)

A Large Language Model (LLM) is an AI system trained on massive text datasets to understand, generate, and manipulate human language. Using deep learning and transformer architectures, LLMs process vast amounts of text, enabling applications such as conversational AI, text summarization, and content generation across various industries.

A Large Language Model is like a well-read librarian who has studied millions of books. While it doesn't create new ideas from scratch, it can retrieve, summarize, and rephrase information, mimicking human-like responses based on the patterns it has learned.

Examples

Chatbots and Virtual Assistants: AI-powered assistants like ChatGPT and Google Bard use LLMs to engage in human-like conversations, answer queries, and provide recommendations across various domains see pg. 528).

Automated Content Creation: Businesses leverage LLMs to generate blog articles, social media posts, and marketing content, streamlining copywriting and enhancing audience engagement with AI-generated text (see pg. 33).

Code Generation and Debugging: Tools like GitHub Copilot use LLMs to assist developers by generating code snippets, suggesting improvements, and identifying errors, increasing productivity in software development.

Foundational Concepts

Large Language Models rely on transformer architectures, specifically models like GPT (Generative Pre-trained Transformer) and BERT (Bidirectional Encoder Representations from Transformers). They undergo pretraining on massive text corpora and then fine-tuning on specialized datasets for improved accuracy. LLMs use tokenization to break down text into smaller units for processing, and attention mechanisms to weigh the relevance of words in context. Scaling laws indicate that increasing model size, data, and computation improves performance, but also raises challenges in bias, interpretability, and computational costs.

Related Terms

Natural Language Processing (NLP): The field of AI that enables machines to process and generate human language (see pg. 346).

Transformer Model: A deep learning architecture that improves contextual language understanding using self-attention mechanisms (see pg. 500).

Generative AI: AI systems designed to create text, images, or other media based on learned data patterns (see pg. 33).

Common Misconceptions

LLMs understand language like humans: While they mimic human-like responses, LLMs lack true comprehension and only generate statistically probable outputs.

LLMs always provide accurate information: These models can generate misleading or biased content based on training data limitations.

Bigger models always perform better: Scaling improves fluency but doesn't guarantee better reasoning or factual accuracy without effective training and fine-tuning.

Historical Context

LLMs evolved from early statistical language models and recurrent neural networks (RNNs). The introduction of transformers by **Vaswani et al. (2017)** revolutionized NLP. **OpenAI**'s GPT models, beginning with GPT-1 (**2018**) and advancing to GPT-4 (**2023**), significantly improved language understanding. **Google**'s **BERT (2018)** enhanced bidirectional language processing, while **T5** and **PaLM** introduced more efficient training paradigms. Today, LLMs continue to expand in size and capability, shaping AI-driven communication and automation.

Practical Implications

LLMs transform industries by enabling real-time translations, customer service automation, and advanced research tools. In healthcare, they assist in medical documentation and diagnostics. In education, AI tutors provide personalized learning. In law, they streamline document analysis. However, concerns around ethical AI, misinformation, and data privacy necessitate responsible deployment. As LLMs continue evolving, research into AI alignment, bias mitigation, and regulatory frameworks will be crucial in ensuring their benefits outweigh their risks.

Latency (HPC)

Latency refers to the time delay between initiating a task and receiving a response in a computing system. In High-Performance Computing (HPC), latency impacts the efficiency of data transfer, memory access, and network communication, directly influencing system performance and application speed.

Latency is like waiting for a letter to arrive by mail. While throughput determines how many letters are sent per hour, latency is the time it takes for a single letter to reach its destination. Lower latency means faster responses in computing, just as express mail speeds up deliveries.

Examples

Scientific Simulations: In climate modeling, low-latency HPC systems ensure that real-time atmospheric changes are processed instantly, enabling accurate weather forecasting and climate predictions.

Financial Trading: High-frequency trading (HFT) relies on ultra-low latency computing to execute trades in microseconds, reducing risk and maximizing profit in volatile stock markets.

AI Model Training: Deep learning frameworks process massive datasets across GPUs. Reducing latency in memory and data access accelerates model training, improving AI performance in applications like speech recognition and autonomous systems.

Foundational Concepts

Latency in HPC is influenced by network latency, memory latency, and processing latency. Network latency is the time taken for data packets to travel between nodes, affected by bandwidth, congestion, and distance. Memory latency occurs when a processor waits for data retrieval from RAM or cache, mitigated by caching strategies and prefetching. Processing latency refers to CPU or GPU execution delays, often minimized through parallel processing and optimized scheduling. Reducing latency bottlenecks is crucial for enhancing HPC efficiency, especially in distributed computing environments.

Related Terms

Throughput: The volume of data processed per unit time, contrasting with latency, which measures delay.

Parallel Computing: The simultaneous execution of multiple tasks to reduce processing latency (see pg. 364).

Edge Computing: A method of processing data closer to the source to reduce network latency (see pg. 192).

Common Misconceptions

Latency and throughput are the same: While related, latency measures delay, whereas throughput measures volume.

More bandwidth always reduces latency: Increased bandwidth improves throughput, but latency also depends on network efficiency and data routing.

Latency is only relevant in networking: It affects memory access, CPU processing, and data storage in all HPC applications.

Historical Context

The challenge of reducing latency emerged with supercomputing in the **1960s**, when **Seymour Cray** designed **Cray-1** to optimize memory access speeds. In the **1980s** and **1990s**, parallel computing helped mitigate latency by distributing workloads across multiple processors. The rise of GPUs and cloud-based HPC in the **2000s** introduced low-latency architectures, enabling real-time applications in AI, finance, and engineering. Today, exascale computing continues to push latency reduction for scientific breakthroughs and AI advancements.

Practical Implications

Reducing latency in HPC accelerates advancements in scientific research, AI, and real-time analytics. In healthcare, low-latency computing enables faster genome sequencing for precision medicine. In manufacturing, it enhances real-time robotic control for automation. In cybersecurity, ultra-low-latency threat detection prevents cyberattacks before they spread. As quantum computing and AI-driven optimization evolve, reducing latency remains critical for maximizing HPC performance and technological innovation.

Latency (XR)

Latency refers to the delay between a user's action in an Extended Reality (XR) environment and the system's response. In Virtual Reality (VR), Augmented Reality (AR), and Mixed Reality (MR), high latency can cause lag, motion sickness, and reduced immersion, affecting user experience and interaction quality.

Latency is like a conversation on a poor phone connection. If there's a delay between speaking and hearing the response, the conversation feels unnatural. Similarly, in XR, high latency causes lag between user movements and system updates, disrupting immersion and responsiveness.

Examples

VR Gaming: Low-latency VR headsets like the Meta Quest 3 ensure seamless motion tracking, reducing dizziness and motion sickness by minimizing response delays between head movements and display updates (see pg. 530).

AR Navigation: AR apps like Google Lens and Apple ARKit rely on minimal latency to overlay real-time navigation data onto the user's camera feed, ensuring accurate directions without noticeable lag.

Remote Collaboration: Platforms like Microsoft Mesh use low-latency XR to create real-time, lifelike virtual meeting spaces where participants interact as if they were physically present.

Foundational Concepts

Latency in XR depends on motion-to-photon latency, the time taken for a movement to be reflected on-screen. Tracking latency affects hand, head, and eye-tracking accuracy, while network latency influences cloud-based XR applications. Refresh rate and frame rate synchronization mitigate latency issues by ensuring smooth visuals. Edge computing and 5G reduce delays in cloud-based XR, while foveated rendering optimizes performance by prioritizing visual detail where the user is looking. Maintaining low latency is essential for avoiding motion sickness and achieving real-time interaction in VR and AR applications.

Related Terms

Frame Rate: The number of frames displayed per second, impacting the smoothness of XR experiences.

Edge Computing: A technology that processes data closer to the user to reduce network latency (see pg. 192).

Motion-to-Photon Latency: The delay between a user's movement and the corresponding update on the display.

Common Misconceptions

Latency is only a network issue: While network delays impact cloud-based XR, hardware and rendering delays also contribute to overall latency.

All XR systems have the same latency: Different devices and refresh rates affect latency, with standalone VR headsets generally having higher latency than PC-tethered systems.

High latency only affects gaming: Motion sickness, interaction lag, and poor hand-tracking affect training simulations, remote work, and healthcare XR applications as well.

Historical Context

Latency concerns in XR date back to the early **1990s** when **NASA**'s Virtual Environment Workstation struggled with motion sickness due to high response lag. In the **2010s**, advances in inertial tracking and low-persistence displays reduced latency in VR headsets like the **Oculus Rift**. 5G and edge computing in the **2020s** further minimized network-induced XR latency, enabling real-time remote collaboration and cloud-based VR rendering. Today, AI-driven motion prediction continues to optimize latency reduction in high-performance XR applications.

Practical Implications

Reducing latency is critical for VR training simulations in medicine, aviation, and military applications, where real-time feedback improves learning outcomes. In AR-assisted surgery, low-latency visual overlays help surgeons navigate procedures with precision. In immersive retail, reducing AR rendering lag enhances virtual try-ons and real-time product visualization. As XR adoption expands, innovations in AI-powered prediction, quantum computing, and ultra-low-latency networking will shape the future of seamless, high-fidelity virtual experiences.

Load Balancing (HPC)

Load balancing refers to the process of distributing computational tasks evenly across multiple processors, servers, or networks to optimize performance, prevent overload, and ensure efficient resource utilization. In High-Performance Computing (HPC), effective load balancing minimizes delays, enhances parallel processing efficiency, and enables large-scale simulations and AI training.

Load balancing is like traffic management on a multi-lane highway. If one lane is congested while others are empty, delays occur. By dynamically directing cars (computational tasks) to the least crowded lanes (processors), traffic (workload) moves smoothly, reducing bottlenecks and improving overall efficiency.

Examples

Scientific Simulations: Climate models and molecular simulations rely on load balancing to distribute computations across supercomputers, preventing idle processors and reducing simulation runtimes.

Cloud Computing Services: Platforms like Amazon Web Services (AWS) and Google Cloud use load balancers to allocate web traffic efficiently, ensuring optimal performance and availability of cloud-based applications.

AI Model Training: Deep learning models, such as GPT-4, require balanced distribution of computations across GPUs and TPUs, accelerating processing times while preventing memory overload and hardware failures.

Foundational Concepts

Load balancing in HPC involves static and dynamic scheduling. Static load balancing assigns tasks before execution, while dynamic load balancing adjusts task distribution in real-time based on processor availability and workload fluctuations. Round-robin scheduling evenly distributes requests, while least connections strategy directs tasks to the least occupied nodes. Parallel computing frameworks, such as MPI (Message Passing Interface) and OpenMP, optimize task allocation in distributed and multi-core computing environments. Efficient load balancing prevents resource wastage, enhances fault tolerance, and ensures high throughput in large-scale computations.

Related Terms

Parallel Computing: The execution of multiple computational tasks simultaneously to improve performance (see pg. 364).

Throughput: The rate at which computational tasks are completed within a given time frame.

Cluster Computing: The use of interconnected computers working together as a single system for high-performance tasks (see pg. 132).

Common Misconceptions

Load balancing is only for cloud computing: While crucial for cloud services, load balancing is fundamental in HPC, AI training, and large-scale simulations.

More processors always improve performance: Without proper load balancing, additional processors may remain idle or inefficiently utilized, leading to wasted resources.

Static load balancing is always better: Dynamic load balancing is often more effective in unpredictable workloads, adjusting to real-time system conditions.

Historical Context

The concept of load balancing emerged in the **1960s,** when early parallel computing systems sought to distribute workloads efficiently. In the **1980s** and **1990s,** supercomputing advancements led to the development of task scheduling algorithms in systems like **Cray** supercomputers. The rise of distributed computing in the **2000s** introduced network load balancing for web traffic. Today, AI-driven autonomous load balancing and predictive workload distribution optimize HPC, cloud services, and real-time AI applications.

Practical Implications

Load balancing is critical in scientific research, where large-scale simulations require efficient computation distribution. In healthcare, AI-driven medical imaging uses GPU load balancing to analyze vast datasets rapidly. In finance, high-frequency trading systems depend on low-latency load balancing for real-time risk analysis. Emerging technologies like edge computing and quantum computing continue to refine load balancing strategies, ensuring optimized resource management, energy efficiency, and high-performance analytics across industries.

Local vs. Global Explanations (XAI)

Local vs. Global Explanations refers to two approaches in Explainable AI (XAI). Local explanations clarify individual predictions made by an AI model, while global explanations provide insights into the overall decision-making process of the model. Both are crucial for transparency, trust, and accountability in AI systems.

Understanding local vs. global explanations is like analyzing a cookbook. A local explanation explains why a specific recipe turned out a certain way, focusing on individual ingredients. A global explanation provides an overview of the cookbook's guiding principles, helping understand how all recipes are structured and executed.

Examples

Healthcare Diagnostics: A local explanation in an AI-driven radiology system justifies why a specific X-ray was flagged for lung disease. A global explanation describes the general patterns the model uses to detect abnormalities across all X-rays.

Loan Approval Systems: A local explanation details why an applicant was denied a loan, showing which factors (e.g., credit score, income) influenced the decision. A global explanation describes how the AI model evaluates creditworthiness across all applicants.

Autonomous Vehicles: A local explanation clarifies why a self-driving car decided to stop at a particular moment. A global explanation provides insight into the AI's general driving logic, such as how it prioritizes pedestrian safety in all situations.

Foundational Concepts

Local explanations focus on individual AI outputs, making them useful for users seeking justification for specific decisions. Methods like LIME (Local Interpretable Model-agnostic Explanations) and SHAP (Shapley Additive Explanations) help identify which features influenced a single prediction. Global explanations, on the other hand, describe the model's overall structure, logic, and decision patterns, often achieved through rule extraction, feature importance analysis, and model visualization. Balancing both explanation types is key to ensuring AI systems are transparent, interpretable, and accountable in real-world applications.

Related Terms

Black-Box AI: AI models, such as deep neural networks, that make decisions without providing human-understandable reasoning (see pg. 118).

Feature Importance: A technique used to measure how much each input factor contributes to an AI model's predictions (see pg. 220).

Causal Explanations: A method that explains AI decisions by identifying cause-and-effect relationships between input variables and outcomes.

Common Misconceptions

Local explanations can replace global ones: Local explanations help users understand single decisions but don't provide insight into system-wide AI behavior.

Global explanations always reveal AI bias: While they highlight decision patterns, deeper bias detection methods are needed to uncover hidden model biases.

All AI models support both explanation types: Some complex models, like deep learning networks, struggle with transparent global explanations, requiring post-hoc analysis.

Historical Context

Interest in XAI grew as AI models became more complex. In the **1990s**, early rule-based AI systems provided explicit global explanations. The rise of deep learning in the **2010s** led to concerns over AI's "black-box" nature, prompting research into interpretable ML methods. **DARPA**'s **Explainable AI (XAI) initiative**, launched in **2016**, emphasized the need for both local and global interpretability. Advances in SHAP, LIME, and counterfactual explanations have since improved AI transparency across industries.

Practical Implications

Local explanations are essential in high-stakes AI applications, such as healthcare and finance, where users need to understand individual predictions. Global explanations help regulators, engineers, and policymakers assess model fairness, bias, and reliability. In autonomous systems, explainable AI improves safety by providing both real-time and system-wide decision insights. As AI adoption grows, ensuring explanation balance will be key to fostering trust, fairness, and ethical AI deployment across industries.

Loss Function (AI)

Loss function is a mathematical function that quantifies the difference between an AI model's predicted output and the actual target value. It guides the learning process by adjusting model parameters to minimize errors, improving accuracy in tasks like classification, regression, and reinforcement learning.

Loss function is like a GPS recalculating a route. If you take a wrong turn (incorrect prediction), the GPS measures the deviation from your destination (target value) and suggests an adjustment (parameter updates) to get you back on the most efficient path.

Examples

Image Classification: In computer vision, models like CNNs use cross-entropy loss to evaluate how well they classify images into categories, such as distinguishing between dogs and cats in an image dataset (see pg. 128).

Speech Recognition: AI-powered voice assistants minimize CTC (Connectionist Temporal Classification) loss to align spoken words with textual transcripts, reducing misinterpretations and improving speech-to-text accuracy (see pg. 460).

Stock Market Prediction: Mean Squared Error (MSE) is used in financial forecasting models to measure the deviation between predicted and actual stock prices, refining predictions by minimizing large errors.

Foundational Concepts

A loss function calculates the error between an AI model's prediction and the actual value, influencing the gradient descent optimization process. Mean Squared Error (MSE) is commonly used for regression, while cross-entropy loss is preferred for classification. In reinforcement learning, reward-based loss functions adjust model behavior based on rewards and penalties. The choice of loss function affects model performance, convergence speed, and stability. Regularization techniques, such as L1 and L2 norms, help prevent overfitting by penalizing large model weights.

Related Terms

Gradient Descent: An optimization algorithm that updates model parameters to minimize the loss function.

Overfitting: A condition where a model memorizes training data instead of generalizing patterns, leading to poor real-world performance (see pg. 362).

Regularization: Techniques like L1 (Lasso) and L2 (Ridge) that prevent excessive model complexity and improve generalization.

Common Misconceptions

Loss and accuracy are the same: Loss quantifies error, while accuracy measures correct predictions; a low loss does not always imply high accuracy.

Lower loss always means a better model: Excessive loss reduction may indicate overfitting, where the model performs well on training data but poorly on unseen data.

All models use the same loss function: Different tasks require specific loss functions, such as categorical cross-entropy for classification and MSE for regression.

Historical Context

The concept of loss functions emerged with early machine learning and statistical modeling. The least squares method, introduced by **Carl Friedrich Gauss** in the early 19th century, laid the foundation for MSE-based regression analysis. The rise of deep learning in the **2010s** led to advances in loss functions like cross-entropy for neural networks and reinforcement learning loss functions for AI-driven decision-making. **AutoML** and **meta-learning** continue to refine loss function selection for optimizing modern AI models.

Practical Implications

A well-chosen loss function ensures AI models achieve high accuracy, stability, and efficiency. In healthcare, medical imaging models use binary cross-entropy to detect diseases. In autonomous driving, self-driving cars leverage reinforcement learning loss to refine real-time decision-making. In natural language processing (NLP), transformers like GPT-4 optimize text generation by minimizing language modeling loss. As AI evolves, the design and optimization of loss functions remain crucial for improving model performance, fairness, and generalization across industries.

Machine-to-Machine (M2M) Communication (IoT)

Machine-to-Machine (M2M) communication refers to the automatic exchange of data between connected devices without human intervention. It enables smart systems to function autonomously, optimizing processes in industries like healthcare, manufacturing, transportation, and IoT networks, improving efficiency, and enabling real-time decision-making.

M2M communication is like two walkie-talkies exchanging messages automatically. Instead of people speaking, sensors and devices send and receive signals, adjusting their behavior based on data without needing human supervision, just like an autopilot system fine-tuning flight controls without a pilot's input.

Examples

Smart Grid Systems: In energy distribution, smart meters use M2M communication to adjust power supply based on demand, preventing overload and optimizing electricity usage.

Industrial Automation: Manufacturing plants utilize M2M-enabled robots that coordinate assembly lines, adjusting speed and production rates in real time to maintain efficiency.

Connected Healthcare: Remote patient monitoring devices transmit vital signs to healthcare providers, enabling real-time medical alerts and predictive diagnostics without manual intervention.

Foundational Concepts

M2M communication relies on sensors, wireless networks, and automated control systems to enable real-time data exchange between devices. These systems use Internet of Things (IoT) protocols, 5G networks, and cloud computing for seamless integration. Embedded SIMs (eSIMs) and LPWAN (Low-Power Wide-Area Networks) facilitate secure, low-energy communication over vast distances. Edge computing enhances M2M processing, reducing latency by analyzing data closer to the source. As AI integrates with M2M networks, predictive analytics and autonomous decision-making become increasingly sophisticated.

Related Terms

Internet of Things (IoT): A network of interconnected smart devices that use M2M communication for automation and data-driven decision-making (see pg. 288 & 290).

Edge Computing: A method of processing data locally on a device rather than relying on central cloud servers, reducing latency in M2M systems (see pg. 192).

Telemetry: The automatic collection and transmission of data from remote sources, a fundamental principle of M2M communication in industries like aerospace and healthcare.

Common Misconceptions

M2M is the same as IoT: While M2M enables IoT, IoT includes a broader ecosystem, incorporating cloud computing, AI, and big data analytics.

M2M requires the internet: M2M communication can occur over cellular networks, Bluetooth, RFID, and proprietary communication protocols without needing an internet connection.

M2M devices always require AI: While AI enhances M2M efficiency, traditional M2M systems can function with predefined logic-based automation.

Historical Context

The concept of M2M communication originated with telemetry systems in the early 20th century, used for remote monitoring in aerospace and military applications. The **1960s** saw M2M adoption in telephone networks and industrial automation. In the **1990s** and **2000s**, advancements in wireless technology and IoT expanded M2M applications, enabling smart cities, connected vehicles, and industrial robotics. The rise of 5G, edge computing, and AI-driven automation has made M2M systems more efficient, scalable, and adaptive.

Practical Implications

M2M communication enhances logistics, transportation, and manufacturing by enabling automated inventory tracking, fleet management, and predictive maintenance. In agriculture, smart irrigation systems optimize water usage based on real-time weather data. In healthcare, wearable sensors detect early signs of diseases and transmit alerts automatically. The integration of AI, blockchain, and quantum computing with M2M communication is shaping the future of autonomous decision-making, cybersecurity, and next-generation industrial automation.

Malware (Malicious Software) (CS)

Malware refers to any software designed to harm, exploit, or disrupt computers, networks, or systems. It includes viruses, worms, ransomware, spyware, and trojans, often used for data theft, financial fraud, espionage, and system damage. Malware spreads through phishing emails, malicious websites, software vulnerabilities, and infected devices.

Malware is like a Trojan horse in ancient warfare—disguised as something harmless, it enters a system unnoticed and unleashes damage from within. Just as soldiers hid inside the horse, malware operates covertly, stealing data, disrupting operations, or controlling devices without user consent.

Examples

Ransomware Attacks: WannaCry and Ryuk ransomware encrypt user files and demand payment for decryption, crippling businesses, hospitals, and government agencies worldwide (see pg. 402).

Banking Trojans: Malware like Zeus infiltrates financial systems, stealing online banking credentials, enabling cybercriminals to transfer money without detection.

Spyware in Smartphones: Pegasus spyware infiltrates mobile devices, secretly accessing calls, messages, and camera feeds, often used for surveillance of high-profile individuals.

Foundational Concepts

Malware operates by exploiting vulnerabilities in software or human behavior. Polymorphic malware constantly alters its code to evade detection by antivirus software. Rootkits embed deep within operating systems, enabling persistent access. Botnets use infected devices to launch large-scale DDoS attacks, overwhelming servers. Advanced persistent threats (APTs) are stealthy, long-term cyberattacks targeting sensitive organizations. Zero-day exploits take advantage of undisclosed security flaws before they are patched. Modern cybersecurity relies on AI-driven malware detection, behavioral analysis, and threat intelligence to combat evolving malware threats.

Related Terms

Phishing: A cyberattack technique where attackers trick users into revealing sensitive information through deceptive emails or websites (see pg. 366).

Zero-Day Vulnerability: A security flaw unknown to software developers, exploited by hackers before a patch is available (see pg. 534).

Botnet: A network of compromised computers controlled remotely to perform malicious activities, such as spam distribution and cyberattacks.

Common Misconceptions

Only Windows devices are affected: While Windows is a frequent target, malware also affects macOS, Linux, Android, and IoT devices.

Antivirus software is enough protection: Modern malware bypasses traditional signature-based detection, requiring AI-powered security and user vigilance.

Malware always causes visible harm: Many malware types, like spyware and keyloggers, operate silently, stealing data without the user's knowledge.

Historical Context

The first malware, the **Creeper worm (1971)**, was a harmless program testing network movement. In the **1980s**, the **Brain virus** became the first PC virus, marking the rise of computer infections. The **2000s** saw ransomware, botnets, and phishing attacks becoming cybercrime tools. **Stuxnet (2010)**, a government-created worm, demonstrated malware's role in cyber warfare. Today, AI-driven malware, deepfake attacks, and IoT vulnerabilities shape the future of cybersecurity threats.

Practical Implications

Malware protection is critical for financial institutions, healthcare, and national security. In business, cyberattacks disrupt operations and result in financial losses. In healthcare, ransomware paralyzes hospital systems, endangering patients. As AI-enhanced malware grows more sophisticated, organizations must adopt real-time threat detection, multi-layered security, and proactive cybersecurity frameworks to prevent breaches. Zero-trust architecture and cloud security solutions play an increasing role in mitigating malware risks in the digital era.

Markov Decision Process (MDP) (AI)

Markov Decision Process (MDP) is a mathematical framework used in reinforcement learning and decision-making where outcomes are partially random and depend on actions taken by an agent. It consists of states, actions, transition probabilities, rewards, and policies, enabling optimal decision-making in uncertain environments.

MDP is like navigating a maze in the dark with only a flashlight. Each move (action) leads to a new location (state) based on probability, and rewards guide the best path. The goal is to maximize rewards while adapting to uncertain surroundings.

Examples

Robotics Navigation: Autonomous robots use MDPs to decide movement strategies, balancing efficiency and avoiding obstacles while navigating unpredictable environments like warehouses or disaster zones.

Healthcare Treatment Plans: AI-driven medical decision-making systems use MDPs to optimize patient treatment plans by predicting how different therapies will affect recovery over time.

Financial Trading: Trading algorithms apply MDPs to model market behavior, determining when to buy or sell stocks by considering uncertainty, historical trends, and potential rewards.

Foundational Concepts

An MDP is defined by a set of states (S), actions (A), transition probabilities (P), and rewards (R). The Markov property states that the future state depends only on the current state and action, not past history. Policy (π) guides action selection to maximize cumulative rewards. Discount factor (γ) determines how much future rewards influence present decisions. Bellman equations help compute optimal policies, forming the foundation of dynamic programming, reinforcement learning, and AI-based decision-making.

Related Terms

Reinforcement Learning (RL): A machine learning paradigm where agents learn optimal strategies through rewards and penalties (see pg. 410).

Bellman Equation: A recursive formula used to calculate the best possible decision-making strategy in an MDP.

Q-Learning: A model-free reinforcement learning algorithm that estimates the value of actions to maximize long-term rewards in an MDP.

Common Misconceptions

MDPs always yield deterministic outcomes: MDPs involve probabilistic transitions, meaning the same action can lead to different outcomes.

All decision processes are MDPs: Not all problems follow the Markov property; some require Partially Observable MDPs (POMDPs) for handling hidden information.

MDPs are only used in AI: While crucial in reinforcement learning, MDPs are widely applied in economics, robotics, and healthcare.

Historical Context

The Markov Decision Process was formalized in the **1950s** by **Richard Bellman**, who introduced dynamic programming to solve sequential decision-making problems. **Andrey Markov**'s earlier work on stochastic processes laid the foundation for MDPs. The **1980s–2000s** saw MDPs applied to AI, robotics, and control systems. With the rise of deep reinforcement learning, companies like **DeepMind** leverage MDPs to train AI in games, healthcare, and autonomous systems.

Practical Implications

MDPs are crucial for robotics, self-driving cars, and AI assistants, helping machines make sequential decisions under uncertainty. In supply chain management, they optimize logistics by balancing demand fluctuations and transportation constraints. In healthcare, AI models improve personalized treatments using MDP-driven adaptive strategies. As AI advances, deep reinforcement learning with MDPs will continue shaping autonomous decision-making, economic modeling, and AI ethics.

Masked Language Modeling (MLM) (AI)

Masked Language Modeling (MLM) is a self-supervised learning technique used in natural language processing (NLP) to train AI models by predicting masked words within a sentence. By randomly masking portions of input text, models learn contextual relationships, improving language understanding, text generation, and machine translation.

MLM is like solving a fill-in-the-blank puzzle. If you read, "The cat sat on the ___," you can predict "mat" using context. Similarly, AI models learn to reconstruct missing words, improving their understanding of sentence structures and meaning.

Examples

Pretraining Language Models: Models like BERT (Bidirectional Encoder Representations from Transformers) use MLM to understand sentence context, enhancing applications like chatbots, summarization, and search engines.

Speech-to-Text Optimization: MLM-trained models improve speech recognition systems by reconstructing missing words from noisy or incomplete transcriptions, enhancing AI-driven voice assistants like Siri and Google Assistant (see pg. 460).

Machine Translation: AI translation models leverage MLM to learn grammatical structures and word relationships across languages, increasing the fluency and accuracy of tools like Google Translate.

Foundational Concepts

MLM is based on self-supervised learning, where words in a sentence are randomly masked, and the AI model predicts them based on surrounding context. Unlike traditional left-to-right models, MLM enables bidirectional learning, improving semantic comprehension. It plays a key role in pretraining deep learning architectures, particularly transformers like BERT, RoBERTa, and T5. Tokenization techniques such as WordPiece and Byte-Pair Encoding help break text into subword units for more efficient learning. MLM enhances contextual embeddings, making AI-generated text more cohesive and accurate.

Related Terms

Self-Supervised Learning: A machine learning approach where models learn patterns from incomplete data without explicit labels (see pg. 430).

Bidirectional Encoding: A technique allowing AI models to process text from both left-to-right and right-to-left, improving contextual understanding.

Tokenization: The process of breaking text into smaller units (tokens), crucial for MLM-based models to handle words, subwords, and characters efficiently.

Common Misconceptions

MLM requires labeled data: Unlike supervised learning, MLM is a self-supervised technique, eliminating the need for manually labeled datasets.

MLM trains AI to memorize words: MLM models learn contextual relationships, not just individual words, improving generalization to unseen text.

MLM works for all AI tasks: While powerful in NLP, MLM is less effective for domains like image or numerical data processing, where other techniques are preferred.

Historical Context

MLM gained prominence with the release of BERT (**2018**) by **Google AI**, introducing bidirectional language modeling for superior NLP performance. Inspired by cloze tests in linguistics, MLM replaced traditional left-to-right prediction methods. Further research led to advancements like **RoBERTa (2019)**, which refined MLM training strategies. Today, MLM-powered AI models drive advancements in chatbots, semantic search, and multilingual translation, shaping the future of context-aware AI systems.

Practical Implications

MLM revolutionized AI-driven search engines, chatbots, and automated writing assistants, making them more contextually aware and human-like. In education, AI models enhance language tutoring and grammar correction. In healthcare, MLM-based NLP assists in medical text analysis and automated documentation. As multimodal AI evolves, MLM principles continue to improve cross-lingual communication, content moderation, and legal document processing, expanding AI's role in real-world applications.

Massive Machine-Type Communications (mMTC) (5G)

Massive Machine-Type Communications (mMTC) refers to a wireless communication standard designed for large-scale Internet of Things (IoT) networks, enabling billions of low-power devices to transmit data with minimal human intervention. It supports smart cities, industrial automation, and remote monitoring applications by ensuring efficient connectivity in dense environments.

mMTC is like an automated postal system handling millions of small packages daily. Each package (data transmission) is lightweight but vital. The system ensures deliveries (communications) reach their destination efficiently without congestion, despite the overwhelming volume of simultaneous transmissions.

Examples

Smart Cities: mMTC enables connected infrastructure such as smart streetlights, traffic monitoring, and waste management sensors, optimizing urban efficiency while reducing costs and energy consumption.

Agricultural IoT: Farmers use mMTC-enabled sensors for soil moisture monitoring, automated irrigation, and livestock tracking, allowing precise resource management and improving crop yields with minimal manual oversight.

Industrial Automation: mMTC-powered smart factories use thousands of connected sensors and machines to monitor real-time production data, predictive maintenance, and supply chain logistics, enhancing efficiency and reducing downtime.

Foundational Concepts

mMTC is a core component of 5G networks, designed to support a vast number of low-power, low-data-rate devices with minimal latency. Unlike traditional human-centric communication, mMTC optimizes network resources for short, infrequent transmissions. Low-power wide-area networks (LPWANs) such as NB-IoT (Narrowband IoT) and LoRaWAN extend connectivity to remote areas with minimal energy consumption. Advanced network slicing and spectrum sharing ensure scalability, while AI-driven traffic management helps prioritize critical communications in dense IoT ecosystems.

Related Terms

Internet of Things (IoT): A network of smart devices that use mMTC to communicate and exchange data autonomously (see pg. 288 & 290).

5G Networks: The next-generation mobile communication standard enabling mMTC, ultra-reliable low-latency communication (URLLC), and enhanced mobile broadband (eMBB) (see pg 2).

Edge Computing: A distributed computing paradigm that processes IoT data closer to the source, reducing network congestion and improving mMTC efficiency (see pg 192).

Common Misconceptions

mMTC requires high data rates: mMTC prioritizes large-scale, low-data transmissions over high-speed connections, making it ideal for IoT devices rather than high-bandwidth applications.

mMTC is only useful for smart cities: While urban applications benefit greatly, mMTC is crucial for agriculture, healthcare, manufacturing, and logistics.

mMTC consumes high energy: mMTC devices are optimized for low power consumption, enabling years of operation on a single battery.

Historical Context

The need for massive IoT connectivity emerged in the early **2010s**, as industries sought efficient ways to integrate billions of devices into wireless networks. The development of 5G standards (3GPP Release 15 and 16) formalized mMTC as a key component. LPWAN technologies, including NB-IoT and LTE-M, laid the groundwork for scalable IoT deployments. Today, mMTC-driven solutions power global initiatives in automation, environmental monitoring, and smart grids, shaping the future of ubiquitous connectivity.

Practical Implications

mMTC enables autonomous monitoring and control in industries ranging from transportation to healthcare. In energy management, smart meters track consumption patterns, optimizing electricity distribution. In telemedicine, wearable devices monitor patient vitals, transmitting data to healthcare providers. As 6G networks and AI-driven IoT evolve, mMTC's role in digital transformation will expand, enabling hyper-connected environments, self-sustaining smart cities, and intelligent automation across the globe.

Massive MIMO (Multiple-Input Multiple-Output) (5G)

Massive MIMO (Multiple-Input Multiple-Output) is an advanced wireless communication technology that enhances network capacity, data rates, and signal reliability by using a large number of antennas at base stations. It plays a key role in 5G and future 6G networks, improving spectral efficiency and reducing interference.

Massive MIMO is like a crowded concert where hundreds of conversations occur simultaneously. Instead of shouting, people use multiple microphones and speakers that direct sound to specific individuals, ensuring clear communication despite the dense environment, just as antennas direct signals efficiently in wireless networks.

Examples

5G Networks: Massive MIMO improves cellular performance by enabling multiple users to connect simultaneously while maintaining high data speeds, reducing congestion in urban areas (see pg 2).

Smart Cities: Public Wi-Fi systems use Massive MIMO to provide reliable connectivity in high-density locations like airports, stadiums, and city centers, ensuring seamless service despite user crowding.

Autonomous Vehicles: Massive MIMO facilitates high-speed vehicle-to-infrastructure (V2I) communication, enabling real-time data exchange for traffic management, navigation, and collision avoidance.

Foundational Concepts

Massive MIMO relies on beamforming, spatial multiplexing, and channel state information (CSI) to efficiently transmit and receive signals. Beamforming directs wireless signals toward specific users, reducing interference. Spatial multiplexing allows multiple data streams to be sent simultaneously over the same frequency band, increasing network capacity. CSI feedback loops optimize real-time signal adjustments based on environmental conditions. Massive MIMO enhances spectral efficiency, minimizes latency, and improves network robustness, making it fundamental to modern wireless communication.

Related Terms

Beamforming: A signal-processing technique that focuses radio waves toward specific users instead of broadcasting in all directions (see pg 102).

Spatial Multiplexing: A method of transmitting multiple data streams simultaneously using separate antennas, increasing throughput without additional bandwidth.

5G New Radio (5G NR): The wireless standard that integrates Massive MIMO to support ultra-fast, low-latency communication (see pg 62).

Common Misconceptions

Massive MIMO only increases speed: While higher data rates are a benefit, Massive MIMO primarily enhances network reliability, spectral efficiency, and interference management.

More antennas always mean better performance: Performance depends on beamforming accuracy, network conditions, and user distribution, not just antenna count.

Massive MIMO is only for 5G: While essential to 5G, it also benefits 4G LTE and will be critical in 6G and future wireless networks.

Historical Context

MIMO technology dates back to the **1970s**, with **Bell Labs** pioneering early multi-antenna systems. In the **1990s** and **2000s**, multi-user MIMO (MU-MIMO) improved wireless performance, paving the way for Massive MIMO, first proposed by **Thomas L. Marzetta** in **2010**. The adoption of 5G standards (3GPP Release 15 and 16) integrated Massive MIMO into modern cellular networks. Ongoing research explores its role in 6G, satellite communication, and AI-driven adaptive networks.

Practical Implications

Massive MIMO is transforming telecommunications, IoT, and edge computing by providing high-speed, low-latency connections for smart homes, industrial automation, and remote healthcare. In rural connectivity, it bridges digital divides by improving network reach. In defense and aerospace, Massive MIMO strengthens secure, anti-jamming military communications. As AI-driven self-optimizing networks evolve, Massive MIMO's role in energy-efficient, high-capacity wireless ecosystems will continue to expand.

Millimeter Wave (mmWave) (5G)

Millimeter wave (mmWave) refers to electromagnetic waves with frequencies between 30 GHz and 300 GHz, enabling high-speed wireless communication with large bandwidth. Used in 5G networks, radar systems, and satellite communications, mmWave supports ultra-fast data transfer but has limited range and penetration.

mmWave is like a high-pressure water hose—delivering an extremely strong and focused stream (high-speed data), but only at close range. Just as water disperses when encountering obstacles, mmWave signals weaken when obstructed by walls, trees, or heavy rain.

Examples

5G Wireless Networks: mmWave enables multi-gigabit internet speeds in urban environments, improving video streaming, gaming, and augmented reality experiences (see pg 2).

Airport Security Scanners: Full-body scanners use mmWave technology to detect concealed objects without physical contact, enhancing airport security screening.

Autonomous Vehicles: mmWave radar sensors provide precise distance measurement and object detection, improving collision avoidance and navigation in self-driving cars.

Foundational Concepts

mmWave operates in the high-frequency spectrum, allowing wider bandwidths and faster data transfer than traditional sub-6 GHz signals. However, short wavelength propagation limits range and penetration, requiring small cell networks, beamforming, and MIMO antennas to ensure connectivity. Beamforming directs mmWave signals precisely toward users, enhancing signal strength and efficiency. Massive MIMO employs multiple antennas to improve coverage, capacity, and reliability. Adaptive signal processing compensates for environmental interference, making mmWave viable for urban 5G deployment.

Related Terms

Beamforming: A technique that focuses wireless signals in specific directions to enhance coverage and reduce interference (see pg 102).

Massive MIMO: A multi-antenna system that improves mmWave transmission efficiency, enabling high-capacity wireless networks (see pg 322).

Small Cells: Low-power base stations that extend mmWave coverage, ensuring seamless 5G connectivity in dense urban areas (see pg 444).

Common Misconceptions

mmWave is only for 5G: While 5G benefits significantly, mmWave is widely used in radar systems, medical imaging, and space communications.

mmWave can penetrate walls: Unlike lower-frequency signals, mmWave has poor penetration, requiring dense network infrastructure for effective indoor coverage.

mmWave causes health risks: mmWave radiation is non-ionizing, meaning it lacks the energy to damage DNA, making it safe for human exposure.

Historical Context

mmWave technology was first explored for military radar systems in the **1940s**. By the **1990s**, it became crucial for satellite communications and remote sensing. 5G mmWave research accelerated in the **2010s**, with major breakthroughs in beamforming and MIMO antennas. The **2019** rollout of 5G networks by **Verizon**, **AT&T**, and other telecom providers marked mmWave's large-scale deployment, driving advancements in next-generation wireless connectivity.

Practical Implications

mmWave enables ultra-fast 5G services, low-latency cloud computing, and high-definition video streaming. In healthcare, mmWave medical imaging offers non-invasive diagnostic tools. In transportation, mmWave radar improves self-driving car safety. As 6G development progresses, mmWave research continues to enhance space exploration, high-frequency trading, and immersive augmented reality applications.

Mining (BC)

Mining is the process of validating and adding new transactions to a blockchain by solving complex mathematical puzzles. It ensures network security, decentralization, and consensus in Proof-of-Work (PoW) blockchains, such as Bitcoin and Ethereum (pre-2.0 upgrade), rewarding miners with cryptocurrency.

Mining is like solving a Sudoku puzzle to earn a prize. The first person to solve it (miner) gets a reward, and once verified by others, the solution (new block) is added to the official record (blockchain), ensuring accuracy and security.

Examples

Bitcoin Mining: Miners use powerful ASIC (Application-Specific Integrated Circuit) machines to solve cryptographic puzzles, validating transactions and securing the Bitcoin network, earning new BTC as rewards.

Ethereum Mining (Pre-2.0): Before transitioning to Proof-of-Stake (PoS), Ethereum miners verified transactions and smart contracts using graphics processing units (GPUs) to maintain the blockchain's integrity and process decentralized applications (DApps).

Monero Mining: Monero, a privacy-focused cryptocurrency, enables CPU-friendly mining, allowing individuals to contribute computational power while maintaining high transaction anonymity.

Foundational Concepts

Mining relies on the Proof-of-Work (PoW) consensus mechanism, where miners compete to solve hash puzzles using computational power. The winning miner adds a new block of transactions to the blockchain ledger and receives a block reward and transaction fees. Hashing algorithms, such as SHA-256 (Bitcoin) and Ethash (Ethereum pre-2.0), ensure secure and immutable transactions. Mining difficulty adjusts dynamically to maintain a consistent block creation time, preventing excessive inflation or network instability.

Related Terms

Proof-of-Work (PoW): A consensus mechanism requiring computational effort to validate transactions, ensuring security in blockchains like Bitcoin.

Hash Rate: The total computational power used by miners to solve cryptographic puzzles, influencing mining speed and network security.

Mining Pool: A collective group of miners pooling computational resources to increase their chances of earning rewards, splitting profits based on contribution.

Common Misconceptions

Mining creates cryptocurrency from nothing: Mining rewards new coins but also secures and verifies transactions, preventing fraud and double-spending.

All cryptocurrencies require mining: Many blockchains, like Ethereum 2.0 and Cardano, use Proof-of-Stake (PoS) instead of mining for validation.

Mining is easy and always profitable: Rising hardware costs, electricity consumption, and difficulty adjustments make solo mining increasingly unprofitable.

Historical Context

Bitcoin mining began in **2009**, when **Satoshi Nakamoto** mined the genesis block, rewarding 50 BTC. Initially feasible on personal computers, mining soon required GPUs and ASICs due to rising difficulty. Mining pools emerged in **2010**, enabling collective rewards. **Ethereum**'s transition to PoS (**2022**) reduced reliance on energy-intensive mining, while **Bitcoin**'s halving events continue to shape mining economics.

Practical Implications

Mining secures decentralized blockchain networks, preventing fraud and enabling trustless financial transactions. In developing regions, crypto mining provides alternative income sources. However, concerns over energy consumption, environmental impact, and centralization of mining power have led to shifts toward eco-friendly consensus models, like Proof-of-Stake (PoS) and green mining solutions using renewable energy. As blockchain technology evolves, mining remains a key driver of digital asset ecosystems and decentralized finance (DeFi).

Mixed Reality (MR) (XR)

Mixed Reality (MR) blends physical and digital environments, allowing real-world objects to interact seamlessly with virtual elements in real time. Unlike Virtual Reality (VR), which is fully immersive, or Augmented Reality (AR), which overlays digital content, MR enables dynamic interaction between the physical and virtual worlds, enhancing human-computer interaction.

MR is like a magician's stage where digital illusions appear real. A user wearing MR glasses can see and manipulate holographic objects alongside physical ones, much like a performer interacting with projected images that respond to movement and touch.

Examples

Medical Training: MR-based simulations allow surgeons to practice complex procedures on virtual patients that respond realistically, improving precision and reducing real-world risks.

Remote Collaboration: Platforms like Microsoft HoloLens enable teams to interact with 3D holograms while discussing designs, aiding industries like architecture, engineering, and automotive development.

Gaming and Entertainment: MR-powered gaming lets users engage with virtual characters and objects in real-world settings, creating immersive experiences beyond traditional screen-based gaming.

Foundational Concepts

MR operates using advanced computer vision, spatial mapping, and AI-driven object recognition to merge physical and virtual environments. SLAM (Simultaneous Localization and Mapping) enables devices to understand and track surroundings in real time. Holographic rendering creates interactive digital objects that respond to human gestures, eye tracking, and environmental changes. 5G and edge computing enhance MR applications by reducing latency, allowing seamless remote collaboration, training, and entertainment experiences. Gesture recognition and haptic feedback further enrich interaction, making digital elements feel tangible.

Related Terms

Augmented Reality (AR): Overlays digital content onto the real world but does not allow interaction between real and virtual objects (see pg 92).

Virtual Reality (VR): Creates a fully immersive digital environment, isolating users from the physical world (see pg. 530).

Holography: A technique that uses light diffraction to create 3D images, central to MR headsets like Microsoft HoloLens and Magic Leap.

Common Misconceptions

MR is just an advanced form of AR: Unlike AR, which only overlays content, MR enables real-time interaction between digital and physical objects.

MR requires expensive hardware: While premium MR headsets exist, mobile-based MR applications are increasingly accessible on smartphones and tablets.

MR is only for gaming: MR has practical applications in education, healthcare, manufacturing, and business, extending far beyond entertainment.

Historical Context

The term Mixed Reality was coined in **1994** by **Paul Milgram** and **Fumio Kishino**, defining a spectrum between real and virtual environments. Early MR prototypes emerged in the **2000s**, but it wasn't until **Microsoft** introduced **HoloLens** (**2016**) that MR gained commercial viability. Companies like **Meta**, **Magic Leap**, and **Apple** have since advanced MR technology, integrating AI, cloud computing, and 5G to improve interactivity and accessibility.

Practical Implications

MR is revolutionizing industries by enhancing remote work, education, and product design. In healthcare, MR assists in surgical planning and patient rehabilitation. In manufacturing, MR-guided assembly reduces errors and improves efficiency. In education, interactive MR learning environments boost engagement and comprehension. As AI-powered MR applications evolve, they will drive innovation in smart cities, digital commerce, and human-machine collaboration, reshaping how people interact with technology.

Mobile IoT (MIoT) (IoT)

Mobile IoT (MIoT) refers to a network of low-power, wide-area (LPWA) connected devices that communicate wirelessly using cellular technologies such as LTE-M and NB-IoT. It enables real-time data exchange in smart cities, logistics, healthcare, and industrial automation, enhancing mobility, scalability, and efficiency.

MIoT is like a fleet of delivery drones connected to a central system. Each drone reports location, battery status, and cargo information in real-time, allowing seamless coordination, just as MIoT devices continuously exchange data over cellular networks without human intervention.

Examples

Smart Transportation: MIoT sensors in vehicles and traffic systems monitor congestion, optimize routes, and improve road safety through real-time communication.

Asset Tracking: Logistics companies use MIoT-enabled GPS trackers on shipping containers, allowing real-time location monitoring, theft prevention, and supply chain optimization.

Remote Healthcare: Wearable MIoT devices track patient vitals, transmitting data to healthcare providers via cellular networks, enabling continuous remote monitoring and predictive diagnosis.

Foundational Concepts

MIoT relies on cellular LPWAN technologies such as NB-IoT (Narrowband IoT) and LTE-M (Long-Term Evolution for Machines), designed for low-power, long-range communication. Unlike traditional Wi-Fi or short-range IoT protocols, MIoT enables real-time connectivity over vast distances. Edge computing enhances efficiency by processing data closer to the source, reducing latency. 5G integration further improves MIoT scalability, low-latency applications, and energy efficiency, making it ideal for smart agriculture, logistics, and industrial automation.

Related Terms

LPWAN (Low-Power Wide-Area Network): A wireless communication technology optimized for long-range, low-power IoT connectivity.

Edge Computing: A distributed computing approach that processes data near the IoT device to reduce network congestion and improve response times (see pg 192).

5G IoT: The next evolution of MIoT, leveraging 5G networks to enhance real-time analytics, ultra-low latency, and high device density (see pg 330).

Common Misconceptions

MIoT requires high bandwidth: MIoT prioritizes energy efficiency and long-range communication, often using low-bandwidth data transmissions for sensors and monitoring devices.

MIoT is only for industrial applications: While crucial in logistics and manufacturing, MIoT is widely used in healthcare, smart homes, and agriculture.

MIoT is just traditional IoT with mobile connectivity: Unlike Wi-Fi-based IoT, MIoT leverages cellular networks, providing greater coverage, security, and reliability.

Historical Context

The concept of Mobile IoT evolved in the **2010s**, as LPWAN technologies like NB-IoT and LTE-M were developed to support battery-powered IoT devices over long distances. **Third Generation Partnership Project** (3GPP) standardized NB-IoT and LTE-M in Release 13 (**2016**), leading to widespread adoption. By **2020**, telecom providers integrated 5G MIoT, unlocking faster, more efficient smart device communication.

Practical Implications

MIoT is transforming industries by enabling real-time monitoring, automation, and predictive analytics. In agriculture, MIoT sensors monitor soil conditions, weather patterns, and irrigation systems, optimizing water usage. In utilities, MIoT-based smart meters enhance energy distribution and grid management. In disaster management, MIoT deploys connected sensors for environmental monitoring, early warning systems, and emergency response coordination, improving resilience and safety.

Modal Window (HCI)

A modal window is a user interface element that appears on top of the main content, requiring users to interact with it before returning to the main interface. It is commonly used for alerts, confirmations, forms, and critical notifications, ensuring user focus and action.

A modal window is like a pop-up conversation with a store clerk—you must respond to the clerk's question before continuing to browse. Similarly, a modal demands user interaction, preventing them from proceeding with other tasks until they acknowledge or dismiss it.

Examples

Online Forms: A login modal appears on a website, requiring users to enter credentials before accessing their accounts, ensuring secure authentication.

Error Messages: A file deletion confirmation modal in operating systems asks users to confirm before permanently removing a file, preventing accidental actions.

E-Commerce Checkout: A modal appears in an online store to verify payment details before completing a purchase, ensuring users have reviewed their order.

Foundational Concepts

Modal windows rely on user interaction constraints to maintain focus on critical tasks. Overlay mechanics prevent background interaction, ensuring attention on the modal's content. Dialog box hierarchy determines how modals behave within an application, with some allowing dismissal (soft modals) while others require mandatory interaction (hard modals). Usability heuristics dictate that modals should be minimally disruptive, provide clear exit options, and enhance user experience, avoiding overuse, which may lead to frustration and accessibility issues.

Related Terms

Popup Window: A separate browser window that opens independently, unlike modals, which are layered within the same interface.

Lightbox: A type of modal used for displaying media, such as images or videos, while dimming the background for focus.

Non-Modal Dialog: A dialog box that allows users to continue interacting with the main application without requiring immediate action.

Common Misconceptions

Modal windows always disrupt user experience: When designed well, modals enhance usability by guiding users toward important actions.

All popups are modal windows: Unlike generic popups, modals appear within the interface, not as separate browser windows.

Modal windows should always be used for alerts: Overuse can frustrate users; alternatives like inline messages or toast notifications may be more effective.

Historical Context

The concept of modals emerged from early GUI designs in the **1980s**, refining user interaction by preventing unintended actions. **Windows**, **MacOS**, and early web applications popularized modals for error handling, file management, and user authentication. As web development evolved, **CSS**, **JavaScript**, and frameworks like **Bootstrap** standardized modals, integrating them into modern UI/UX design. Today, modal design is shaped by usability research, mobile responsiveness, and accessibility best practices.

Practical Implications

Modal windows improve usability and workflow efficiency when used appropriately. In healthcare applications, modals alert users about critical patient data updates. In finance, modals verify transactions to prevent fraud. In software applications, modals streamline workflows, such as confirming file uploads or user preferences. However, poor modal design can lead to user frustration and accessibility challenges, emphasizing the need for responsive, user-friendly modals that enhance, rather than disrupt, digital interactions.

Model (AI)

A model in artificial intelligence and machine learning is a mathematical representation of a system that learns patterns from data to make predictions or decisions. It consists of parameters adjusted during training to optimize performance on a given task, such as image recognition or language processing.

A model is like a recipe for baking a cake. Just as a recipe provides step-by-step instructions based on past cooking experiences, a model uses learned patterns from data to generate outputs, ensuring consistent and accurate results when faced with new inputs.

Examples

Image Recognition: AI models trained on large datasets of images can recognize and classify objects, enabling applications such as facial recognition, medical imaging diagnostics, and automated quality control in manufacturing (see pg 276).

Language Processing: Natural language processing (NLP) models, like GPT and BERT, analyze text to enable chatbots, search engines, and translation services that understand human language (see pg 346).

Financial Forecasting: Machine learning models process market trends, economic indicators, and historical data to predict stock prices, credit risks, and financial fraud detection, assisting businesses and investors.

Foundational Concepts

A model is built using training data to learn relationships between inputs and outputs. Supervised learning models rely on labeled data, while unsupervised learning models detect patterns without predefined labels. Deep learning models, structured as neural networks, process vast amounts of data for complex tasks like speech recognition. Optimization techniques such as gradient descent adjust model parameters to minimize loss functions, improving accuracy. Bias-variance tradeoff ensures models generalize well without overfitting or underfitting the data.

Related Terms

Algorithm: A set of rules or calculations that guide how a model processes data and makes predictions.

Neural Network: A type of machine learning model inspired by the human brain, consisting of interconnected nodes (neurons) that process information (see pg 352).

Training Data: A dataset used to teach a model patterns, relationships, and behaviors before it is deployed for real-world use.

Common Misconceptions

A model is the same as an algorithm: A model is the trained outcome of an algorithm applied to data, whereas an algorithm is the process used to train the model.

More data always improves a model: While more data can enhance accuracy, poor-quality or biased data can lead to incorrect predictions.

A model makes perfect predictions: No model is 100% accurate; models operate on probabilities and approximations based on training data.

Historical Context

The concept of models in AI dates back to early statistical learning theories from the **1950s**, with pioneers like **Alan Turing** and **Marvin Minsky** exploring machine intelligence. The development of neural networks in the **1980s** and deep learning breakthroughs in the **2010s** led to models like **AlexNet**, **ResNet**, and **Transformers**, revolutionizing computer vision, NLP, and reinforcement learning. Modern models, such as **GPT-4** and **DALL·E**, showcase the power of large-scale deep learning architectures trained on vast datasets.

Practical Implications

AI models drive innovation across industries, from healthcare (diagnosing diseases from medical scans) to autonomous vehicles (predicting and responding to road conditions). In retail, recommendation models personalize shopping experiences. In cybersecurity, models detect fraud and prevent cyberattacks. As AI advances, the focus on ethical AI, model interpretability, and reducing biases becomes crucial to ensuring fair and responsible decision-making in real-world applications.

Model Transparency (XAI)

Model transparency refers to the degree to which a machine learning model's internal workings, decision-making processes, and predictions are understandable to humans. Transparent models allow users to inspect, interpret, and trust the outputs, fostering accountability, fairness, and ethical AI deployment.

Model transparency is like a well-explained recipe. Instead of just serving a dish, the chef shares the ingredients and steps taken to prepare it. Similarly, a transparent model reveals its data sources, feature importance, and decision logic, making its predictions easier to understand and trust.

Examples

Healthcare Diagnostics: Transparent AI models in medical imaging help doctors understand how diagnoses are made, ensuring trust in AI-assisted disease detection and improving patient outcomes.

Financial Loan Decisions: Banks use explainable AI models to assess creditworthiness, enabling regulators and customers to understand why a loan was approved or denied and ensuring fair lending practices.

Autonomous Vehicles: Self-driving cars must provide transparent reasoning for decisions, such as why they stopped or changed lanes, ensuring safety and regulatory compliance.

Foundational Concepts

Model transparency is central to Explainable AI (XAI), ensuring that AI-driven decisions can be audited, understood, and trusted. Interpretable models like decision trees and linear regression provide clear logic, while black-box models like deep neural networks require post-hoc explanation techniques like SHAP (Shapley Additive Explanations) and LIME (Local Interpretable Model-Agnostic Explanations). Regulatory frameworks like the EU AI Act and GDPR demand transparency in AI models affecting human rights, finance, and healthcare.

Related Terms

Explainable AI (XAI): A field focused on creating AI systems whose decisions can be understood by humans (see pg 27).

Interpretability: The ability to understand how an AI model makes predictions, often requiring simplified representations (see pg 286).

Algorithmic Accountability: Ensuring AI systems are responsible for their decisions, preventing unfair bias and discrimination (see pg 64).

Common Misconceptions

Transparency means AI reveals all data: While transparency improves explainability, sensitive data like user identities or trade secrets may still be protected.

Complex models cannot be transparent: Techniques like SHAP, feature attribution, and decision visualization make even complex deep learning models more interpretable.

Transparency eliminates bias: While transparency helps identify bias, it does not automatically correct it—fairness audits and bias mitigation are still needed.

Historical Context

The need for model transparency grew with the rise of machine learning and AI in critical applications during the **2010s**. Researchers like **Cynthia Rudin** emphasized interpretable AI over post-hoc explanations. In **2016**, the **GDPR**'s **"Right to Explanation"** sparked debate on AI decision accountability. Regulatory agencies like **NIST** and the **EU AI Act** now mandate transparency in high-risk AI applications, ensuring fairness and ethical deployment.

Practical Implications

Model transparency ensures trust, fairness, and regulatory compliance across industries. In healthcare, it improves patient confidence in AI-driven diagnoses. In criminal justice, transparent AI prevents biased sentencing predictions. In finance, regulators demand transparency in AI-driven loan approvals and fraud detection. Businesses adopting transparent AI benefit from higher user trust, reduced legal risks, and better model debugging, making AI more aligned with human values and ethical considerations.

Monoclonal Antibodies (mAbs) (BT)

Monoclonal antibodies (mAbs) are laboratory-produced molecules designed to mimic the immune system's ability to fight off pathogens. Each monoclonal antibody is engineered to bind to a specific antigen, blocking harmful biological processes or marking cells for immune destruction.

Monoclonal antibodies are like highly trained sniffer dogs, each trained to detect and neutralize a particular scent. Instead of general immune responses, they precisely target specific molecules, making them invaluable for treating diseases like cancer, autoimmune disorders, and viral infections.

Examples

Cancer Therapy: Monoclonal antibodies like Herceptin (trastuzumab) target HER2-positive breast cancer cells, preventing their growth and signaling the immune system to destroy them.

Autoimmune Diseases: Drugs like Rituximab treat rheumatoid arthritis and multiple sclerosis by depleting overactive immune cells, reducing inflammation and tissue damage.

Infectious Diseases: Monoclonal antibodies such as Regeneron's COVID-19 therapy neutralize SARS-CoV-2, reducing viral load and preventing severe disease in high-risk patients.

Foundational Concepts

Monoclonal antibodies are produced using hybridoma technology, where B cells from an immunized animal are fused with myeloma cells to create a hybrid cell line that mass-produces identical antibodies. These can be humanized or fully human for better compatibility. Monoclonal antibodies function by blocking receptors, marking cells for immune destruction, or neutralizing toxins. Their specificity makes them powerful therapeutic tools in oncology, immunology, and infectious disease treatment.

Related Terms

Polyclonal Antibodies: A mixture of antibodies produced by different B cells, recognizing multiple sites on an antigen.

Immunotherapy: A treatment approach that uses the immune system, including monoclonal antibodies, to fight diseases like cancer.

Cytokine Storm: An excessive immune response that monoclonal antibodies can regulate by blocking inflammatory pathways.

Common Misconceptions

Monoclonal antibodies are vaccines: Unlike vaccines, monoclonal antibodies provide immediate but temporary immunity rather than training the immune system for long-term protection.

They cure diseases completely: While monoclonal antibodies are highly effective, they often manage rather than cure diseases, requiring repeated doses.

All monoclonal antibodies work the same way: They function in different mechanisms, such as blocking receptors, signaling immune responses, or delivering toxic payloads to target cells.

Historical Context

Monoclonal antibody technology was pioneered by **César Milstein** and **Georges Köhler** in **1975**, earning them the **Nobel Prize** in **1984**. The first FDA-approved monoclonal antibody, **Muromonab-CD3** (OKT3), was introduced in **1986** for organ transplant rejection. Over time, humanized and fully human antibodies were developed, reducing immune reactions. In the 21st century, monoclonal antibodies revolutionized oncology, autoimmune treatments, and infectious disease therapies, including COVID-19.

Practical Implications

Monoclonal antibodies are a cornerstone of precision medicine, offering targeted therapies with fewer side effects than traditional treatments. In cancer care, they enhance chemotherapy efficacy or act as stand-alone treatments. In autoimmune diseases, they modulate the immune system to prevent tissue damage. Biotech companies and pharmaceutical firms continue to develop next-generation monoclonal antibodies, including bispecific antibodies that target multiple pathways and antibody-drug conjugates for more effective cancer treatment.

Multi-Factor Authentication (MFA) (CS)

Multi-Factor Authentication (MFA) is a security mechanism that requires users to verify their identity using two or more factors before gaining access to a system. These factors typically include something you know (password), something you have (smartphone), or something you are (fingerprint or facial recognition).

MFA is like using multiple locks on a door. Instead of relying on just a key (password), a security system might also require a fingerprint scan or a one-time code sent to your phone, ensuring only authorized users can gain access.

Examples

Online Banking: Banks use MFA to secure customer accounts by requiring both a password and a one-time authentication code sent via SMS or email before completing a transaction.

Corporate Networks: Businesses protect sensitive data by implementing MFA for employee logins, requiring a password plus biometric verification or a security token for remote access.

E-Commerce Security: Online retailers like Amazon use MFA to protect user accounts by prompting customers to verify their identity via an authentication app or an SMS code before making a purchase or changing account details.

Foundational Concepts

MFA enhances security by requiring authentication from at least two different categories: knowledge (passwords, PINs), possession (smartphone, security key), and inherence (biometrics, facial recognition). This method reduces the risk of unauthorized access, even if one factor is compromised. Time-based One-Time Passwords (TOTP) and push notifications are common MFA techniques. Zero Trust Security models also incorporate MFA to ensure users are continuously authenticated when accessing sensitive systems.

Related Terms

Two-Factor Authentication (2FA): A subset of MFA that requires exactly two authentication factors, such as a password and a phone-based code.

Biometric Authentication: A security process that verifies identity using unique biological traits, such as fingerprints, retina scans, or voice recognition.

Phishing-Resistant Authentication: MFA methods designed to prevent phishing attacks, often using hardware tokens or cryptographic authentication (see pg. 366).

Common Misconceptions

MFA is the same as 2FA: While 2FA requires exactly two factors, MFA can include two or more, incorporating additional layers like biometrics.

MFA makes accounts unhackable: While it significantly reduces risk, no system is completely foolproof against social engineering, SIM swapping, or advanced cyber threats.

MFA is inconvenient: Many modern MFA solutions, like biometric authentication and push notifications, are designed to be seamless and user-friendly.

Historical Context

The concept of multi-factor authentication dates back to **1977**, when the first two-factor authentication system was introduced using passwords and keycards. In the **1990s**, **RSA SecureID** pioneered one-time passcode authentication. With the rise of cloud computing, data breaches, and identity theft, **Google**, **Microsoft**, and **Apple** incorporated MFA as a standard security feature. The adoption of **FIDO2** and **WebAuthn** protocols in the **2010s** further improved phishing-resistant authentication methods.

Practical Implications

MFA is a critical defense against cyber threats, protecting user accounts, corporate systems, and financial transactions. In healthcare, MFA safeguards electronic health records from unauthorized access. Governments use MFA for e-voting and secure citizen authentication. The growing use of passwordless authentication (such as biometrics or physical security keys) is shaping the future of MFA, balancing security with convenience while combating emerging cyber threats like credential stuffing and deepfake-based identity fraud.

Multimodal AI (GenAI)

Multimodal AI refers to artificial intelligence that can process and integrate information from multiple input sources, such as text, images, audio, and video, to generate meaningful responses. This enables more human-like understanding and interaction, enhancing AI applications in areas like chatbots, healthcare, and robotics.

Multimodal AI is like how humans experience the world. Just as we use sight, sound, and touch to understand our surroundings, multimodal AI combines different data sources to create more contextually aware and intelligent responses, improving decision-making and problem-solving across various fields.

Examples

Virtual Assistants: AI-powered assistants like Alexa and Siri use multimodal AI to understand voice commands, process text inputs, and recognize images, enhancing user interactions and accessibility (see pg. 528).

Healthcare Diagnostics: AI models analyze medical images, patient records, and speech data to assist doctors in diagnosing diseases more accurately by combining multiple sources of information.

Autonomous Vehicles: Self-driving cars use camera feeds, LiDAR, radar, and GPS data to navigate roads safely, detecting obstacles and interpreting traffic signals through multimodal AI processing.

Foundational Concepts

Multimodal AI is based on deep learning architectures that can simultaneously process multiple types of input data. It relies on fusion techniques, where information from different modalities is combined to improve AI's understanding. Transformer-based models, such as CLIP and GPT-4V, leverage cross-modal learning to analyze relationships between text, images, and speech. Neural networks and attention mechanisms help the model focus on relevant aspects of each input, making multimodal AI more effective in complex real-world applications.

Related Terms

Computer Vision: A field of AI that enables machines to interpret and process visual data from images or videos.

Natural Language Processing (NLP): AI's ability to analyze and generate human language, often combined with other modalities in multimodal AI (see pg 346).

Sensor Fusion: A technique where data from multiple sensors (e.g., cameras, LiDAR, microphones) is integrated to improve AI decision-making.

Common Misconceptions

Multimodal AI is just combining inputs: It does more than process multiple data types—it learns relationships between them to generate context-aware responses.

Multimodal AI is only for chatbots: While useful in chatbots, it also powers self-driving cars, medical AI, and industrial automation.

It requires perfect data from all sources: AI can still function with incomplete data, leveraging advanced fusion techniques to compensate for missing inputs.

Historical Context

Multimodal AI evolved from advances in deep learning, image recognition, and speech processing. Early research in computer vision and NLP laid the foundation, with **Google**'s CLIP (**2021**) and **DALL·E** (**2021**) demonstrating cross-modal learning. **OpenAI** and **Meta** pioneered multimodal AI for image-text generation and real-world interaction, influencing modern AI assistants and interactive applications in healthcare and robotics.

Practical Implications

Multimodal AI enhances user experiences, decision-making, and automation in industries like healthcare, retail, and transportation. AI-powered customer service agents can process voice and visual cues for better interactions. Augmented reality applications improve education and entertainment through interactive AI. As AI models continue to evolve, multimodal learning will shape the future of AI-driven communication, automation, and problem-solving, leading to more natural and intuitive human-computer interactions.

Natural Language Generation (NLG) (AI)

Natural Language Generation (NLG) is a branch of artificial intelligence that enables machines to transform structured data into human-like text. It automates content creation, summarization, and storytelling, allowing AI to produce coherent, context-aware responses in applications such as chatbots, automated journalism, and personalized reports.

NLG is like a skilled writer who crafts articles based on given facts. Just as a journalist turns raw data into a compelling story, NLG processes structured input—such as numbers, tables, or keywords—into fluent, meaningful sentences that a human can easily understand.

Examples

Chatbots & Virtual Assistants: AI-powered chatbots like ChatGPT, Siri, and Alexa generate natural language responses based on user queries, improving engagement and accessibility in customer service and automation (see pg. 528).

Financial & Business Reports: NLG tools analyze large datasets to create automated financial summaries, business reports, and personalized insights without requiring human intervention.

Automated Journalism: News organizations use NLG to generate real-time sports updates, weather forecasts, and financial reports, reducing manual effort and increasing content speed.

Foundational Concepts

NLG operates through three main stages: content determination, sentence structuring, and language realization. Deep learning models, such as transformers and recurrent neural networks (RNNs), play a crucial role in making AI-generated text contextually relevant and grammatically sound. Template-based approaches provide structured output, while pre-trained language models like GPT and BERT enable more fluid and adaptive text generation. Semantic analysis and discourse planning further enhance NLG's coherence and relevance across various domains.

Related Terms

Natural Language Processing (NLP): The broader field encompassing language understanding, translation, and generation by AI (see pg 346).

Text-to-Speech (TTS): Converts AI-generated text into spoken words, enhancing accessibility in voice assistants (see pg 490).

Summarization AI: Uses NLG techniques to condense long texts into concise, meaningful summaries.

Common Misconceptions

NLG is just text prediction: Unlike simple autocomplete models, NLG generates full, meaningful narratives, not just isolated word predictions.

NLG always creates perfect human-like text: AI-generated text still requires refinement, contextual accuracy, and bias control to match human writing.

NLG can fully replace human writers: While NLG accelerates content creation, human oversight is necessary for quality, creativity, and contextual nuance.

Historical Context

NLG's origins trace back to rule-based systems in the **1960s**, evolving into statistical models and deep learning techniques. Early AI systems used template-driven text generation, while the **2000s** saw advances in NLP and machine learning. **OpenAI**'s GPT models (**2018**-present) revolutionized context-aware NLG, enabling chatbots, AI writing assistants, and automated content tools to generate increasingly natural text. Recent breakthroughs in transformer-based models have made AI-generated text indistinguishable from human writing in many cases.

Practical Implications

NLG streamlines automated communication, content creation, and real-time reporting across industries. In healthcare, AI-generated patient reports improve efficiency. E-commerce platforms use NLG for personalized product descriptions. In legal and financial industries, AI automates complex contract summarization and market analysis. As NLG advances, human-AI collaboration in writing, journalism, and business intelligence will continue to expand, enhancing productivity while maintaining the need for ethical oversight and fact-checking in AI-generated content.

Natural Language Processing (NLP) (GenAI)

Natural Language Processing (NLP) is a branch of artificial intelligence that enables computers to understand, interpret, generate, and respond to human language. It combines linguistics and machine learning to process text and speech for applications like chatbots, voice assistants, sentiment analysis, and automated translation.

NLP is like a multilingual translator who not only understands words but also grasps meaning, context, and intent. Just as a human comprehends a conversation by analyzing tone, structure, and meaning, NLP enables machines to process and respond to text or speech accurately.

Examples

Chatbots & Virtual Assistants: NLP powers AI-driven assistants like Siri, Alexa, and ChatGPT, allowing them to process user queries and generate human-like responses (see pg. 528).

Machine Translation: Tools like Google Translate leverage NLP to convert text between languages while maintaining context and meaning.

Sentiment Analysis: Businesses use NLP to analyze social media posts, reviews, and feedback, detecting emotions and opinions to improve customer engagement and decision-making.

Foundational Concepts

NLP relies on syntax analysis, semantic understanding, and contextual modeling to interpret human language. Machine learning models, including deep learning and transformers, enhance NLP's ability to process and generate text. Tokenization, part-of-speech tagging, and named entity recognition break down sentences into components for analysis. Word embeddings, such as Word2Vec and BERT, help models understand relationships between words. Pre-trained AI models use self-supervised learning to improve comprehension across different languages and domains.

Related Terms

Natural Language Understanding (NLU): A subfield of NLP focused on interpreting the meaning and intent behind text or speech.

Natural Language Generation (NLG): The counterpart of NLP that enables AI to generate human-like text based on structured or unstructured data.

Speech Recognition: Converts spoken language into text, forming the foundation of voice assistants and automated transcription services.

Common Misconceptions

NLP perfectly understands language: While advanced, NLP models lack true human-like comprehension and can struggle with sarcasm, slang, or ambiguous statements.

All NLP models work the same way: Different NLP techniques—rule-based, statistical, and neural network-based approaches—vary in accuracy and effectiveness.

NLP doesn't require large datasets: Modern NLP models, especially deep learning-based transformers, require massive datasets for training and improving accuracy.

Historical Context

NLP has evolved from rule-based symbolic AI in the **1950s** to statistical models in the **1990s** and deep learning-based approaches in the **2010s**. **Alan Turing** (**1950**) introduced the **Turing Test**, influencing NLP's development. The **1970s** saw early chatbots like **ELIZA**, while **Google**, **OpenAI**, and **DeepMind** pioneered modern large-scale NLP models. The introduction of transformer models (e.g., BERT, GPT) revolutionized NLP by improving context-aware language understanding.

Practical Implications

NLP enhances healthcare, finance, customer service, and education. In medicine, AI-powered NLP analyzes clinical records and diagnoses diseases. In finance, NLP-driven trading algorithms interpret market news and investor sentiment. Customer service chatbots reduce response times, while educational tools personalize learning experiences. As NLP continues advancing, ethical considerations, bias mitigation, and multilingual accessibility remain critical challenges for researchers and industry leaders.

Net Metering (CET)

Net metering is a billing arrangement that allows owners of solar panels and other renewable energy systems to send excess electricity back to the grid in exchange for credits. These credits offset the energy consumed from the grid when solar generation is insufficient.

Net metering is like a savings account for electricity. When solar panels produce more power than needed, the extra energy is "deposited" onto the grid. Later, when solar production is low, homeowners "withdraw" electricity from the grid using the stored credits.

Examples

Residential Solar Systems: Homeowners with rooftop solar panels generate excess electricity during the day and receive credits to reduce their electricity bills.

Commercial Buildings: Businesses install solar arrays to cut energy costs, exporting surplus power to the grid and balancing energy usage during peak hours.

Community Solar Projects: Shared solar farms allow multiple users to benefit from net metering, distributing credits among participants based on their share of energy production.

Foundational Concepts

Net metering operates on bidirectional electricity flow, enabling distributed energy resources to interact with the grid. Smart meters track both energy production and consumption. Utilities use billing credits to compensate users at either retail or wholesale rates. Policies vary by location, with some caps on credit rollovers or compensation structures. Grid reliability and stability are considered to ensure that distributed energy sources do not disrupt overall power distribution.

Related Terms

Feed-in Tariff: A policy that pays renewable energy producers for feeding electricity into the grid at a fixed rate.

Time-of-Use (TOU) Pricing: A billing model where electricity costs fluctuate based on demand, affecting net metering savings.

Distributed Energy Resources (DERs): Small-scale power sources, like rooftop solar and wind turbines (see pg. 532), that feed energy into the grid.

Common Misconceptions

Net metering provides free electricity: Homeowners still pay fixed grid fees even if their electricity bill is reduced to zero.

Solar users always receive full retail credit: Some utilities offer lower wholesale rates for excess energy, reducing financial returns.

Net metering is unlimited: Many regions impose caps on participation or limit credit rollovers, restricting long-term energy storage benefits.

Historical Context

Net metering policies emerged in the **1980s** as solar technology expanded. The **U.S. Public Utility Regulatory Policies Act** (PURPA) of **1978** encouraged small-scale renewable energy adoption. By the **1990s**, states like **California** and **Minnesota** pioneered net metering laws. As solar panel efficiency improved, global adoption increased, with countries like **Germany**, **Australia**, and **India** implementing net metering frameworks to support renewable energy transitions.

Practical Implications

Net metering reduces electricity costs, incentivizes solar adoption, and enhances grid resilience. In residential and commercial sectors, it allows energy independence and lowers dependence on fossil fuels. Utility companies face grid management challenges, leading some to revise compensation models. As battery storage becomes more affordable, hybrid systems combining solar and energy storage could reshape net metering policies, enhancing self-sufficiency and reducing reliance on the traditional power grid.

Network Slicing (5G)

Network slicing is a 5G technology that allows operators to divide a single physical network into multiple virtual networks tailored for different applications. Each slice has unique performance characteristics, such as low latency or high bandwidth, optimizing network resources for diverse use cases.

Network slicing is like building multiple highways on the same road. Some lanes are dedicated to high-speed vehicles, others to emergency services, and some for public transport. Similarly, network slices allocate different resources for streaming, autonomous vehicles, and smart factories.

Examples

Autonomous Vehicles: A dedicated low-latency slice ensures real-time communication between vehicles, improving traffic safety and coordination.

Smart Cities: Utility and infrastructure services use network slices for efficient monitoring, controlling streetlights, and managing traffic signals.

Healthcare: Remote surgeries and telemedicine require ultra-reliable, low-latency network slices to ensure real-time video streaming and robotic precision.

Foundational Concepts

Network slicing relies on virtualization and software-defined networking (SDN) to allocate resources dynamically. Multi-access edge computing (MEC) enhances network performance by processing data closer to users. Operators use orchestration platforms to manage slices efficiently, ensuring optimized performance for massive IoT, ultra-reliable low-latency communications (URLLC), and enhanced mobile broadband (eMBB). This enables customized connectivity while maintaining overall network efficiency.

Related Terms

Software-Defined Networking (SDN): A network architecture that centralizes control, enabling flexible and programmable network slicing.

Multi-Access Edge Computing (MEC): A technique that processes data closer to end users, reducing latency and improving performance (see pg 192).

Virtual Network Functions (VNF): Software-based functions that replace traditional network hardware, allowing dynamic resource allocation.

Common Misconceptions

Network slicing is just bandwidth allocation: It involves customized resource management, not just dividing speed or bandwidth.

All 5G networks automatically support slicing: Network slicing requires orchestration and infrastructure upgrades, not all networks implement it.

One slice can serve all applications: Different industries require customized slices, with specific latency, speed, and security configurations.

Historical Context

The concept of network slicing emerged with 5G standardization by the **3rd Generation Partnership Project** (3GPP). Early virtualization techniques in 4G LTE paved the way, but full implementation became feasible with SDN and NFV (Network Function Virtualization). In **2018**, major telecom providers, including **Ericsson**, **Nokia**, and **Huawei**, began trials. By **2020**, network slicing was recognized as a core feature of 5G deployments worldwide.

Practical Implications

Network slicing enhances efficiency, reduces congestion, and improves security by isolating network resources. In manufacturing, it supports real-time automation. In entertainment, it guarantees lag-free streaming and gaming. Governments use dedicated slices for secure communications. As 5G adoption grows, custom network slices will enable hyper-personalized connectivity, transforming transportation, healthcare, and industrial automation.

Neural Networks (AI)

Neural networks are a class of machine learning models inspired by the structure of the human brain. They consist of layers of interconnected nodes (neurons) that process and learn from data, enabling tasks like image recognition, natural language processing, and autonomous decision-making.

A neural network is like a team of detectives solving a case. Each detective (neuron) gathers clues (data), shares findings with colleagues (connected neurons), and refines conclusions based on feedback. Over time, the team improves at identifying patterns and making accurate deductions.

Examples

Image Recognition: Neural networks power facial recognition, medical imaging, and autonomous vehicle perception by learning complex visual patterns (see pg 276).

Speech-to-Text Systems: Virtual assistants like Siri and Alexa use neural networks to convert spoken language into text with high accuracy (see pg. 460).

Fraud Detection: Banks leverage neural networks to analyze transaction patterns and detect anomalies, preventing fraudulent activities.

Foundational Concepts

Neural networks rely on artificial neurons arranged in layers: input, hidden, and output layers. Each neuron applies weights and activation functions to incoming data, refining patterns through backpropagation and gradient descent. Deep learning extends this concept, using multiple hidden layers to solve complex problems. Convolutional Neural Networks (CNNs) specialize in image tasks, while Recurrent Neural Networks (RNNs) process sequential data, such as text and speech. These architectures enable adaptive learning from vast datasets.

Related Terms

Deep Learning: A subset of machine learning that employs multi-layered neural networks to model complex data representations (see pg 178).

Backpropagation: A training technique that adjusts neuron weights by minimizing errors through iterative feedback.

Artificial Neuron: The basic unit of a neural network, mimicking biological neurons by processing and transmitting data signals.

Common Misconceptions

Neural networks think like humans: They identify patterns but lack reasoning or consciousness.

More layers always improve performance: Excessive layers can cause overfitting and require more data for training.

All AI systems use neural networks: Many AI models rely on alternative techniques, such as rule-based systems or decision trees.

Historical Context

Neural networks trace back to the **1950s**, when **Warren McCulloch** and **Walter Pitts** proposed artificial neurons. **Frank Rosenblatt** developed the perceptron in the **1950s**, but limitations stalled progress. The backpropagation algorithm, refined in the **1980s** by **Geoffrey Hinton**, reignited interest. With the rise of big data and GPUs, deep learning flourished, leading to breakthroughs in AI applications, including **AlphaGo**, **GPT**, and self-driving technology.

Practical Implications

Neural networks revolutionize healthcare, detecting diseases from medical scans. In finance, they predict stock trends and assess credit risk. Autonomous systems, from drones to robots, rely on neural networks for decision-making. As models become more powerful, challenges in interpretability, ethics, and computational efficiency must be addressed to ensure responsible deployment in critical sectors.

Neuromorphic Computing (AI)

Neuromorphic computing is a computational approach that mimics the structure and function of the human brain using artificial neurons and synapses. It enables highly efficient, adaptive, and parallel processing, making it ideal for energy-efficient AI, robotics, and real-time decision-making systems.

Neuromorphic computing is like a self-learning musical orchestra where each musician (neuron) adapts their tune based on the performance of others. Instead of following rigid, pre-written instructions, they continuously refine their melodies in real time, improving efficiency and harmony without external direction.

Examples

Edge AI and IoT Devices: Neuromorphic chips enable low-power, real-time AI processing in wearables, smart sensors, and autonomous drones, reducing dependence on cloud computing.

Medical Diagnostics: Brain-inspired computing accelerates image recognition in healthcare, aiding in disease detection from MRI and CT scans with higher efficiency and lower energy consumption.

Autonomous Systems: Self-driving cars and robots use neuromorphic processors for real-time sensor fusion, allowing them to react instantly to changes in their environment.

Foundational Concepts

Neuromorphic computing is built on spiking neural networks (SNNs), which mimic biological neurons by transmitting data as discrete spikes rather than continuous signals. Unlike traditional von Neumann architectures, neuromorphic chips integrate memory and processing units, reducing energy consumption and increasing speed. Event-driven processing allows computations to happen only when needed, improving efficiency. Plasticity, inspired by synaptic learning in the brain, enables the system to adapt dynamically to new patterns, making it ideal for unsupervised learning and real-time inference.

Related Terms

Spiking Neural Networks (SNNs): A neural network model where information is transmitted as spikes, mimicking biological neurons (see pg 352).

Edge AI: AI processing performed directly on devices rather than in the cloud, benefiting from neuromorphic efficiency.

Neuromorphic Chips: Specialized hardware designed to replicate brain-like computation, such as Intel's Loihi and IBM's TrueNorth.

Common Misconceptions

Neuromorphic computing is the same as deep learning: While both use artificial neurons, neuromorphic systems are event-driven and energy-efficient, unlike traditional deep learning models.

It replaces conventional computing: Neuromorphic systems complement but do not entirely replace classical AI or von Neumann architectures.

It requires massive datasets: Unlike deep learning, neuromorphic computing excels at real-time learning with minimal data.

Historical Context

Neuromorphic computing was first conceptualized in the **1980s** by **Carver Mead**, who proposed mimicking biological neurons in silicon. **IBM's TrueNorth (2014)** and **Intel's Loihi (2017)** marked milestones in commercial neuromorphic chips. The development of spiking neural networks and event-driven computation further advanced the field. Recent breakthroughs in brain-inspired architectures have positioned neuromorphic computing as a key enabler of low-power AI applications.

Practical Implications

Neuromorphic computing is transforming AI at the edge, enabling real-time, low-power processing in smartphones, IoT devices, and autonomous systems. In biomedical research, it enhances brain-machine interfaces for prosthetics and neurotherapy. Cybersecurity benefits from neuromorphic chips' ability to detect anomalies in real-time. As industries push for efficient, adaptive AI, neuromorphic computing is set to redefine robotics, smart infrastructure, and energy-conscious AI models.

Neuron (AI)

A neuron in AI is a fundamental computational unit in artificial neural networks (ANNs), modeled after biological neurons. It receives input, processes it using a mathematical function, and transmits an output to other neurons, enabling pattern recognition, decision-making, and deep learning models.

An AI neuron is like a light switch with a dimmer—it takes in multiple electrical signals (inputs), adjusts the brightness (activation function), and passes the appropriate light level (output) to other switches (neurons), forming a network of interconnected decisions.

Examples

Image Recognition: AI neurons process pixel values in images, identifying patterns to classify objects like faces, animals, or medical anomalies (see pg 276).

Speech-to-Text Conversion: AI models use neuron layers to recognize speech patterns, converting spoken words into written text in applications like voice assistants and transcription services (see pg 460).

Financial Fraud Detection: Neurons analyze banking transactions to detect unusual spending behaviors, reducing fraud by identifying irregularities in real time.

Foundational Concepts

AI neurons are inspired by biological neurons, where synapses transmit signals between nerve cells. In artificial neural networks (ANNs), neurons receive weighted inputs, apply an activation function, and send outputs to the next layer. The weights adjust during training to refine predictions. Deep learning uses multiple layers of neurons to detect complex patterns. Backpropagation, an algorithm for optimizing weights, enhances learning by minimizing errors. The strength of neural networks lies in their non-linearity, enabling them to model intricate relationships in data.

Related Terms

Artificial Neural Network (ANN): A computational model consisting of interconnected AI neurons used in machine learning (see pg 352).

Activation Function: A function (e.g., ReLU, sigmoid) that determines whether a neuron should "fire" based on its input (see pg 70).

Backpropagation: A method for adjusting neuron weights during training to improve accuracy in neural networks.

Common Misconceptions

AI neurons function like human neurons: AI neurons are mathematical functions, not biological cells, and lack consciousness or organic processing.

More neurons always mean better AI: While deeper networks can improve learning, too many neurons can lead to overfitting, making models less generalizable.

Neurons process data sequentially: Unlike traditional computing, neurons in ANNs process information in parallel, enhancing efficiency.

Historical Context

Inspired by biological neuroscience, AI neurons were first introduced in **1943** by **Warren McCulloch** and **Walter Pitts**, who created a simple mathematical model of a neuron. **Frank Rosenblatt** developed the Perceptron in **1958**, an early neural network. The backpropagation algorithm, introduced by **Geoffrey Hinton** in the **1980s**, revolutionized deep learning. Modern AI advancements, such as transformer models and convolutional neural networks (CNNs), build upon neuron-based architectures for language processing, vision, and generative AI.

Practical Implications

AI neurons power speech recognition, medical diagnostics, and self-driving cars, enabling complex decision-making in real time. Healthcare AI assists in diagnosing diseases, while autonomous systems use AI neurons to analyze sensory data for navigation. In finance, neural networks optimize algorithmic trading and risk assessment. As neural networks grow, they revolutionize robotics, natural language processing (NLP), and personalized recommendations, making AI systems more adaptive and efficient.

Node (BC)

A node in blockchain technology is any computer or device connected to the blockchain network that participates in verifying, storing, and maintaining the distributed ledger. Nodes ensure data integrity, enable transactions, and validate consensus mechanisms to keep the network secure and decentralized.

A blockchain node is like a librarian in a vast digital library—each librarian holds a copy of every book (ledger), checks new additions (transactions), and ensures all books remain accurate and consistent with the others in the system.

Examples

Bitcoin Full Nodes: Full nodes in the Bitcoin network store the entire transaction history, validate new transactions, and enforce consensus rules to maintain blockchain integrity.

Ethereum Smart Contract Nodes: Ethereum nodes execute smart contracts, verifying and storing transaction data while enabling decentralized applications (dApps) to function securely.

Supply Chain Nodes: Companies use blockchain nodes to track goods movement, ensuring authenticity and transparency by verifying product origin, ownership, and compliance across a distributed network.

Foundational Concepts

A blockchain node is a critical component in a decentralized ledger, responsible for verifying transactions, maintaining network security, and enabling consensus mechanisms. There are full nodes, which store and validate the entire blockchain, light nodes, which rely on full nodes for data verification, and mining nodes, which validate transactions through proof-of-work (PoW) or proof-of-stake (PoS). Nodes communicate across a peer-to-peer (P2P) network, ensuring blockchain data remains immutable, tamper-proof, and synchronized across all participants.

Related Terms

Consensus Mechanism: The process nodes use to validate transactions and reach agreement, such as Proof of Work (PoW) or Proof of Stake (PoS) (see pg 146).

Distributed Ledger: A decentralized database replicated across multiple nodes, ensuring transparency and data security in blockchain networks (see pg 188).

Mining: The computational process where nodes solve cryptographic puzzles to validate transactions and add new blocks to the blockchain (see pg 326).

Common Misconceptions

Nodes are miners: Not all nodes mine cryptocurrency; some only validate and store blockchain data.

All nodes store the full blockchain: Light nodes only store relevant transaction data, relying on full nodes for verification.

Running a node is the same as staking: While staking supports blockchain security, a node's primary function is to validate transactions and store ledger data.

Historical Context

The concept of nodes in blockchain originated with **Bitcoin** (**2009**), developed by **Satoshi Nakamoto**, where full nodes maintained the distributed ledger. The **Ethereum** network (**2015**) expanded node functionality to support smart contracts and dApps. Over time, innovations such as sharding, sidechains, and layer-2 scaling solutions have introduced new node architectures, optimizing blockchain efficiency, scalability, and security.

Practical Implications

Nodes power cryptocurrency networks, decentralized finance (DeFi), and enterprise blockchain solutions, ensuring secure transactions, transparency, and autonomy from central authorities. Financial institutions use nodes to support real-time settlement, while governments explore blockchain nodes for digital identity and voting systems. In healthcare, nodes enhance patient data security through immutable records. By decentralizing trust, nodes strengthen data integrity, reduce fraud, and enable global, censorship-resistant networks.

Output Layer (AI)

The output layer in a neural network is the final layer that produces the model's predictions. It receives processed data from previous layers, applies activation functions, and generates results in forms such as classifications, probabilities, or continuous values based on the given input.

The output layer is like a voting machine in an election—it gathers opinions from different groups (hidden layers), processes them, and announces the final decision, whether it's selecting a candidate, recognizing an image, or predicting future trends.

Examples

Image Recognition: In a neural network trained for facial recognition, the output layer classifies an image as a specific person by assigning probability values to each potential match (see pg 276).

Sentiment Analysis: In natural language processing, the output layer of a model determines whether a text expresses positive, neutral, or negative sentiment by applying probability scores to each category.

Stock Price Prediction: A financial forecasting model uses the output layer to generate continuous values, predicting stock prices based on historical trends and market data.

Foundational Concepts

The output layer plays a critical role in determining the final outcome of a neural network by processing the aggregated information from the hidden layers. It applies an activation function, such as softmax for classification or linear activation for regression. The number of neurons in the output layer corresponds to the number of possible outputs. During training, the model optimizes the output layer using backpropagation, adjusting weights to minimize errors using a loss function, ensuring accurate and reliable predictions.

Related Terms

Hidden Layer: Intermediate layers in a neural network that process input data and extract features before passing it to the output layer.

Activation Function: A mathematical function applied to neurons in the output layer, such as softmax for probability distributions or sigmoid for binary classification (see pg 70).

Loss Function: A metric that evaluates how well the output layer's predictions align with actual values, guiding model optimization through backpropagation (see pg 310).

Common Misconceptions

The output layer always produces one answer: Some models, like multi-label classification networks, generate multiple outputs simultaneously.

The output layer decides on its own: It does not make decisions independently but relies on processed information from hidden layers.

The number of neurons in the output layer is arbitrary: The number of neurons must match the number of possible output classes or regression targets.

Historical Context

The concept of layered neural networks dates back to **Frank Rosenblatt**'s **Perceptron** (**1958**), where a simple neural model produced binary outputs. The backpropagation algorithm, introduced in the **1980s** by **Rumelhart**, **Hinton**, and **Williams**, revolutionized training, enabling complex deep learning architectures. Today, output layers vary in complexity, supporting multi-class classification, object detection, and generative models like **GPT** and **DALL·E**.

Practical Implications

The output layer is fundamental in AI applications like medical diagnosis, fraud detection, and language translation, ensuring accurate and interpretable predictions. Self-driving cars rely on output layers to detect and classify objects, while chatbots use output layers to generate coherent responses. In healthcare, AI models analyze X-rays and output predictions of diseases, aiding doctors in diagnostics. By optimizing output layers, AI achieves higher accuracy, better generalization, and enhanced decision-making across various industries.

Overfitting (AI)

Overfitting occurs when a machine learning model learns the training data too well, capturing noise and minor fluctuations instead of general patterns. This results in poor generalization, meaning the model performs well on training data but fails on new, unseen data.

Overfitting is like memorizing answers for a test instead of understanding the subject. A student who memorizes specific problems may excel on practice tests but struggle with slightly different questions in an actual exam because they lack a broader understanding of the concepts.

Examples

Medical Diagnosis: An AI model trained on a limited dataset of medical images may recognize patterns specific to those images but fail to diagnose new patients due to overfitting.

Stock Market Prediction: A financial AI model may fit historical stock market data too closely, capturing random fluctuations rather than underlying trends, leading to poor future predictions.

Facial Recognition: An overfitted facial recognition system may work well on known images but struggle with new faces or slight variations in lighting, angles, or expressions (see pg 214).

Foundational Concepts

Overfitting arises when a model has too many parameters relative to the available data, causing it to memorize noise instead of identifying general trends. This can occur in deep learning, decision trees, and other models. Techniques such as regularization, dropout layers, and cross-validation help mitigate overfitting by ensuring the model generalizes well. A balance between bias and variance is essential: too much bias leads to underfitting, while too much variance results in overfitting.

Related Terms

Underfitting: The opposite of overfitting, where a model is too simple and fails to capture patterns in the data (see pg 508).

Regularization: Techniques like L1 and L2 regularization help reduce overfitting by penalizing overly complex models.

Cross-Validation: A method of training a model on different data subsets to test its generalization ability and prevent overfitting.

Common Misconceptions

Overfitting only happens in deep learning: It can occur in any machine learning model, including decision trees, regression models, and neural networks.

More data always prevents overfitting: While more data helps, models can still overfit if they are overly complex or not properly regularized.

Overfitting is always bad: In some cases, slight overfitting can be acceptable if the goal is high accuracy on specific datasets.

Historical Context

Overfitting has been a recognized problem since the early days of statistical modeling and machine learning. In the **1980s**, researchers developed regularization techniques to prevent overfitting in neural networks. The introduction of dropout layers in deep learning (**2014**) by **Geoffrey Hinton** and **Nitish Srivastava** further addressed this issue. Today, transfer learning and data augmentation are widely used to improve generalization.

Practical Implications

Overfitting impacts finance, healthcare, autonomous systems, and cybersecurity by reducing model reliability. In autonomous vehicles, an overfitted model might fail to recognize new road conditions, causing safety risks. Fraud detection systems must generalize well to detect emerging fraud patterns. In natural language processing, models trained on biased datasets may overfit to specific language patterns, failing to understand broader contexts. Addressing overfitting ensures AI models remain robust, accurate, and adaptable in real-world applications.

Parallel Computing (HPC)

Parallel computing is a computational technique that divides complex tasks into smaller sub-tasks, processing them simultaneously across multiple processors or cores. This approach significantly enhances computing speed and efficiency, making it essential for high-performance computing, artificial intelligence, and large-scale simulations.

Parallel computing is like a team of chefs in a kitchen preparing a meal. Instead of one person handling every task, multiple chefs work on different dishes at the same time, reducing the overall cooking time while ensuring the final meal is completed efficiently.

Examples

Scientific Simulations: Climate modeling uses parallel computing to process vast datasets, predicting weather patterns and environmental changes with higher accuracy and speed.

Artificial Intelligence Training: Deep learning models, such as those used in image recognition and natural language processing, leverage parallel computing to accelerate training on massive datasets using GPUs and TPUs.

Financial Risk Analysis: Large-scale financial institutions utilize parallel computing to perform real-time risk assessments, analyzing millions of transactions per second to detect fraud and market trends.

Foundational Concepts

Parallel computing is based on decomposing tasks into multiple subtasks that run simultaneously on different processors. It consists of data parallelism, where the same operation is applied to different data subsets, and task parallelism, where different tasks execute independently. Message passing and shared memory architectures allow processors to communicate efficiently. Load balancing ensures optimal resource utilization, while synchronization mechanisms coordinate execution. High-performance computing frameworks, such as MPI (Message Passing Interface) and CUDA, enable parallelism in supercomputing and AI workloads.

Related Terms

Distributed Computing: A computing paradigm where tasks are processed across multiple interconnected computers instead of a single system.

Multithreading: A technique that allows multiple threads to run concurrently within a single processor, improving execution efficiency.

GPU Acceleration: The use of graphics processing units (GPUs) to execute many operations simultaneously, significantly enhancing performance in AI and gaming applications.

Common Misconceptions

Parallel computing is only for supercomputers: While high-performance computing benefits greatly, modern consumer devices, such as smartphones and gaming consoles, also utilize parallel processing for efficiency.

More processors always mean better performance: Poorly optimized parallel programs may suffer from synchronization overhead or load imbalance, leading to inefficiencies.

All tasks can be parallelized: Some problems are inherently sequential, requiring step-by-step execution, limiting the benefits of parallel computing.

Historical Context

Parallel computing has roots in early supercomputing, with pioneers like **Seymour Cray** developing multiprocessor systems in the **1960s**. The **1980s** saw advancements in massively parallel architectures, such as **Connection Machine CM-1**. The rise of GPUs in the **2000s**, particularly with **NVIDIA**'s **CUDA** framework, revolutionized AI and deep learning. Today, exascale computing and quantum computing push parallelism to unprecedented levels.

Practical Implications

Parallel computing drives advancements in scientific research, artificial intelligence, cryptography, and real-time analytics. In healthcare, it enables faster genome sequencing for personalized medicine. In autonomous systems, it allows real-time processing of sensor data for self-driving cars. Cybersecurity benefits from rapid encryption and decryption of data. As computing demands grow, cloud computing providers leverage parallel architectures to offer scalable, high-speed computing solutions, ensuring efficiency across industries.

Phishing (CS)

Phishing is a cyberattack method where attackers impersonate trusted entities to trick individuals into revealing sensitive information, such as passwords, credit card details, or personal data. This is typically done through fraudulent emails, fake websites, or deceptive messages designed to exploit human trust.

Phishing is like a fisherman casting a baited hook into the water, hoping an unsuspecting fish will bite. Similarly, cybercriminals send fake emails or links to lure victims into providing their credentials, allowing attackers to access their accounts or steal valuable information.

Examples

Email Phishing: Attackers send emails posing as banks or online services, urging recipients to click on malicious links that steal login credentials.

Spear Phishing: A targeted attack where hackers customize messages for a specific individual or organization, often using personal details to increase credibility.

Smishing (SMS Phishing): Fraudulent text messages claim to be from legitimate institutions, prompting users to click malicious links or provide sensitive information.

Foundational Concepts

Phishing exploits social engineering, manipulating human psychology to deceive victims. Attackers use spoofing techniques to make emails or websites appear authentic. Credential harvesting occurs when users unknowingly enter their login details into fake portals. Some phishing schemes involve malware deployment, where clicking a link installs spyware or ransomware. Security measures such as multi-factor authentication (MFA), email filtering, and employee training help mitigate phishing risks. Advanced detection tools, including machine learning-based anomaly detection, identify and block phishing attempts before they reach users.

Related Terms

Social Engineering: Psychological manipulation used to trick individuals into divulging confidential information.

Spoofing: The act of disguising a malicious source as a trusted one, such as fake email addresses or cloned websites.

Ransomware: Malware that encrypts a victim's data, often deployed via phishing attacks, demanding payment for decryption (see pg 402).

Common Misconceptions

Only naive users fall for phishing: Even cybersecurity professionals can be deceived by sophisticated phishing tactics.

Phishing only happens via email: Attacks also occur through text messages (smishing), phone calls (vishing), and social media.

Antivirus software alone prevents phishing: While helpful, phishing relies on human deception, making education and vigilance crucial.

Historical Context

Phishing traces back to the **1990s**, when attackers impersonated AOL employees to steal passwords. In the **2000s**, spear phishing became a major cyber threat, targeting businesses and government agencies. High-profile breaches, such as the **2016 Democratic National Committee** (DNC) hack, showcased the power of phishing in cyber espionage. Today, AI-driven phishing detection tools help counter increasingly sophisticated attacks.

Practical Implications

Phishing affects banking, e-commerce, corporate security, and government agencies. Businesses implement employee training programs to recognize phishing attempts. Financial institutions develop fraud detection algorithms to monitor suspicious activities. Cybersecurity frameworks, such as zero-trust architectures, minimize unauthorized access even if credentials are compromised. With growing AI-driven phishing campaigns, continuous advancements in security awareness and AI-driven threat detection are crucial to protecting individuals and organizations from financial loss and data breaches.

Photovoltaic (PV) Cells (CET)

Photovoltaic (PV) cells are semiconductor devices that convert sunlight directly into electricity through the photovoltaic effect. When sunlight hits the cell, it excites electrons, generating an electric current. PV cells are the fundamental units of solar panels, widely used for renewable energy generation.

PV cells are like small solar-powered calculators—when exposed to light, they generate electricity without moving parts or fuel. Just as calculators operate without batteries in daylight, PV cells continuously convert sunlight into electrical power, providing clean, sustainable energy for homes, businesses, and industries.

Examples

Residential Solar Panels: Homeowners install solar panels made of PV cells to generate electricity, reducing dependence on traditional power grids and lowering utility bills.

Solar Farms: Large-scale PV installations produce electricity for public grids, supplying renewable energy to cities and reducing carbon footprints.

Portable Solar Chargers: Compact PV cells power mobile devices, enabling users to charge phones, laptops, and small electronics in remote areas without access to electricity.

Foundational Concepts

PV cells function through the photovoltaic effect, where photons (light particles) strike a semiconductor material, typically silicon, freeing electrons and creating an electric current. They are categorized into monocrystalline, polycrystalline, and thin-film cells, each with different efficiencies. Inverters convert the direct current (DC) generated into alternating current (AC) for household and commercial use. Net metering allows users to feed excess electricity back into the grid. Advances in perovskite solar cells and bifacial PV technology improve efficiency and affordability.

Related Terms

Solar Panel: An assembly of multiple PV cells connected to generate electricity.

Net Metering: A system that allows PV cell users to send surplus electricity back to the grid for credit.

Perovskite Solar Cells: A newer, high-efficiency alternative to traditional silicon-based PV cells.

Common Misconceptions

PV cells need constant sunlight: They still generate power on cloudy days, though at reduced efficiency.

Solar panels store energy: PV cells generate electricity but require batteries or grid connections for energy storage.

Solar power is inefficient: Modern PV cells exceed 20% efficiency, with new materials pushing even higher performance.

Historical Context

The photovoltaic effect was discovered by **Alexandre Edmond Becquerel** in **1839**. In **1954, Bell Labs** developed the first practical silicon PV cell, achieving 6% efficiency. The **1970s** energy crisis accelerated solar research, leading to improved PV technologies. Space agencies pioneered PV use in satellites. Government incentives and climate policies in the **2000s** drove mass adoption, making solar energy mainstream.

Practical Implications

PV cells are revolutionizing renewable energy, reducing dependence on fossil fuels. In urban planning, smart grids integrate PV-generated electricity. Developing nations use PV for off-grid electrification, bringing power to remote communities. Electric vehicles (EVs) explore PV-integrated charging systems. The falling cost of PV cells accelerates global sustainability efforts, making solar power a crucial component of carbon neutrality goals.

Policy or Q-function (AI)

A policy in reinforcement learning defines the strategy an agent uses to determine its next action based on a given state. The Q-function (action-value function) estimates the expected cumulative reward of an action taken in a specific state, helping optimize decision-making in dynamic environments.

A policy is like a GPS navigation system—given a current location (state), it recommends the best route (action). The Q-function is like a traffic prediction app, estimating the best route based on past traffic data, optimizing choices to reach the destination efficiently.

Examples

Autonomous Vehicles: A self-driving car uses a policy to decide when to accelerate, turn, or brake based on real-time sensor data, while the Q-function helps determine the best action by evaluating future traffic patterns.

Robotic Process Automation: Industrial robots optimize movement sequences using Q-functions to determine the most efficient paths, minimizing errors and improving assembly-line productivity.

Game AI: Video game agents use Q-functions to predict winning moves, adjusting strategies dynamically to defeat opponents and improve their decision-making over multiple rounds.

Foundational Concepts

The policy represents a mapping from states to actions and can be deterministic (always selects the best action) or stochastic (chooses actions with probabilities). The Q-function calculates the expected return of an action given a state and a policy. Reinforcement learning algorithms, such as Q-learning and Deep Q-Networks (DQN), use trial-and-error learning to refine the Q-function, improving decision-making. Bellman equations are used to iteratively update Q-values, balancing exploitation (choosing the best-known action) and exploration (trying new actions to discover better outcomes).

Related Terms

Reinforcement Learning: A machine learning paradigm where agents learn optimal actions by interacting with an environment and receiving rewards (see pg 410).

Value Function: A function estimating the expected long-term reward of a given state, used alongside Q-functions to guide learning (see pg. 522).

Deep Q-Network (DQN): A reinforcement learning algorithm that uses neural networks to approximate Q-values, enabling decision-making in complex environments.

Common Misconceptions

Q-functions always give perfect decisions: They are estimates that improve over time but can be inaccurate, especially in complex environments.

Policies are always fixed: Policies evolve as the agent learns, adapting based on new experiences and reward feedback.

Q-learning doesn't require exploration: Without exploration, Q-functions may become biased, preventing discovery of optimal strategies.

Historical Context

Richard Bellman developed the **Bellman equation** in the **1950s**, laying the groundwork for dynamic programming. **Watkins** and **Dayan** introduced Q-learning in **1989**, a breakthrough in model-free reinforcement learning. The **DeepMind** team revolutionized Q-learning with Deep Q-Networks (DQN) in **2015**, achieving superhuman performance in **Atari** games, proving the effectiveness of combining reinforcement learning with deep learning.

Practical Implications

Q-functions and policies are fundamental to AI-driven decision-making in robotics, finance, healthcare, and gaming. Autonomous systems use policies to optimize real-time actions, while Q-functions enhance predictive analytics. In stock trading, reinforcement learning models improve investment decisions by evaluating long-term gains. Healthcare AI optimizes treatment plans by balancing risks and rewards. The growing integration of deep reinforcement learning into AI research ensures continuous advancements in intelligent decision-making systems.

Post-Hoc Explanation (XAI)

A post-hoc explanation refers to the process of interpreting and explaining the decisions of an already trained AI model, rather than designing the model to be inherently interpretable. These explanations help users understand AI behavior without modifying the underlying complex, often opaque, black-box models.

Post-hoc explanations are like reverse-engineering a magic trick—rather than knowing the secret behind the trick from the beginning, one studies its effects and works backward to figure out how it was done. This helps make AI outputs more transparent and trustworthy.

Examples

Healthcare Diagnostics: AI models predicting diseases from X-rays use post-hoc explanations like saliency maps to highlight critical image areas that influenced the decision, helping doctors verify the diagnosis.

Financial Credit Scoring: Post-hoc methods explain why a loan application was denied by identifying key factors, such as low credit score or high debt-to-income ratio, making AI-based lending more transparent.

Autonomous Vehicles: Self-driving AI decisions, such as braking or lane changes, can be explained post-hoc using decision heatmaps, improving regulatory compliance and safety in accident investigations.

Foundational Concepts

Post-hoc explanations use interpretability techniques to understand black-box AI models after training. Common methods include SHAP (Shapley Additive Explanations), which assigns importance scores to input features, and LIME (Local Interpretable Model-agnostic Explanations), which builds simpler models to approximate complex AI decisions. These techniques do not change the model but enhance user trust and accountability. AI ethics and compliance require post-hoc explanations, especially in sensitive applications like healthcare and finance, where human oversight is critical.

Related Terms

Explainable AI (XAI): The broader field focusing on making AI models interpretable and transparent (see pg 27).

Model-Agnostic Methods: Techniques like LIME that work with any machine learning model to generate explanations.

Counterfactual Explanations: Alternative scenario-based explanations showing how a slight change in input could lead to different AI decisions (see pg 156).

Common Misconceptions

Post-hoc explanations change the AI model: They only provide insights into existing models without modifying them.

They make AI fully transparent: They help interpret decisions but do not eliminate black-box behavior entirely.

All AI models need post-hoc explanations: Some simpler models, like decision trees, are inherently interpretable and do not require them.

Historical Context

Post-hoc explanations became crucial as deep learning and complex AI models gained adoption in the **2010s**. SHAP and LIME, developed by **Scott Lundberg** and **Marco Tulio Ribeiro**, respectively, became widely used in AI interpretability. The rise of AI ethics frameworks, like EU's **GDPR** and the **U.S. AI Bill of Rights**, further emphasized the need for transparent AI explanations, influencing research in Explainable AI (XAI).

Practical Implications

Post-hoc explanations enhance trust and accountability in high-stakes AI applications, such as finance, law, and medicine. They help regulators and auditors ensure AI fairness and bias mitigation. In business AI, they assist customer support teams in understanding AI-driven recommendations. As AI adoption expands, post-hoc explanations will be vital for AI governance, compliance, and ethical decision-making, ensuring AI systems align with human values and legal standards.

Predictive Coding (ANI)

Predictive coding is a computational framework where the brain—or artificial neural networks—processes information by predicting incoming sensory data and correcting errors between predictions and reality. This hierarchical approach minimizes processing load, improving efficiency in perception, decision-making, and machine learning models.

Predictive coding is like autocorrect on a smartphone—it anticipates the next word based on previous input. If the prediction is wrong, it adjusts based on actual user input. Similarly, AI and the brain continually refine predictions based on new sensory or computational feedback.

Examples

Autonomous Vehicles: Self-driving cars use predictive coding to anticipate pedestrian movements and other vehicles' behavior, reducing reaction times and preventing accidents.

Speech Recognition: AI-powered assistants, like Siri or Google Assistant, predict speech patterns to enhance real-time transcription accuracy by minimizing error corrections (see pg 460).

Medical Imaging: AI systems analyze MRI scans using predictive coding, highlighting anomalies by detecting deviations from expected patterns in healthy tissue structures.

Foundational Concepts

Predictive coding is rooted in Bayesian inference, where systems update beliefs based on new data. It operates within hierarchical neural networks, passing predictions downward while sending error signals upward when discrepancies occur. Error minimization is crucial—if predictions align well, less energy is used for correction. In AI, generative models leverage predictive coding for efficient learning, particularly in unsupervised learning and reinforcement learning. Neuroscientists study predictive coding to understand human perception and cognition, influencing AI development in computer vision and natural language processing.

Related Terms

Bayesian Inference: A statistical method updating probabilities based on new data, fundamental to predictive coding.

Generative Models: AI models like GANs or VAEs that predict or generate data based on learned distributions (see pg 33).

Hierarchical Neural Networks: Multi-layered AI architectures processing predictions and errors iteratively, mimicking predictive coding (see pg 352).

Common Misconceptions

Predictive coding applies only to AI: It originates in neuroscience and is used to understand human perception and cognition.

It eliminates errors completely: Predictive coding minimizes errors but cannot remove them entirely, as some variability in data is unpredictable.

Only deep learning models use it: Classical machine learning models also incorporate predictive Bayesian principles for refinement.

Historical Context

Predictive coding was first proposed in neuroscience by **Rao** and **Ballard** (**1999**) as a theory of brain function, explaining perception as an error correction process. AI researchers later adapted it into hierarchical generative models to enhance deep learning efficiency. With the rise of Bayesian neural networks and reinforcement learning, predictive coding has become essential in fields like computer vision, robotics, and AI-powered healthcare.

Practical Implications

Predictive coding enhances AI efficiency and decision-making, reducing computational cost in image recognition, speech processing, and robotics. In healthcare, it improves diagnostic accuracy by modeling expected vs. abnormal patterns in medical scans. In autonomous systems, it enables real-time adjustments by forecasting environmental changes. As AI advances, predictive coding will be crucial for adaptive learning, real-time processing, and energy-efficient neural architectures in AI and cognitive science applications.

Privacy (RAI)

Privacy in Responsible AI refers to the protection of individuals' data from unauthorized access, misuse, or exposure. It ensures that AI systems process personal information securely and transparently, adhering to legal, ethical, and technical standards such as data minimization, encryption, and differential privacy.

Privacy is like closing your curtains at home—you choose what others can see while still interacting with the outside world. AI systems must ensure that user data remains secure and controlled, allowing useful interactions without exposing sensitive personal information.

Examples

Healthcare AI: AI-driven medical platforms ensure patient data privacy by anonymizing records, enabling AI to detect diseases without exposing identities.

Online Advertising: AI-driven ad networks use privacy-preserving algorithms to deliver personalized content without directly accessing users' identifiable data.

Smart Assistants: Devices like Alexa or Siri use on-device processing to handle queries while minimizing the amount of personal data sent to cloud servers.

Foundational Concepts

Privacy in AI relies on data protection principles such as differential privacy, which introduces controlled noise to datasets to prevent individual identification. Federated learning enables AI models to train on decentralized data sources without exposing raw data. Encryption techniques like homomorphic encryption allow computations on encrypted data without decryption, preserving confidentiality. Legal frameworks such as GDPR and CCPA set global standards for AI data privacy. AI must balance data utility and security to ensure responsible decision-making while protecting personal information.

Related Terms

Differential Privacy: A technique adding statistical noise to datasets to prevent individual identification while maintaining data utility.

Federated Learning: A method allowing AI models to train across multiple devices without centralizing raw data, enhancing privacy.

Homomorphic Encryption: A cryptographic approach enabling AI to analyze encrypted data without exposing its original content.

Common Misconceptions

AI privacy means no data collection: AI can still function with privacy-preserving methods like anonymous data processing and on-device computations.

Encryption makes AI less effective: AI can perform encrypted computations without accessing raw data, maintaining both privacy and accuracy.

Privacy laws restrict AI innovation: Privacy regulations encourage ethical AI development, fostering trust and adoption in AI-driven services.

Historical Context

The concept of privacy in AI evolved with early computing, but concerns escalated with big data and machine learning. The General Data Protection Regulation (**GDPR**) was introduced in **2018** to address AI-related privacy risks. **Google**'s differential privacy research and **Apple**'s on-device machine learning helped advance AI privacy practices. The emergence of federated learning in **2017** marked a shift toward decentralized AI models that enhance privacy while maintaining performance.

Practical Implications

Privacy is crucial in healthcare, finance, and government AI applications to ensure secure and ethical decision-making. Data breaches and AI surveillance concerns push industries toward privacy-enhancing technologies. AI-driven cybersecurity tools use privacy-preserving methods to detect fraud while safeguarding sensitive information. With growing AI adoption, privacy ensures trust, compliance, and user safety, shaping the future of ethical AI across industries.

Prompt Engineering (GenAI)

Prompt engineering is the practice of designing and refining input queries or instructions to optimize an AI model's responses. By carefully structuring prompts, users can influence language models, chatbots, and generative AI to produce more accurate, relevant, and context-aware outputs.

Prompt engineering is like asking a chef to prepare a dish—the clearer and more detailed the request, the better the result. Just as a vague order may lead to an unexpected meal, an unclear prompt can result in AI-generated content that lacks precision or relevance.

Examples

Chatbots and Virtual Assistants: Customer support chatbots use optimized prompts to generate responses that are clear, informative, and aligned with user intent (see pg. 528).

Content Generation: Writers and marketers use structured prompts to generate high-quality text, such as blog posts or product descriptions, with AI-powered tools like ChatGPT.

Programming Assistance: Developers use carefully designed prompts in AI-powered coding assistants like GitHub Copilot to receive contextually relevant code suggestions.

Foundational Concepts

Prompt engineering relies on natural language processing (NLP) principles, where AI models interpret and generate text based on structured user input. Effective prompts use context setting, examples, and constraints to improve response accuracy. Few-shot learning allows AI to learn from minimal examples within the prompt, enhancing task adaptability. Tokenization affects how AI interprets prompts, influencing response coherence. Temperature and top-k sampling control randomness in responses, balancing creativity and precision. By refining prompts, users can fine-tune AI performance without modifying underlying model architecture.

Related Terms

Natural Language Processing (NLP): The field of AI that enables machines to understand and generate human language (see pg 346).

Few-Shot Learning: A technique where AI learns from a small number of examples provided within the prompt.

Tokenization: The process of breaking text into smaller units, affecting how AI models interpret and generate responses.

Common Misconceptions

AI understands prompts like a human: AI processes text statistically, not conceptually—it generates responses based on patterns in training data.

More words in a prompt always improve results: Concise, well-structured prompts are often more effective than long, ambiguous ones.

Prompt engineering is unnecessary with advanced AI: Even powerful models require well-crafted prompts for optimal performance and consistency.

Historical Context

Prompt engineering became critical with the rise of transformer-based AI models, particularly **OpenAI**'s GPT series. Early AI models required extensive training, but few-shot and zero-shot learning, introduced with GPT-3, highlighted the importance of prompt design. Mid-**2020s** advancements in reinforcement learning from human feedback (RLHF) further refined AI's responsiveness to well-engineered prompts. With tools like **ChatGPT**, **Bard** (now **Gemini**), and **Claude**, prompt engineering evolved into a skill for optimizing AI performance without modifying model weights.

Practical Implications

Prompt engineering improves efficiency in AI applications, from automating customer interactions to enhancing creativity in writing, coding, and research. It enables domain-specific AI customization without additional training. In education, well-crafted prompts help AI tutors deliver more context-aware learning experiences. Business applications include AI-powered market analysis, legal document drafting, and report generation. As AI adoption grows, prompt engineering remains a key skill, ensuring AI tools produce reliable, accurate, and safe outputs across industries.

Prototyping (HCI)

Prototyping is the process of creating early models of a user interface, system, or product to test functionality, usability, and design before full development. In human-computer interaction (HCI), prototyping helps refine user experiences by identifying pain points, interaction flows, and design improvements iteratively.

Prototyping is like sketching a house before construction—it allows designers to visualize, test, and adjust their ideas before committing to the final build. Just as an architect revises blueprints based on feedback, designers refine prototypes to enhance usability and functionality in interactive systems.

Examples

UI/UX Design: Tech companies create interactive wireframes of mobile apps and websites to test usability before investing in full-scale development (see pg 518 & 520).

Voice Assistants: Engineers prototype speech recognition models for virtual assistants like Siri and Alexa, refining how users interact with AI-driven voice commands (see pg. 528).

Automotive Interfaces: Car manufacturers develop dashboard screen prototypes to evaluate driver interaction with navigation, entertainment, and safety features before production.

Foundational Concepts

Prototyping relies on iterative design, where early models are tested, evaluated, and refined. Low-fidelity prototypes, such as paper sketches, provide conceptual validation, while high-fidelity prototypes simulate real user experiences through interactive mockups and coded simulations. Usability testing ensures designs align with user expectations, and feedback loops help refine functionality. Rapid prototyping methods, including Wizard of Oz testing, allow designers to assess experiences without full AI or system implementation. The goal is to enhance user satisfaction, accessibility, and intuitive interaction in digital environments.

Related Terms

Wireframing: A visual representation of an interface's layout, focusing on structure and navigation rather than detailed aesthetics.

User-Centered Design (UCD): A design approach prioritizing user needs and behaviors throughout the development process.

A/B Testing: A method of comparing two design versions by analyzing user interactions to determine the most effective option.

Common Misconceptions

Prototypes must be high-tech: Basic sketches or simple wireframes are often enough for early testing.

Prototyping is only for designers: Developers, researchers, and stakeholders all contribute to prototype evaluation and improvement.

Prototypes guarantee final design success: While they reduce risk, user behavior in real-world applications may still require further iterations.

Historical Context

Prototyping in HCI evolved from software engineering and industrial design, becoming a core UX/UI practice in the **1980s. Donald Norman,** a pioneer in human-centered design, emphasized the need for early testing to prevent usability failures. The rise of agile development in the **2000s** accelerated rapid prototyping techniques, integrating user feedback cycles into product design. Modern tools like **Figma, Sketch,** and **Adobe XD** enable real-time collaborative prototyping, shaping today's digital experience industry.

Practical Implications

Prototyping improves user experience design by ensuring interfaces are intuitive, efficient, and user-friendly. In software development, prototypes reduce costly late-stage revisions by identifying flaws early. In AI systems, they help refine chatbot dialogues, machine-learning interfaces, and voice command interactions. Industries such as healthcare, automotive, and smart home technology use prototyping to validate human-computer interactions, ensuring safety, efficiency, and accessibility. As digital interfaces become more complex, prototyping remains an essential tool for designing human-centered, adaptive technologies.

Python (AI)

Python is a high-level, interpreted programming language known for its simplicity, readability, and versatility. It supports multiple programming paradigms, including object-oriented, functional, and procedural programming. Python is widely used in web development, data science, artificial intelligence, automation, and software engineering, making it one of the most popular languages globally.

Python is like a Swiss Army knife for programmers—it provides an extensive set of built-in tools and libraries, making it easy to solve a variety of problems, from automating simple tasks to building advanced machine learning models and web applications.

Examples

Data Science & AI: Python is the primary language for machine learning and data analysis, with libraries like TensorFlow, NumPy, and Pandas helping scientists process and visualize data.

Web Development: Frameworks such as Django and Flask allow developers to build robust, scalable web applications quickly, making Python a top choice for startups and enterprises.

Automation & Scripting: Python automates repetitive tasks, such as file management, web scraping, and system monitoring, enhancing productivity and efficiency across industries.

Foundational Concepts

Python follows the principle of readability, with an emphasis on clean syntax and code indentation rather than braces. It is dynamically typed, allowing flexible variable handling. The extensive standard library and third-party modules provide powerful tools for various applications. Garbage collection ensures efficient memory management, and Python's interpreted nature allows quick debugging. Virtual environments help manage dependencies, making it easy to develop and deploy applications. Python's cross-platform compatibility enables developers to write code that runs on multiple operating systems without modification.

Related Terms

JavaScript: A language often used alongside Python for web applications, particularly in front-end development.

Machine Learning: A field that heavily relies on Python due to its extensive AI and deep learning libraries (see pg 45).

Object-Oriented Programming (OOP): A programming paradigm that Python supports, allowing the use of classes and objects to structure code.

Common Misconceptions

Python is slow: While Python is not as fast as compiled languages like C++, its performance is optimized using libraries such as NumPy and Cython.

Python is only for beginners: While Python is beginner-friendly, it is also used in complex AI research, cloud computing, and large-scale applications.

Python is not suitable for mobile development: While it's not the primary language for mobile apps, frameworks like Kivy and BeeWare enable mobile development with Python.

Historical Context

Python was created in **1991** by **Guido van Rossum**, aiming to provide a simple yet powerful language. Inspired by **ABC** and **C**, it evolved into a multi-purpose language used worldwide. The introduction of Python 2 (**2000**) and Python 3 (**2008**) marked significant milestones, improving Unicode support, performance, and syntax enhancements. Python's popularity surged with the rise of machine learning and data science, solidifying its status as a leading programming language in modern computing.

Practical Implications

Python is a key enabler of technological innovation. In finance, it powers algorithmic trading and fraud detection. In healthcare, it helps process medical images and genomic data. Python plays a pivotal role in cybersecurity, automating penetration testing and security analysis. Its use in education has made programming more accessible worldwide. With its continuous community-driven evolution, Python remains a dominant force in software development, AI, and cloud computing, ensuring its relevance for years to come.

PyTorch (AI)

PyTorch is an open-source deep learning framework developed by Meta AI that provides flexible and efficient tools for tensor computation, neural network training, and artificial intelligence research. It is widely used for computer vision, natural language processing (NLP), and reinforcement learning due to its dynamic computational graph and ease of use.

PyTorch is like a laboratory notebook for AI research—scientists can easily experiment, adjust, and iterate without being constrained by rigid structures. Unlike static frameworks, PyTorch allows real-time model modification, making it ideal for rapid prototyping and debugging.

Examples

Computer Vision: PyTorch powers advanced image recognition systems in medical diagnostics, autonomous vehicles, and security surveillance, utilizing deep convolutional networks for accurate object detection.

Natural Language Processing: PyTorch is the backbone of NLP models like ChatGPT and BERT, enabling tasks such as sentiment analysis, translation, and chatbots with its robust sequence modeling capabilities (see pg 346).

Reinforcement Learning: PyTorch supports deep reinforcement learning in robotics, gaming, and financial trading, allowing models to learn from interactions and optimize decision-making strategies (see pg 410).

Foundational Concepts

PyTorch is built around tensor-based computation, similar to NumPy but optimized for GPU acceleration. It employs an autograd system, which dynamically computes gradients, enabling efficient backpropagation for deep learning. The TorchScript feature allows models to transition seamlessly between development and production. PyTorch's modular neural network library, torch.nn, simplifies complex architectures, while its data handling utilities streamline large-scale training. Dataloader and Dataset classes help manage training datasets, ensuring efficiency. Its strong community support and integration with libraries like Hugging Face and FastAI make it a leading AI research tool.

Related Terms

TensorFlow: A deep learning framework developed by Google, offering static graph computation for large-scale AI applications (see pg 482).

CUDA: A parallel computing platform by NVIDIA, enabling PyTorch to leverage GPUs for accelerated deep learning tasks.

Autograd: PyTorch's automatic differentiation engine, which computes gradients dynamically for efficient neural network optimization.

Common Misconceptions

PyTorch is only for research: While it excels in research, PyTorch's TorchScript and ONNX allow smooth deployment in production environments.

PyTorch is slow: With CUDA acceleration and tensor optimizations, PyTorch achieves high-speed performance comparable to TensorFlow.

PyTorch lacks industry adoption: Major companies like Tesla, Microsoft, and Meta use PyTorch for AI applications.

Historical Context

PyTorch was released in **2016** by **Meta AI** (formerly **Facebook AI Research**) as an evolution of Torch, an earlier deep learning framework. It quickly gained popularity due to its intuitive syntax and dynamic computation graph, addressing TensorFlow's limitations at the time. The PyTorch 1.0 release (**2018**) introduced production-ready features, making it suitable for deployment. In **2022**, PyTorch joined the **Linux Foundation**, ensuring open-source governance and long-term sustainability. Today, PyTorch remains a leading AI framework, widely adopted in academia and industry.

Practical Implications

PyTorch drives breakthroughs in AI research, medical imaging, and autonomous systems. In healthcare, it aids in diagnosing diseases through deep learning-based medical image analysis. In robotics, it helps train adaptive models for navigation and human-robot interactions. AI-powered finance applications, such as fraud detection and risk assessment, rely on PyTorch for fast, accurate predictions. Its role in generative AI, including image synthesis and deepfake detection, showcases its versatility. With ongoing advancements in AI, PyTorch continues shaping the future of intelligent systems and automation.

Quantum Algorithm (QC)

A quantum algorithm is a set of instructions designed to be executed on a quantum computer, leveraging quantum superposition, entanglement, and interference to perform computations exponentially faster than classical algorithms. These algorithms solve complex problems in cryptography, optimization, and simulation, which are infeasible for classical computers.

A quantum algorithm is like searching for a hidden treasure in an enormous ocean. While a classical diver explores one spot at a time, a quantum diver can explore multiple locations simultaneously, increasing the chance of finding the treasure exponentially faster than the classical approach.

Examples

Shor's Algorithm: This quantum algorithm efficiently factors large numbers, threatening modern cryptographic systems. It could break RSA encryption, a fundamental security protocol used in banking and digital communications.

Grover's Algorithm: Used for searching unsorted databases, Grover's algorithm provides a quadratic speedup, enabling faster solutions for AI, data mining, and cybersecurity applications.

Quantum Simulations: Quantum computers simulate molecular interactions and quantum materials, accelerating breakthroughs in drug discovery, nanotechnology, and superconductors, outperforming classical simulations.

Foundational Concepts

Quantum algorithms exploit qubits, which can exist in superposition, representing multiple states at once. Entanglement links qubits, allowing them to influence each other instantaneously, enhancing computational power. Quantum interference ensures that correct solutions reinforce while incorrect paths cancel out. These principles enable exponential speedups over classical counterparts. Quantum gates manipulate qubits, constructing complex algorithms. Hybrid quantum-classical computing combines quantum processing with classical optimization for real-world problem-solving.

Related Terms

Quantum Computing: The hardware and theoretical framework enabling quantum algorithms through qubits and quantum gates (see pg 52).

Qubit: The fundamental unit of quantum information, capable of superposition and entanglement, enabling quantum parallelism (see pg 400).

Quantum Supremacy: The milestone where a quantum computer outperforms the best classical supercomputers on a specific task (see pg 398).

Common Misconceptions

Quantum algorithms replace classical computing: Quantum algorithms augment rather than replace classical computing, excelling in specialized tasks like cryptography and simulations.

Quantum computing is universally faster: Not all problems benefit from quantum algorithms—only specific cases like search, optimization, and cryptography see exponential speedups.

Quantum computing is ready for large-scale use: While progress is rapid, quantum systems still face error correction and hardware scalability challenges.

Historical Context

Quantum algorithms originated with **Richard Feynman** (**1982**), who proposed quantum computers for simulating quantum mechanics. **Peter Shor** (**1994**) revolutionized cryptography by creating **Shor's algorithm** for efficient integer factorization. **Lov Grover** (**1996**) introduced **Grover's algorithm**, speeding up database searches. In **2019**, **Google** claimed quantum supremacy, demonstrating a quantum computer solving a problem exponentially faster than classical machines. **IBM**, **Microsoft**, and startups like **Rigetti** continue refining quantum hardware and software, making quantum algorithms increasingly practical.

Practical Implications

Quantum algorithms have transformative applications in finance, optimizing portfolios and risk analysis. In medicine, they accelerate drug discovery and protein folding simulations, expediting treatments for diseases. Cybersecurity faces a paradigm shift, as quantum algorithms could break classical encryption, necessitating post-quantum cryptographic methods. Artificial intelligence benefits from quantum-enhanced machine learning, improving pattern recognition and optimization. As quantum hardware advances, industries must adapt, integrating quantum algorithms to solve previously intractable problems.

Quantum Annealing (QC)

Quantum annealing is an optimization technique that leverages quantum mechanics to find the lowest-energy state of a system, solving complex combinatorial problems. It relies on quantum tunneling and superposition to explore multiple solutions simultaneously, outperforming classical methods in optimization, logistics, and machine learning applications.

Quantum annealing is like navigating a vast landscape of mountains and valleys in total darkness. While classical methods take slow, step-by-step routes over obstacles, quantum annealing "tunnels" through barriers, reaching the lowest valley—the optimal solution—much faster than conventional approaches.

Examples

Supply Chain Optimization: Companies use quantum annealing to minimize logistics costs, improving delivery routes and warehouse distribution, resulting in faster, more efficient supply chains.

Financial Portfolio Optimization: Banks apply quantum annealing to find optimal investment portfolios, balancing risk and return across multiple assets faster than traditional algorithms.

Drug Discovery: Quantum annealing helps pharmaceutical researchers analyze molecular interactions, accelerating the identification of new drug candidates for treating diseases.

Foundational Concepts

Quantum annealing exploits qubits in superposition, allowing multiple states to be processed at once. Unlike gate-based quantum computing, which performs discrete operations, quantum annealing gradually transitions toward the lowest-energy solution using quantum tunneling. This process avoids getting stuck in local minima, a limitation of classical optimization methods. Adiabatic quantum computing is a related approach, ensuring the system remains in its lowest-energy state during computation. D-Wave Systems pioneered commercial quantum annealers, demonstrating applications in machine learning, scheduling, and cryptography.

Related Terms

Quantum Tunneling: A quantum phenomenon allowing particles to pass through energy barriers, enabling faster optimization.

Adiabatic Quantum Computing: A theoretical model closely related to quantum annealing, designed to maintain an optimal state throughout the computation.

Quantum Optimization: The broader field of using quantum computing techniques to solve complex optimization problems faster than classical methods.

Common Misconceptions

Quantum annealing solves all problems: It excels at optimization problems but is not a general-purpose quantum computing approach.

It replaces classical computers: Quantum annealers complement, rather than replace, classical computing, improving specific problem domains.

All quantum computers use annealing: Gate-based quantum computing, such as that used by IBM and Google, differs fundamentally from quantum annealing.

Historical Context

Quantum annealing was first theorized in the **1980s**, with **D-Wave Systems** launching the first commercial quantum annealer in **2011**. **NASA, Google**, and **Lockheed Martin** have explored its applications in machine learning and optimization. In **2019**, researchers demonstrated quantum annealing's ability to solve real-world problems faster than classical methods. While still limited in scope, ongoing advances in hardware, superconducting qubits, and hybrid quantum-classical systems continue expanding quantum annealing's potential.

Practical Implications

Quantum annealing is revolutionizing industries requiring complex optimization. Manufacturing benefits from faster scheduling and resource allocation, while logistics firms optimize fleet management. Healthcare researchers use it to analyze protein folding and molecular interactions, improving drug design. Cybersecurity specialists explore its potential for enhancing encryption techniques. Though still in early stages, quantum annealing is poised to transform industries by solving problems previously deemed computationally impossible.

Quantum Circuit (QC)

A quantum circuit is a model for quantum computation, consisting of qubits manipulated using quantum gates in a structured sequence. These circuits harness superposition, entanglement, and interference to perform calculations exponentially faster than classical circuits for cryptography, optimization, and machine learning tasks.

A quantum circuit is like a musical composition, where each quantum gate is a musical note that transforms the melody. Unlike classical compositions, which follow a linear sequence, quantum circuits allow notes to exist in multiple harmonies simultaneously, creating intricate quantum computations beyond classical capabilities.

Examples

Cryptography: Quantum circuits implement Shor's algorithm, which can efficiently factor large numbers, potentially breaking classical encryption methods like RSA.

Drug Discovery: By simulating quantum molecular interactions, quantum circuits help researchers model complex chemical reactions faster than classical computers.

Optimization Problems: Quantum circuits improve supply chain logistics, financial modeling, and traffic management by solving combinatorial optimization problems exponentially faster than classical approaches.

Foundational Concepts

A quantum circuit consists of qubits, the fundamental units of quantum information, and quantum gates, which manipulate qubits in specific ways. Superposition allows qubits to exist in multiple states simultaneously, while entanglement links qubits, enabling correlated operations. Quantum circuits are executed using quantum hardware, such as superconducting qubits or trapped ions. Algorithms like Grover's search and Shor's factoring demonstrate their computational advantages. Quantum error correction is a crucial challenge, as qubits are highly susceptible to noise and decoherence.

Related Terms

Quantum Gate: A fundamental operation that modifies qubits, analogous to classical logic gates but exploiting quantum properties (see pg 396).

Superposition: A quantum state where qubits exist in multiple values simultaneously, enabling parallel computations (see pg 466).

Quantum Entanglement: A phenomenon where qubits become correlated, influencing each other instantaneously regardless of distance (see pg 198).

Common Misconceptions

Quantum circuits replace classical computers: They complement, rather than replace, classical computing for specialized tasks.

All quantum computers use the same circuits: Different quantum architectures (e.g., gate-based vs. annealing) impact circuit design and performance.

Quantum circuits always outperform classical circuits: Quantum speedup applies to specific problem domains, not general-purpose computing.

Historical Context

Quantum circuits emerged from **Richard Feynman**'s **1981** proposal that quantum mechanics could enhance computing. **David Deutsch** formalized the concept in **1985**, defining the first universal quantum **Turing machine**. **Peter Shor**'s **1994** factoring algorithm demonstrated practical quantum advantage, leading to experimental quantum gate implementations. **IBM**, **Google**, and **Rigetti** have since developed scalable quantum processors, increasing qubit counts and circuit complexity.

Practical Implications

Quantum circuits are transforming industries reliant on complex computations. Finance applications include portfolio optimization and risk assessment. Cybersecurity faces new challenges, as quantum circuits threaten traditional encryption methods. Healthcare researchers leverage them for drug discovery and genetic analysis. While still in early development, quantum circuits promise breakthroughs in artificial intelligence, materials science, and fundamental physics, making them a cornerstone of next-generation computing.

Quantum Decoherence (QC)

Quantum decoherence occurs when a quantum system loses its quantum properties due to interactions with its environment. This process causes superposition and entanglement to collapse, making the system behave classically. Decoherence is a major challenge in quantum computing, quantum cryptography, and quantum sensing applications.

Quantum decoherence is like a sandcastle exposed to waves. Initially, the castle has well-defined structures, much like a quantum system in superposition. As waves (environmental noise) hit, the castle gradually loses its form, just as quantum coherence is lost, making the system behave classically.

Examples

Quantum Computing Stability: Quantum decoherence limits the ability of qubits to maintain coherence, reducing the accuracy of quantum computations in IBM and Google's quantum processors.

Quantum Cryptography Security: Secure communication protocols, such as quantum key distribution (QKD), must counteract decoherence effects to ensure that transmitted information remains protected.

Quantum Sensors: Highly sensitive quantum sensors, used in medical imaging and gravitational wave detection, must mitigate decoherence to maintain precision.

Foundational Concepts

Quantum decoherence results from the interaction between a quantum system and its surrounding environment, leading to information loss. Wavefunction collapse occurs when quantum states become distinguishable due to measurement or noise. Decoherence time determines how long a system can maintain its quantum properties before classical behavior emerges. Quantum error correction techniques, such as surface codes and topological qubits, help mitigate decoherence. Researchers explore low-temperature environments and superconducting materials to reduce decoherence and improve quantum system stability.

Related Terms

Qubit: The fundamental unit of quantum information, highly sensitive to decoherence (see pg 400).

Superposition: The quantum phenomenon where a particle exists in multiple states simultaneously, lost due to decoherence (see pg 466).

Quantum Error Correction: A set of techniques designed to counteract decoherence and preserve quantum information (see pg 394).

Common Misconceptions

Decoherence destroys quantum information: The information is not destroyed but becomes entangled with the environment, making it inaccessible.

Decoherence and measurement are the same: While measurement collapses a quantum state, decoherence is a gradual process due to environmental interaction.

Quantum computers will always overcome decoherence: Quantum error correction helps but does not eliminate decoherence completely.

Historical Context

Decoherence theory was introduced by **Hugh Everett (1957)** in his many-worlds interpretation, later formalized by **Wojciech Zurek** in the **1980s**. Zurek's research explained how classicality emerges from quantum mechanics, influencing fields like quantum computing and information theory. Decoherence remains a key challenge in scalable quantum computing, leading to the development of fault-tolerant quantum processors.

Practical Implications

Quantum decoherence limits quantum computer scalability, requiring error correction techniques and low-temperature environments to extend qubit coherence times. In quantum cryptography, decoherence poses security risks, necessitating error-resilient quantum communication. Quantum sensors and metrology rely on minimizing decoherence to improve sensitivity in navigation, medical imaging, and fundamental physics experiments. Future advancements in material science, superconducting circuits, and topological qubits aim to mitigate decoherence and unlock quantum technologies' full potential.

Quantum Error Correction (QEC) (QC)

Quantum error correction (QEC) is a set of techniques that protect quantum information from errors caused by decoherence, noise, and faulty quantum operations. Unlike classical error correction, QEC handles errors without directly measuring qubits, preserving their superposition and entanglement while maintaining computational integrity in quantum computers.

Quantum error correction is like autocorrect for quantum computers. Just as autocorrect fixes typos without changing the meaning of a sentence, QEC corrects quantum errors without collapsing delicate quantum states, ensuring computations proceed accurately despite environmental interference or hardware imperfections.

Examples

Fault-Tolerant Quantum Computing: Quantum computers, such as IBM's and Google's, use QEC to correct errors in superconducting qubits, enabling more reliable quantum computations.

Quantum Cryptography: Secure quantum communication systems employ error correction codes to ensure quantum key distribution (QKD) remains immune to transmission noise and adversarial attacks.

Quantum Sensors and Metrology: High-precision quantum sensors, used in medical imaging and gravitational wave detection, rely on QEC to maintain measurement accuracy despite quantum noise.

Foundational Concepts

Quantum error correction is based on redundant encoding of quantum information across multiple physical qubits to create logical qubits that resist errors. Shor's code and surface codes are widely used error-correcting techniques. Entanglement and syndrome measurement allow the detection and correction of errors without disturbing quantum coherence. Decoherence-free subspaces and topological qubits help reduce errors. QEC is crucial for fault-tolerant quantum computation, ensuring that quantum operations remain accurate as hardware scales.

Related Terms

Qubit: The fundamental unit of quantum information, requiring error correction for reliable operations (see pg 400).

Decoherence: The process by which quantum states lose coherence due to environmental interaction, causing computational errors (see pg 392).

Surface Code: A leading quantum error correction method that arranges qubits in a grid-like structure to protect against noise.

Common Misconceptions

Quantum error correction eliminates all errors: QEC reduces, but does not entirely eliminate, quantum errors.

QEC is the same as classical error correction: Unlike classical methods, QEC must correct errors without direct measurement.

All quantum computers use QEC: Many current quantum systems operate without error correction, relying instead on short-lived, noisy qubits.

Historical Context

Peter Shor introduced the first quantum error correction code in **1995**, proving that quantum information can be protected. **Andrew Steane** developed additional codes, improving quantum fault tolerance. Surface codes, introduced in the early **2000s**, became the leading approach due to their practical hardware implementations. Today, **IBM**, **Google**, and **Microsoft** focus on scalable quantum error correction to enable long-term quantum computing advancements.

Practical Implications

Quantum error correction is essential for scaling quantum computers beyond noisy intermediate-scale quantum (NISQ) devices. In secure communications, QEC enhances quantum cryptography by ensuring message integrity. Quantum sensors, such as those in space navigation and MRI machines, use QEC to maintain precision. The future of fault-tolerant quantum computing depends on advancements in hardware-efficient error correction codes, which will drive breakthroughs in drug discovery, financial modeling, and artificial intelligence optimization.

Quantum Gate (QC)

A quantum gate is a fundamental operation in quantum computing, manipulating qubits similarly to how classical logic gates operate on bits. Unlike classical gates, quantum gates utilize superposition, entanglement, and unitary transformations, enabling computations that exploit quantum parallelism to solve complex problems efficiently.

A quantum gate is like a choreographed dance move—each step must be precise and reversible to maintain the quantum system's integrity. Just as dancers coordinate movements to create intricate routines, quantum gates manipulate qubits in ways that preserve and harness their unique quantum properties.

Examples

Shor's Algorithm: Quantum gates enable factoring large numbers exponentially faster than classical computers, with applications in cryptography and security.

Quantum Machine Learning: Quantum circuits with quantum gates help speed up optimization tasks and data classification for AI models.

Simulating Molecules: Quantum gates enable the simulation of molecular interactions, helping researchers design new drugs and understand quantum chemistry.

Foundational Concepts

Quantum gates rely on unitary operations, which preserve quantum information by reversibly transforming qubits. The Hadamard gate creates superposition, the CNOT gate establishes entanglement, and the Pauli gates (X, Y, Z) apply quantum state rotations. Unlike classical gates, which are irreversible, quantum gates follow the principles of linear algebra and matrix transformations, ensuring computational reversibility. The universality theorem states that a set of fundamental quantum gates can construct any quantum algorithm, making them essential for building quantum circuits.

Related Terms

Qubit: The basic unit of quantum information, manipulated by quantum gates (see pg 400).

Quantum Circuit: A sequence of quantum gates that perform computational tasks (see pg 390).

Entanglement: A quantum phenomenon where qubits become interconnected, influencing each other regardless of distance (see pg 198).

Common Misconceptions

Quantum gates are like classical logic gates: While they share a name, quantum gates operate reversibly and probabilistically, unlike classical gates.

Quantum gates amplify computation speed directly: The advantage comes from quantum parallelism, not just individual gate operations.

Quantum gates always produce deterministic outputs: The results are often probabilistic, requiring multiple measurements to extract meaningful results.

Historical Context

Richard Feynman (1982) proposed quantum computing, leading to gate-based models. **David Deutsch (1985)** formalized the quantum circuit model, introducing universal quantum computation. **The Hadamard and Toffoli gates** emerged as key components, with the first experimental quantum logic gates implemented in the **1990s** using trapped ions. Companies like **IBM**, **Google**, and **Rigetti** continue refining quantum gate operations, advancing fault-tolerant quantum computing.

Practical Implications

Quantum gates power algorithms for factorization (Shor's), database searching (Grover's), and quantum simulation. In finance, they can potentially optimize portfolio management. In pharmaceuticals, they can potentially accelerate drug discovery by simulating molecular structures. As quantum hardware improves, fault-tolerant quantum gates will unlock unprecedented computing power, revolutionizing AI, materials science, and cybersecurity.

Quantum Supremacy (QC)

Quantum supremacy refers to the point at which a quantum computer can solve a problem that is practically impossible for even the most powerful classical supercomputers. This milestone demonstrates the advantage of quantum computation over traditional computing in specific tasks.

Quantum supremacy is like a race between a quantum sprinter and a classical marathon runner. While classical computers take a long, methodical approach, quantum computers can take many possible routes simultaneously, reaching the finish line exponentially faster for certain problems.

Examples

Random Circuit Sampling: Google's Sycamore processor performed a calculation in seconds that would take classical supercomputers thousands of years, demonstrating quantum supremacy in **2019**.

Quantum Cryptanalysis: Future quantum computers may break classical encryption using Shor's algorithm, rendering traditional cryptographic security obsolete.

Material Simulation: Quantum supremacy allows simulation of quantum materials, enabling the discovery of new superconductors and molecules that classical computers struggle to model.

Foundational Concepts

Quantum supremacy is based on superposition, where qubits exist in multiple states simultaneously, and entanglement, which enables instant correlations between qubits. Unlike classical bits, which process one calculation at a time, quantum computers use quantum gates to explore multiple solutions in parallel. The challenge is achieving low error rates and scalability to outperform classical systems. While quantum supremacy does not mean general-purpose quantum computing, it marks a breakthrough in computational complexity for specific tasks.

Related Terms

Qubit: The fundamental unit of quantum information, enabling quantum superposition and entanglement (see pg 400).

Quantum Speedup: The advantage of quantum computers over classical ones in solving complex problems faster.

Quantum Algorithm: A computational method that leverages quantum principles to solve problems more efficiently than classical algorithms (see pg 386).

Common Misconceptions

Quantum supremacy means replacing all classical computers: Quantum supremacy applies to specific problems, not general computing tasks.

Quantum computers instantly solve all problems: Many problems still lack efficient quantum algorithms, and classical computers remain superior in most applications.

Quantum supremacy equals practical usability: The milestone only proves feasibility—current quantum systems still face error correction and scalability challenges.

Historical Context

In **2012**, physicist **John Preskill** coined the term quantum supremacy, predicting a future milestone where quantum computers outperform classical ones. In **2019**, **Google** announced achieving quantum supremacy with its **Sycamore processor**, completing a complex task in 200 seconds that would take the world's fastest supercomputer 10,000 years. Other companies, including **IBM** and **Honeywell**, continue advancing quantum architectures, refining hardware and algorithms to achieve real-world quantum advantages.

Practical Implications

Quantum supremacy accelerates drug discovery, financial modeling, and artificial intelligence. Cryptography faces disruption, as quantum computers threaten RSA encryption. In logistics and optimization, quantum algorithms could revolutionize traffic routing and supply chains. However, the need for fault-tolerant quantum computing remains a barrier to widespread adoption.

Qubit (Quantum Bit) (QC)

A qubit (quantum bit) is the fundamental unit of quantum information, analogous to a classical bit but with quantum properties. Unlike classical bits that exist as 0 or 1, a qubit can be in a superposition of both states, enabling parallel computation and enhanced processing power.

A qubit is like a spinning coin, where classical bits are like a coin lying flat as either heads (0) or tails (1). A qubit remains in a superposition of heads and tails until measured, enabling multiple possibilities simultaneously.

Examples

Quantum Cryptography: Qubits enable secure encryption methods like quantum key distribution (QKD), where eavesdropping disrupts quantum states, making interception detectable.

Drug Discovery: Qubits simulate molecular interactions more efficiently than classical computers, accelerating pharmaceutical research and material science.

Artificial Intelligence: Quantum-enhanced AI algorithms leverage qubits for faster machine learning, enabling pattern recognition and optimization at unprecedented speeds.

Foundational Concepts

Qubits leverage superposition, meaning they exist in multiple states simultaneously, and entanglement, where two qubits become linked, allowing changes to one to instantaneously affect the other. Quantum interference helps refine computations by canceling out incorrect paths. Unlike classical computing, qubits rely on quantum gates to manipulate data. Due to quantum decoherence, maintaining stable qubits requires error correction techniques to reduce noise and extend coherence times.

Related Terms

Superposition: A quantum state allowing qubits to be both 0 and 1 simultaneously, increasing processing power (see pg 466).

Entanglement: A quantum phenomenon where two qubits share an instantaneous connection, regardless of distance (see pg 198).

Quantum Circuit: A sequence of quantum gates applied to qubits to perform computations (see pg 390).

Common Misconceptions

Qubits replace classical bits completely: Quantum computers enhance, not replace, classical computing for specific tasks.

Qubits always hold multiple values: Superposition only persists until measurement, at which point the qubit collapses to 0 or 1.

Qubits enable instant problem-solving: While qubits allow faster processing, quantum systems still require complex error correction and improvements in stability.

Historical Context

The concept of qubits emerged in the **1980s**, with physicist **Richard Feynman** proposing quantum computing for simulating nature. **David Deutsch** formalized quantum computation, showing qubits' advantages over classical bits. In **1994, Peter Shor** developed **Shor's algorithm**, proving that qubits could factor large numbers exponentially faster than classical computers. **IBM**, **Google**, and **D-Wave** have since developed quantum processors, refining qubit stability and coherence times.

Practical Implications

Qubits enable breakthroughs in cybersecurity, with quantum-safe encryption protecting sensitive data. In finance, quantum models optimize risk assessment and portfolio management. Optimization problems, such as logistics and supply chain routing, benefit from qubits' ability to process multiple outcomes simultaneously. However, practical implementation requires advances in error correction and scalable quantum hardware before widespread adoption is feasible.

Ransomware (CS)

Ransomware is a type of malicious software (malware) that encrypts or locks files and systems, demanding payment (ransom) from victims to restore access. It can spread via phishing emails, malicious links, or software vulnerabilities, affecting individuals, businesses, and critical infrastructure.

Ransomware is like a digital hostage situation—imagine locking your house, but a thief changes the locks and demands money for the new key. You're trapped, unable to enter unless you pay, yet there's no guarantee the criminal will unlock the door.

Examples

Hospital Cyberattack: Ransomware attacks on hospitals disrupt patient care, medical records, and operations, forcing some facilities to pay ransom to regain control.

Corporate Data Breach: Businesses experience data encryption and operational shutdowns, with attackers threatening to leak sensitive information unless ransom demands are met.

Government Infrastructure Attack: Ransomware has targeted city services, police departments, and utilities, causing widespread disruptions and financial losses.

Foundational Concepts

Ransomware exploits encryption algorithms to make files inaccessible without a decryption key. Attackers often demand payment in cryptocurrency for anonymity. Phishing tactics and social engineering are commonly used to trick users into downloading malware. Advanced ransomware strains utilize double extortion, where files are encrypted and also stolen, with threats to release sensitive data if the ransom is unpaid. Organizations use backup strategies, endpoint security, and network segmentation to mitigate risks and minimize damage.

Related Terms

Malware: Any malicious software designed to harm, exploit, or steal data (see pg. 314).

Phishing: A social engineering attack that deceives users into revealing sensitive information or downloading malware (see pg. 366).

Encryption: The process of encoding data to prevent unauthorized access, often misused in ransomware attacks (see pg. 194).

Common Misconceptions

Paying the ransom guarantees file recovery: Many victims never recover their data, even after payment.

Only large companies are targeted: Individuals and small businesses are frequent victims.

Antivirus software completely prevents ransomware: While security software helps, phishing attacks and human error remain major risks.

Historical Context

Ransomware first emerged in the late **1980s** with the **AIDS Trojan**, demanding payment via postal mail. **CryptoLocker (2013)** popularized modern ransomware, encrypting files and demanding **Bitcoin** payments. **WannaCry (2017)** affected over 200,000 systems worldwide, exploiting **Windows** vulnerabilities. **Ryuk, Maze**, and **Conti** became dominant ransomware groups, demanding millions in ransom. Law enforcement agencies like **FBI** and **Interpol** now actively combat ransomware through cyber task forces and coordinated takedowns.

Practical Implications

Ransomware poses a major threat to businesses, governments, and individuals, causing financial losses, reputational damage, and operational shutdowns. Cyber insurance, regular backups, and zero-trust security models are crucial in mitigating risks. Governments enforce ransomware regulations and reporting mandates, while law enforcement collaborates internationally to track and dismantle ransomware groups. However, as ransomware techniques evolve, cybersecurity defenses must continuously adapt.

Recommendation Engine (ANI)

A recommendation engine is an AI-powered system that analyzes user behavior and preferences to suggest relevant content, products, or services. It is widely used in e-commerce, streaming platforms, and social media to enhance user experience and increase engagement through personalized recommendations.

A recommendation engine is like a personal shopping assistant who observes your interests and browsing habits, then suggests items you might like. Just as a bookstore clerk recommends books based on past purchases, AI systems analyze data to tailor suggestions for users.

Examples

Streaming Services: Platforms like Netflix and Spotify use recommendation engines to suggest movies, shows, or songs based on user preferences and historical interactions.

E-commerce Platforms: Amazon and eBay recommend products by analyzing past purchases, browsing history, and similar customer behaviors, increasing sales and engagement.

Online Learning Platforms: Coursera and Duolingo use recommendation engines to suggest courses, quizzes, or learning paths suited to a user's interests and progress.

Foundational Concepts

Recommendation engines rely on collaborative filtering, which compares user preferences to others with similar tastes, and content-based filtering, which analyzes item attributes to suggest similar options. Hybrid models combine both techniques for more accurate recommendations. Machine learning and deep learning algorithms improve predictions by detecting patterns in vast datasets. User behavior tracking, natural language processing, and graph-based models further enhance recommendation accuracy. Ethical concerns include data privacy, bias in recommendations, and filter bubbles, where users see only content reinforcing their existing preferences.

Related Terms

Collaborative Filtering: A technique that suggests items by identifying users with similar interests.

Content-Based Filtering: A method that recommends items based on their attributes and a user's past interactions.

Personalization Algorithm: AI-driven methods that tailor content, products, or services to an individual user's preferences.

Common Misconceptions

Recommendation engines are always accurate: While they improve suggestions, they can sometimes produce irrelevant results.

Only big companies use them: Many small businesses and startups implement recommendation engines through AI-as-a-service platforms.

They invade user privacy: While they analyze user data, ethical recommendation engines use anonymized and consent-based data.

Historical Context

Early recommendation engines emerged in the **1990s**, with collaborative filtering algorithms pioneered by **GroupLens Research**. **Amazon** popularized recommendations in e-commerce, while **Netflix** revolutionized content suggestions with its **Netflix Prize (2006-2009)**, encouraging innovations in recommendation algorithms. Advancements in deep learning further enhanced recommendation accuracy. Today, AI-driven recommendation systems are integral to digital marketing, media, and user engagement strategies, influencing billions of interactions daily.

Practical Implications

Recommendation engines drive engagement, retention, and sales across industries. In retail, they increase revenue by personalizing shopping experiences. In media, they help platforms keep users engaged with tailored content. Healthcare recommendation systems assist in personalized treatment plans, while education platforms adapt learning materials to individual progress. However, concerns about data ethics, user privacy, and algorithmic bias remain, requiring continuous improvements in AI transparency and fairness.

Recurrent Neural Network (RNN) (AI)

A Recurrent Neural Network (RNN) is a type of artificial neural network designed for sequential data processing. Unlike traditional neural networks, it retains memory of past inputs by incorporating recurrent connections, making it effective for tasks like time series forecasting, natural language processing, and speech recognition.

An RNN is like a storyteller who remembers past events while narrating a new story. Just as a writer recalls previous plot points when crafting new sentences, an RNN processes sequential data by using memory from previous inputs to influence current predictions.

Examples

Speech Recognition: Virtual assistants like Siri and Google Assistant use RNNs to process spoken words sequentially, converting speech into text while considering context (see pg. 460).

Language Translation: Google Translate utilizes RNNs in sequence-to-sequence models, preserving context across long sentences to generate accurate translations.

Stock Price Prediction: Financial institutions use RNNs to analyze historical stock market trends and predict future prices by capturing dependencies in time-series data.

Foundational Concepts

RNNs rely on feedback loops where the output of one step serves as input for the next, enabling temporal dependency modeling. A hidden state stores past information, but standard RNNs suffer from vanishing gradient problems, making them ineffective for long sequences. To address this, Long Short-Term Memory (LSTM) and Gated Recurrent Unit (GRU) architectures were introduced, improving memory retention. RNNs are widely used in speech-to-text conversion, handwriting recognition, and music generation, where previous information influences the current output.

Related Terms

Long Short-Term Memory (LSTM): A specialized RNN variant designed to retain long-term dependencies using memory cells and gating mechanisms.

Gated Recurrent Unit (GRU): A simplified version of LSTM that also solves vanishing gradients but with fewer parameters, improving computational efficiency.

Transformer Model: A modern deep learning architecture that replaces RNNs for many tasks by using attention mechanisms to process sequential data more efficiently (see pg. 500).

Common Misconceptions

RNNs remember all past inputs indefinitely: Standard RNNs struggle with long-term dependencies due to vanishing gradients, requiring LSTMs or GRUs for improvement.

RNNs are the best choice for all sequential data: While useful, Transformers outperform RNNs in many NLP tasks due to their parallel processing ability.

RNNs process sequences instantaneously: Unlike feedforward networks, RNNs process data step by step, making them computationally intensive for long sequences.

Historical Context

The concept of RNNs dates back to the **1980s**, with early work by **John Hopfield** and **David Rumelhart** on neural memory. In **1997**, **Sepp Hochreiter** and **Jürgen Schmidhuber** introduced LSTM networks, addressing RNN limitations. GRUs, proposed by **Kyunghyun Cho et al.** in **2014**, provided a simpler alternative. Despite advancements, RNNs were largely replaced by Transformer models (introduced by **Vaswani et al.** in **2017**) for tasks like machine translation and text generation.

Practical Implications

RNNs revolutionized speech recognition, sentiment analysis, and financial forecasting by enabling models to learn from sequential data. They are widely used in autonomous driving systems for predicting vehicle movement patterns and in chatbots for generating context-aware responses. However, the rise of Transformers has shifted AI research focus, reducing reliance on RNNs in some domains. Despite this, RNNs remain crucial in applications where sequential processing and real-time inference are necessary, such as robotics and biosignal analysis.

Regression (AI)

Regression is a statistical and machine learning technique used to model relationships between dependent and independent variables. It predicts continuous numerical outcomes based on input features. Common types include linear regression, logistic regression, polynomial regression, and ridge regression, widely used in finance, healthcare, and engineering.

Regression is like predicting house prices based on past sales data. Just as a real estate agent estimates a home's value by considering size, location, and age, regression algorithms analyze historical data to forecast future trends in stock prices, sales, or temperature.

Examples

House Price Prediction: Real estate platforms use regression to estimate property values based on location, square footage, and market trends, helping buyers and sellers make informed decisions.

Sales Forecasting: Businesses predict future revenue by analyzing historical sales data, seasonality, and economic indicators, allowing them to optimize inventory and marketing strategies.

Healthcare Risk Assessment: Insurance companies use regression to determine patient health risks based on factors like age, lifestyle, and medical history, influencing policy pricing.

Foundational Concepts

Regression is based on mathematical models that find patterns in numerical data. Linear regression establishes a straight-line relationship between variables, while polynomial regression captures more complex, curved trends. Logistic regression, though classified under regression models, is used for binary classification tasks. Loss functions like Mean Squared Error (MSE) or Mean Absolute Error (MAE) help optimize predictions by reducing differences between actual and predicted values. Regression is widely applied in econometrics, risk analysis, and machine learning models to infer relationships and make quantitative predictions.

Related Terms

Linear Regression: A regression method that models the relationship between dependent and independent variables using a straight-line equation.

Logistic Regression: A classification algorithm that predicts probabilities of categorical outcomes, commonly used in spam detection and medical diagnosis.

Overfitting: A common issue where a regression model learns noise instead of actual patterns, leading to poor generalization on new data (see pg. 362).

Common Misconceptions

Regression is only for linear relationships: While linear regression is common, other forms like polynomial and ridge regression handle non-linear patterns.

Regression is only for continuous data: While standard regression predicts numerical values, logistic regression applies regression concepts to classification tasks.

More features always improve regression models: Including too many variables can cause overfitting, reducing model accuracy on unseen data.

Historical Context

Regression traces back to **Francis Galton**, who coined the term in the 19th century while studying hereditary traits. **Karl Pearson** later formalized the mathematical foundation with correlation coefficients. In the 20th century, regression became a key tool in econometrics, medical research, and artificial intelligence. The rise of machine learning in the 21st century expanded regression techniques, integrating them with neural networks, decision trees, and deep learning architectures.

Practical Implications

Regression is essential in predictive analytics, enabling businesses to anticipate sales trends, detect fraud, and optimize resource allocation. In healthcare, it aids in disease prediction and treatment cost estimation. Financial institutions use it to forecast market trends and credit risk. Regression is also used in climate modeling, traffic prediction, and sports analytics to analyze patterns and make data-driven decisions. As AI advances, regression remains a core analytical method, powering automated insights in various industries.

Reinforcement Learning (RL) (AI)

Reinforcement Learning (RL) is a machine learning approach where an agent learns to make decisions by interacting with an environment and receiving rewards or penalties. Through trial and error, the agent improves its strategy to maximize cumulative rewards, making RL useful for complex, sequential decision-making tasks.

Reinforcement Learning is like training a dog with treats. If the dog sits on command, it gets a treat (reward). If it disobeys, it gets no reward. Over time, the dog learns which actions result in treats and adjusts its behavior accordingly.

Examples

Autonomous Vehicles: Self-driving cars use RL to navigate traffic, avoid obstacles, and optimize fuel efficiency by continuously learning from road conditions and driver behavior.

Game AI: RL powers AI agents in video games, enabling them to learn strategies, improve gameplay, and adapt to human opponents through continuous interaction.

Robotics: Robots in manufacturing use RL to improve efficiency, learning optimal movements to reduce material waste and speed up production processes (see pg. 98).

Foundational Concepts

Reinforcement Learning is based on trial-and-error learning, where an agent interacts with an environment and learns through reward-based feedback. It relies on key elements: states (agent's current situation), actions (decisions it can make), and rewards (positive or negative feedback). Algorithms like Q-learning and Deep Q Networks (DQN) use a reward signal to optimize the agent's policy (strategy). Exploration vs. exploitation is a critical trade-off, balancing between trying new actions and refining known strategies for higher rewards.

Related Terms

Markov Decision Process (MDP): A mathematical framework for modeling RL problems with states, actions, and rewards.

Deep Reinforcement Learning: Combines deep learning with RL to handle high-dimensional data, used in applications like AlphaGo and robotics (see pg. 178 & 410).

Policy Gradient: A method where the agent directly optimizes its policy instead of relying on value functions like in Q-learning.

Common Misconceptions

RL learns instantly: Unlike supervised learning, RL takes thousands of iterations to achieve optimal performance.

RL is only for games: While famous for AlphaGo and Atari, RL is widely applied in robotics, finance, and healthcare.

More training always improves RL models: Overtraining can cause overfitting to specific scenarios, reducing generalization to new environments.

Historical Context

Reinforcement Learning was inspired by behavioral psychology, particularly **B.F. Skinner**'s work on operant conditioning. Early RL concepts emerged in the **1950s**, but the Q-learning algorithm by **Chris Watkins (1989)** was a breakthrough. The field evolved with **DeepMind**'s **AlphaGo (2016)**, which used **Deep RL** to defeat human champions. RL is now a cornerstone of AI research, powering advancements in robotics, finance, and autonomous systems.

Practical Implications

Reinforcement Learning is transforming autonomous systems, personalized recommendations, and robotics. In finance, RL optimizes algorithmic trading strategies. In healthcare, it enhances treatment plans by learning from patient responses. RL also improves smart grids, industrial automation, and logistics by dynamically adjusting operations. As RL scales with deep learning, its applications will expand into AI-driven assistants, resource optimization, and scientific discovery, revolutionizing decision-making in numerous fields.

Renewable Energy (CET)

Renewable Energy refers to energy generated from naturally replenishing sources such as solar, wind, hydro, geothermal, and biomass. Unlike fossil fuels, these energy sources do not deplete over time and produce minimal greenhouse gas emissions, making them crucial for sustainable energy systems and climate change mitigation.

Renewable Energy is like a perpetual water fountain that refills itself naturally. Unlike a battery that eventually drains, renewable sources—like the sun, wind, and rivers—continuously provide power, ensuring a long-term, sustainable supply of electricity without running out.

Examples

Solar Power: Photovoltaic panels convert sunlight into electricity, providing power for homes, businesses, and even entire cities while reducing dependence on fossil fuels.

Wind Energy: Wind turbines harness airflow to generate electricity, making wind farms a key component of national renewable energy grids and sustainable infrastructure (see pg. 532).

Hydropower: Flowing water from dams and rivers drives turbines, producing electricity in a reliable, large-scale manner, widely used in countries with abundant water resources.

Foundational Concepts

Renewable Energy is based on natural cycles that replenish energy sources. Solar radiation powers solar panels, wind currents drive turbines, and water cycles enable hydropower. Unlike fossil fuels, which release carbon dioxide, renewables produce clean energy with minimal environmental impact. Energy storage solutions, like batteries and smart grids, help manage fluctuations in supply and demand. Governments incentivize clean energy adoption through feed-in tariffs, tax credits, and infrastructure investments to transition toward a low-carbon future.

Related Terms

Sustainability: The principle of using resources efficiently to meet present needs without compromising future generations' ability to meet theirs.

Smart Grid: A digitalized power grid that optimizes energy distribution by integrating renewables, energy storage, and real-time monitoring (see pg. 450).

Energy Transition: The global shift from fossil fuels to renewable energy to combat climate change and resource depletion.

Common Misconceptions

Renewables are unreliable: While solar and wind are weather-dependent, energy storage and grid balancing ensure a stable supply.

Renewable energy is expensive: Costs have dramatically decreased, with solar and wind power now cheaper than fossil fuels in many regions.

Hydropower is always sustainable: Large-scale dams can disrupt ecosystems, making run-of-river hydropower a more sustainable alternative.

Historical Context

Humans have harnessed wind and water energy for centuries, from windmills in ancient Persia to hydropower mills in Europe. The modern renewable energy movement gained traction in the **1970s** oil crisis, pushing research into solar panels, wind turbines, and biofuels. **The Kyoto Protocol (1997)** and **Paris Agreement (2015)** emphasized carbon reduction, accelerating renewable energy policies. Today, countries worldwide are investing in green energy technologies to meet net-zero carbon goals.

Practical Implications

Renewable Energy is revolutionizing power generation, reducing emissions, and promoting energy independence. In urban planning, cities integrate solar panels and electric vehicle charging stations. Developing nations use off-grid solar systems to provide electricity to remote areas. Corporations invest in clean energy to meet sustainability targets. As storage technology improves, renewables will replace fossil fuels, transforming global energy markets and reducing climate impact.

Responsive Design (HCI)

Responsive Design is an approach to web and application development that ensures interfaces adapt seamlessly to different screen sizes, resolutions, and devices. It uses fluid grids, flexible images, and media queries to optimize user experience across desktops, tablets, and smartphones without requiring separate designs.

Responsive Design is like water in a container—it naturally takes the shape of whatever space it is in. Whether viewed on a small phone screen or a large desktop monitor, a responsive website adjusts fluidly, ensuring a consistent and user-friendly experience.

Examples

E-commerce Websites: Online stores like Amazon and eBay use Responsive Design to provide a smooth shopping experience on mobile, tablet, and desktop devices, ensuring images, buttons, and text adjust to screen size.

News Portals: Media outlets like BBC and The New York Times implement Responsive Design so readers can access news seamlessly from various devices without needing a separate mobile version.

E-learning Platforms: Online courses on Coursera and Udemy use Responsive Design to ensure lessons, videos, and quizzes are accessible across different devices, maintaining usability and readability.

Foundational Concepts

Responsive Design is based on three core principles: fluid grids, flexible images, and media queries. Fluid grids ensure content scales proportionally rather than being fixed at specific pixel dimensions. Flexible images resize dynamically to fit the layout without distortion. Media queries enable styles to adjust based on screen width, resolution, and orientation. This ensures a consistent user experience across devices. Mobile-first design prioritizes smaller screens before scaling up, improving performance and accessibility for all users.

Related Terms

Adaptive Design: Unlike Responsive Design, Adaptive Design creates separate layouts for different screen sizes instead of a single flexible layout.

Progressive Enhancement: A design strategy that builds a basic, functional experience first, then adds advanced features for larger screens.

Viewport Meta Tag: A crucial HTML tag that ensures a web page scales correctly on mobile devices, improving readability and usability.

Common Misconceptions

Responsive Design is only for mobile: It adapts to all screen sizes, not just mobile.

It makes websites slower: Proper optimization ensures efficient loading despite dynamic resizing.

Separate mobile websites are better: Responsive Design eliminates the need for multiple versions of a site, reducing maintenance effort.

Historical Context

Responsive Design emerged as a response to mobile internet growth. **Ethan Marcotte** coined the term in **2010**, outlining principles in an article for **A List Apart**. Before this, developers created separate mobile sites, leading to higher costs and maintenance complexity. The rise of smartphones and tablets made fluid, adaptable designs essential. Advances in **CSS3** and **HTML5** facilitated Responsive Design, influencing modern UX/UI standards. Today, it is a default practice in web development, ensuring accessibility across all devices.

Practical Implications

Responsive Design is critical in digital accessibility, SEO, and user retention. Websites that adapt to multiple devices rank higher in search engines, reducing bounce rates and improving engagement. Businesses save costs by maintaining one website instead of separate versions for different platforms. It enhances user experience, accessibility, and brand consistency, making digital platforms more inclusive and scalable for evolving technologies.

Reward Signal (AI)

A Reward Signal is a numerical value that represents feedback in reinforcement learning (RL). It guides an AI agent's learning process by indicating the success or failure of an action. The agent aims to maximize cumulative rewards over time to optimize its behavior.

A Reward Signal is like a gold star in a classroom—students (AI agents) adjust their behavior based on praise (positive reward) or correction (negative reward). Just as students strive for more gold stars, AI systems refine their actions to maximize rewards.

Examples

Self-Driving Cars: Reward signals guide autonomous vehicles by reinforcing safe driving behaviors, such as staying in lanes and maintaining optimal speed, while penalizing unsafe actions like abrupt braking.

Game AI: In video games, RL-based AI opponents learn strategies by receiving reward signals for winning battles, avoiding damage, or completing objectives, leading to more adaptive gameplay.

Robotic Manipulation: Robots in warehouses receive rewards for successfully picking and placing objects while avoiding collisions, helping improve efficiency in logistics and automation (see pg. 98).

Foundational Concepts

Reward Signals are central to reinforcement learning, where an agent interacts with an environment and learns by trial and error. The agent's objective is to maximize the cumulative reward, known as the return. The reward function defines how rewards are given based on the agent's actions. Temporal Difference Learning (TD Learning) helps the agent estimate future rewards, allowing for long-term planning. Exploration vs. Exploitation is a key challenge, as the agent must balance trying new actions with sticking to known rewarding behaviors.

Related Terms

Policy: The strategy an agent follows to decide on actions based on past rewards and observations (see pg. 370).

Q-Learning: A method in RL where an agent learns the optimal action-value function to maximize future rewards (see pg. 410).

Markov Decision Process (MDP): A mathematical framework defining states, actions, rewards, and transitions, essential for modeling reinforcement learning problems.

Common Misconceptions

All rewards are immediate: Many RL problems involve delayed rewards, meaning actions may not have immediate consequences.

Negative rewards are always bad: Negative rewards (or penalties) are useful for discouraging undesired behaviors rather than always being harmful.

More rewards always improve learning: Poorly designed reward functions can lead to undesired behaviors, such as agents exploiting loopholes rather than solving tasks properly.

Historical Context

The concept of reward-driven learning originates from behavioral psychology, particularly **B.F. Skinner**'s reinforcement theory. In computer science, **Richard Sutton** and **Andrew Barto** developed reinforcement learning frameworks in the **1980s**. RL gained popularity with Deep Q-Networks (DQN) by **DeepMind** in **2015**, where an agent learned to play **Atari** games using only reward signals. Today, reward-based AI is fundamental to robotics, autonomous systems, and artificial intelligence research.

Practical Implications

Reward signals enable AI in robotics, gaming, and finance to optimize decision-making. In healthcare, RL-based AI recommends treatments by rewarding effective interventions. In energy management, AI receives rewards for minimizing power consumption while maintaining efficiency. Reward signals also help in chatbots and recommendation systems, improving interactions based on user feedback. However, ensuring well-designed reward structures is crucial, as poorly shaped rewards can lead to unintended AI behaviors.

Robot Ethics (RT)

Robot Ethics refers to the moral principles and guidelines governing the design, deployment, and interaction of robots in human environments. It addresses issues such as autonomous decision-making, accountability, fairness, privacy, and the impact of robotics on society, ensuring that robots operate ethically and responsibly.

Robot Ethics is like teaching a child the difference between right and wrong. Just as children must learn appropriate behaviors and consequences, robots must be programmed with ethical principles to ensure they act responsibly, respect human rights, and avoid causing harm in real-world interactions.

Examples

Autonomous Weapons: Ethical concerns arise when AI-powered military drones make independent attack decisions. Policies are needed to ensure accountability and compliance with humanitarian laws.

Caregiving Robots: AI-driven robots assist elderly and disabled individuals, but ethical concerns include privacy, autonomy, and emotional dependency, requiring regulations on data use and decision-making limits.

Workplace Automation: AI-powered robotic systems replace human workers, raising ethical concerns about job displacement, economic inequality, and fair labor practices, necessitating policies for workforce adaptation.

Foundational Concepts

Robot Ethics is based on moral philosophy, AI safety, and legal frameworks that guide AI behavior. Asimov's Three Laws of Robotics, a theoretical foundation, suggests that robots must not harm humans. Machine learning transparency ensures that AI decisions remain explainable and fair. Value alignment focuses on aligning robots' objectives with human values, preventing unintended consequences. Bias mitigation is crucial, as poorly trained AI can reinforce discrimination. Regulatory frameworks, such as the EU AI Act, help enforce ethical guidelines in robotic development.

Related Terms

AI Ethics: The broader study of ethical concerns in AI, including bias, privacy, and decision-making fairness (see pg. 204).

Explainable AI (XAI): AI systems designed to provide transparent and interpretable decision-making, crucial for ethical robotics (see pg. 27).

Human-Robot Interaction (HRI): The study of how humans and robots communicate, ensuring robots behave safely and appropriately.

Common Misconceptions

All robots have built-in ethics: Robots only follow programmed rules; they lack intrinsic morality.

Ethical robots eliminate human responsibility: Human developers and policymakers remain accountable for robot behavior and outcomes.

Robots will always act in human interest: Without careful design, AI-driven robots may optimize for efficiency over ethics, leading to unintended consequences.

Historical Context

Robot Ethics gained prominence in **1942** when **Isaac Asimov** introduced **the Three Laws of Robotics**. By the late 20th century, ethical AI debates intensified with increasing automation. In the **2000s**, advancements in autonomous systems prompted concerns about military drones, self-driving cars, and care robots. **The IEEE Global Initiative on Ethics of Autonomous Systems** and **EU AI regulations** established guidelines for responsible robotics, emphasizing transparency, fairness, and accountability in AI-driven automation.

Practical Implications

Robot Ethics influences healthcare, military, and industrial robotics. In healthcare, ensuring that AI-powered assistants prioritize patient well-being is critical. In law enforcement, facial recognition and robotic policing raise concerns about bias and privacy. In manufacturing, automation must be designed to augment human workforces rather than replace them unfairly. As robots become more autonomous, ethical frameworks are essential to prevent unintended harm, algorithmic bias, and human displacement, ensuring that robotics benefits society rather than exacerbating inequalities.

Robustness (RAI)

Robustness in Responsible AI refers to an AI system's ability to perform reliably under various conditions, including adversarial attacks, data shifts, and unexpected inputs. A robust AI system maintains accuracy, fairness, and security across different environments, ensuring consistent and ethical decision-making without unintended failures.

Robustness is like a well-trained athlete performing in different weather conditions. Just as a runner must adapt to wind, rain, or extreme heat without compromising performance, AI systems must function reliably across varying data inputs, ensuring fairness and resilience in unpredictable real-world scenarios.

Examples

Autonomous Vehicles: AI-powered self-driving cars must function reliably in varied weather, road conditions, and traffic patterns, preventing accidents and ensuring passenger safety.

Healthcare AI Diagnostics: AI systems analyzing medical images must remain robust against diverse patient demographics, imaging techniques, and data quality variations to prevent biases and diagnostic errors.

Financial Fraud Detection: AI-based fraud detection must detect sophisticated, evolving fraud tactics while avoiding false positives that could block legitimate transactions, ensuring financial security and customer trust.

Foundational Concepts

Robustness in AI relies on adversarial training, domain generalization, and model interpretability to ensure consistent performance. Adversarial robustness enables AI models to resist deceptive inputs, while generalization techniques ensure adaptability to unseen data distributions. Bias mitigation prevents discriminatory behavior, ensuring fairness across diverse populations. Error tolerance allows AI to recover from minor disruptions, preventing critical failures. Redundancy mechanisms, such as ensemble learning, enhance reliability. Regulatory frameworks, including EU AI Act guidelines, encourage AI developers to prioritize robustness, ensuring models align with ethical standards.

Related Terms

Adversarial Robustness: AI's ability to withstand maliciously crafted inputs designed to exploit system weaknesses.

Fairness in AI: Ensuring AI models make equitable and unbiased decisions across different demographic groups (see pg. 216).

Model Generalization: The ability of an AI system to perform well on unseen data distributions, preventing overfitting to training data.

Common Misconceptions

Robustness eliminates bias completely: While robustness minimizes failures, fairness and bias mitigation still require active intervention.

AI is naturally robust once trained: AI models must be continuously tested, retrained, and adapted to maintain robustness in evolving conditions.

Robust AI is immune to cyberattacks: While robustness improves security, AI models must still incorporate encryption, monitoring, and defensive mechanisms to prevent adversarial manipulation.

Historical Context

The concept of robust AI emerged as machine learning models began facing adversarial attacks and real-world deployment challenges. Early discussions on robustness date back to **1990s** control theory, but concerns grew in the **2010s** with adversarial attacks in image classification and fraud detection. In **2017**, **Google Brain** and **OpenAI** introduced techniques to enhance adversarial robustness. Regulatory bodies, including **ISO** and the **EU AI Act**, now emphasize AI robustness as a critical component of trustworthy AI governance.

Practical Implications

Robustness is critical in healthcare, finance, and cybersecurity, ensuring AI reliability in high-stakes environments. In critical infrastructure, robust AI prevents malfunctions in power grids and autonomous defense systems. In social media moderation, robustness reduces false content removals, preventing biases in enforcement policies. As AI adoption grows, robustness safeguards against adversarial manipulation, data bias, and unintended ethical violations, ensuring AI systems remain trustworthy, secure, and responsible across global applications.

Saliency Map (XAI)

A saliency map is a visualization technique used in Explainable AI (XAI) to highlight which parts of an input—such as an image, text, or dataset—are most influential in an AI model's decision-making process. By assigning importance to different regions, it helps interpret and diagnose AI behavior.

A saliency map is like a heatmap on a sports field, showing where a player has spent the most time. Just as coaches use it to understand movement patterns, AI researchers use saliency maps to see which areas of data influence an algorithm's decision the most.

Examples

Medical Imaging: Saliency maps help interpret AI-powered diagnoses by showing which parts of an X-ray, MRI, or CT scan influenced the model's decision, ensuring trust and accuracy in medical AI.

Autonomous Vehicles: Self-driving cars use saliency maps to highlight critical objects, such as pedestrians or stop signs, ensuring the AI model prioritizes relevant visual cues for decision-making.

Fraud Detection: AI models in finance use saliency maps to identify anomalies in transaction data, highlighting suspicious activities that require further human investigation.

Foundational Concepts

Saliency maps rely on gradient-based methods, attention mechanisms, and feature attribution techniques to determine the influence of individual inputs. Gradient-weighted class activation mapping (Grad-CAM) visualizes which areas of an image drive an AI's prediction. Layer-wise relevance propagation (LRP) distributes model decisions backward to highlight key features. Attention-based saliency methods, common in natural language processing, identify the most important words in AI-generated text summaries. Saliency mapping enhances transparency by revealing biases, errors, and potential misinterpretations in deep learning models.

Related Terms

Explainable AI (XAI): A field of AI that focuses on making AI decision-making interpretable, transparent, and understandable for humans (see pg. 27).

Feature Attribution: A technique used to identify which input features contribute most to an AI model's output (see pg. 220).

Grad-CAM: A visual explanation method that highlights which regions in an image influenced a deep learning model's decision.

Common Misconceptions

Saliency maps provide exact explanations: They highlight important regions but do not fully explain why a model made a decision.

Saliency maps eliminate AI bias: They expose biases in AI decisions, but fairness still requires additional model audits and bias correction techniques.

Saliency maps work perfectly for all AI models: Some models, especially black-box neural networks, still produce ambiguous or misleading saliency maps.

Historical Context

The concept of saliency dates back to human visual attention research in psychology. In AI, early methods such as backpropagation-based visualization emerged in the **2010s** to improve model interpretability. In **2016**, **Grad-CAM** became widely used for visualizing convolutional neural networks (CNNs). Advances in attention-based AI models, such as transformers, introduced new saliency mapping techniques, making explainability a key focus in AI ethics and regulation. Organizations like **DARPA** and the **EU AI Act** emphasize saliency maps in responsible AI development.

Practical Implications

Saliency maps improve AI trustworthiness, regulatory compliance, and model debugging across industries. In healthcare, they enable doctors to verify AI diagnoses before making treatment decisions. In finance, they help auditors understand fraud detection models. In legal AI, saliency maps explain why an AI system flagged a document as relevant, ensuring algorithmic transparency in legal decision-making. As AI adoption grows, saliency maps play a crucial role in human-AI collaboration, fairness assessments, and regulatory alignment to ensure ethical AI deployment.

Scalability (HPC)

Scalability refers to a system's ability to efficiently handle increasing workloads by expanding resources, such as computing power, memory, or network capacity. In High-Performance Computing (HPC), scalability ensures that as demand grows, performance remains optimal, whether by adding more processors or optimizing software architectures.

Scalability is like a restaurant kitchen—a small staff works fine for a few customers, but when orders increase, hiring more chefs and using efficient workflows prevents delays. Similarly, HPC systems expand resources to manage larger computational tasks without performance degradation.

Examples

Cloud Computing: Cloud platforms like Amazon Web Services (AWS) and Google Cloud scale up or down based on workload demands, optimizing resources for cost and performance.

Scientific Simulations: HPC systems scale to handle massive climate models, requiring thousands of processors to simulate weather patterns, ocean currents, and atmospheric changes efficiently.

Machine Learning Training: Training large AI models, like GPT-4 or deep neural networks, requires scalability to distribute workloads across multiple GPUs or TPUs to accelerate computation.

Foundational Concepts

Scalability in HPC relies on parallel computing, distributed systems, and load balancing to ensure efficiency as workloads increase. Strong scaling maintains execution speed by distributing a fixed workload across more resources, while weak scaling increases resources to match growing workloads. Amdahl's Law and Gustafson's Law define the limits of scalability, highlighting bottlenecks in parallel processing. Elastic computing allows cloud platforms to dynamically adjust resources in response to real-time demand, making HPC adaptable to fluctuating workloads.

Related Terms

Parallel Processing: The division of large computational tasks into smaller parts, executed simultaneously across multiple processors (see pg. 364).

Load Balancing: The distribution of workloads across computing resources to prevent bottlenecks and optimize performance.

Elastic Computing: A cloud computing feature that automatically scales up or down based on real-time demand.

Common Misconceptions

Scalability guarantees better performance: Adding resources doesn't always improve efficiency; bottlenecks may still exist.

Only cloud systems are scalable: Scalability applies to on-premise HPC clusters, supercomputers, and AI models, not just cloud-based systems.

Scaling horizontally and vertically are the same: Horizontal scaling adds more machines, while vertical scaling increases the power of existing machines.

Historical Context

The concept of scalability emerged in early supercomputing, where researchers developed parallel computing models to process massive datasets. The **Cray-1 supercomputer** (**1976**) demonstrated early scalable architectures, followed by advances in distributed computing in the **1990s**. The rise of cloud computing (**2000s**) transformed scalability, enabling on-demand resource allocation. Companies like **Google, Amazon**, and **Microsoft** pioneered scalable AI and cloud platforms, leveraging HPC for large-scale applications. Exascale computing, capable of a billion billion calculations per second, represents the latest milestone in scalable HPC.

Practical Implications

Scalability impacts AI, finance, healthcare, and engineering by enabling large-scale computations. In financial trading, scalable HPC systems process real-time transactions and risk assessments. In healthcare, scalable genomics platforms analyze DNA sequences across millions of patients. In autonomous vehicles, real-time AI models require scalable infrastructure to process sensor data efficiently. Scalability ensures technological advancements remain feasible, making high-performance AI, scientific research, and enterprise applications cost-effective and efficient.

Scikit Learn (AI)

Scikit-Learn is an open-source Python library that provides efficient tools for machine learning, data preprocessing, and model evaluation. Built on NumPy, SciPy, and Matplotlib, it enables supervised and unsupervised learning with algorithms like regression, classification, clustering, and dimensionality reduction, making it a widely used tool in AI research and industry.

Scikit-Learn is like a Swiss Army knife for machine learning—it provides multiple built-in tools that allow developers to quickly apply different techniques without building everything from scratch. Whether solving classification problems or predicting trends, it simplifies AI development.

Examples

Spam Detection: Email services use Scikit-Learn to train models that classify emails as spam or legitimate, improving filtering based on text analysis and pattern recognition.

Customer Segmentation: Businesses apply clustering algorithms from Scikit-Learn to analyze customer purchasing behavior, creating targeted marketing strategies based on groups with similar preferences.

Medical Diagnosis: Hospitals use Scikit-Learn's classification models to predict diseases based on symptoms, genetic data, and imaging, assisting doctors in early diagnosis and personalized treatment planning.

Foundational Concepts

Scikit-Learn is built on core machine learning principles, including supervised learning (where models learn from labeled data) and unsupervised learning (where patterns emerge from unlabeled data). It offers data preprocessing tools like feature scaling and missing value imputation. Model selection relies on cross-validation, ensuring robustness. Hyperparameter tuning optimizes algorithm performance, while dimensionality reduction techniques like Principal Component Analysis (PCA) improve computational efficiency. Its modular design allows seamless integration with other AI frameworks like TensorFlow and PyTorch.

Related Terms

NumPy: A foundational library for numerical computing, providing fast array operations used in Scikit-Learn.

Pandas: A data manipulation library used with Scikit-Learn for preprocessing structured datasets.

TensorFlow: A deep learning framework that complements Scikit-Learn, used for more complex neural network models (see pg. 482).

Common Misconceptions

Scikit-Learn is for deep learning: It primarily supports traditional machine learning models, not deep learning, which requires TensorFlow or PyTorch.

Scikit-Learn is slow: While optimized for CPU-based tasks, it may not match the speed of GPU-accelerated frameworks for large-scale data.

Only experts can use it: Scikit-Learn is designed for both beginners and professionals, offering a simple API and extensive documentation.

Historical Context

Developed as part of the **Google Summer of Code** (**2007**), Scikit-Learn was officially released in **2010** by **David Cournapeau** and improved by a community of developers. It built upon the SciPy ecosystem, bringing machine learning capabilities to **Python**. Over the years, it has become an industry standard, widely adopted by companies like **Spotify**, **Airbnb**, and **JPMorgan Chase**. Continuous updates have expanded its functionalities, making it essential for AI development.

Practical Implications

Scikit-Learn accelerates AI adoption in finance, healthcare, e-commerce, and cybersecurity. In finance, it enables fraud detection by identifying anomalous transactions. In healthcare, it enhances predictive analytics for patient outcomes. In e-commerce, it improves recommendation systems, helping businesses personalize user experiences. Its simplicity allows rapid prototyping of AI models, making machine learning accessible to researchers, engineers, and data scientists across various domains.

Self-Regulating AI Systems (ANI)

Self-Regulating AI Systems are artificial intelligence models that autonomously monitor, adjust, and optimize their behavior to maintain efficiency, fairness, and ethical compliance. They use feedback loops, adaptive learning, and error correction mechanisms to improve performance while preventing harmful or biased decision-making in dynamic environments.

Self-Regulating AI is like a self-driving car with an internal safety monitor—constantly adjusting its speed, direction, and braking based on traffic and road conditions. It corrects errors and adapts to changes, ensuring a smooth and safe ride without human intervention.

Examples

Autonomous Healthcare Diagnostics: AI-powered medical imaging systems self-regulate by adjusting scan analysis thresholds based on patient data variability, improving accuracy while minimizing false positives.

Financial Fraud Detection: Banking AI systems continuously refine fraud detection rules by analyzing new patterns, reducing both false alarms and undetected fraud, ensuring compliance with evolving regulations.

Smart Grid Energy Management: Self-regulating AI optimizes renewable energy distribution by dynamically adjusting supply-demand algorithms, improving efficiency in power grids while minimizing outages (see pg. 450).

Foundational Concepts

Self-Regulating AI Systems rely on reinforcement learning, adaptive optimization, and real-time feedback mechanisms to ensure robustness. Explainability is critical, as these systems must justify autonomous decisions. Ethical AI principles, such as bias mitigation and fairness, guide their self-improvement processes. Continuous monitoring allows AI models to detect anomalies, retrain on new data, and avoid unintended consequences. Integration with human oversight mechanisms ensures alignment with user-defined goals while maintaining autonomy. These self-regulating frameworks enhance trust and safety in high-stakes applications.

Related Terms

Reinforcement Learning: A learning paradigm where AI agents adjust behavior based on reward signals (see pg. 410).

Explainable AI (XAI): Methods ensuring AI decisions are transparent, interpretable, and accountable (see pg. 27).

Bias Mitigation: Techniques that detect and correct biases in AI systems to ensure fairness (see pg. 104).

Common Misconceptions

Self-regulation means full autonomy: These AI systems still require human oversight to prevent unintended behaviors.

Self-regulating AI is bias-free: While it corrects biases, it does not eliminate them entirely without external intervention.

All AI systems self-regulate: Most AI models lack real-time adaptation and require manual updates.

Historical Context

The concept of self-regulating AI emerged from control theory and cybernetics in the mid-20th century. **Norbert Wiener**'s work on feedback loops laid the foundation for adaptive systems. Modern advances in deep learning, reinforcement learning, and explainable AI have enabled practical self-regulating mechanisms. Companies like **Google DeepMind** and **OpenAI** have pioneered self-correcting models in fields like natural language processing and robotics. Increasing concerns about AI ethics and safety have further accelerated research in autonomous self-regulation.

Practical Implications

Self-regulating AI enhances reliability, transparency, and efficiency in critical sectors. In autonomous vehicles, these systems improve navigation safety by adapting to unpredictable road conditions. Cybersecurity AI detects and mitigates threats in real-time, reducing human intervention. Personalized education platforms dynamically adjust learning paths to match student progress. As AI becomes more autonomous, self-regulation ensures alignment with ethical and legal standards, promoting responsible AI adoption in industries like finance, healthcare, and smart infrastructure.

Self-Supervised Learning (AI)

Self-Supervised Learning (SSL) is a machine learning paradigm where models learn patterns and relationships from unlabeled data by creating their own supervision signals. By predicting missing or transformed parts of data, SSL reduces reliance on human-labeled datasets and improves AI generalization and efficiency.

Self-Supervised Learning is like a child learning a language by hearing conversations rather than using flashcards. Instead of relying on explicit lessons, the child deduces grammar and meaning from context, enabling natural learning without external labeling.

Examples

Natural Language Processing: Models like GPT and BERT use SSL to predict missing words in sentences, enabling better context understanding and text generation (see pg. 346).

Computer Vision: SSL helps AI recognize objects by learning from cropped, rotated, or occluded images, improving its ability to generalize without labeled data.

Healthcare Diagnostics: AI systems use SSL to analyze unlabeled medical scans, identifying abnormalities by learning patterns within datasets rather than relying on manually annotated images.

Foundational Concepts

Self-Supervised Learning builds on unsupervised learning, where AI extracts structure from unlabeled data. It often relies on contrastive learning, autoencoders, and masked modeling to predict hidden or transformed data. SSL reduces dependency on expensive labeled datasets, making AI training more scalable. Techniques like self-distillation enable models to refine themselves over time. By leveraging large-scale pretraining, SSL improves AI's ability to adapt across domains, enhancing transfer learning and generalization in real-world applications.

Related Terms

Unsupervised Learning: AI learns without explicit labels, discovering hidden patterns and clusters in data (see pg. 514).

Contrastive Learning: A technique that trains AI by comparing similar and dissimilar data points to enhance differentiation (see pg. 148).

Transfer Learning: AI models apply knowledge from one task to another, improving performance with minimal new data.

Common Misconceptions

SSL eliminates the need for labeled data: While it reduces reliance, some labeled data is still needed for fine-tuning.

SSL only applies to vision and language: It is also used in healthcare, finance, and robotics for anomaly detection and autonomous learning.

SSL models are always self-sufficient: They require substantial computing power for training and manual tuning for optimization.

Historical Context

Self-Supervised Learning evolved from unsupervised learning and deep learning innovations. Early advancements in autoencoders and self-predictive models laid the groundwork. Breakthroughs like **Word2Vec (2013)**, **BERT (2018)**, and **SimCLR (2020)** demonstrated SSL's potential. **Meta AI**, **Google DeepMind**, and **OpenAI** continue advancing SSL, making AI more adaptive and data-efficient.

Practical Implications

Self-Supervised Learning democratizes AI by reducing the need for large labeled datasets, making AI accessible in low-resource domains like healthcare and scientific research. It enhances robust AI models, making them less prone to overfitting and better at generalizing to unseen data. SSL also accelerates autonomous learning in robotics, cybersecurity, and finance, where real-time adaptation is crucial. By minimizing human intervention in data labeling, SSL makes AI more scalable and cost-effective for large-scale applications.

Self-training (AI)

Self-training is a semi-supervised learning technique where a model iteratively trains itself using a small set of labeled data and a large set of unlabeled data. The model labels the unlabeled data, refines its predictions, and re-trains to improve performance with minimal human intervention.

Self-training is like a student teaching themselves a subject using only a few textbook examples. Initially, they learn from a teacher's guidance but then attempt exercises independently, refining their understanding through self-correction and additional practice, gradually improving their grasp of the material.

Examples

Speech Recognition: AI models improve transcription accuracy by training on a small dataset of labeled audio clips and generating additional pseudo-labels from unlabeled recordings (see pg. 460).

Medical Diagnosis: Self-training enhances AI in radiology and pathology, where models use limited expert-annotated images to classify new medical scans with minimal human input.

Fraud Detection: Banks use self-training models to identify fraudulent transactions, leveraging a small set of labeled fraud cases to analyze larger datasets for hidden patterns.

Foundational Concepts

Self-training is based on semi-supervised learning, where models use both labeled and unlabeled data to improve accuracy. It employs pseudo-labeling, where the model assigns labels to unknown data and retrains using its own predictions. This approach enhances model generalization, efficiency, and adaptability in data-scarce environments. Self-training is often combined with active learning, where AI selectively queries humans for difficult cases. By iteratively refining its predictions, self-training allows models to scale learning with minimal manual effort while maintaining high performance.

Related Terms

Semi-Supervised Learning: A learning method using both labeled and unlabeled data to enhance AI training (see pg. 436).

Pseudo-Labeling: The process where AI generates its own labels for unlabeled data to expand training datasets.

Active Learning: AI selects uncertain or difficult cases for human labeling to improve accuracy efficiently.

Common Misconceptions

Self-training eliminates the need for labeled data: It reduces reliance but still requires a small labeled dataset for initial learning.

Self-training guarantees perfect results: Errors in pseudo-labeling can propagate, requiring confidence thresholds for reliable learning.

Self-training only applies to text and images: It is used in finance, cybersecurity, and scientific research where large unlabeled datasets exist.

Historical Context

Self-training traces back to early semi-supervised learning research in the **1990s**, where decision trees and neural networks leveraged unlabeled data. **Yarowsky (1995)** demonstrated self-training for natural language processing, influencing modern techniques. Advances in deep learning, transformer models, and unsupervised pretraining have accelerated self-training adoption in fields like computer vision and speech recognition.

Practical Implications

Self-training enhances AI scalability, enabling systems to learn from vast amounts of unlabeled data with minimal human supervision. In healthcare, it aids in disease detection and drug discovery, while in autonomous driving, it refines AI's ability to interpret real-world traffic scenarios. Financial institutions use self-training to identify fraud and market trends. By reducing the need for costly labeled datasets, self-training makes AI more accessible, adaptable, and efficient for real-world applications.

Semi-Structured Data (AI)

Semi-structured data is information that does not conform to a strict relational database format but has some organizational properties. It lacks a rigid schema like structured data but contains markers, tags, or metadata that provide context, making it easier to analyze than unstructured data.

Semi-structured data is like a well-organized notebook with handwritten notes and highlighted sections. While it does not follow a fixed format like a spreadsheet, headings, labels, and underlined text help identify key information, making it easier to find and process than a completely unstructured diary.

Examples

Email Data: Emails include both structured components (timestamps, sender, recipient) and unstructured text (email body), making them a prime example of semi-structured data.

JSON & XML Files: These formats store data with nested elements and tags, allowing flexible storage and retrieval while retaining some structure.

Sensor Data in IoT: Devices like smart thermostats or wearable health trackers generate data with structured timestamps and unstructured logs, making it semi-structured.

Foundational Concepts

Semi-structured data bridges structured and unstructured data, allowing flexible storage and retrieval. It is commonly stored in NoSQL databases, XML, JSON, and data lakes, where schema definitions are dynamic rather than fixed. Metadata plays a key role in organizing the data, enabling machine learning models and AI systems to extract insights. Unlike relational databases, which require predefined table structures, semi-structured data allows for scalability and adaptability in handling evolving datasets. Natural language processing (NLP) and text analytics are often used to extract meaning from semi-structured sources.

Related Terms

Structured Data: Highly organized data stored in relational databases with predefined schemas, such as SQL tables (see pg. 462).

Unstructured Data: Data without any predefined format, such as raw text, videos, or images, requiring more advanced processing techniques (see pg. 512).

NoSQL Databases: Databases optimized for semi-structured and unstructured data, offering scalability and schema flexibility.

Common Misconceptions

Semi-structured data is completely unorganized: It does have tags, labels, or markers to provide structure.

Semi-structured data requires relational databases: NoSQL databases like MongoDB handle semi-structured data more efficiently.

It is difficult to analyze: With modern AI and data processing tools, semi-structured data can be analyzed effectively for insights.

Historical Context

Semi-structured data gained prominence in the **1990s** as organizations sought more flexible storage solutions beyond relational databases. The rise of **XML**, **JSON**, and big data technologies enabled easier processing of semi-structured datasets. The development of **NoSQL** databases like **MongoDB**, **CouchDB**, and **Apache Cassandra** allowed organizations to scale data storage without fixed schemas. Advances in natural language processing (NLP) and data lakes have further enhanced the usability of semi-structured data in AI and analytics.

Practical Implications

Semi-structured data plays a vital role in web technologies, big data analytics, and AI. In e-commerce, product reviews and customer interactions contain structured ratings and unstructured text, helping businesses analyze sentiment. Healthcare systems use semi-structured patient records with a mix of medical codes and clinical notes to enhance diagnostics. In cybersecurity, logs from firewalls and network devices, which combine structured timestamps with unstructured error messages, help detect threats. Its adaptability makes it essential for real-time analytics and AI-driven decision-making across industries.

Semi-Supervised Learning (AI)

Semi-supervised learning is a machine learning approach that leverages a small amount of labeled data along with a large set of unlabeled data to improve model training. It bridges the gap between supervised learning, which relies on labeled examples, and unsupervised learning, which works without explicit labels.

Semi-supervised learning is like a student learning a new subject with only a few examples from a teacher but figuring out the rest through self-study and pattern recognition. The limited guidance helps them generalize knowledge, reducing the need for exhaustive instruction.

Examples

Medical Image Classification: A small number of labeled X-ray images can train an AI model, while a vast number of unlabeled scans help refine classification accuracy.

Speech Recognition: AI systems use transcribed speech samples to learn patterns and apply them to large amounts of unlabeled voice data, improving recognition capabilities (see pg. 460).

Fraud Detection in Finance: Models learn from limited labeled fraudulent transactions and refine detection by analyzing vast amounts of unlabeled transaction data for suspicious patterns.

Foundational Concepts

Semi-supervised learning utilizes self-training, pseudo-labeling, and graph-based models to make use of both labeled and unlabeled data. Consistency regularization ensures that predictions remain stable when data is slightly altered. Generative models, such as Variational Autoencoders (VAEs) and Generative Adversarial Networks (GANs), can create synthetic labeled examples to enhance learning. By combining clustering techniques and neural network representations, semi-supervised learning improves performance in domains where labeled data is expensive or scarce, such as biomedical research, natural language processing, and cybersecurity.

Related Terms

Supervised Learning: Requires fully labeled data for model training and is commonly used in classification and regression tasks (see pg. 468).

Unsupervised Learning: Extracts patterns from unlabeled data using clustering, dimensionality reduction, or anomaly detection (see pg. 514).

Self-Supervised Learning: A subfield of machine learning where models generate their own labels from raw data, often used in pretraining AI systems (see pg. 430).

Common Misconceptions

It requires equal amounts of labeled and unlabeled data: Even a small portion of labeled data can significantly improve learning.

It is as accurate as supervised learning: While effective, semi-supervised models may not always match fully supervised models in accuracy.

It only works for image data: It is widely applied in text processing, fraud detection, and speech recognition as well.

Historical Context

Semi-supervised learning gained traction in the **1990s** and early **2000s**, as researchers sought alternatives to supervised learning, which requires large labeled datasets. Techniques like co-training and self-training were developed to leverage unlabeled data. The rise of deep learning in the **2010s** enhanced semi-supervised approaches, enabling pseudo-labeling and consistency training. **Google**, **OpenAI**, and **DeepMind** have applied semi-supervised learning in NLP and vision models, improving AI performance with limited labeled data.

Practical Implications

Semi-supervised learning is widely used in healthcare, finance, cybersecurity, and natural language processing. Medical diagnostics benefit from AI models trained on limited labeled cases while analyzing vast amounts of patient data. Fraud detection algorithms learn from confirmed fraud cases and identify emerging threats from unlabeled transactions. Search engines and recommendation systems refine content suggestions by learning from both user-labeled preferences and anonymous browsing data. As labeled data remains expensive, semi-supervised learning enables cost-effective and scalable AI development across industries.

Sensor (IoT)

A sensor is a device that detects and measures physical, chemical, or biological properties in its environment and converts them into digital signals for analysis. In the Internet of Things (IoT), sensors enable real-time data collection for automation, monitoring, and decision-making in smart systems.

A sensor is like a human's five senses—seeing, hearing, touching, smelling, and tasting—translating external stimuli into signals for the brain. Similarly, sensors detect environmental changes, such as temperature, motion, or pressure, and convert them into data that computers and IoT systems can process.

Examples

Smart Home Automation: Motion sensors detect movement, triggering smart lighting, while temperature sensors adjust climate control in smart thermostats.

Industrial Monitoring: IoT sensors in factories track machine vibrations and temperature, preventing failures through predictive maintenance and improving efficiency.

Healthcare Wearables: Heart rate and oxygen sensors in smartwatches monitor patient health, providing real-time alerts and tracking fitness levels over time.

Foundational Concepts

Sensors function by detecting changes in physical, environmental, or biological conditions and converting them into electrical signals for processing. They use transducers to transform measurements into digital data. Wireless communication technologies, such as Wi-Fi, Bluetooth, and LoRaWAN, transmit sensor data to IoT platforms for real-time analysis. Edge computing enables local processing, reducing latency, while machine learning models help interpret sensor outputs for anomaly detection and automation. Power efficiency and sensor calibration ensure long-term accuracy and reliability in various applications.

Related Terms

Actuator: A device that responds to sensor data by triggering actions, such as opening a valve or adjusting a motor (see pg. 72).

Edge Computing: A computing paradigm that processes sensor data locally rather than in a centralized cloud to reduce latency (see pg. 192).

Wireless Sensor Network (WSN): A network of sensors communicating wirelessly to collect and transmit data for IoT applications.

Common Misconceptions

Sensors always provide perfect accuracy: Many require calibration to maintain accuracy and may be affected by environmental factors.

All sensors are wired devices: Wireless IoT sensors operate on low-power networks for remote applications.

Sensors only measure physical changes: Advanced sensors can detect chemical, biological, and even behavioral patterns in AI-powered applications.

Historical Context

The concept of sensors dates back to early electromechanical measuring instruments, evolving significantly in the 20th century with the rise of semiconductor technology. The **1980s** and **1990s** saw the emergence of MEMS (Microelectromechanical Systems), enabling miniaturized sensors. The rise of IoT in the **2010s** integrated sensors into smart cities, healthcare, and industrial automation. Innovations in nanotechnology and AI-driven analytics continue to refine sensor accuracy, efficiency, and scalability.

Practical Implications

IoT sensors revolutionize industries by enabling real-time monitoring, automation, and predictive analytics. In healthcare, they improve patient monitoring and early diagnosis. In agriculture, soil moisture and climate sensors enhance precision farming. In smart cities, sensors optimize traffic control, energy usage, and public safety. As 5G, AI, and edge computing advance, sensor capabilities will expand, fostering smarter, more responsive environments across sectors.

Six Degrees of Freedom (6DoF) (XR)

Six Degrees of Freedom (6DoF) refers to the ability of an object to move freely in three-dimensional space, encompassing three translational movements (forward/backward, left/right, up/down) and three rotational movements (pitch, yaw, roll). In Extended Reality (XR), 6DoF enables users to interact naturally within virtual environments.

Moving in 6DoF is like flying a drone—it can go forward, backward, up, and down while also tilting, turning, or rotating. Unlike a car restricted to a road (3DoF), a drone freely navigates space in six independent directions.

Examples

Virtual Reality (VR) Gaming: VR headsets like the Meta Quest allow users to move freely in 3D space, letting them dodge, lean, or interact naturally within immersive environments (see pg. 530).

Robotics & Drones: Autonomous drones navigate using 6DoF, allowing precise movements for deliveries, inspections, and rescue missions in complex environments (see pg. 98).

Medical Simulations: 6DoF-powered surgical training systems let medical professionals practice procedures with realistic motion tracking, improving precision and learning outcomes.

Foundational Concepts

6DoF tracking relies on motion sensors, cameras, and inertial measurement units (IMUs) to map an object's position and orientation in real-time. Positional tracking uses inside-out tracking (headset cameras) or outside-in tracking (external sensors). Computer vision and AI-driven algorithms help refine movement accuracy. 6DoF interaction is crucial in virtual reality (VR), augmented reality (AR), and mixed reality (MR), making digital environments feel natural. Devices without 6DoF tracking provide only 3DoF, limiting motion to rotational movement without real-world positioning.

Related Terms

3DoF: Allows movement in three rotational axes (yaw, pitch, roll) but lacks spatial positioning, limiting interaction realism.

Inside-out Tracking: A method where onboard sensors, such as cameras, track movement without external devices.

Spatial Computing: The ability of machines to understand and interact with 3D environments, crucial for immersive 6DoF applications.

Common Misconceptions

6DoF is only for gaming: It's widely used in robotics, engineering, and medical training for realistic spatial interaction.

All VR headsets support 6DoF: Some only offer 3DoF, meaning users can look around but not physically move within a scene.

6DoF means full-body tracking: While it tracks head and controller movement, additional sensors are required for full-body motion capture.

Historical Context

The 6DoF concept originates from mechanical engineering and aerospace, describing aircraft motion. In the **1980s**, **NASA** incorporated 6DoF tracking for astronaut training. Early VR systems like the **VPL DataGlove** in the **1990s** used basic tracking but lacked full immersion. With IMU advancements, 6DoF tracking became central to modern VR, AR, and robotics, with devices like the **HTC Vive** (**2016**) revolutionizing consumer-level interaction.

Practical Implications

6DoF enhances realism in immersive technologies, revolutionizing VR gaming, professional training, and industrial automation. In architecture, it allows precise 3D modeling and design visualization. In defense and aerospace, military simulations and drone navigation depend on 6DoF tracking for maneuverability. As AI, haptics, and spatial computing evolve, 6DoF will be fundamental to creating fully interactive digital experiences, bridging the gap between virtual and real-world interactions.

SLAM (Simultaneous Localization and Mapping) (RT)

Simultaneous Localization and Mapping (SLAM) is a computational process that enables a system—such as a robot, drone, or augmented reality (AR) device—to map an unknown environment while simultaneously tracking its position within it. SLAM is crucial for autonomous navigation and spatial understanding in dynamic, GPS-restricted environments.

SLAM is like a blindfolded traveler using only touch and memory to navigate a room while drawing a map. As they move, they continuously update their understanding of both the environment and their location, refining the accuracy of their mental map over time.

Examples

Autonomous Vehicles: Self-driving cars use SLAM to detect obstacles, recognize roadways, and navigate without relying on GPS, ensuring safe and efficient movement through city streets and highways.

Augmented Reality (AR) & Virtual Reality (VR): AR applications like Microsoft HoloLens or Apple's ARKit use SLAM to overlay digital objects onto the real world, allowing for seamless interaction and object stability in immersive experiences (see pg. 92 & 530).

Robotic Navigation: Industrial and service robots rely on SLAM to move through warehouses, hospitals, or homes, adapting to dynamic environments and avoiding obstacles while optimizing routes (see pg. 98).

Foundational Concepts

SLAM involves sensor fusion, combining data from LiDAR, cameras, IMUs (inertial measurement units), and GPS to construct a real-time map. It relies on feature extraction to recognize objects, track key points, and build a consistent representation of the environment. Probabilistic algorithms like the Kalman filter or particle filters refine position estimates. Loop closure detection ensures the system recognizes when it has returned to a known area, preventing map drift. SLAM is widely used in robotics, drones, and extended reality (XR) applications.

Related Terms

LiDAR: A remote sensing technology that uses laser pulses to measure distances and create high-resolution spatial maps.

Sensor Fusion: The process of combining data from multiple sensors (e.g., cameras, IMUs, depth sensors) to improve environmental understanding.

Odometry: The use of motion data from sensors to estimate an object's position, often used alongside SLAM for tracking movement.

Common Misconceptions

SLAM only works with LiDAR: While LiDAR enhances SLAM, vision-based and depth-camera SLAM approaches (e.g., ORB-SLAM) can achieve similar results without laser-based sensors.

SLAM is only for robots: SLAM is essential for AR, VR, drones, and smart devices, not just autonomous robots.

SLAM provides perfect maps: SLAM maps are probabilistic and constantly adjusted; environmental changes can impact accuracy.

Historical Context

SLAM research began in the **1980s** with early applications in robotics and autonomous exploration. **The Kalman filter**, introduced in **1960** by **Rudolf Kálmán**, laid the foundation for SLAM's probabilistic approach. **The Monte Carlo Localization** (MCL) method emerged in the **1990s**, improving real-time navigation. Advances in computer vision led to the development of Visual SLAM (V-SLAM), which enabled applications in AR and VR. Companies like **Google** (Tango), **Apple** (ARKit), and **OpenCV** have significantly advanced SLAM technology.

Practical Implications

SLAM revolutionizes autonomous navigation, immersive computing, and robotic efficiency. In urban environments, it enables precise indoor navigation where GPS signals are weak. In logistics, warehouse robots use SLAM to optimize movement, reducing costs. In healthcare, SLAM-powered robotic assistants aid in patient care and surgery. Drones in agriculture and inspection leverage SLAM to scan landscapes and infrastructure autonomously. As AI-driven perception systems improve, SLAM will be essential in smart cities, human-robot collaboration, and the evolution of augmented reality experiences.

Small Cell (5G)

Small cell is a low-power wireless access point that enhances network coverage and capacity in localized areas. Used in 5G and LTE networks, small cells reduce congestion, improve data speeds, and enable efficient communication by complementing traditional macro cell towers, particularly in dense urban environments.

A small cell is like a network of mini water stations placed around a city to provide localized water distribution. Instead of relying solely on large reservoirs (macro towers), these smaller stations ensure efficient delivery, reducing congestion and enhancing service where needed most.

Examples

Urban 5G Deployment: Small cells installed on streetlights and buildings improve high-speed connectivity in busy metropolitan areas, ensuring smooth streaming and low-latency applications like smart city infrastructure.

Indoor Wireless Coverage: Offices, shopping malls, and stadiums use small cells to enhance network reliability, allowing users to maintain strong signals without relying solely on distant macro towers.

Industrial IoT Connectivity: Factories and warehouses leverage small cells to support IoT devices and autonomous systems, enabling seamless machine-to-machine communication in automated production environments.

Foundational Concepts

Small cells rely on millimeter-wave (mmWave) frequencies, beamforming, and massive MIMO to provide high-speed, low-latency connections. Unlike macro towers, which cover large geographic areas, small cells focus on localized coverage, improving bandwidth efficiency. They operate in three types: femtocells (for homes and small offices), picocells (for larger buildings), and microcells (for public spaces). Small cells offload network traffic from macro towers, ensuring seamless user experiences in high-density areas while supporting the edge computing required for autonomous vehicles, augmented reality (AR), and smart city applications.

Related Terms

Macrocell: A large cellular tower covering wide geographical areas, serving as the backbone of mobile networks.

Beamforming: A technology that directs wireless signals towards users, improving efficiency and reducing interference (see pg. 102).

Edge Computing: Processing data closer to the source (e.g., small cells) rather than relying on distant cloud servers, reducing latency (see pg. 192).

Common Misconceptions

Small cells replace macro towers: Small cells complement rather than replace macrocells, enhancing coverage where towers struggle.

Small cells only work with 5G: While crucial for 5G, small cells also improve 4G LTE connectivity.

Small cells have unlimited range: Their range is limited to short distances, making them ideal for urban, indoor, and high-traffic areas.

Historical Context

The development of small cells began in the early **2000s** to improve indoor coverage and mobile broadband. **Femtocells** were first introduced as home-based network extenders. As mobile data consumption surged, telecom providers integrated picocells and microcells into urban networks. The rollout of 4G LTE accelerated small cell adoption, but 5G deployment made them essential. Companies like **Qualcomm**, **Ericsson**, and **Nokia** have pioneered small cell technology, enabling low-latency applications, private 5G networks, and smart infrastructure in cities worldwide.

Practical Implications

Small cells drive 5G adoption, smart city development, and industrial automation. In transportation, they enhance vehicle-to-everything (V2X) communication, enabling autonomous driving and intelligent traffic systems. Healthcare benefits from small cells through connected medical devices and remote monitoring in hospitals. Retail and entertainment venues use small cells for augmented reality shopping, immersive experiences, and reliable customer connectivity. As network demand grows, small cells will play a critical role in next-generation communication, ensuring faster, more reliable wireless networks across urban and rural landscapes.

Smart Contract (BC)

A smart contract is a self-executing program stored on a blockchain that automatically enforces the terms of an agreement. These contracts eliminate intermediaries by executing predefined conditions, ensuring secure, transparent, and tamper-proof transactions in areas like finance, supply chain, and digital identity management.

A smart contract is like a vending machine—you insert the required amount, and the machine delivers your product automatically, without needing a cashier. Similarly, smart contracts execute transactions without human intervention, ensuring trust, security, and automation in digital agreements.

Examples

Decentralized Finance (DeFi): Smart contracts facilitate automated lending, borrowing, and trading without banks. Platforms like Uniswap use them to enable peer-to-peer cryptocurrency exchanges, eliminating intermediaries.

Supply Chain Management: Companies use smart contracts to track shipments, verify authenticity, and automate payments when goods reach a destination, ensuring transparency and reducing fraud.

Real Estate Transactions: Smart contracts enable secure property transfers by automating ownership verification, escrow services, and payments, reducing paperwork and legal costs.

Foundational Concepts

Smart contracts rely on blockchain technology to ensure immutability, security, and automation. They use if-then logic to execute agreements without central authorities. The execution is validated through decentralized consensus mechanisms like proof-of-work (PoW) or proof-of-stake (PoS). Ethereum pioneered smart contract deployment with its Solidity programming language. Unlike traditional contracts, smart contracts eliminate the risk of manipulation or fraud, making them essential for decentralized applications (dApps), tokenization, and self-governing ecosystems.

Related Terms

Blockchain: A decentralized ledger that records transactions securely, enabling trustless smart contract execution (see pg. 18).

Decentralized Application (dApp): A blockchain-based application that operates via smart contracts without central control.

Gas Fees: The computational cost required to execute smart contracts on blockchain networks like Ethereum.

Common Misconceptions

Smart contracts require legal approval: They are not traditional legal documents but rather enforceable code stored on a blockchain.

Smart contracts are always secure: Bugs in coding or poor implementation can lead to vulnerabilities and exploits, as seen in past DeFi hacks.

Only Ethereum supports smart contracts: While Ethereum is the most popular, networks like Binance Smart Chain, Solana, and Cardano also support them.

Historical Context

The idea of smart contracts was first proposed by **Nick Szabo** in **1994** as a way to facilitate digital agreements. However, they became practical with **Ethereum**'s launch in **2015**, which introduced the Solidity programming language for blockchain automation. **Ethereum Virtual Machine** (EVM) allowed decentralized contract execution, revolutionizing finance, gaming, and governance. The rise of **DeFi (2020-2021)** demonstrated smart contracts' power, while security concerns, such as the **DAO hack (2016)**, highlighted their risks, leading to increased focus on audits and security protocols.

Practical Implications

Smart contracts revolutionize industries by reducing costs, enhancing transparency, and eliminating intermediaries. In banking, they enable automated loans, insurance claims, and payments. Governments use them for identity verification, tax collection, and public records management. In gaming and digital ownership, NFTs (non-fungible tokens) rely on smart contracts for ownership tracking. As Web3 and metaverse applications grow, smart contracts will underpin digital economies, enabling trustless interactions and decentralized governance while requiring robust security measures and regulatory frameworks.

Smart Device (IoT)

A smart device is an internet-connected electronic device that can collect, process, and transmit data, often using artificial intelligence (AI) and automation. These devices interact with users or other systems, enabling seamless communication in homes, industries, healthcare, and cities, forming the backbone of the Internet of Things (IoT).

A smart device is like a digital assistant—just as a personal secretary anticipates needs, schedules tasks, and provides information, smart devices learn user behavior, automate actions, and interact with other devices to enhance convenience, efficiency, and personalization in daily life.

Examples

Smart Home Assistants: Devices like Amazon Echo and Google Nest use AI to control smart appliances, provide information, and respond to voice commands, enhancing home automation.

Wearable Health Trackers: Smartwatches and fitness bands monitor heart rate, track activity, and send health alerts, integrating data into medical applications for real-time health management.

Smart Industrial Sensors: Factories use connected sensors to track machine performance, detect faults, and optimize energy usage, improving efficiency and reducing operational costs.

Foundational Concepts

A smart device operates using embedded sensors, microprocessors, and wireless communication technologies such as Wi-Fi, Bluetooth, and 5G. These devices rely on machine learning algorithms to analyze data, predict outcomes, and automate responses. They interact through cloud computing and edge computing, ensuring real-time processing and decision-making. Smart devices can function independently or within a network, enabling autonomous control, remote access, and adaptive learning to enhance efficiency, security, and convenience in various domains.

Related Terms

Internet of Things (IoT): A network of interconnected smart devices that collect, share, and analyze data for automation and efficiency (see pg. 288 & 290).

Edge Computing: A technology that processes data closer to the device, reducing latency and enhancing real-time responsiveness in smart devices (see pg. 192).

Artificial Intelligence (AI): Enables smart devices to learn from data, make predictions, and automate tasks based on user preferences and behavior (see pg. 7).

Common Misconceptions

Smart devices always require internet access: While many smart devices use cloud connectivity, some function with local AI and edge computing.

All smart devices are AI-powered: Not all smart devices use AI; some operate using predefined automation rules.

Smart devices are completely secure: Cybersecurity risks exist, and regular updates, encryption, and authentication are essential to prevent data breaches.

Historical Context

The evolution of smart devices began with the first internet-connected toaster (**1990**), followed by **IBM**'s **Simon** (**1994**), the first smartphone. The rise of Wi-Fi, cloud computing, and AI in the early **2000s** accelerated smart device adoption. **Apple**'s **Siri** (**2011**), **Amazon Echo** (**2014**), and **Google Nest** (**2016**) revolutionized smart homes, while industrial IoT applications transformed manufacturing, healthcare, and cities. Today, smart devices integrate AI, blockchain, and 5G for enhanced automation, security, and connectivity.

Practical Implications

Smart devices revolutionize daily life, industries, and healthcare by improving efficiency, convenience, and automation. In smart homes, they control lighting, security, and energy use. In transportation, smart sensors optimize traffic flow and enable self-driving cars. Healthcare benefits from remote patient monitoring and AI-assisted diagnostics. Businesses use smart devices for predictive maintenance, automated inventory tracking, and personalized customer experiences. As IoT adoption grows, smart devices will continue shaping digital transformation, demanding improved cybersecurity, ethical AI, and regulatory frameworks for responsible deployment.

Smart Grid (CET)

A smart grid is an advanced electricity network that integrates digital communication, automation, and real-time data analytics to optimize energy distribution. It enables efficient energy management, two-way power flow, and renewable energy integration, improving reliability, reducing energy waste, and supporting sustainable power generation.

A smart grid is like a modern traffic system—just as smart traffic lights adjust in real time to ease congestion, smart grids dynamically balance electricity supply and demand, rerouting power efficiently while incorporating renewable sources like solar and wind energy.

Examples

Renewable Energy Integration: Smart grids allow real-time adjustment of solar and wind power supply, balancing energy fluctuations to ensure stable distribution without overloading the system.

Demand Response Systems: Smart meters enable homes and industries to adjust power usage based on peak demand pricing, reducing strain on the grid and lowering costs.

Automated Fault Detection: Using sensors and AI, smart grids detect outages and reroute electricity, restoring power faster while reducing maintenance costs and downtime.

Foundational Concepts

A smart grid combines IoT, AI-driven analytics, and automated controls to enhance energy efficiency. It utilizes smart meters and sensors to monitor electricity usage and optimize distribution. Distributed energy resources (DERs), such as rooftop solar panels and electric vehicle batteries, can supply power back to the grid. Microgrids function as localized power systems that operate independently if needed. Smart grids also enhance grid resilience against cyber threats, natural disasters, and fluctuating energy demand.

Related Terms

Microgrid: A self-sufficient energy system that can operate independently or in coordination with the main grid.

Demand Response: A system that adjusts power consumption based on real-time grid needs, optimizing energy use and reducing costs.

Distributed Energy Resources (DERs): Small-scale power sources, such as solar panels or wind turbines (see pg. 532), that contribute energy to the smart grid.

Common Misconceptions

Smart grids only benefit renewable energy: While they enhance clean energy integration, they also improve efficiency, reliability, and security in traditional power networks.

Smart grids eliminate power outages: While they reduce downtime with automation, extreme weather or cyberattacks can still cause disruptions.

Smart meters invade privacy: These devices only track energy usage, not personal activities, ensuring secure and encrypted data collection.

Historical Context

The concept of smart grids emerged in the early **2000s** as governments and energy companies sought more resilient and efficient power systems. The **U.S. Department of Energy** (DOE) and **European Commission** launched major smart grid initiatives, integrating AI, IoT, and automation to modernize traditional power infrastructure. The rise of renewable energy, electric vehicles, and decentralized energy production accelerated smart grid adoption. Today, nations worldwide are investing in next-generation grids to enhance sustainability, security, and efficiency.

Practical Implications

Smart grids revolutionize energy management by reducing costs, improving reliability, and lowering carbon emissions. In residential areas, they help consumers optimize power use with smart appliances and real-time pricing. In industrial sectors, they prevent energy waste and enhance operational efficiency. Governments leverage smart grids for national energy security, ensuring faster recovery from outages and better cybersecurity defenses. As energy demand grows, smart grids play a critical role in achieving global sustainability goals while supporting the transition to a clean, decentralized energy future.

Social Engineering (CS)

Social engineering is a cybersecurity attack method that manipulates human psychology to deceive individuals into divulging sensitive information, granting unauthorized access, or performing certain actions. Instead of exploiting technical vulnerabilities, attackers trick users into compromising security through deception, persuasion, or coercion.

Social engineering is like a digital con artist who gains trust to steal information. Just as a thief might impersonate a maintenance worker to enter a secured building, cybercriminals pose as trusted entities—such as IT support or a bank—to extract sensitive data.

Examples

Phishing Emails: Attackers send fraudulent emails impersonating legitimate companies, urging users to click malicious links or provide login credentials, leading to data breaches (see pg. 366).

Pretexting Attacks: A scammer pretends to be a trusted figure, such as an HR employee, to request sensitive data like Social Security numbers or account credentials.

Baiting and Quid Pro Quo Attacks: Malicious USB devices labeled "Confidential Payroll Data" are left in offices, tempting employees to plug them in, unknowingly installing malware.

Foundational Concepts

Social engineering leverages human emotions, trust, and cognitive biases to bypass security controls. Attackers exploit authority, urgency, curiosity, and fear to manipulate victims. Phishing, spear-phishing, and pretexting are common tactics. Unlike brute-force attacks, social engineering relies on psychological deception rather than technical hacking. Organizations use security awareness training, two-factor authentication (2FA), and behavioral analytics to mitigate these threats. AI-driven fraud detection and user behavior analysis help identify suspicious interactions and prevent data breaches.

Related Terms

Phishing: Fraudulent messages designed to trick recipients into revealing sensitive information, often through emails or fake websites (see pg. 366).

Social Engineering Penetration Testing: A security assessment that simulates social engineering attacks to identify vulnerabilities in human security defenses.

Multi-Factor Authentication (MFA): A security method that requires users to verify their identity through multiple credentials, reducing the success rate of social engineering attacks (see pg. 340).

Common Misconceptions

Social engineering only happens online: It also occurs through phone calls, in-person interactions, and physical deception (e.g., tailgating into secure areas).

Only non-tech-savvy users fall for social engineering: Even IT professionals and executives can be targeted through advanced, personalized attacks like spear phishing.

Strong passwords prevent social engineering: While passwords help, human deception bypasses even the strongest authentication measures, making training and awareness essential.

Historical Context

Social engineering techniques have existed for centuries, evolving with technology. The **Kevin Mitnick** case in the **1990s** demonstrated how psychological manipulation could bypass security measures. Early phishing attacks emerged in the **2000s**, often targeting email users with fake banking alerts. In **2016**, cybercriminals used social engineering to breach the **Democratic National Committee** (DNC). Today, attackers leverage deepfake technology, AI-powered scams, and business email compromise (BEC) fraud to deceive even the most vigilant users.

Practical Implications

Social engineering is a top cybersecurity threat in finance, healthcare, government, and corporate sectors. Cybercriminals use it to steal credentials, execute fraud, and launch ransomware attacks. Organizations combat it with employee training, anti-phishing software, and behavioral analytics. In critical infrastructure, social engineering attacks could disrupt power grids, emergency services, and national security. As AI deepfake scams increase, businesses and individuals must stay vigilant against evolving manipulation tactics, reinforcing cybersecurity policies to protect against deception-based threats.

Soft Robotics (RT)

Soft robotics is a field of robotics that focuses on flexible, deformable materials instead of traditional rigid components. Inspired by biological organisms, soft robots use elastic, fluidic, or pneumatic structures to adapt, grip, and move in ways that conventional robots cannot, making them ideal for delicate and complex tasks.

Soft robotics is like an octopus compared to a hard-shelled crab. While traditional robots have rigid joints like a crab's legs, soft robots bend, stretch, and conform to their surroundings, much like an octopus using its flexible tentacles to explore and manipulate objects.

Examples

Medical Assistive Devices: Soft robotic exoskeletons help stroke patients regain movement by gently guiding limbs, providing rehabilitation with adaptable support rather than rigid frames.

Industrial Automation: Soft robotic grippers are used in food processing to handle fragile items like eggs or produce, preventing damage while maintaining efficiency in sorting and packaging.

Search and Rescue Operations: Soft robots navigate rubble and tight spaces after disasters, reaching trapped individuals or assessing hazardous environments where rigid robots would struggle.

Foundational Concepts

Soft robotics mimics nature, using biomimicry, fluidic actuation, and material science to create adaptable machines. Unlike traditional robots, soft robots use elastomers, pneumatic actuators, and shape-memory materials to achieve flexible motion. Compliant mechanisms allow them to interact safely with humans and fragile objects. Advances in biohybrid robotics, where living tissues integrate with soft robotic structures, push the boundaries of organic-machine interfaces. Artificial intelligence (AI) and machine learning optimize movement control, making soft robots more autonomous in unpredictable environments.

Related Terms

Biomimicry: The design of robots inspired by natural organisms, such as soft-bodied animals like octopuses and worms.

Actuators: Mechanisms that enable movement in robots; soft actuators use air, fluid, or shape-memory materials instead of motors and gears (see pg. 72).

Haptics: The technology that enables tactile feedback in soft robots, improving their ability to interact with objects and humans safely (see pg. 260).

Common Misconceptions

Soft robots are weak and inefficient: While they lack rigidity, soft robots excel in adaptability and safe interaction, making them ideal for fragile or biocompatible applications.

Soft robotics is just traditional robotics with flexible parts: Soft robots require different design principles, using fluidic control, material engineering, and AI-driven learning rather than mechanical joints and rigid actuators.

Soft robots cannot handle industrial tasks: Industries like agriculture, medicine, and logistics are increasingly using soft robotic grippers, exosuits, and prosthetics for high-efficiency automation.

Historical Context

Soft robotics emerged from biologically inspired robotics in the early **2000s**. **Harvard**'s **Wyss Institute** pioneered pneumatic soft actuators, leading to advancements in wearable robotics and assistive devices. In **2011**, researchers developed octopus-inspired robotic arms, revolutionizing underwater robotics. By **2016**, **DARPA** and **NASA** explored soft robots for space exploration and rescue missions. Today, **MIT**, **Stanford**, and **ETH Zurich** continue leading soft robotics innovation in healthcare, automation, and human-robot interaction.

Practical Implications

Soft robotics is transforming healthcare, manufacturing, and disaster response. In medicine, robotic gloves help paralyzed individuals regain mobility, while soft endoscopes assist in minimally invasive surgery. Manufacturing sectors adopt soft grippers for handling fragile products, increasing efficiency and reducing waste. In disaster relief, soft robots navigate unstructured environments, aiding rescue teams. As AI-driven soft robotics improve adaptability and dexterity, their applications expand into personal assistance, prosthetics, and biohybrid robotics, revolutionizing human-robot collaboration across industries.

Software-Defined Networking (SDN) (5G)

Software-Defined Networking (SDN) is a network architecture that separates the control plane from the data plane, enabling centralized network management through software. This approach enhances network flexibility, automation, and scalability, making it easier to optimize traffic flow and dynamically adjust resources based on real-time demands.

SDN is like a GPS navigation system for a network. Instead of individual cars (network devices) making independent routing decisions, SDN acts as a central traffic controller, optimizing paths, rerouting congestion, and adjusting flows in real-time for improved performance and efficiency.

Examples

Data Center Management: Cloud providers use SDN to dynamically allocate bandwidth and optimize data traffic, ensuring efficient resource utilization and cost reduction for businesses hosting applications.

5G Network Optimization: Telecom operators deploy SDN to manage mobile data traffic, dynamically routing user requests and prioritizing critical applications to enhance connectivity and reduce latency.

Cybersecurity Enforcement: Enterprises use SDN for automated threat detection and response, instantly isolating compromised devices and mitigating attacks without manual intervention.

Foundational Concepts

SDN decentralizes network control, shifting decision-making from hardware to software-based controllers. This separation of control plane (decision-making) and data plane (packet forwarding) allows for programmability, automation, and dynamic configuration. Northbound APIs connect the SDN controller to applications, enabling policy-based management, while Southbound APIs communicate with physical or virtual network devices. Network function virtualization (NFV) complements SDN by replacing hardware-based network services with software-based alternatives, increasing adaptability and reducing infrastructure costs.

Related Terms

Network Function Virtualization (NFV): Virtualizes firewalls, load balancers, and routers, allowing SDN to deploy network functions on-demand.

OpenFlow: A standard protocol enabling SDN controllers to communicate with switches, directing how packets should be forwarded.

Intent-Based Networking (IBN): Uses AI to automate and optimize SDN, translating business policies into network configurations with minimal human intervention.

Common Misconceptions

SDN replaces all network hardware: SDN does not eliminate hardware; it optimizes its usage through software-based control.

SDN is only for large-scale networks: While SDN benefits large enterprises and data centers, it also enhances small-scale network automation and security.

SDN is inherently secure: While SDN enhances security through centralized control, it requires strong authentication to prevent controller vulnerabilities.

Historical Context

SDN concepts emerged in the **1990s** but gained traction in **2008** with the **OpenFlow** protocol at **Stanford University**, marking the shift toward programmable networks. **Google** pioneered SDN deployment in **2012** for its data centers, demonstrating massive efficiency gains. The ONF (Open Networking Foundation) and industry leaders like **Cisco**, **VMware**, and **Huawei** expanded SDN adoption, driving the development of hybrid cloud solutions and automated networking frameworks.

Practical Implications

SDN revolutionizes network management, security, and cloud computing. In enterprise IT, it enables automated traffic control, cost efficiency, and real-time monitoring. In cloud computing, SDN supports multi-cloud networking, dynamic provisioning, and application-aware routing. In telecommunications, SDN enhances 5G deployment, reduces latency, and improves bandwidth utilization. As AI-driven SDN evolves, it paves the way for self-healing networks, autonomous security protocols, and fully software-defined infrastructures, transforming how organizations manage digital connectivity.

Spatial Audio (XR)

Spatial audio is a sound technology that simulates a three-dimensional auditory environment, allowing listeners to perceive sound from different directions as they would in real life. Using directional cues and head tracking, spatial audio enhances immersion in virtual reality, gaming, and entertainment applications.

Spatial audio is like standing in the middle of an orchestra—instead of hearing music as flat stereo sound, you can pinpoint where each instrument is located, whether it's behind, above, or beside you, making the experience more lifelike and immersive.

Examples

Virtual Reality (VR) & Gaming: Spatial audio enhances VR games by providing realistic directional sounds, allowing players to detect approaching enemies or environmental cues with 360-degree precision (see pg. 530).

Cinema & Streaming: Streaming platforms like Apple Music and Netflix use spatial audio to create immersive surround sound experiences, making movies and music feel more dynamic and engaging.

Hearing Aids & Assistive Technology: Modern hearing aids leverage spatial audio to enhance speech clarity in noisy environments, allowing users to focus on specific sound sources in real-time.

Foundational Concepts

Spatial audio relies on binaural audio processing, head-related transfer functions (HRTF), and object-based audio encoding to replicate real-world sound perception. Binaural audio mimics natural hearing by adjusting sound waves based on ear positioning. HRTF accounts for how sound interacts with the head and ears, creating realistic directional cues. Object-based audio formats like Dolby Atmos and MPEG-H encode sound sources with precise spatial coordinates, allowing audio playback systems to render 3D soundscapes dynamically.

Related Terms

Binaural Audio: A recording technique that simulates 3D sound perception by capturing how audio reaches both ears.

Head-Related Transfer Function (HRTF): A set of mathematical filters that replicate how sound waves are altered by the shape of the head and ears.

Dolby Atmos: A spatial audio format that places individual sound objects in a 3D space, creating immersive sound environments.

Common Misconceptions

Spatial audio is the same as surround sound: Unlike traditional surround sound, spatial audio enables sound movement and adapts based on listener position.

It requires expensive equipment: While high-end headphones enhance the experience, many smartphones and streaming platforms support spatial audio with standard headphones.

Only useful for entertainment: Spatial audio is also applied in assistive technologies, automotive safety systems, and teleconferencing.

Historical Context

The foundation of spatial audio traces back to binaural recording techniques developed in the **1930s**. In the **1990s**, researchers at **NASA** and **Dolby** pioneered 3D audio rendering for VR and cinema. The launch of **Dolby Atmos** in **2012** revolutionized spatial sound in theaters. **Apple** integrated head-tracked spatial audio in **2020**, further popularizing the technology. Advances in AI-driven sound modeling and real-time rendering continue to refine spatial audio applications in gaming, virtual environments, and assistive hearing.

Practical Implications

Spatial audio redefines immersive experiences in VR, gaming, music, and film by providing dynamic, lifelike soundscapes. In healthcare, spatial audio assists in hearing aid design and auditory therapy. The automotive industry applies spatial audio for 360-degree awareness in driver assistance systems. In teleconferencing, spatial audio improves clarity by placing voices in virtual space, reducing listener fatigue. As spatial computing and AI-driven sound synthesis evolve, spatial audio will become a core technology in augmented and mixed reality environments.

Speech to Text (GenAI)

Speech to text is a technology that converts spoken language into written text using natural language processing (NLP) and machine learning. It is widely used in voice assistants, transcription services, and accessibility tools, enabling hands-free communication, automated documentation, and real-time translation.

Speech to text is like a real-time typist for your voice—instead of manually writing or typing, you simply speak, and the system converts your words into text almost instantly, making it easier to interact with technology through natural conversation.

Examples

Voice Assistants: Virtual assistants like Siri, Google Assistant, and Alexa use speech-to-text technology to interpret voice commands, enabling users to set reminders, send messages, and control smart devices hands-free (see pg. 528).

Automated Transcription Services: Services like Otter.ai and Google Docs Voice Typing convert spoken content from meetings, interviews, and lectures into written text, saving time and improving accessibility.

Live Captioning & Accessibility: Speech-to-text is used in real-time captioning for TV broadcasts, video conferencing, and assistive tools, enhancing accessibility for individuals with hearing impairments.

Foundational Concepts

Speech-to-text technology relies on automatic speech recognition (ASR), deep learning, and phonetic analysis to process spoken words. ASR systems break speech into phonemes, the smallest units of sound, and match them to pre-trained language models. Neural networks refine transcription accuracy by learning from large datasets of human speech. Contextual NLP models improve word prediction and grammar correction, ensuring that transcriptions reflect natural speech patterns. Advances in transformer-based architectures, such as Whisper by OpenAI, have enhanced multilingual transcription and real-time processing.

Related Terms

Automatic Speech Recognition (ASR): The core technology behind speech-to-text, analyzing audio input to convert it into written text (see pg. 460).

Natural Language Processing (NLP): A field of AI that enables machines to understand, interpret, and generate human language (see pg. 346).

Speech Synthesis: The inverse of speech-to-text, converting written text into spoken audio, commonly used in text-to-speech (TTS) systems (see pg. 490).

Common Misconceptions

Speech-to-text is 100% accurate: While AI models have improved, background noise, accents, and complex jargon can still cause errors.

Only useful for dictation: Speech-to-text has broader applications in accessibility, customer service, and real-time communication.

Does not require internet: Some offline models exist, but most cloud-based services rely on online processing for higher accuracy.

Historical Context

The foundation of speech-to-text began in the **1950s** with **Bell Labs'** "**Audrey**" system, which recognized digits spoken aloud. In the **1970s**, **IBM**'s "**Shoebox**" system expanded to a small vocabulary of words. The **1990s** saw improvements with Hidden Markov Models (HMMs), which laid the groundwork for modern ASR algorithms. The emergence of deep learning in the **2010s**, particularly **Google's DeepMind** and **OpenAI's Whisper**, revolutionized speech recognition by achieving near-human transcription accuracy. Today, real-time multilingual speech-to-text applications are widely used in AI-driven communication platforms.

Practical Implications

Speech-to-text technology transforms communication in industries like healthcare, finance, and customer support by automating documentation, voice commands, and accessibility services. In education, it enhances note-taking and language learning, while in law enforcement, it aids in interrogation transcriptions and courtroom proceedings. The integration of AI-powered ASR into IoT devices has also enabled voice-controlled smart homes and hands-free navigation in autonomous vehicles. As models improve, speech-to-text will play an essential role in bridging language barriers, increasing digital inclusivity, and enhancing human-computer interactions.

Structured Data (AI)

Structured data refers to highly organized information stored in a fixed format, often in relational databases, spreadsheets, or tables. It follows a predefined schema, making it easy to search, filter, and analyze. Common examples include customer records, financial transactions, and product inventories.

Structured data is like a well-organized library, where every book is labeled, categorized, and shelved systematically. Just as a librarian can quickly locate a book using a catalog, structured data enables computers to retrieve specific information efficiently using predefined rules.

Examples

Banking Transactions: Financial institutions store customer account details, transaction histories, and credit scores in structured databases to process payments, detect fraud, and generate financial reports.

E-commerce Inventory Management: Online retailers maintain product details, pricing, and stock levels in structured databases, allowing real-time updates and seamless search functionality for customers.

Healthcare Records: Hospitals use structured databases to store patient demographics, diagnoses, and medication history, ensuring accurate retrieval and compliance with electronic health record (EHR) standards.

Foundational Concepts

Structured data relies on relational database management systems (RDBMS), where information is stored in tables with predefined columns and rows. Each row (record) represents a unique data entry, while each column (attribute) defines a specific data type. Structured Query Language (SQL) is commonly used to manage and query structured data efficiently. The use of schemas ensures data integrity and consistency, making structured data ideal for transactional systems, reporting, and business intelligence applications.

Related Terms

Relational Database: A database model that organizes data into tables with predefined relationships, ensuring structured storage.

Unstructured Data: Data that lacks a predefined format, such as text documents, images, and videos, making it harder to search and analyze (see pg. 512).

SQL (Structured Query Language): A programming language used to query, manipulate, and manage structured data in relational databases.

Common Misconceptions

All data is structured: While structured data is widely used, most data (over 80%) is unstructured, including emails, videos, and social media content.

Structured data is only for large enterprises: Small businesses also use structured data in CRM systems, sales tracking, and customer support logs.

Structured data cannot be modified: While structured data follows predefined schemas, it can be updated, altered, or expanded as needed.

Historical Context

Structured data has its roots in early computing systems of the **1960s**, with **IBM**'s hierarchical and network databases laying the groundwork. The relational database model, introduced by **Edgar F. Codd** in **1970**, revolutionized data storage, leading to the development of SQL-based RDBMS like **Oracle**, **MySQL**, and **PostgreSQL**. Over time, advancements in cloud computing, data analytics, and real-time processing have further optimized structured data management.

Practical Implications

Structured data is fundamental to business intelligence, machine learning, and automation. In finance, it enables fraud detection and risk assessment. In marketing, it helps segment customer demographics for targeted advertising. Governments use structured data for census records, tax filings, and law enforcement databases. As AI-driven analytics grow, structured data will continue to power predictive modeling, operational efficiency, and decision-making across industries.

Supercomputer (HPC)

A supercomputer is a high-performance computing system capable of processing vast amounts of data and executing complex calculations at incredible speeds. It leverages parallel processing, specialized hardware, and optimized algorithms to tackle computationally intensive tasks in scientific research, artificial intelligence, and climate modeling.

A supercomputer is like a massive team of expert problem solvers working simultaneously. Instead of relying on a single brain, it distributes tasks across thousands of processors, much like a team of scientists analyzing different parts of a project to solve a problem faster.

Examples

Weather Forecasting: Supercomputers process climate models, atmospheric simulations, and real-time satellite data to predict hurricanes, storms, and global temperature changes with high accuracy.

Drug Discovery: Pharmaceutical companies use supercomputers to simulate molecular interactions, accelerating the development of new medications and reducing the time needed for clinical trials.

Artificial Intelligence Training: AI researchers train deep learning models on massive datasets, improving natural language processing, image recognition, and autonomous systems in industries like robotics and healthcare.

Foundational Concepts

Supercomputers rely on parallel computing, where thousands of processors execute multiple tasks simultaneously, increasing computational efficiency. High-performance computing (HPC) architectures optimize data flow and minimize latency. Vector processing accelerates mathematical operations, while interconnect networks ensure rapid communication between processing units. Cooling systems and energy efficiency are critical due to the immense power consumption and heat generation of these machines.

Related Terms

Parallel Processing: A technique where multiple processors handle different parts of a problem simultaneously, significantly boosting speed (see pg. 364).

Quantum Computing: A next-generation computing model leveraging quantum mechanics to solve complex problems beyond supercomputing capabilities (see pg. 52).

Exascale Computing: The next milestone in supercomputing, achieving a quintillion (10^{18}) calculations per second for even greater computational power.

Common Misconceptions

Supercomputers are just large personal computers: Unlike PCs, supercomputers use thousands of processors, optimized algorithms, and specialized cooling systems.

Only governments use supercomputers: While governments own many, corporations, universities, and research institutions also operate supercomputers.

Supercomputers solve any problem instantly: While powerful, they require highly optimized code and algorithms to leverage their full potential.

Historical Context

Supercomputing dates back to the **1960s**, with **Seymour Cray** developing the first commercial supercomputer, the **CDC 6600**. The **Cray-1** (**1976**) set a new standard for high-speed computing. The TOP500 list, introduced in **1993**, ranks the world's most powerful supercomputers. Recent advancements include the **Fugaku supercomputer** in **Japan** and the **Frontier system**, the first exascale supercomputer, developed in **2022**.

Practical Implications

Supercomputers drive scientific discovery, engineering, and AI advancements. In medicine, they enable genomic analysis and pandemic response simulations. In energy, they optimize nuclear fusion research and climate impact studies. Governments use them for national security, cryptography, and defense simulations. As AI and big data grow, supercomputers will remain essential for advancing technology, solving global challenges, and shaping the future of computing.

Superposition (QC)

Superposition is a fundamental principle of quantum mechanics where a quantum system exists in multiple states simultaneously until measured. In quantum computing, a qubit can represent both 0 and 1 at the same time, enabling exponentially faster computations compared to classical bits.

Superposition is like a spinning coin that exists in both heads and tails until it lands. While spinning, the outcome is uncertain, and both possibilities coexist. Similarly, a qubit remains in multiple states until observed, collapsing into a single definite state.

Examples

Quantum Computing: Superposition enables quantum computers to process vast amounts of data simultaneously, revolutionizing fields such as cryptography, AI, and optimization (see pg. 52).

Quantum Cryptography: Secure communication protocols like quantum key distribution (QKD) use superposition to detect eavesdropping, ensuring encrypted data remains unbreakable.

Molecular Simulations: Superposition allows quantum simulations of molecular interactions, aiding drug discovery and material science research by computing multiple outcomes simultaneously.

Foundational Concepts

Superposition is central to quantum mechanics and relies on wave-particle duality, meaning particles like electrons or photons exhibit multiple states at once. This is mathematically described using probability amplitudes in a Hilbert space. When measured, a qubit's wavefunction collapses into a single definite state. Quantum interference—the ability of quantum states to amplify or cancel out each other—further enhances computational power in quantum algorithms.

Related Terms

Qubit: The fundamental unit of quantum computing, capable of existing in superposition states.

Quantum Entanglement: A phenomenon where two qubits become correlated, influencing each other instantly regardless of distance.

Wavefunction Collapse: The process where a quantum system loses its superposition and settles into a single state upon measurement.

Common Misconceptions

Superposition means a qubit is in two places at once: Instead, a qubit holds a probabilistic combination of states, not physically existing in two places.

Observing superposition preserves it: Measurement causes wavefunction collapse, forcing the system into a single state.

Superposition guarantees faster computation: Only certain quantum algorithms leverage superposition for speedups; not all problems benefit.

Historical Context

Superposition was first introduced in quantum mechanics by **Erwin Schrödinger** in the **1920s**. His Schrödinger's cat thought experiment illustrated quantum uncertainty. **Richard Feynman** later proposed quantum computing in the **1980s**, recognizing superposition's potential in solving complex problems. The first experimental qubits demonstrating superposition were created in the late **1990s**, paving the way for modern quantum computing.

Practical Implications

Superposition is the backbone of quantum computing, enabling faster solutions for problems like factorization, optimization, and simulations. In AI, it enhances machine learning models by speeding up data processing. In finance, it optimizes portfolios by simulating multiple market conditions. Future applications include quantum networks, advanced encryption, and material discovery, making superposition a critical concept in shaping the next era of technology.

Supervised Learning (AI)

Supervised Learning is a machine learning paradigm where an algorithm learns from labeled data. A model maps inputs to outputs using a dataset with known correct answers. It continuously adjusts its parameters to minimize error and improve accuracy in predicting outcomes for new data.

Supervised Learning is like teaching a child with flashcards. By showing a child an image of an animal with its name, they learn to associate the two. Over time, they recognize new animals based on prior knowledge, just as models generalize from labeled training data.

Examples

Spam Detection: Email services use Supervised Learning to classify emails as spam or legitimate by learning from past labeled examples, ensuring better filtering over time.

Medical Diagnosis: AI models trained on medical images detect diseases like cancer by recognizing patterns in labeled X-rays, assisting doctors in early diagnosis and treatment planning.

Fraud Detection: Financial institutions train machine learning models on past fraudulent and legitimate transactions, enabling real-time fraud prevention by flagging suspicious activity.

Foundational Concepts

Supervised Learning relies on training data with labeled outputs, where an algorithm iteratively learns patterns through gradient descent and optimization techniques. It uses loss functions to measure errors and improve predictions. Common models include decision trees, support vector machines, and neural networks. Overfitting occurs when a model learns noise instead of patterns, requiring regularization and cross-validation to maintain generalizability.

Related Terms

Unsupervised Learning: A machine learning approach where data lacks labeled outputs, and the model finds hidden patterns or structures autonomously.

Neural Networks: Computational models inspired by the human brain, commonly used in Supervised Learning for pattern recognition tasks like image classification.

Overfitting: When a model memorizes training data rather than generalizing patterns, leading to poor performance on new data.

Common Misconceptions

Supervised Learning is fully automated: It requires human-labeled data, which can be labor-intensive.

More data always improves accuracy: Poorly labeled or biased data can degrade performance, leading to inaccurate models.

Supervised Learning works for all tasks: Some problems, like clustering or anomaly detection, are better suited for unsupervised or reinforcement learning.

Historical Context

Supervised Learning dates back to early statistical models in the **1950s**, with **Frank Rosenblatt**'s Perceptron (**1958**) being a major milestone. The development of Support Vector Machines (SVMs) in the **1990s** and deep learning breakthroughs in the **2000s** and **2010s**—notably with convolutional neural networks—have revolutionized the field. Modern advancements leverage big data and GPU-accelerated training to create highly accurate AI models.

Practical Implications

Supervised Learning drives innovations in healthcare, finance, and autonomous systems. In customer service, chatbots trained on labeled conversations provide realistic responses. In autonomous vehicles, models learn to recognize road signs and pedestrians for safe navigation. It also enhances personalized recommendations, improving user experiences on platforms like Netflix and Amazon. Despite its success, challenges like data bias and scalability remain, requiring ongoing research and refinement.

Surrogate Model (XAI)

A surrogate model is a simplified, interpretable model that approximates the behavior of a more complex, often opaque machine learning model. It is used in Explainable AI (XAI) to provide insights into how a model makes predictions while preserving accuracy and interpretability.

A surrogate model is like a tour guide explaining a foreign language movie—while the original movie might be complex and difficult to follow, the guide translates and summarizes key points, allowing viewers to understand the storyline without grasping every detail of the language.

Examples

Healthcare Diagnostics: A deep learning model predicts disease likelihood, but a surrogate decision tree explains which symptoms or biomarkers contribute most to the diagnosis.

Financial Credit Scoring: A black-box AI model determines credit risk, but a surrogate logistic regression model highlights which factors, such as income or debt-to-income ratio, influence approval decisions.

Autonomous Vehicles: Neural networks guide self-driving cars, but rule-based surrogate models can explain how the AI prioritizes obstacles, speed adjustments, and lane changes.

Foundational Concepts

Surrogate models leverage simpler algorithms like decision trees, linear regression, or rule-based models to approximate complex AI predictions. They help in model interpretability, debugging, and regulatory compliance, ensuring AI decisions can be auditable and trustworthy. Surrogate models can be local, explaining individual predictions, or global, summarizing the entire AI system. Methods such as LIME (Local Interpretable Model-Agnostic Explanations) and SHAP (Shapley Additive Explanations) create surrogate models to improve transparency.

Related Terms

Explainable AI (XAI): A field focused on making AI decisions interpretable and understandable for users (see pg. 27).

Black-Box Model: A complex AI model, such as deep neural networks, whose internal workings are not easily interpretable (see pg. 118).

Model-Agnostic Interpretation: Techniques that can be applied to any AI model type, including decision trees, SHAP, and LIME (see pg. 27).

Common Misconceptions

Surrogate models replace AI models: They only approximate them for explainability, not deployment.

Surrogate models are always accurate: They simplify complex relationships and may miss nuanced interactions.

All AI models need a surrogate: Some AI models, like decision trees, are inherently interpretable and do not require surrogates.

Historical Context

The need for explainable AI emerged in the **2010s**, as deep learning models became widely adopted but lacked transparency. LIME and SHAP, developed in the mid-**2010s**, became popular methods for generating surrogate models. Researchers like **Zachary Lipton** and **Cynthia Rudin** emphasized AI interpretability in high-risk fields like healthcare and finance, leading to regulatory discussions, such as **EU AI transparency** requirements.

Practical Implications

Surrogate models enhance trust and transparency in AI-driven industries like healthcare, finance, and law enforcement. They help in bias detection, ensuring AI models make fair, ethical decisions. In regulated sectors, such as GDPR compliance, surrogate models justify AI predictions for audits. By improving explainability, they bridge the gap between AI performance and human understanding, fostering broader adoption and responsible deployment of machine learning systems.

Sustainability (RAI)

Sustainability in Responsible AI refers to the development and deployment of artificial intelligence systems in a way that minimizes environmental impact, promotes social equity, and ensures long-term economic viability. It involves reducing AI's carbon footprint, ensuring fair resource use, and prioritizing ethical AI governance to benefit future generations.

Sustainability in AI is like fuel-efficient cars in transportation—just as hybrid and electric vehicles reduce carbon emissions while improving mobility, sustainable AI optimizes computing power while reducing energy consumption, ensuring progress without harming the environment or exacerbating social inequalities.

Examples

Energy-Efficient AI Models: Companies like Google use AI to optimize data center cooling systems, reducing electricity consumption and lowering their carbon footprint.

Fair AI in Hiring: AI-powered hiring platforms incorporate bias-mitigation techniques to ensure fair employment practices, promoting workplace diversity and sustainability in hiring decisions (see pg. 216).

Agricultural Optimization: AI-powered precision farming systems optimize water usage and reduce pesticide overuse, enhancing crop yields while minimizing environmental harm.

Foundational Concepts

Sustainable AI focuses on reducing energy consumption, optimizing computational resources, and ensuring equitable access to AI technologies. Key approaches include green computing, where AI models are trained using renewable energy, and model pruning, which reduces unnecessary computations. Sustainable AI also considers algorithmic fairness, ensuring that models do not reinforce existing biases or inequalities. Organizations use carbon accounting metrics to track AI's environmental impact, and responsible AI frameworks advocate for transparent and accountable decision-making processes in AI-driven systems.

Related Terms

Green AI: AI development practices that prioritize energy efficiency and sustainability over sheer computational power.

Ethical AI: AI frameworks designed to ensure fairness, transparency, and accountability in decision-making (see pg. 204).

Bias Mitigation: Techniques used to reduce discriminatory effects in AI models, ensuring fair and inclusive outcomes (see pg. 104).

Common Misconceptions

AI is inherently sustainable: AI models require massive computational resources, contributing to energy-intensive processes.

Sustainability only concerns energy use: It also includes social equity, algorithmic fairness, and ethical considerations.

Smaller models are always sustainable: Some optimized AI models still reinforce biases or require frequent retraining, negating sustainability benefits.

Historical Context

The discussion on AI sustainability gained traction in the early **2020s**, as researchers highlighted the environmental costs of large-scale AI training. Studies on carbon emissions from AI models by **OpenAI** and **MIT** led to the **Green AI** movement. Organizations like the **AI for Good** initiative and the **Partnership on AI** pushed for sustainable AI policies, emphasizing energy-efficient training methods and the ethical deployment of AI technologies.

Practical Implications

Sustainability in AI ensures long-term viability by balancing innovation with ethical responsibility. In corporate AI adoption, companies prioritize carbon-neutral AI to align with global sustainability goals. Governments incorporate AI policies that enforce environmental regulations, while researchers focus on lightweight models that achieve efficiency with minimal energy consumption. In developing nations, sustainable AI ensures equitable access without exacerbating resource disparities. By integrating sustainability into AI practices, businesses and policymakers create a future-proof and ethical AI ecosystem.

Swarm Robotics (RT)

Swarm robotics is an approach to robotic coordination inspired by natural swarm intelligence, where multiple simple robots work together to complete complex tasks. These robots communicate and collaborate without centralized control, using local interactions and decentralized decision-making to achieve global objectives efficiently and adaptively.

Swarm robotics is like a colony of ants, where each individual follows simple rules but, collectively, they achieve sophisticated tasks such as foraging or nest construction. Similarly, swarm robots operate autonomously but collaborate to complete missions that would be impossible for a single robot.

Examples

Disaster Response: Swarm robots can be deployed in search and rescue operations, spreading out to locate survivors and relay real-time data to human responders.

Agriculture Automation: Small autonomous drones in precision farming monitor crop health, optimize irrigation, and manage pests efficiently through coordinated behavior.

Warehouse Logistics: Swarm robots optimize supply chains, moving products in warehouses autonomously, reducing human labor costs, and increasing efficiency in large-scale distribution centers.

Foundational Concepts

Swarm robotics is based on distributed control, where no single robot dictates the group's behavior. Instead, robots follow simple rules, enabling emergent collective intelligence. Self-organization allows these systems to function without centralized oversight, while local communication—using sensors or wireless signals—enables robots to share information and adapt dynamically. Scalability is a key feature, allowing swarms to increase or decrease in size based on task complexity. These principles ensure swarm robotics systems are resilient, flexible, and robust, even in unpredictable environments.

Related Terms

Multi-Agent Systems: Computational systems where multiple autonomous entities collaborate, similar to swarm robotics but often involving software agents.

Bio-Inspired AI: AI techniques modeled after biological systems, including swarm intelligence derived from ant colonies and flocking birds.

Decentralized Control: A system where decision-making is distributed across multiple agents instead of a central authority, essential in swarm robotics.

Common Misconceptions

Swarm robots always have a leader: Unlike traditional robotic systems, swarm robots lack a centralized controller, making decisions autonomously.

More robots mean better performance: Adding more robots does not always improve efficiency—without proper coordination, resource competition or interference may reduce effectiveness.

Swarm robotics is only theoretical: Swarm robotics is already used in real-world applications, including autonomous drones, logistics, and surveillance.

Historical Context

Swarm robotics emerged from swarm intelligence research in the **1990s**, drawing inspiration from ant colonies, flocking birds, and decentralized biological systems. Early research by **Gerardo Beni** and **Jing Wang** in **1989** introduced the concept. The **DARPA**-funded research and advances in machine learning and distributed AI have since enabled real-world implementations. Modern swarm robotics is driven by advances in embedded computing, miniaturization, and wireless communication, allowing scalable, adaptive, and autonomous robotic swarms to operate in dynamic environments.

Practical Implications

Swarm robotics has transformative potential across multiple industries. In space exploration, NASA explores self-organizing swarms for planetary missions. Defense applications use robotic swarms for autonomous surveillance and reconnaissance. In environmental monitoring, swarms of robots can track pollution levels, ocean currents, or forest health. The decentralized nature of swarm robotics enhances fault tolerance and adaptability, making it ideal for applications requiring autonomous decision-making in unpredictable environments.

Synthetic Biology (BT)

Synthetic biology is an interdisciplinary field that applies engineering principles to biological systems to create new organisms, modify existing ones, or design biological components with novel functions. It integrates genetic engineering, computational modeling, and automation to develop innovations in medicine, agriculture, and environmental science.

Synthetic biology is like programming DNA, similar to how software developers write code for computers. Scientists rearrange and design genetic sequences to make living cells perform specific functions—such as producing medicine, breaking down pollutants, or enhancing crop yields—just as software enables machines to perform complex tasks.

Examples

Medical Therapies: Synthetic biology enables genetically engineered bacteria to produce insulin and other pharmaceuticals, revolutionizing drug production and personalized medicine.

Sustainable Agriculture: Genetically modified crops can be engineered to resist pests, survive droughts, and improve nutrient content, enhancing global food security.

Biodegradable Plastics: Engineered microbes can convert organic waste into biodegradable materials, reducing plastic pollution and offering sustainable alternatives to petroleum-based plastics.

Foundational Concepts

Synthetic biology combines genetic engineering, bioinformatics, and systems biology to manipulate biological functions at the DNA level. Scientists use CRISPR gene-editing, DNA synthesis, and metabolic engineering to redesign cellular processes. A key principle is modularity, where genetic circuits function like programmable parts. Standardized genetic components, called biobricks, allow researchers to build custom biological systems. Computational modeling aids in designing and predicting genetic interactions before implementation, ensuring efficiency and precision in biological modifications.

Related Terms

Genetic Engineering: The direct modification of an organism's DNA to introduce or remove specific traits.

Metabolic Engineering: Optimizing cellular pathways to enhance production of desired compounds, such as biofuels or pharmaceuticals.

Biocomputing: The use of biological molecules like DNA to perform computational tasks, merging synthetic biology with computing.

Common Misconceptions

Synthetic biology creates artificial life: Scientists modify existing biological systems rather than creating life from scratch.

Genetic modifications are unsafe: Many synthetic biology applications follow rigorous safety and regulatory protocols before deployment.

It is only used for GMOs: While genetic modification is a key aspect, synthetic biology also applies to biomedical advancements, biofuels, and sustainable materials.

Historical Context

The roots of synthetic biology trace back to genetic engineering breakthroughs in the **1970s**, including recombinant DNA technology. In the **2000s**, **Drew Endy** and **Craig Venter** pioneered biobricks and the first synthetic genome, respectively. **The Human Genome Project** accelerated advancements in DNA synthesis and bioinformatics, enabling more precise genetic design. Over time, synthetic biology expanded into personalized medicine, sustainable agriculture, and environmental bioremediation, driven by automation and AI-driven gene sequencing.

Practical Implications

Synthetic biology has the potential to transform multiple industries. In healthcare, it allows for customized gene therapies and bioengineered drugs. In environmental science, it supports carbon sequestration and bio-based energy production. Synthetic microbes can remediate oil spills and plastic waste, improving sustainability. In food production, lab-grown meat and engineered crops address food security challenges. With advances in AI and automation, synthetic biology is set to drive new medical treatments, climate solutions, and resource-efficient manufacturing.

Synthetic Data (AI)

Synthetic data refers to artificially generated data that mimics real-world datasets without containing any original or sensitive information. It is created using algorithms, statistical models, or generative AI to train machine learning systems while preserving privacy, improving accessibility, and reducing bias in data-driven applications.

Synthetic data is like a flight simulator for AI—just as pilots train in a simulated environment that mimics real-world conditions without actual risk, AI models learn from synthetic datasets that reflect real data patterns while avoiding security, privacy, or ethical concerns.

Examples

Healthcare AI Development: Synthetic patient records are used to train AI models for medical diagnosis and drug discovery without exposing real patient data, ensuring compliance with privacy regulations.

Autonomous Vehicles: Self-driving car models train on synthetic traffic scenarios to learn how to respond to complex road conditions, improving safety before real-world deployment.

Fraud Detection: Banks use synthetic transaction data to train fraud detection algorithms, ensuring financial security while avoiding risks associated with exposing sensitive customer information.

Foundational Concepts

Synthetic data is generated using mathematical models, deep learning, or generative adversarial networks (GANs) to resemble real-world datasets. Unlike anonymized data, which removes personally identifiable information, synthetic data is created from scratch, preserving statistical properties without direct duplication. Privacy-preserving AI techniques, such as differential privacy and federated learning, enhance synthetic data's security benefits. Its use extends to bias mitigation, dataset augmentation, and AI explainability, making it essential for safe and ethical machine learning training.

Related Terms

Generative Adversarial Networks (GANs): AI models that create synthetic data by pitting two neural networks against each other (see pg. 240).

Differential Privacy: A technique ensuring data privacy by adding statistical noise to datasets, reducing the risk of individual re-identification.

Data Augmentation: The process of artificially expanding training datasets using transformations, such as rotation or cropping, to improve AI model performance.

Common Misconceptions

Synthetic data is fake: It accurately represents real-world patterns without copying original records.

It replaces real data: Synthetic data complements real data, often improving AI training where real datasets are scarce or sensitive.

Synthetic data is less accurate: Properly generated synthetic datasets maintain statistical integrity and can even improve AI model robustness.

Historical Context

The concept of synthetic data emerged in the **1990s** for statistical analysis but gained traction with the rise of AI and privacy regulations. **Alan Turing** first envisioned synthetic intelligence, while modern advancements in GANs, variational autoencoders (VAEs), and privacy-preserving AI have propelled its adoption. The General Data Protection Regulation (**GDPR**) and similar laws increased demand for synthetic data to enable safe AI training without privacy violations.

Practical Implications

Synthetic data has transformative potential across finance, healthcare, cybersecurity, and AI research. In healthcare, it enables AI-powered diagnostics while ensuring patient confidentiality. In autonomous systems, synthetic data accelerates vehicle training without real-world risks. Fraud prevention and security benefit from safe data simulations. As AI requires vast datasets, synthetic data ensures ethical AI development while reducing data acquisition costs and compliance risks.

Tactile Sensors (RT)

Tactile sensors are electronic devices that detect and measure physical interactions such as pressure, texture, temperature, and force. They mimic the human sense of touch, enabling robots, prosthetics, and smart devices to interact with objects and environments more accurately and safely.

Tactile sensors are like a pianist's fingertips—just as a pianist feels each key's resistance and adjusts pressure to create the perfect melody, robots and prosthetic hands use tactile sensors to detect force, texture, and temperature, ensuring precise, delicate interactions with objects.

Examples

Robotic Surgery: Tactile sensors in robotic-assisted surgery provide real-time force feedback, helping surgeons perform delicate operations with enhanced precision and control.

Prosthetic Limbs: Advanced bionic hands with tactile sensors allow amputees to feel pressure and texture, improving grip strength and dexterity in daily activities.

Smart Packaging: Retail and logistics industries use tactile sensors in automated warehouses to detect fragile items, adjusting handling force to prevent damage during shipping.

Foundational Concepts

Tactile sensors work by detecting mechanical deformations when in contact with objects. They utilize capacitive, resistive, piezoelectric, and optical sensing techniques to measure force, temperature, and texture. Haptic feedback systems integrate tactile sensors with actuators to simulate real-time touch sensations. Machine learning algorithms enhance sensor-driven robotics, improving their ability to recognize and manipulate objects with precision, adaptability, and safety in dynamic environments.

Related Terms

Haptic Feedback: A system that uses vibrations or force feedback to simulate touch sensations in virtual or robotic environments (see pg. 260).

Force Sensors: Devices that measure the amount of pressure or force applied, often used alongside tactile sensors in robotics.

Electronic Skin (E-Skin): A flexible, sensor-embedded material that replicates human skin's ability to feel pressure, heat, and texture.

Common Misconceptions

Tactile sensors only measure pressure: They also detect texture, temperature, vibration, and slip to improve robotic and prosthetic functionality.

They work the same as touchscreens: Unlike capacitive touchscreens, tactile sensors detect dynamic interactions, such as grip force and surface roughness.

Only robots use tactile sensors: They are also used in wearables, prosthetics, and consumer electronics to enhance user experiences.

Historical Context

The concept of tactile sensing originated in biomechanics and robotics in the **1970s**, inspired by human skin's sensitivity. **NASA** and **MIT** developed early tactile sensors for robotic grippers and space exploration. Advances in artificial skin and flexible electronics in the **1990s** and **2000s** led to applications in prosthetics and medical robotics. Today, AI-powered tactile sensors enable real-time object recognition and adaptive robotic interactions across industries.

Practical Implications

Tactile sensors enhance human-robot interaction, making automation safer and more intuitive. In healthcare, prosthetics with haptic feedback improve quality of life. Manufacturing robots use tactile sensors for quality control, precision assembly, and safe human collaboration. Wearable technology integrates these sensors for fitness tracking and virtual reality applications. As AI and robotics advance, tactile sensing will drive innovations in medical devices, autonomous systems, and human-AI interfaces.

TensorFlow (AI)

TensorFlow is an open-source machine learning framework developed by Google for building, training, and deploying artificial intelligence (AI) models. It supports deep learning, neural networks, and large-scale computations, making it essential for computer vision, natural language processing, and predictive analytics in research and industry applications.

TensorFlow is like a universal AI toolkit—just as a chef uses various kitchen tools to prepare different dishes, AI developers use TensorFlow's flexible components to design, train, and optimize models for tasks such as speech recognition, medical diagnosis, and autonomous systems.

Examples

Image Recognition: TensorFlow powers facial recognition systems, object detection models, and medical imaging AI, helping companies improve security, automation, and diagnostics (see pg. 276).

Speech-to-Text Conversion: AI-driven voice assistants, including Google Assistant and automated transcription services, use TensorFlow to process, understand, and convert spoken language into text (see pg. 460).

Predictive Analytics: Financial institutions and retailers use TensorFlow-based models for fraud detection, demand forecasting, and customer behavior analysis, enabling data-driven decision-making.

Foundational Concepts

TensorFlow operates using tensor-based computations, where data is represented as multi-dimensional arrays. It employs computational graphs, optimizing the flow of data through various layers of a neural network. TensorFlow supports both CPU and GPU acceleration, improving model training speed. Its key features include automatic differentiation, which helps AI models learn by adjusting weights, and TensorFlow Extended (TFX), which streamlines model deployment in production. Keras, a high-level API within TensorFlow, simplifies deep learning development for researchers and practitioners.

Related Terms

PyTorch: An alternative deep learning framework developed by Meta, known for its dynamic computation graphs and flexibility in research.

Keras: A high-level neural network API within TensorFlow, simplifying deep learning model creation and experimentation.

AutoML: A suite of tools that enable automatic machine learning, allowing TensorFlow to optimize models without manual tuning (see pg. 96).

Common Misconceptions

TensorFlow is only for deep learning: While widely used for neural networks, TensorFlow also supports traditional machine learning models and general numerical computation.

It is difficult to learn: With Keras and pre-built models, TensorFlow is accessible even to beginners in AI and machine learning.

TensorFlow is only for research: Major industries use TensorFlow in real-world applications, including healthcare, finance, and cybersecurity.

Historical Context

TensorFlow was developed by **Google Brain** and released as open-source software in **2015**. It evolved from **DistBelief**, Google's earlier deep learning system. TensorFlow 2.0 (**2019**) introduced easier model building, integration with Keras, and improved GPU support. Over the years, TensorFlow has become one of the most widely used AI frameworks, enabling breakthroughs in computer vision, reinforcement learning, and generative AI.

Practical Implications

TensorFlow has transformed AI development, making deep learning scalable, efficient, and accessible. In healthcare, it assists in early disease detection and personalized treatments. Autonomous vehicles rely on TensorFlow models for object detection and navigation. Businesses leverage it for customer insights, recommendation systems, and fraud prevention. As AI continues advancing, TensorFlow's versatile ecosystem will remain crucial for innovations in robotics, AI-driven automation, and generative models.

Text Data (AI)

Text data refers to structured or unstructured information stored as words, sentences, or symbols, often derived from documents, websites, emails, and social media. It is a fundamental component of natural language processing (NLP), search engines, and AI-driven communication technologies.

Text data is like a vast digital library—just as books contain knowledge in written form, AI systems process and analyze text data to extract meaning, identify patterns, and generate insights for applications like chatbots, recommendation systems, and sentiment analysis.

Examples

Chatbots and Virtual Assistants: AI models process text data from user inputs to generate natural, human-like responses, enhancing customer service and digital interactions (see pg. 528).

Sentiment Analysis: Businesses use AI to analyze social media posts, reviews, and surveys, helping them gauge public opinion and improve products.

Automated Content Summarization: AI models extract key points from news articles, legal documents, or research papers, enabling users to quickly grasp critical information without reading the full text (see pg. 488).

Foundational Concepts

Text data is categorized into structured, semi-structured, and unstructured formats. Tokenization breaks text into words or phrases for analysis, while vectorization converts words into numerical representations. Natural language processing (NLP) applies machine learning algorithms to interpret and analyze text, enabling semantic understanding, text classification, and language modeling. Named entity recognition (NER) identifies people, locations, and objects in text, while sentiment analysis determines emotional tone. Large language models (LLMs) use deep learning architectures like transformers to generate human-like text.

Related Terms

Natural Language Processing (NLP): The field of AI that enables machines to understand and process human language (see pg. 346).

Large Language Models (LLMs): Advanced AI models, such as GPT, trained on massive text datasets to generate and analyze text (see pg. 300).

Text Mining: The process of extracting patterns, insights, and relationships from large amounts of text data.

Common Misconceptions

Text data is always structured: Most text data is unstructured, requiring AI techniques for organization and analysis.

Text analysis only involves word matching: Modern AI uses deep learning to grasp context, tone, and intent beyond basic keyword searches.

Only English text is useful for AI: AI processes multilingual text, aiding in global translation, cross-cultural insights, and diverse applications.

Historical Context

Text data analysis dates back to early information retrieval systems, including the **1950s**-era **IBM** search systems. In the **1990s**, search engines like **Google** revolutionized text-based indexing and retrieval. The rise of NLP and deep learning in the **2010s** enabled breakthroughs like machine translation, text summarization, and AI-generated content. Transformer-based models, introduced by Google's **2017 Attention Is All You Need** paper, led to today's powerful language models, advancing text understanding and AI-driven communication.

Practical Implications

Text data fuels AI-driven automation, impacting industries such as healthcare, finance, and e-commerce. AI-powered chatbots streamline customer interactions, while legal and medical AI systems analyze documents for faster decision-making. Text analytics helps detect fake news, cyber threats, and compliance risks. As AI evolves, text data will play an even greater role in knowledge extraction, automated storytelling, and personalized digital experiences.

Text Generation (AI)

Text generation refers to the process of using artificial intelligence models to automatically produce human-like text. It is widely used in chatbots, content creation, machine translation, and automated summarization. Advanced AI techniques, such as deep learning and natural language processing (NLP), enable models to generate coherent, context-aware text.

Text generation is like a digital ghostwriter—just as an author creates compelling narratives based on prior knowledge, AI models generate meaningful text by learning from vast amounts of written content, adapting style, tone, and structure to match various applications.

Examples

Chatbots and Virtual Assistants: AI-powered assistants like ChatGPT and Google Bard use text generation to produce conversational responses that mimic human interaction (see pg. 528).

Automated News and Content Creation: AI tools generate articles, reports, and marketing copy, helping organizations automate content production with minimal human intervention.

Code Generation: AI models, such as GitHub Copilot, assist programmers by generating code snippets and auto-completing functions based on contextual input.

Foundational Concepts

Text generation relies on deep learning architectures such as transformers, which enable AI to understand and generate human-like text. Large language models (LLMs), trained on massive datasets, utilize context embeddings and attention mechanisms to produce coherent responses. Recurrent neural networks (RNNs) and long short-term memory (LSTM) networks were earlier techniques, but transformers, particularly GPT and BERT-based models, have become dominant. Temperature settings control output randomness, and fine-tuning adapts models for specific applications, improving accuracy and relevance.

Related Terms

Natural Language Processing (NLP): The field of AI focused on understanding and generating human language (see pg. 346).

Large Language Models (LLMs): AI models trained on vast datasets to produce coherent, contextually accurate text (see pg. 300).

Generative Adversarial Networks (GANs): AI models that generate new data, including realistic text, by learning from existing samples (see pg. 240).

Common Misconceptions

AI-generated text is always accurate: AI models can produce hallucinations, generating plausible but incorrect information.

Text generation is simple word prediction: Advanced models understand context, grammar, and semantics, making output more sophisticated than basic autocomplete systems.

AI-generated content is indistinguishable from human writing: While AI can mimic human style, it often lacks deep understanding, creativity, and original thought.

Historical Context

Early text generation models were based on rule-based systems and statistical methods. In the **2010s**, deep learning and neural networks revolutionized NLP, leading to the development of transformers with **Google**'s **2017** paper **Attention Is All You Need**. **OpenAI**'s GPT models further advanced text generation, making AI-written content indistinguishable from human text in many applications. Modern models, such as GPT-4 and **Claude**, continue to refine AI's ability to generate complex, meaningful text.

Practical Implications

Text generation is transforming content creation, customer service, programming, and education. AI-powered content platforms streamline marketing and journalism, while AI chatbots improve customer engagement. In education, AI helps students learn languages, summarize information, and generate reports. Code generation tools boost developer productivity. However, ethical concerns, such as misinformation, plagiarism, and AI bias, require responsible implementation. As AI models evolve, text generation will become increasingly integral to automated knowledge processing and communication systems.

Text Summarization (ANI)

Text summarization is the process of using artificial intelligence techniques to generate concise and meaningful summaries from longer pieces of text while retaining key information. It can be performed through extractive methods, which pull key sentences, or abstractive methods, which rephrase content in a shorter form.

Text summarization is like turning a long speech into a short news headline—it extracts the most critical details, just as a journalist condenses a press conference into a few impactful sentences while preserving the original meaning.

Examples

News Summarization: AI-powered systems generate shortened versions of news articles, allowing readers to grasp key points without reading the full text.

Legal Document Analysis: AI helps lawyers and researchers summarize lengthy legal documents, saving time while maintaining essential case details.

Academic Research Summarization: AI extracts key findings from research papers, enabling students and professionals to quickly review large volumes of literature.

Foundational Concepts

Text summarization relies on natural language processing (NLP) and deep learning models to extract or generate concise content. Extractive summarization selects and ranks important sentences from the original text, while abstractive summarization rewrites information in a condensed form using transformer models like BERT and GPT. Techniques such as TF-IDF (term frequency-inverse document frequency) and attention mechanisms help models determine the most relevant information. Fine-tuning with domain-specific data improves summary relevance and accuracy.

Related Terms

Natural Language Processing (NLP): A branch of AI focused on understanding and processing human language.

Extractive Summarization: A method that selects key sentences directly from the text.

Abstractive Summarization: A technique that rewrites content using AI-generated language.

Common Misconceptions

Summarization is just keyword extraction: AI-driven summarization preserves context and meaning, not just keywords.

Extractive summarization is always accurate: It can sometimes miss important context by simply selecting sentences.

AI summarization fully replaces human summarization: While AI can generate summaries, human oversight is often needed for accuracy and nuance.

Historical Context

Early text summarization relied on statistical methods and rule-based approaches. In the **1990s**, machine learning models improved extraction techniques. With deep learning and transformers emerging in the **2010s**, AI-powered abstractive summarization became feasible. **Google**'s **BERT** (**2018**) and **OpenAI**'s GPT models revolutionized the field by enabling human-like text understanding and summarization. Today, models like T5 (Text-to-Text Transfer Transformer) continue to refine AI-generated summaries.

Practical Implications

Text summarization enhances content consumption, research, legal analysis, and news reporting. Businesses use AI to summarize customer feedback, while medical professionals leverage summarization for patient records. Automated content generation helps in journalism and digital marketing, creating concise, engaging summaries. AI-powered tools improve reading efficiency, decision-making, and knowledge retrieval, though concerns about bias, hallucinations, and loss of nuance require careful implementation. As AI evolves, summarization will play a crucial role in managing information overload across industries.

Text to Speech (TTS) (GenAI)

Text to Speech (TTS) is an AI-driven technology that converts written text into spoken audio. Using natural language processing (NLP) and deep learning, TTS synthesizes human-like speech from digital text, making content more accessible for visually impaired users, automated assistants, and interactive applications.

TTS is like a voice actor reading a script on demand—it takes written words and transforms them into spoken language, much like a narrator bringing a book to life in an audiobook.

Examples

Voice Assistants: AI-powered assistants like Siri, Alexa, and Google Assistant use TTS to respond to user queries with spoken words, enabling hands-free interaction (see pg. 528).

Audiobooks & E-Learning: TTS generates natural-sounding narration for audiobooks and educational content, improving accessibility for students and individuals with reading difficulties.

Accessibility Tools: TTS assists visually impaired users by reading out webpages, emails, and digital documents, enhancing independence in daily tasks.

Foundational Concepts

TTS relies on speech synthesis and NLP to transform text into natural-sounding speech. Concatenative synthesis stitches together recorded speech fragments, while parametric synthesis uses algorithms to generate sound waves. Modern deep learning models like WaveNet and Tacotron improve speech fluidity by modeling intonation, pitch, and rhythm. Prosody modeling ensures speech sounds natural, while text preprocessing handles abbreviations, punctuation, and phonetics.

Related Terms

Natural Language Processing (NLP): AI techniques that enable computers to understand and generate human language (see pg. 346).

Speech Recognition: The inverse of TTS, converting spoken language into text for applications like voice commands and transcription (see pg. 460).

Deep Learning: Neural networks used to improve TTS models by enhancing speech realism and adaptability (see pg. 178).

Common Misconceptions

TTS is robotic-sounding: Modern AI-driven TTS produces natural, expressive voices, mimicking human speech patterns.

TTS understands context fully: While advanced, TTS systems rely on predefined linguistic rules and can misinterpret ambiguous text.

All TTS systems are the same: Variations exist in voice quality, language support, and adaptability across different TTS models.

Historical Context

Early TTS systems in the **1950s**-60s used basic phoneme synthesis to produce robotic speech. In the **1990s**, concatenative synthesis improved voice quality by combining recorded sound snippets. **Google's WaveNet (2016)** and **Tacotron (2017)** revolutionized neural TTS, producing more natural, human-like speech. Today, companies like **OpenAI**, **Google**, and **Amazon** continue to enhance TTS capabilities for applications in assistive technology, entertainment, and AI assistants.

Practical Implications

TTS enhances digital accessibility, customer service, and automation. In healthcare, it supports patient communication for those with speech impairments. Businesses use TTS in interactive voice response (IVR) systems to automate customer support. In education, AI-generated speech aids language learning and auditory comprehension. Future developments will focus on personalized voice cloning, multilingual support, and emotional intonation, broadening AI's role in human-computer interaction.

Throughput (HPC)

Throughput refers to the amount of data, computations, or tasks processed by a system within a given time frame. In high-performance computing (HPC), throughput measures the efficiency of a system, indicating how quickly it can complete workloads such as simulations, data analysis, and machine learning training.

Throughput is like water flowing through a pipeline—a wider pipe or better water pressure increases the volume delivered per second, just as optimizing computing power, memory bandwidth, and parallel processing boosts system performance.

Examples

Scientific Simulations: Climate modeling and molecular dynamics simulations rely on high-throughput HPC systems to process vast amounts of data and run complex calculations efficiently.

AI Model Training: Machine learning models require high data throughput to handle large datasets, optimizing neural network training for applications like speech recognition and computer vision.

Financial Trading Systems: High-frequency trading platforms depend on low-latency, high-throughput computing to execute transactions within milliseconds, maximizing efficiency and profitability in dynamic markets.

Foundational Concepts

Throughput in HPC is influenced by parallel processing, network bandwidth, and memory efficiency. Latency measures delay, while throughput defines processing capacity—a system with high throughput and low latency is optimal. Scalability enables distributed computing to increase throughput by adding computational nodes. I/O bottlenecks, memory bandwidth, and processor clock speed also impact performance.

Related Terms

Latency: The time delay before a process starts; lower latency improves overall throughput.

Parallel Computing: A technique that divides tasks into smaller parts, enabling simultaneous execution for higher throughput (see pg. 364).

Bandwidth: The maximum data transfer capacity of a system, crucial for optimizing throughput in HPC environments.

Common Misconceptions

More CPU cores always mean higher throughput: Without optimized memory and parallel algorithms, additional cores may not enhance throughput.

Throughput is the same as speed: While related, speed focuses on single-task execution time, while throughput measures overall task completion over time.

Low latency equals high throughput: A system can have low latency but limited throughput if its processing capacity is restricted.

Historical Context

Throughput became critical with the rise of supercomputing in the **1960s**, pioneered by **Cray Research**. The **1980s**-90s introduced parallel processing, boosting computational throughput. Modern HPC systems, such as exascale computing, achieve unprecedented data throughput for applications like genomics, AI, and space exploration.

Practical Implications

HPC throughput advancements revolutionize fields like healthcare, finance, and AI research. Faster genetic sequencing, real-time analytics, and autonomous vehicle simulations depend on high-throughput computing. Cloud-based HPC solutions improve throughput scalability, allowing businesses and researchers to process large datasets efficiently. Future innovations will focus on quantum computing and neuromorphic architectures, further enhancing throughput efficiency.

Tokenization (BC)

Tokenization in blockchain technology refers to the process of converting real-world or digital assets into blockchain-based tokens that can be traded, stored, or transferred. These tokens represent ownership, access rights, or value and can be fungible (e.g., cryptocurrencies) or non-fungible (NFTs).

Tokenization is like converting physical cash into digital credits in an online payment system. Just as a digital wallet holds credits redeemable for real goods, blockchain tokens digitally represent ownership of tangible or intangible assets such as real estate, art, or company shares.

Examples

Real Estate Tokenization: Properties can be divided into digital tokens, allowing investors to purchase fractional ownership, making real estate investments more accessible and liquid.

Supply Chain Management: Tokenized assets track goods along global supply chains, ensuring transparency, authenticity, and efficiency by recording ownership transfers on an immutable blockchain.

Art and Collectibles: Artists use NFTs (Non-Fungible Tokens) to tokenize digital or physical artworks, enabling secure transactions, royalties, and proof of ownership.

Foundational Concepts

Tokenization relies on blockchain technology, a decentralized ledger that records and verifies transactions securely. Smart contracts automate token creation, distribution, and exchange. Fungible tokens (e.g., cryptocurrencies like Bitcoin) are interchangeable, while non-fungible tokens (NFTs) are unique and store metadata. Security tokens comply with financial regulations, representing shares, bonds, or legal assets on a blockchain.

Related Terms

Smart Contracts: Self-executing contracts coded on a blockchain that automate transactions without intermediaries (see pg. 446).

NFTs (Non-Fungible Tokens): Unique digital tokens that verify ownership of assets like art, music, and real estate.

Stablecoins: Cryptocurrencies pegged to real-world assets (e.g., USD) to maintain price stability.

Common Misconceptions

Tokenization equals cryptocurrency: While cryptocurrencies use tokens, tokenization extends beyond digital currency to physical assets, intellectual property, and financial instruments.

Tokenized assets have no intrinsic value: The value of a token depends on underlying assets, smart contracts, and market demand.

All tokens are decentralized: Some security tokens comply with centralized financial regulations, requiring legal oversight.

Historical Context

The concept of tokenization emerged with **Bitcoin (2009)**, introducing fungible digital assets. **Ethereum (2015)** pioneered smart contracts, enabling tokenized assets beyond currency. The **2017** NFT boom revolutionized digital ownership, while **DeFi** (Decentralized Finance) applications continue expanding tokenization into finance and governance.

Practical Implications

Tokenization democratizes access to assets, allowing fractional ownership of high-value investments like real estate and stocks. It enhances security and transparency in finance, supply chains, and digital rights management. As governments regulate digital assets, tokenization will integrate with traditional financial systems, driving new economic models and decentralized finance (DeFi) innovation.

Train vs. Test (AI)

Train vs. Test refers to the process of splitting a dataset into two parts: the training set, used to teach a machine learning model patterns and relationships, and the test set, used to evaluate the model's ability to generalize to unseen data.

Training a model is like teaching a student using a textbook, while testing is like giving the student an exam. The textbook (training data) helps them learn concepts, and the exam (test data) measures how well they apply their knowledge to new questions.

Examples

Spam Email Detection: A model is trained on thousands of labeled emails (spam vs. non-spam) and tested on a separate set of emails to measure how well it filters out spam.

Medical Diagnosis AI: An AI system learns from patient medical records to predict diseases and is tested on a different dataset to assess its accuracy in diagnosing real-world cases.

Autonomous Vehicles: AI models train on labeled road scenarios and are tested on new driving conditions to evaluate their ability to recognize traffic signs and obstacles.

Foundational Concepts

The training set helps a model learn patterns using supervised, unsupervised, or reinforcement learning techniques. The test set evaluates the model's accuracy, recall, precision, and F1 score. A separate validation set is often used to tune hyperparameters and prevent overfitting, which happens when a model memorizes training data instead of generalizing. To ensure fairness, data is typically split using cross-validation methods such as k-fold validation.

Related Terms

Overfitting: When a model performs well on training data but poorly on new data due to memorization rather than generalization (see pg. 362).

Cross-Validation: A technique where data is split multiple times to improve model evaluation and reduce bias.

Hyperparameter Tuning: Adjusting settings like learning rate and batch size to optimize model performance.

Common Misconceptions

The bigger the training set, the better the model: More data helps, but data quality, diversity, and proper validation matter more than sheer volume.

Test data should be used to tweak the model: Test sets should remain untouched until final evaluation, while validation sets guide improvements.

A high training accuracy means a great model: A model can memorize training data but fail on new examples, leading to poor real-world performance.

Historical Context

Early machine learning research, such as **Frank Rosenblatt**'s Perceptron (**1958**), highlighted the need for separate training and evaluation phases. The **1980s-1990s** neural network boom emphasized cross-validation techniques. The rise of deep learning (**2010s**) with models like **AlexNet** and **GPT** required large-scale data splits to avoid overfitting and improve generalization.

Practical Implications

Train vs. test splits are crucial in finance, healthcare, cybersecurity, and autonomous systems. In fraud detection, training models on historical transactions and testing on new data prevents false positives. In healthcare AI, proper data partitioning ensures robust disease prediction. In autonomous driving, rigorous testing avoids unsafe real-world deployments. Ensuring a fair, unbiased split prevents ethical concerns like AI discrimination in hiring or medical diagnoses.

Transfer Learning (ML)

Transfer Learning is a technique where knowledge learned in one task or domain (often from a large, general dataset) is reused to accelerate learning in another, typically smaller or more specific, task. Instead of starting from scratch, a model begins with pretrained representations and then adapts to the new problem, saving time, data, and compute.

It's like hiring a seasoned chef into a new kitchen: they already know how to chop, sauté, and season; you only need to teach the house specials.

Examples

Medical Imaging: Start from a model pretrained on millions of natural images, then fine-tune to detect pathologies in chest X-rays or retinal scans.

Customer Support NLP: Take a general language model and adapt it to classify tickets or draft helpful replies in a specific company's tone.

Manufacturing Vision: Begin with a detection model trained on generic objects, then adapt it to spot hairline defects on a particular production line.

Foundational Concepts

Transfer typically follows a **pretraining → adaptation** pattern. In **pretraining**, a model learns broadly useful features (e.g., edges, textures, syntax, semantics) from large datasets; during **fine-tuning**, those features are adjusted on task-specific data to improve accuracy. This "pretrain then fine-tune" workflow is now standard in language and vision systems.

Common modes include **feature extraction** (freeze most layers, train a shallow head), **full fine-tuning** (update all layers on the target task), and **parameter-efficient tuning** (adapters/LoRA/prompting) that adds or tweaks a small number of parameters. When source and target data differ meaningfully, **domain adaptation** (e.g., augmentations, style transfer, or distribution-alignment losses) helps bridge the gap. Good transfer depends on **representation quality**, **data similarity**, and **regularization** to avoid overfitting.

Related Terms

Pretraining: Learning general features from large, diverse data.

Fine-Tuning: Task-specific adaptation of a pretrained model.

Feature Extraction: Using pretrained layers as fixed encoders for new tasks.

Domain Adaptation: Techniques to handle shifts between source and target domains.

Self-Supervised Learning: Label-free pretraining that often improves transfer (see pg. 430).

Few-Shot Learning: Adapting with very limited labeled examples.

Representation Learning: Learning feature spaces that transfer well.

Foundation Model: Broadly pretrained model intended for many downstream tasks.

Common Misconceptions

Transfer always helps: Negative transfer can occur when source and target are too dissimilar; careful evaluation is required.

With transfer, you don't need labels: It reduces labeling needs but doesn't remove them. Small, high-quality labels still matter for adaptation.

Bigger pretraining is always better: Scale helps, but match to task/domain, quality of data, and tuning strategy often matter more.

Fine-tuning = changing all weights: Many effective methods alter only a small subset of parameters.

Historical Context

Early reuse appeared in classic ML via hand-engineered features. The modern surge came with deep learning: image models pretrained on large datasets and language models pretrained on massive corpora proved that broad representations could be adapted quickly to many tasks. Today, transfer learning underpins vision, speech, and NLP, increasingly via **self-supervised** and **multimodal pretraining**.

Practical Implications

Transfer Learning speeds up development, boosts accuracy with limited data, and lowers compute and labeling costs, and the one reason it's now a default starting point for many AI projects. In practice, teams choose a suitable pretrained backbone, decide how much to tune (features vs. full model), and use regularization and validation to guard against overfitting or domain mismatch. Done well, transfer reduces manual labeling burden and makes model training more scalable.

Transformer Architecture (AI)

Transformer architecture is a deep learning model that processes input data in parallel rather than sequentially, making it highly efficient for natural language processing (NLP) and other AI tasks. It utilizes self-attention mechanisms to weigh different words in a sequence, improving context understanding and long-range dependencies.

A transformer is like a group discussion where every participant (word) listens to all others at once, rather than waiting for a turn. This allows faster and more effective communication, unlike traditional sequential models that process words one after another like a telephone game.

Examples

Machine Translation: Transformers power Google Translate, allowing it to translate entire sentences by considering context rather than word-by-word translations, significantly improving accuracy.

Chatbots and Virtual Assistants: AI assistants like ChatGPT and Alexa use transformers to understand questions and generate human-like responses, making conversations more fluid and coherent (see pg. 528).

Image Captioning: Models like Vision Transformers (ViTs) analyze images and generate text descriptions, helping visually impaired users interpret visual content through AI-powered narration.

Foundational Concepts

At its core, the transformer model relies on self-attention mechanisms, where each word in a sentence is compared with all others to determine contextual importance. This differs from recurrent neural networks (RNNs) and convolutional neural networks (CNNs), which process data sequentially or in fixed windows. Transformers use positional encoding to retain word order and multi-head attention to capture multiple relationships simultaneously. The encoder-decoder structure is used for tasks like translation, while encoder-only or decoder-only models serve other NLP applications.

Related Terms

Self-Attention: The ability of a model to weigh the importance of different words in a sentence when making predictions.

BERT: A transformer-based model optimized for understanding text by pre-training on large datasets and fine-tuning for tasks like sentiment analysis.

GPT: A decoder-only transformer trained to generate text, widely used for chatbots, content generation, and summarization.

Common Misconceptions

Transformers only work for text: While originally designed for NLP, transformers are now widely used in computer vision, drug discovery, and robotics.

Bigger models are always better: Larger models require more data and computing power but don't always outperform smaller, well-optimized ones.

Transformers understand language like humans: Despite producing coherent text, transformers lack true comprehension and rely solely on statistical patterns.

Historical Context

Transformers were introduced in **2017** by **Vaswani et al.** in the paper **Attention Is All You Need**. The model outperformed LSTMs and RNNs in NLP tasks, leading to innovations like **BERT (2018)** and GPT-3 (**2020**). Over time, transformers expanded into multimodal AI, influencing models like **DALL·E** for image generation and **AlphaFold** for protein structure prediction.

Practical Implications

Transformers power search engines, AI assistants, medical diagnostics, and financial forecasting. They enhance content moderation on social media, enabling fact-checking and spam detection. In healthcare, transformers analyze medical texts and assist doctors in diagnosing conditions. The architecture's rapid growth also raises concerns about AI bias, misinformation, and computational energy consumption, driving research into ethical AI development and efficient model scaling.

Transparency (RAI)

Transparency in AI refers to the ability to clearly explain how an AI system makes decisions. It ensures that AI models, data, and decision-making processes are understandable, interpretable, and accountable to users, regulators, and stakeholders, promoting trust and responsible AI deployment.

AI transparency is like a cooking recipe—just as knowing the ingredients and steps used in a dish helps people understand how it was made, transparency in AI allows users to see what data and logic an AI system uses to arrive at its conclusions.

Examples

AI in Hiring: Transparency ensures that AI-driven recruitment tools do not introduce bias, allowing companies to justify hiring decisions and ensure fair candidate evaluations (see pg. 216).

Medical Diagnosis Systems: Transparent AI models in healthcare help doctors understand how an AI arrives at a diagnosis, ensuring that medical professionals trust and validate AI-assisted recommendations.

Financial Risk Assessment: AI-driven credit scoring models must be transparent so individuals understand why they were approved or denied loans, reducing potential discrimination in lending.

Foundational Concepts

Transparency in AI is achieved through explainability, interpretability, and documentation. Explainability ensures users understand why AI makes specific decisions. Interpretability allows researchers to analyze internal model mechanics. Algorithmic accountability ensures AI systems can be audited for fairness and bias. Model cards and datasheets for datasets help document AI's capabilities, limitations, and ethical considerations. Regulatory frameworks, such as EU AI Act and U.S. AI Bill of Rights, emphasize transparency to ensure ethical AI use.

Related Terms

Explainability: The ability to describe how an AI model arrives at its decisions in human-understandable terms (see pg. 27).

Fairness: Ensuring that AI decisions are free from bias and do not disproportionately impact specific groups (see pg. 216).

Accountability: The responsibility of organizations to monitor, audit, and correct AI-driven outcomes that may have unintended consequences (see pg. 64).

Common Misconceptions

Transparency means revealing AI source code: AI transparency doesn't always require exposing proprietary algorithms but instead focuses on explaining how decisions are made.

More transparency always leads to better trust: If explanations are overly complex, transparency efforts may fail to enhance trust.

All AI models can be fully transparent: Some complex models, like deep neural networks, are inherently less interpretable, requiring additional explainability techniques.

Historical Context

AI transparency gained importance with early machine learning models, but deep learning's "black box" nature raised concerns. The **2016 COMPAS** controversy highlighted biased AI in criminal justice, leading to demands for explainable AI. The **GDPR (2018)** introduced the right to explanation, reinforcing transparency in AI decision-making. Organizations like **OpenAI**, **Google**, and **IBM** developed AI interpretability tools, making AI decision-making more accessible.

Practical Implications

Transparency in AI builds public trust, regulatory compliance, and ethical responsibility. In healthcare, it ensures doctors can verify AI diagnoses. In finance, it promotes fairness in credit scoring and fraud detection. In law enforcement, transparency prevents AI-driven racial profiling. Companies adopting transparent AI enhance user confidence, regulatory alignment, and market competitiveness, making AI safer and more accountable for societal impact.

Trustworthiness (XAI)

Trustworthiness in AI refers to the reliability, fairness, and transparency of AI systems, ensuring they operate ethically, without bias, and with accountability. A trustworthy AI system prioritizes safety, fairness, privacy, and robustness, fostering confidence among users, regulators, and society.

Trustworthy AI is like a well-trained guide dog—it must be reliable, fair, and predictable in assisting its user, making decisions that are explainable, safe, and aligned with the individual's best interests while following ethical and legal guidelines.

Examples

AI in Autonomous Vehicles: A trustworthy AI-powered car ensures safety by accurately recognizing pedestrians, obeying traffic laws, and responding predictably in emergencies.

AI in Healthcare Diagnostics: Medical AI models must be trustworthy by providing accurate, explainable, and unbiased diagnoses to support doctors without making errors that could endanger patients.

AI in Finance: Trustworthy AI in banking ensures that credit scoring models do not discriminate, transactions remain secure, and fraud detection systems operate without bias.

Foundational Concepts

Trustworthy AI is built on transparency, fairness, privacy, accountability, and robustness. Transparency ensures AI decisions are understandable, while fairness prevents bias and discrimination. Privacy safeguards user data, and accountability ensures AI outcomes can be traced and audited. Robustness guarantees the AI remains reliable even under unforeseen conditions. Regulatory frameworks like the EU AI Act and NIST AI Risk Management Framework guide organizations in implementing AI systems that prioritize ethical responsibility and human-centered decision-making.

Related Terms

Explainability: The ability of an AI model to provide understandable reasons for its decisions (see pg. 27).

Bias Mitigation: Techniques used to reduce unfair discrimination in AI models (see pg. 104).

AI Governance: The policies and frameworks ensuring AI systems adhere to ethical, legal, and safety standards (see pg. 80).

Common Misconceptions

Trustworthy AI guarantees perfect decisions: Trustworthiness enhances reliability, but AI models can still make mistakes and require human oversight.

Trust in AI means revealing all data: Transparency doesn't always mean exposing all data; it focuses on making AI understandable and accountable.

All AI models can be fully trusted: AI systems require continuous monitoring and validation to remain trustworthy, especially in evolving environments.

Historical Context

The importance of trustworthy AI grew as AI systems became more complex and impactful. Concerns over biased AI models, like the **COMPAS** risk assessment tool in criminal justice, raised awareness about fairness and accountability. In response, organizations like **IBM**, **Google**, and **OpenAI** developed AI ethics principles. The **GDPR** (**2018**) and emerging regulations like the **EU AI Act** (**2023**) emphasize trustworthiness through transparency and fairness.

Practical Implications

Trustworthy AI enhances public confidence, regulatory compliance, and ethical AI deployment. In healthcare, it ensures patients trust AI-based diagnoses. In finance, it prevents biased lending decisions. In law enforcement, it reduces AI-driven racial profiling. Companies prioritizing AI trustworthiness benefit from user adoption, reduced legal risks, and long-term credibility, making AI safer and more reliable across industries.

Ultra-Reliable Low-Latency Communications (URLLC) (5G)

URLLC is a critical component of 5G and beyond networks, designed to provide highly reliable and low-latency data transmission. It ensures near-instantaneous communication with minimal delay, making it essential for mission-critical applications, such as autonomous systems, industrial automation, and remote medical procedures.

URLLC is like a reflexive emergency braking system in a car—it must react in real time with zero tolerance for delays or errors. Just as a split-second delay can mean a collision, high-latency communication could result in AI malfunctions or system failures.

Examples

Autonomous Vehicles: URLLC enables self-driving cars to communicate with traffic systems and other vehicles in real time, ensuring safe navigation, collision avoidance, and adaptive driving responses.

Remote Surgery: Surgeons can perform robotic-assisted procedures across continents using URLLC-powered networks, ensuring precise, real-time control without lag, enhancing patient safety.

Smart Grid Systems: URLLC ensures stable and instant communication between energy grids, optimizing power distribution and preventing outages by detecting and correcting faults in milliseconds (see pg. 450).

Foundational Concepts

URLLC relies on high reliability (99.999% uptime) and ultra-low latency (<1 millisecond) to support time-sensitive AI applications. It employs edge computing to reduce the distance data must travel, ensuring real-time responsiveness. Network slicing allows dedicated communication channels for mission-critical AI-driven services. Error correction techniques and multiple-input multiple-output (MIMO) technology ensure continuous, uninterrupted connectivity even in dense environments. Together, these features enable seamless AI communication, vital for automation, robotics, and immersive digital experiences.

Related Terms

Edge Computing: Processing data closer to the source instead of relying on distant cloud servers, reducing latency (see pg. 192).

Massive Machine-Type Communication (mMTC): A 5G feature enabling large-scale device connectivity, often working alongside URLLC (see pg. 320).

Network Slicing: A technique in 5G that allocates specific network resources for different applications, ensuring reliable communication (see pg. 350).

Common Misconceptions

URLLC is just fast internet: Unlike standard broadband, URLLC prioritizes reliability and consistency, not just speed.

Only useful for streaming: URLLC is designed for critical AI and IoT applications, not consumer entertainment.

5G automatically provides URLLC: URLLC is a specific feature of 5G, requiring custom network configurations for optimal performance.

Historical Context

The **3rd Generation Partnership Project** (3GPP) introduced URLLC in 5G Release 15 (**2018**) as a solution for AI-driven automation. Early applications included robotics and industrial IoT. Companies like **Ericsson**, **Nokia**, and **Qualcomm** pioneered URLLC innovations in manufacturing, transportation, and healthcare. As AI expanded into real-time systems, **6G** research aims to further enhance URLLC with sub-millisecond latencies and AI-powered network optimizations.

Practical Implications

URLLC enables autonomous AI systems, real-time automation, and AI-human collaboration. In manufacturing, robots synchronize for precision assembly. In healthcare, AI-driven diagnostics and telemedicine become instantaneous. In disaster response, drones relay real-time data for immediate intervention. Future 6G networks will push URLLC capabilities, driving innovations in AI-driven automation, smart cities, and cyber-physical systems.

Underfitting (AI)

Underfitting occurs when a machine learning model is too simple to capture the underlying patterns in the training data. It results in poor performance on both training and test data, leading to high bias and failure to generalize to unseen examples.

Underfitting is like using a straight line to fit a complex curve—it fails to capture important variations in the data. Just as a simple rule cannot describe a complicated system, an underfit model lacks the complexity needed to make accurate predictions.

Examples

Medical Diagnosis: If an AI model trained to detect diseases is too simplistic, it may fail to identify rare symptoms, leading to incorrect diagnoses.

Stock Market Predictions: A financial model that only considers past prices but ignores economic indicators may perform poorly, failing to adapt to market trends.

Autonomous Vehicles: A self-driving car's AI using only basic rules for object detection might not recognize complex traffic situations, increasing accident risks.

Foundational Concepts

Underfitting is caused by excessive regularization, insufficient model complexity, or lack of training data. In supervised learning, a high-bias model is too simplistic, leading to poor performance across all datasets. Addressing underfitting involves choosing more complex models, increasing training iterations, and improving feature selection. Regularization techniques like L1 and L2 penalties should be carefully tuned to avoid making the model too rigid. Cross-validation helps detect underfitting by evaluating model performance on different data subsets.

Related Terms

Overfitting: The opposite of underfitting, where a model becomes too complex and captures noise rather than patterns (see pg. 362).

Bias-Variance Tradeoff: A fundamental concept in machine learning where reducing bias (underfitting) increases variance, and vice versa.

Regularization: Techniques like Lasso and Ridge regression that help control model complexity to prevent overfitting or underfitting.

Common Misconceptions

Underfitting only happens with simple models: Even deep learning models can underfit if they are not trained long enough or lack sufficient data.

Adding more data always fixes underfitting: If the model is too simple, increasing data won't improve learning without adjusting complexity.

Underfitting and overfitting can't coexist: Some models can underfit on training data while overfitting on validation data, requiring fine-tuning.

Historical Context

The bias-variance tradeoff was first conceptualized in statistical learning theory and later applied in machine learning. Early regression models in the 20th century highlighted underfitting as a limitation of overly simplistic models. The rise of neural networks in the 21st century shifted focus to overfitting, but underfitting remains relevant in low-capacity models and highly constrained AI systems.

Practical Implications

Underfitting limits AI performance in fields requiring precise pattern recognition, such as healthcare, finance, and robotics. A simplistic fraud detection system may miss sophisticated scams. An AI tutor that generalizes too much may fail to adapt to students' individual learning needs. In autonomous systems, underfitting can lead to erroneous decision-making, compromising safety. Optimizing hyperparameters, feature selection, and model architecture is crucial to balancing complexity and generalization in AI development.

Unlabeled Data (AI)

Unlabeled data refers to raw information that has not been annotated with predefined categories or labels. It lacks explicit classifications, making it challenging for supervised learning models but valuable for unsupervised and semi-supervised learning techniques in AI and machine learning applications.

Unlabeled data is like a pile of unsorted puzzle pieces without a reference image. Unlike labeled data, which provides clear instructions, unlabeled data requires algorithms to identify patterns and structure on their own, making it essential for self-learning AI models.

Examples

Customer Behavior Analysis: Retail companies analyze unlabeled transaction data to detect spending patterns and segment customers, improving marketing strategies.

Anomaly Detection in Cybersecurity: AI models trained on network logs without labels can identify suspicious activity or potential security threats without predefined attack signatures.

Medical Image Processing: AI systems scan massive datasets of X-rays and MRIs to uncover patterns that help predict diseases without explicit diagnostic labels.

Foundational Concepts

Unlabeled data is essential for unsupervised learning, where models find hidden patterns, clusters, or anomalies without predefined outputs. It plays a crucial role in self-supervised learning, where AI generates its own labels from data. Semi-supervised learning combines labeled and unlabeled data to improve model accuracy with minimal manual labeling. Representation learning helps extract meaningful features from raw data, enabling AI to understand relationships without human input. Handling unlabeled data effectively requires dimensionality reduction techniques, such as principal component analysis (PCA) and autoencoders.

Related Terms

Labeled Data: Data that includes explicit labels or classifications, used in supervised learning (see pg. 298).

Self-Supervised Learning: A method where AI generates pseudo-labels from unlabeled data to train itself (see pg. 430).

Clustering: A technique in unsupervised learning where similar data points are grouped without predefined categories (see pg. 134).

Common Misconceptions

Unlabeled data is useless without labeling: AI can extract meaningful insights from patterns, structures, and anomalies without human-labeled annotations.

Labeled data is always superior: Some AI models perform better when trained on a mix of labeled and unlabeled data, reducing bias.

Only supervised learning is useful for AI applications: Many breakthroughs, including self-supervised and generative models, rely on unlabeled data.

Historical Context

The use of unlabeled data in AI dates back to early clustering algorithms in the **1950s**. The rise of neural networks and self-supervised learning in the **2010s** accelerated its importance. Deep learning models like **GPT** and **BERT** demonstrated the power of learning from massive, unlabeled datasets, enabling AI to generate human-like text and speech. Advances in unsupervised learning and contrastive learning continue to make unlabeled data a cornerstone of AI development.

Practical Implications

Unlabeled data drives AI innovation in search engines, recommendation systems, and fraud detection. In autonomous vehicles, AI models use unlabeled road images to improve object detection and navigation. Healthcare applications rely on unsupervised learning to detect early-stage diseases. Reducing reliance on human-labeled data lowers costs, enhances scalability, and accelerates AI development. The ability to process unlabeled data expands AI's adaptability, making it more autonomous and capable of handling real-world challenges.

Unstructured Data (AI)

Unstructured data refers to information that lacks a predefined format or organization, making it difficult for traditional databases to process. It includes text, images, audio, and video, requiring advanced AI techniques like natural language processing (NLP) and computer vision to extract meaningful insights.

Unstructured data is like a box of assorted puzzle pieces with no reference image. Unlike structured data, which fits neatly into rows and columns, unstructured data requires AI to recognize patterns and meaning, making it essential for modern data-driven applications.

Examples

Social Media Analysis: AI analyzes tweets, posts, and comments to detect trends, sentiment, and misinformation in real-time.

Healthcare Diagnostics: Medical imaging AI interprets X-rays, MRIs, and CT scans to detect abnormalities, assisting doctors with faster diagnoses.

Customer Support Chatbots: AI processes voice recordings and text conversations to enhance automated customer service and improve user interactions (see pg. 528).

Foundational Concepts

Unstructured data is processed using machine learning, deep learning, and big data analytics. Natural language processing (NLP) is used for analyzing text, while computer vision interprets images and video. Feature extraction converts raw data into meaningful attributes for AI models. Vector embeddings allow AI to represent unstructured data in mathematical space. Neural networks, convolutional neural networks (CNNs), and recurrent neural networks (RNNs) help process different types of unstructured data, improving AI's ability to understand, classify, and generate meaningful content.

Related Terms

Structured Data: Data organized in predefined formats, such as tables, making it easy to store and query (see pg. 462).

Semi-Structured Data: A hybrid format containing both structured and unstructured elements, such as JSON or XML files (see pg. 434).

Big Data: Large and complex datasets, including unstructured data, requiring specialized tools for processing and analysis.

Common Misconceptions

Unstructured data is useless without AI: While AI enhances processing, humans have long extracted insights from text, images, and videos manually.

Unstructured data is completely random: It follows hidden structures, such as grammatical rules in language or patterns in images, which AI can recognize.

Only structured data is valuable for businesses: Unstructured data drives innovations in AI-powered applications, from voice assistants to fraud detection.

Historical Context

The rise of digital content in the **1990s** and **2000s**, including emails, social media, and multimedia, led to an explosion of unstructured data. AI-driven analytics became essential for processing this data at scale. The development of NLP models, deep learning, and cloud computing in the **2010s** allowed businesses to extract insights from unstructured sources. Technologies like **GPT**, **BERT**, and computer vision algorithms have advanced AI's ability to interpret and generate human-like content from unstructured data.

Practical Implications

Unstructured data fuels AI applications in healthcare, finance, security, and marketing. AI models analyze legal documents, medical scans, and security footage to detect fraud and threats. In customer service, AI-powered chatbots improve interactions by understanding natural language. Businesses leverage text analytics, speech recognition, and image classification to gain competitive insights. Managing unstructured data enhances automation, decision-making, and predictive analytics, shaping the future of AI-driven industries.

Unsupervised Learning (AI)

Unsupervised learning is a machine learning approach where an AI system identifies patterns and relationships in data without labeled examples. Unlike supervised learning, it doesn't rely on predefined outputs, making it useful for tasks such as clustering, anomaly detection, and dimensionality reduction.

Unsupervised learning is like exploring a new city without a map. Instead of following predefined routes, you identify patterns—like noticing which streets have the most shops or which neighborhoods look similar—allowing you to navigate based on observed relationships rather than explicit instructions.

Examples

Customer Segmentation: Businesses use clustering algorithms to analyze shopping habits, grouping customers into similar behavioral categories for personalized marketing.

Anomaly Detection: AI detects fraudulent transactions by recognizing unusual spending behaviors in financial data, helping to prevent fraud.

Medical Image Analysis: AI clusters MRI scans into similar medical conditions, assisting doctors in identifying diseases without predefined labels.

Foundational Concepts

Unsupervised learning relies on clustering, dimensionality reduction, and association rule learning. Clustering groups similar data points, while dimensionality reduction simplifies complex datasets without losing essential information. K-means, hierarchical clustering, and Gaussian mixture models are common clustering techniques. Principal Component Analysis (PCA) and t-SNE are used for dimensionality reduction. Unlike supervised learning, which requires labeled datasets, unsupervised learning finds hidden patterns in raw data, making it valuable for data exploration and feature extraction in AI applications.

Related Terms

Supervised Learning: AI learns from labeled data, mapping inputs to outputs with explicit instructions (see pg. 468).

Semi-Supervised Learning: A hybrid approach that combines small amounts of labeled data with larger sets of unlabeled data (see pg. 436).

Reinforcement Learning: AI learns through trial and error, receiving rewards or penalties based on its actions (see pg. 410).

Common Misconceptions

Unsupervised learning requires no human intervention: While it doesn't use labeled data, human interpretation is often needed to validate results.

It produces perfect groupings: Unsupervised learning identifies structures but may not always yield meaningful classifications without additional tuning.

Only deep learning can perform unsupervised learning: Classical methods like K-means and PCA are widely used for unsupervised tasks.

Historical Context

Early work on clustering and statistical pattern recognition laid the foundation for unsupervised learning. Neural networks in the **1980s** and **1990s** introduced self-organizing maps (SOMs). K-means clustering (**1957**) and PCA (**1901**) remain key methods today. Modern advancements in autoencoders, GANs, and contrastive learning have expanded unsupervised learning's capabilities, making it critical for big data analysis, anomaly detection, and AI-driven insights.

Practical Implications

Unsupervised learning is essential in cybersecurity, healthcare, finance, and e-commerce. It detects fraud, identifies hidden market trends, and enhances personalized recommendations. AI-driven drug discovery, genomics, and climate modeling leverage unsupervised learning to uncover new scientific insights. As datasets grow, unsupervised learning's ability to extract knowledge from raw data will play an increasing role in AI applications, driving innovations across industries.

Usability (HCI)

Usability refers to the ease with which users can interact with a system, product, or interface to achieve their goals efficiently, effectively, and satisfactorily. It focuses on user-centered design principles, ensuring that systems are intuitive, accessible, and responsive to minimize errors and enhance the user experience.

Usability is like a well-designed door handle—it should be easy to use without instructions. If a door requires excessive effort or confusion to open, it fails in usability. Similarly, well-designed software should be intuitive and allow users to complete tasks seamlessly.

Examples

Web & Mobile Applications: Apps like Google Search or Spotify prioritize usability by offering intuitive navigation, clear layouts, and fast response times, making it easy for users to complete tasks without frustration.

Healthcare Interfaces: Medical software must ensure usability for doctors and nurses, providing easy access to patient data, clear alerts, and simple workflows to reduce errors in high-stakes environments.

Self-Driving Car Interfaces: Autonomous vehicles need user-friendly dashboards that allow drivers to monitor system status and intervene if needed, ensuring safety and confidence in human-AI interaction.

Foundational Concepts

Usability is guided by five key principles: learnability, efficiency, memorability, error handling, and satisfaction. A system should be easy to learn, allow fast and effective task completion, remain usable even after a break, minimize user errors, and provide a positive experience. Human-Computer Interaction (HCI) and User Experience (UX) Design are foundational fields influencing usability research. Methods such as usability testing, heuristic evaluation, and A/B testing help refine systems to meet user needs effectively.

Related Terms

User Experience (UX): A broader concept encompassing usability, accessibility, and emotional impact of an interaction (see pg. 518).

Accessibility: Ensuring that digital products are usable by people with disabilities, following guidelines like WCAG (Web Content Accessibility Guidelines).

Cognitive Load: The mental effort required to use a system; lower cognitive load improves usability (see pg. 140).

Common Misconceptions

Usability is just about aesthetics: While design matters, usability prioritizes functionality and ease of use over visual appeal.

If users can figure it out, it's usable: A system may be learnable but not necessarily efficient or intuitive.

Usability only applies to digital products: It also applies to physical products, services, and real-world systems.

Historical Context

Usability research dates back to early computing interfaces in the **1970s**, where researchers like **Donald Norman** and **Jakob Nielsen** shaped usability principles. The **1980s** saw advancements in graphical user interfaces (GUIs) with systems like **Apple Macintosh** prioritizing ease of use. The **2000s** brought mobile usability challenges, leading to new design paradigms for touchscreens and voice interfaces. Today, usability plays a crucial role in AI, augmented reality, and IoT applications, ensuring seamless human-technology interactions.

Practical Implications

Usability is essential in software design, AI-driven systems, automation, and assistive technologies. Poor usability can result in user frustration, decreased adoption, and financial losses. In AI applications, usability ensures that models produce interpretable results, enhancing trust and decision-making. In healthcare, usability-driven interfaces reduce medical errors. In e-commerce, intuitive design improves sales conversion rates. As AI and automation evolve, usability remains key in making advanced systems accessible and beneficial for all users.

User Experience (UX) (HCI)

User Experience (UX) refers to the overall interaction and perception a person has when using a digital product, system, or service. It encompasses usability, accessibility, efficiency, and emotional satisfaction, ensuring that technology is intuitive, enjoyable, and meets user needs effectively.

UX is like visiting a well-designed store—products are easy to find, the checkout process is smooth, and customer service is helpful. If a store is cluttered, confusing, or slow, customers leave frustrated. Similarly, a poor UX in software leads to frustration and abandonment.

Examples

Mobile Apps & Websites: Platforms like Amazon and Netflix use UX design to ensure smooth navigation, personalized recommendations, and fast-loading pages, enhancing user satisfaction.

Healthcare Systems: Medical applications require intuitive interfaces for doctors and nurses to quickly access patient data, ensuring efficient decision-making and reducing errors in critical situations.

Smart Home Devices: UX plays a crucial role in devices like Amazon Echo or Google Nest, ensuring that voice assistants respond accurately, quickly, and in a human-friendly manner.

Foundational Concepts

UX is built upon user-centered design (UCD) principles, prioritizing user needs and behaviors. It involves research, wireframing, prototyping, usability testing, and iteration to improve a product. Gestalt principles, cognitive load theory, and affordances guide how users interact with digital products. Emotional design, introduced by Donald Norman, highlights how aesthetics and functionality shape user perceptions. Accessibility, measured by WCAG guidelines, ensures inclusivity, while interaction design (IxD) focuses on how users engage with a product's interface.

Related Terms

Usability: The ease with which users can interact with a system to achieve goals efficiently (see pg. 516).

Human-Computer Interaction (HCI): The interdisciplinary study of how humans interact with computers and technology (see pg. 39).

Information Architecture (IA): The organization and structuring of digital content to enhance findability and navigation.

Common Misconceptions

UX is just about aesthetics: While visual design matters, UX includes functionality, accessibility, and efficiency.

Good UX means no user training is needed: Some complex systems require onboarding, even with great UX.

UX is the same as UI: UX focuses on the overall experience, while UI (User Interface) pertains specifically to visual and interactive elements.

Historical Context

UX has its roots in early computing interfaces and industrial design. **Donald Norman** popularized the term "User Experience" in the **1990s**, emphasizing human-centered design. Early systems like **Apple Macintosh (1984)** revolutionized UX by introducing graphical user interfaces (GUIs). The rise of mobile computing and AI-driven experiences has pushed UX beyond traditional interfaces, incorporating voice, gestures, and adaptive design to enhance user interactions.

Practical Implications

UX design impacts e-commerce, healthcare, finance, AI interfaces, and smart devices. In AI-driven applications, UX ensures users understand and trust AI recommendations. In financial platforms, UX design improves engagement and transaction efficiency. Poor UX can result in loss of customers, increased support costs, and decreased trust in technology. As AI and automation evolve, UX will shape how humans interact with intelligent systems, ensuring that technology remains accessible, efficient, and user-friendly.

User Interface (UI) (HCI)

User Interface (UI) refers to the graphical, auditory, or tactile elements that allow users to interact with a digital system. It includes buttons, menus, icons, voice commands, and touch gestures, ensuring intuitive and efficient communication between humans and computers. A well-designed UI enhances usability and accessibility.

UI is like a car's dashboard—steering wheels, pedals, and buttons must be easy to locate and use. A poorly designed dashboard makes driving frustrating, just as a complex UI confuses users and reduces efficiency in software applications.

Examples

Mobile Apps & Websites: Platforms like Facebook, Instagram, and Google rely on clean, responsive UI elements, ensuring users can navigate seamlessly with minimal effort.

Video Games: Gaming interfaces include HUDs (Heads-Up Displays), control menus, and interactive elements that help players understand game mechanics without disrupting immersion.

Smart Home Devices: UI plays a vital role in voice assistants like Alexa and Google Home, where voice and screen-based interfaces allow users to control devices effortlessly.

Foundational Concepts

UI design follows human-computer interaction (HCI) principles, ensuring systems are intuitive, accessible, and visually appealing. Gestalt principles influence how users perceive layout and design. Affordances and signifiers help users understand possible actions, while feedback mechanisms like animations or alerts confirm interactions. Consistency ensures users can predict system behavior, and responsive design adapts interfaces across different devices. UI accessibility, guided by WCAG standards, ensures inclusivity for users with disabilities.

Related Terms

User Experience (UX): Encompasses the overall experience a user has with a system, including UI design, usability, and satisfaction (see pg. 518).

Graphical User Interface (GUI): A visual-based UI that includes windows, icons, and menus, commonly found in operating systems and applications.

Voice User Interface (VUI): Allows interaction through speech, commonly used in smart assistants like Siri, Alexa, and Google Assistant.

Common Misconceptions

UI and UX are the same: UI focuses on the interface's visual and interactive elements, while UX considers the overall user journey and experience.

Good UI means no learning curve: Some complex tools require onboarding, even with an intuitive UI.

UI only applies to screens: UI also includes voice, gesture, and physical interfaces like car dashboards or ATM keypads.

Historical Context

UI design has evolved from command-line interfaces (CLI) in early computers to graphical user interfaces (GUI) introduced by **Xerox PARC** and later popularized by **Apple** and **Microsoft**. The **1984 Macintosh** revolutionized GUI with its icon-based interface. Touchscreen interfaces emerged with **Palm PDAs** and the **iPhone** (**2007**), while voice interfaces like **Alexa** (**2014**) expanded UI beyond screens. Today, UI integrates AI-driven personalization, augmented reality (AR), and multimodal interactions.

Practical Implications

UI impacts software, mobile apps, gaming, healthcare, and AI systems. A well-designed UI reduces cognitive load, improves engagement, and enhances accessibility. In e-commerce, UI optimization drives higher conversion rates. In healthcare, UI ensures that medical interfaces are easy to navigate, preventing errors. AI-powered UI customization adapts interfaces to user preferences, improving efficiency. As augmented reality (AR) and virtual reality (VR) evolve, UI will play a crucial role in shaping immersive digital experiences.

Value Function (AI)

A value function in reinforcement learning (RL) estimates the expected cumulative reward an agent will receive when following a particular policy from a given state. It helps the agent determine which actions lead to long-term rewards rather than just immediate gains.

A value function is like a GPS predicting the fastest route to a destination. Instead of focusing only on the next turn, it considers the entire journey, estimating the best path based on current road conditions, traffic, and potential delays.

Examples

Robotics Navigation: A robot uses value functions to assess different movement strategies, maximizing efficiency while avoiding obstacles and reducing energy consumption.

Stock Market Predictions: Reinforcement learning models apply value functions to estimate the long-term profitability of different investment strategies, helping traders make informed decisions.

Video Game AI: Game agents evaluate value functions to determine optimal strategies, such as deciding when to attack or defend based on future rewards and risks.

Foundational Concepts

Value functions are critical in reinforcement learning and are often used in conjunction with policy optimization and Q-learning. The state-value function (V) calculates the expected return from a given state, while the action-value function (Q) estimates the value of taking a specific action in that state. Bellman equations recursively define these functions, enabling algorithms to refine their reward predictions over time. Dynamic programming and temporal difference learning methods help approximate value functions efficiently.

Related Terms

Q-Learning: A reinforcement learning algorithm that estimates the value of action-state pairs using an action-value function.

Policy: The strategy an agent follows to determine actions based on states, either deterministic or probabilistic (see pg. 370).

Bellman Equation: A recursive formula used to update value functions based on expected future rewards.

Common Misconceptions

Value functions guarantee optimal decisions: They provide estimates but require further optimization for the best results.

They only work for simple environments: Value functions are scalable and can be applied to complex, multi-agent systems.

Immediate rewards are always better: Value functions prioritize long-term cumulative rewards over short-term gains.

Historical Context

Value functions have roots in dynamic programming, introduced by **Richard Bellman** in the **1950s**. His **Bellman equation** provided a foundation for reinforcement learning. Later, Q-learning (**1989**) by **Chris Watkins** extended value-based learning. Deep reinforcement learning, popularized by **DeepMind's AlphaGo (2016)**, further advanced value function applications in AI.

Practical Implications

Value functions enable autonomous systems, financial models, and AI-driven decision-making. In self-driving cars, they assess route efficiency and collision risk. In healthcare, value-based AI helps optimize patient treatment plans. AI-driven logistics use value functions to reduce delivery time and cost. By improving long-term decision-making, value functions enhance AI reliability across industries.

Video Data (AI)

Video data consists of sequences of images (frames) combined with audio and metadata, representing motion, sound, and context. It is used in machine learning, computer vision, and artificial intelligence to analyze activities, detect objects, and extract meaningful insights from dynamic visual information.

Video data is like a flipbook where each page is a frame. When flipped quickly, the images create the illusion of movement, just as a video sequence does. Unlike a single image, video adds time as a dimension, capturing ongoing events and transitions.

Examples

Surveillance & Security: AI-powered video analysis detects anomalies, identifies individuals, and alerts security personnel to suspicious activities in real time.

Autonomous Vehicles: Self-driving cars use video data from cameras to recognize objects, track pedestrians, and navigate roads safely under different environmental conditions.

Healthcare Diagnostics: AI models analyze medical videos, such as endoscopic procedures, to detect abnormalities and assist doctors in diagnosing conditions with greater accuracy.

Foundational Concepts

Video data is composed of frames (individual images) played in sequence to represent motion. Each frame contains spatial information, while the sequence provides temporal information. AI models process video using computer vision, deep learning, and motion analysis techniques. Convolutional Neural Networks (CNNs) extract spatial features, while Recurrent Neural Networks (RNNs) and Transformers handle temporal dependencies. Optical flow measures pixel movement between frames, aiding in motion tracking. Video data requires compression techniques, such as MPEG and H.264, to reduce storage and transmission costs.

Related Terms

Computer Vision: A field of AI that enables machines to interpret visual data, including images and videos.

Object Detection: Identifying and classifying objects within video frames, often used in surveillance and autonomous driving.

Frame Rate: The number of frames per second (FPS) in a video, affecting smoothness and accuracy in motion analysis.

Common Misconceptions

Video data is just a collection of images: Unlike static images, video contains temporal relationships, requiring specialized AI techniques for analysis.

Higher resolution always means better AI performance: Processing high-resolution video demands more computational resources, which may not always improve results.

AI can always interpret video accurately: AI models may struggle with low-light conditions, occlusions, and rapid motion, leading to errors.

Historical Context

Video data has evolved from analog film (**1920s**) to digital formats (**1990s**). The rise of computer vision (**1960s**) laid the groundwork for video analysis. The development of deep learning (**2010s**), especially CNNs and Transformers, revolutionized video understanding. Breakthroughs like YOLO (**2016**) enabled real-time object detection in videos, while Transformer-based models (**2020s**) further improved video comprehension.

Practical Implications

Video data is transforming security, entertainment, healthcare, and robotics. AI-driven surveillance systems improve public safety, while video streaming services use AI for personalized recommendations. Sports analytics leverage video for performance tracking, and robotics rely on video data for real-time decision-making. AI-powered video synthesis raises ethical concerns regarding deepfakes, highlighting the need for responsible AI in video data applications.

Video Summarization (ANI)

Video summarization is an AI-driven technique that extracts the most relevant segments from a video to create a condensed version while retaining key information. It is widely used in surveillance, media, and education to enhance content consumption and save time.

Video summarization is like condensing a long movie into a trailer. Instead of watching the entire film, you get the highlights—major plot points, key scenes, and essential dialogues—without losing the essence of the original content. Similarly, AI-based video summarization extracts crucial frames from lengthy footage.

Examples

Security Surveillance: AI-powered video summarization helps security teams review hours of surveillance footage by extracting important events, such as unusual movements or unauthorized access.

Educational Content: Online learning platforms use summarization to generate concise lecture recaps, allowing students to review key concepts without rewatching full-length videos.

News and Sports Highlights: AI-driven summarization extracts crucial moments from live sports events or news reports, enabling viewers to catch up quickly on significant developments.

Foundational Concepts

Video summarization relies on computer vision, deep learning, and natural language processing (NLP) to identify key moments. Techniques include extractive summarization, which selects representative frames, and abstractive summarization, which generates new content descriptions. Recurrent Neural Networks (RNNs), Transformers, and Convolutional Neural Networks (CNNs) are commonly used for feature extraction and event detection. Optical flow analysis helps track motion changes between frames, while attention mechanisms prioritize significant parts of a video. Summarization models often incorporate reinforcement learning to optimize selection criteria for video highlights.

Related Terms

Computer Vision: A field of AI that enables machines to process and interpret visual data from images and videos.

Feature Extraction: The process of identifying and selecting important elements from a video, such as objects, faces, or motion patterns.

Temporal Segmentation: Dividing a video into meaningful sections based on scene changes, transitions, or detected events.

Common Misconceptions

Video summarization is just speeding up a video: Unlike fast-forwarding, AI-driven summarization selects the most informative moments, not just accelerating playback.

Summarized videos always capture full context: While AI prioritizes key events, it may omit nuances that require human interpretation.

Only long videos need summarization: Even short clips can benefit from summarization for more efficient viewing and quick analysis.

Historical Context

Early video summarization techniques (**1990s**) relied on simple scene cuts and metadata-based selection. The emergence of machine learning (**2000s**) improved object and event recognition. The deep learning revolution (**2010s**) introduced CNNs and RNNs, enabling more sophisticated summaries. Transformer-based models (**2020s**) further enhanced content understanding, allowing contextual video summarization in applications like surveillance and content recommendation.

Practical Implications

Video summarization is transforming content consumption across industries. In security, it enhances surveillance efficiency by summarizing hours of footage. In media, it enables automatic generation of news and sports highlights. In education, AI-powered summarization helps students quickly review lectures. Additionally, social media platforms use summarization for automatic clip generation, improving content engagement. The ability to condense vast amounts of video data into meaningful summaries enhances decision-making, accessibility, and productivity across multiple domains.

Virtual Assistant (ANI)

A virtual assistant is an AI-powered software application that performs tasks, provides information, and automates processes based on user input. Using natural language processing (NLP), machine learning, and speech recognition, virtual assistants help with scheduling, answering queries, controlling smart devices, and enhancing customer service interactions.

A virtual assistant is like a personal secretary who listens, understands, and acts on your commands. Just as an efficient secretary organizes schedules, takes notes, and responds to calls, an AI-powered virtual assistant manages tasks like setting reminders, answering questions, and automating workflows.

Examples

Smart Home Automation: Virtual assistants like Alexa or Google Assistant control smart home devices, adjusting lights, thermostats, and security systems through voice commands.

Customer Support Chatbots: Businesses use AI-powered virtual assistants to handle customer inquiries, resolving common issues and escalating complex cases to human representatives.

Productivity Enhancement: Virtual assistants like Siri and Cortana assist professionals by setting meetings, drafting emails, and providing real-time information, improving workflow efficiency.

Foundational Concepts

Virtual assistants rely on natural language processing (NLP), speech recognition, and deep learning to interpret and respond to user queries. Machine learning enables them to improve accuracy over time. Context awareness helps maintain conversational flow, while sentiment analysis refines responses. Integration with APIs allows them to access real-time data, such as weather updates or stock prices. Many assistants use speech synthesis for natural voice interactions and multimodal interfaces for enhanced user experience, including text, voice, and visual responses.

Related Terms

Natural Language Processing (NLP): A branch of AI that enables virtual assistants to understand, interpret, and generate human language (see pg. 346).

Conversational AI: AI systems designed to engage in human-like dialogues through text or speech, improving interactions with users.

Speech Recognition: A technology that converts spoken language into text, allowing virtual assistants to process and respond to voice commands (see pg. 460).

Common Misconceptions

Virtual assistants are the same as chatbots: While both use AI, virtual assistants are more advanced, providing context-aware and multimodal responses beyond simple chat interactions.

They always require voice input: Many virtual assistants also function via text commands and integrate into messaging platforms or applications.

They perfectly understand human language: While advanced, virtual assistants can still misinterpret ambiguous phrases or struggle with regional accents and complex queries.

Historical Context

Early virtual assistants (**1990s**) used rule-based systems with limited capabilities. The introduction of NLP and deep learning (**2010s**) led to intelligent assistants like **Siri** (**2011**), **Google Assistant** (**2016**), and **Alexa** (**2014**). Advances in transformer-based models (**2020s**) have enhanced conversational AI, enabling assistants to generate more natural, human-like interactions across multiple domains.

Practical Implications

Virtual assistants have revolutionized customer service, personal productivity, and smart home technology. Businesses leverage AI-driven assistants for automated customer support, reducing operational costs. In healthcare, AI-powered assistants schedule appointments and provide medical guidance. In education, virtual tutors help students with coursework. The widespread adoption of virtual assistants is reshaping user interaction paradigms, making AI an integral part of everyday digital experiences. However, data privacy concerns and AI bias must be addressed to ensure ethical deployment in sensitive domains.

Virtual Reality (VR) (XR)

Virtual Reality (VR) is a computer-generated simulation that immerses users in an interactive, three-dimensional environment. Using head-mounted displays (HMDs), motion tracking, and spatial audio, VR allows users to experience and interact with virtual worlds as if they were physically present.

Experiencing VR is like stepping into a dream where everything feels real but is entirely digital. Just as reading a novel transports readers to different worlds using imagination, VR places users in interactive environments where they can see, hear, and move as if inside an alternate reality.

Examples

Medical Training: VR allows surgeons to practice complex procedures in a risk-free virtual environment, improving precision and confidence before performing real-world surgeries.

Gaming and Entertainment: Immersive VR games, such as Beat Saber and Half-Life: Alyx, provide players with a highly interactive experience that responds to their movements.

Workplace Training: Industries like aviation and construction use VR to simulate high-risk environments, allowing trainees to gain hands-on experience without real-world dangers.

Foundational Concepts

Virtual Reality relies on computer vision, 3D modeling, and motion tracking to create immersive digital experiences. Head-mounted displays (HMDs) provide stereoscopic visuals, while spatial audio enhances realism by simulating sound direction. Haptic feedback adds a sense of touch, increasing immersion. Positional tracking follows user movements, adjusting the virtual environment accordingly. Advanced AI algorithms can generate adaptive and interactive VR environments, while real-time rendering ensures smooth visual experiences.

Related Terms

Augmented Reality (AR): A technology that overlays digital elements onto the real world, rather than creating a fully immersive environment like VR (see pg. 92).

Mixed Reality (MR): A hybrid of VR and AR, allowing digital and physical objects to interact in real-time (see pg. 328).

360-Degree Video: A panoramic video format that allows viewers to look around in all directions but lacks interactive elements compared to VR.

Common Misconceptions

VR and AR are the same: Unlike AR, which enhances reality with digital overlays, VR completely replaces reality with a simulated environment.

VR is only for gaming: While gaming is a major application, VR is widely used in healthcare, education, and industrial training.

VR causes motion sickness for everyone: Modern VR systems reduce motion sickness through higher frame rates, better tracking, and optimized content design.

Historical Context

The concept of VR dates back to the **1960s**, when **Ivan Sutherland** developed the first head-mounted display (HMD). In the **1990s**, companies like **Nintendo** and **Sega** experimented with consumer VR, but limited technology hindered adoption. The **2010s** saw major advancements with **Oculus Rift (2012)**, **HTC Vive (2016)**, and **PlayStation VR (2016)**, making VR mainstream. Today, AI-driven VR experiences and wireless headsets continue to improve immersion and accessibility.

Practical Implications

Virtual Reality is transforming multiple industries. In education, students can explore historical sites or conduct virtual science experiments. Retail companies use VR for virtual shopping experiences, allowing customers to try products digitally. In therapy, VR helps patients overcome phobias and PTSD through exposure therapy. The rise of metaverse platforms further integrates VR into social interaction, remote work, and entertainment. As hardware becomes more affordable, VR adoption will continue expanding, reshaping digital experiences and human-computer interaction.

Wind Turbine (CET)

A wind turbine is a device that converts kinetic energy from the wind into mechanical power, which is then transformed into electricity using a generator. Wind turbines are commonly used in renewable energy production, providing a sustainable, low-carbon alternative to fossil fuel-based power generation.

A wind turbine is like a windmill, but instead of grinding grain, it generates electricity. Just as a bicycle dynamo converts wheel motion into light, a wind turbine captures wind movement and transforms it into electrical energy, helping to power homes, businesses, and even entire cities.

Examples

Offshore Wind Farms: Countries like the UK and Denmark deploy offshore wind turbines in coastal waters, harnessing stronger, more consistent winds for large-scale electricity production.

Rural Electrification: Remote communities without access to traditional power grids use small wind turbines to generate electricity for homes, schools, and businesses.

Hybrid Renewable Systems: Wind turbines are often integrated with solar panels and battery storage to provide stable, continuous power in microgrid and off-grid applications.

Foundational Concepts

Wind turbines operate on the principles of aerodynamics and electromagnetic induction. The blades are designed to maximize lift and minimize drag, causing rotation. This mechanical motion is transferred through a shaft and gearbox to drive a generator, producing electricity. The power output depends on wind speed, blade size, and turbine efficiency. Modern wind turbines include yaw systems to optimize orientation and pitch control to adjust blade angles for maximum efficiency. Grid integration requires power converters and inverters to ensure stable voltage and frequency.

Related Terms

Renewable Energy: A category of energy sources derived from natural processes, such as wind, solar, and hydro power, which replenish naturally.

Aerodynamics: The study of airflow and forces acting on objects, crucial for wind turbine blade design to maximize efficiency.

Energy Storage: Technologies such as batteries and pumped hydro storage, used to store excess wind energy for later use when wind speeds are low.

Common Misconceptions

Wind turbines work in all weather: Wind turbines require optimal wind speeds (usually 12–55 mph) and shut down during extreme storms or very low wind conditions.

Turbines are noisy and harmful to wildlife: Modern wind turbines are designed to minimize noise and reduce bird and bat collisions through improved site selection and technology.

Wind energy is unreliable: Energy storage systems and grid management strategies help ensure continuous power supply, even during low-wind periods.

Historical Context

The first windmills date back to 7th-century Persia and were later improved in Europe for agriculture. The first electricity-generating wind turbine was built by **Charles F. Brush** in **1887**. Danish scientist **Poul la Cour** further advanced wind power in the early 20th century. The **1970s** energy crisis accelerated research into modern wind technology. By the **2000s**, countries like **Germany, China**, and the **United States** led large-scale wind farm deployments. Today, offshore wind projects and floating wind turbines represent the next frontier in wind energy expansion.

Practical Implications

Wind turbines play a crucial role in global decarbonization efforts. Countries transitioning to renewable energy increasingly invest in wind power to reduce reliance on fossil fuels. In agriculture, wind energy helps power irrigation systems and farm equipment. Corporations and governments are adopting wind power in sustainability initiatives, lowering carbon footprints. As energy storage technology improves, wind turbines will become even more viable for consistent, large-scale electricity production. Future AI-driven predictive maintenance and smart grid integration will enhance wind energy's efficiency and reliability.

Zero-Day Exploit (CS)

A zero-day exploit is a cyberattack that targets a previously unknown software vulnerability before developers have had the chance to create and distribute a fix. Because the flaw is undiscovered by the vendor, attackers can exploit the weakness without facing immediate defenses, making such attacks highly dangerous.

A zero-day exploit is like a thief finding an unlocked window in a house before the homeowner knows it exists. Since no alarm is set, the thief can enter undetected. Similarly, hackers use unknown software vulnerabilities to infiltrate systems before security patches are developed.

Examples

Stuxnet (2010): This zero-day exploit was used in a state-sponsored cyberattack to disrupt Iran's nuclear program by targeting industrial control systems with previously unknown vulnerabilities.

Microsoft Exchange Hack (2021): Attackers exploited zero-day vulnerabilities in Microsoft Exchange servers, allowing them to gain unauthorized access to email accounts and install malware on affected systems.

Apple iOS Exploits (2023): Multiple zero-day vulnerabilities in iOS allowed hackers to execute remote attacks, potentially exposing user data before Apple could release emergency security updates.

Foundational Concepts

Zero-day exploits take advantage of unknown security flaws in software, operating systems, or hardware. Hackers, cybercriminals, and state-sponsored attackers seek out these vulnerabilities before developers release patches. Ethical hackers and cybersecurity researchers may also discover zero-day flaws but report them to vendors rather than exploiting them. Zero-day exploits are sold on the black market or used in advanced persistent threats (APTs). Once a flaw is known, developers must issue a security patch to protect users from further attacks.

Related Terms

Zero-Day Vulnerability: A software flaw that is unknown to the developer and can be exploited by hackers.

Exploit Kit: A collection of automated tools used by hackers to scan for and exploit vulnerabilities in systems.

Patch Management: The process of updating software to fix security vulnerabilities and prevent zero-day exploits.

Common Misconceptions

Zero-day exploits only target large corporations: Small businesses and individuals can also be victims, especially through phishing emails and malware.

Zero-day exploits are rare: While sophisticated attacks are less common, zero-day vulnerabilities are frequently discovered and actively sought by hackers.

Antivirus software stops zero-day exploits: Traditional signature-based security may fail since the attack is unknown and has no existing defense.

Historical Context

Zero-day exploits became widely recognized in the early **2000s**, when attackers started using them in targeted cyber warfare and espionage operations. The **Stuxnet worm (2010)** was a landmark case, demonstrating how governments could use zero-day exploits for sabotage. Over time, exploit markets emerged, with cybercriminals and nation-states purchasing zero-day vulnerabilities for millions of dollars. Bug bounty programs by companies like **Google** and **Microsoft** incentivize ethical hackers to report flaws instead of selling them on the black market.

Practical Implications

Zero-day exploits pose serious risks to national security, financial institutions, and personal data privacy. Governments and corporations invest heavily in cyber threat intelligence to detect and prevent such attacks. AI-driven security systems and real-time behavioral analysis are emerging as critical defense mechanisms. Users must stay vigilant by applying software updates promptly to reduce the risk of zero-day attacks. As cyber warfare and hacking tools evolve, zero-day exploits will remain a major threat to digital infrastructure worldwide.

Index

For Product Safety Concerns and Information please contact our EU
representative GPSR@taylorandfrancis.com
Taylor & Francis Verlag GmbH, Kaufingerstraße 24, 80331 München, Germany

www.ingramcontent.com/pod-product-compliance
Lightning Source LLC
Chambersburg PA
CBHW060946210326
41598CB00031B/4731

* 9 7 8 1 0 4 1 1 6 0 7 2 4 *